B. L. D´ooge

Selections from Urbis Romae viri inlustres

B. L. D´ooge

Selections from Urbis Romae viri inlustres

ISBN/EAN: 9783742861023

Manufactured in Europe, USA, Canada, Australia, Japa

Cover: Foto ©Paul-Georg Meister /pixelio.de

Manufactured and distributed by brebook publishing software (www.brebook.com)

B. L. D'ooge

Selections from Urbis Romae viri inlustres

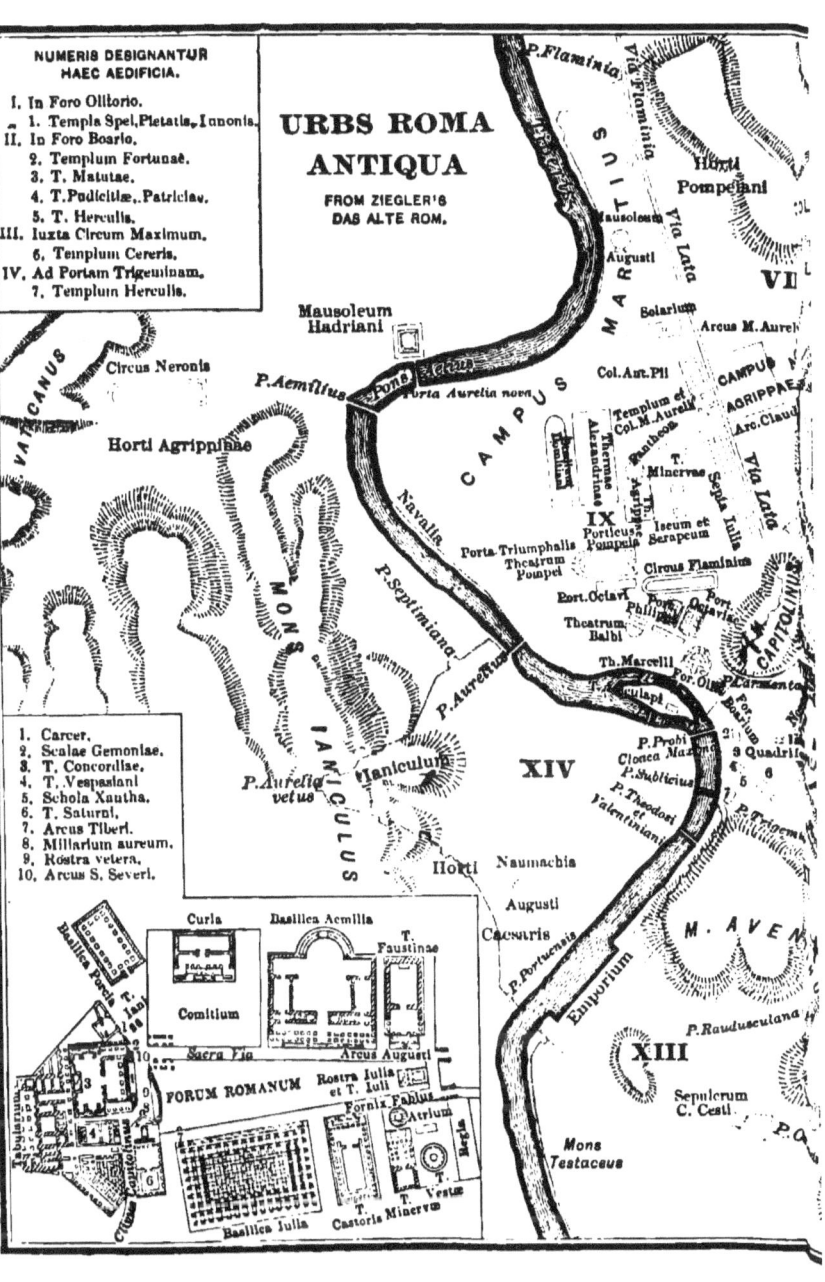

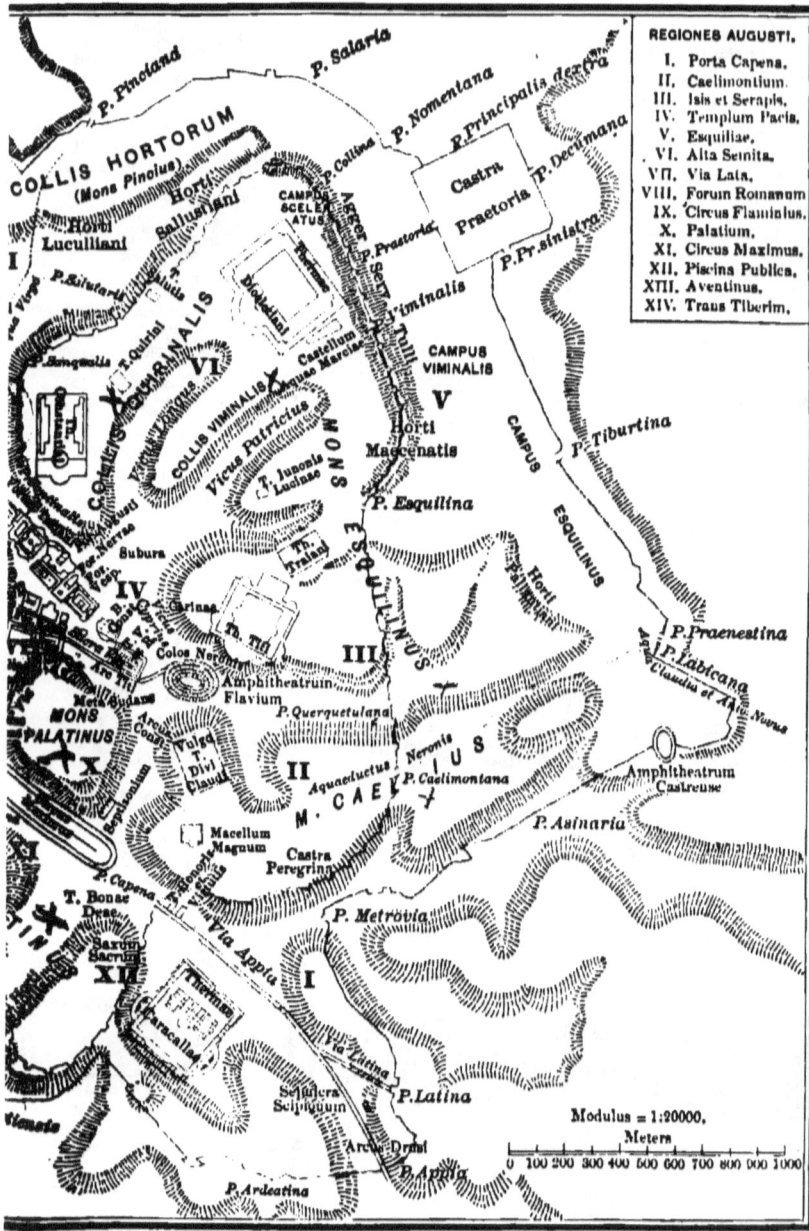

SCHOOL CLASSICS
EDITED UNDER THE SUPERVISION OF
WILLIAM C. COLLAR AND JOHN TETLOW

SELECTIONS

FROM

URBIS ROMAE VIRI INLUSTRES

WITH

NOTES, ILLUSTRATIONS, MAPS, PROSE EXERCISES,
WORD GROUPS, AND VOCABULARY

BY

B. L. D'OOGE, M.A.
MICHIGAN STATE NORMAL SCHOOL

BOSTON, U.S.A., AND LONDON
GINN & COMPANY, PUBLISHERS
1897

PREFACE.

LONG before the report of the Committee of Ten gave expression to the thought, teachers of Latin throughout the country felt the need of a proper stepping-stone from the work of the first year to Caesar. The recommendation of the Committee, therefore, that such books as the *Breviary of Eutropius*, *Gradatim*, and *Viri Romae* should be read as introductory to *Caesar* or *Nepos* was most heartily received.

Viri Romae is a comparatively new book to American schools, though it has long enjoyed great and deserved popularity in the schools of France and Germany. It is a compilation made from Cicero, Livy, Sallust, Seneca, Valerius Maximus, and other Roman writers, by Charles François Lhomond, Professor Emeritus of the University of Paris (1727–1794). It is simplified Latin, but not manufactured Latin. Much is taken verbatim from the authors named, and such changes as occur consist in the omission of unnecessary details and in the removal of difficulties in order and syntax. The style of the authors has been necessarily somewhat changed, but the Latin is pure and the expressions classical.

The real and lively interest that the book inspires commends it to favor. The toilsome acquisition of grammar and syntax during the first year creates an urgent need for an interesting and easy author, whose perusal shall fix the foundations of the language firmly in the mind. *Caesar's Gallic War*, by its difficulty and lack of intrinsic interest, has discouraged and overwhelmed many a promising pupil at this stage of his progress. The *Viri Romae*, under the form of biography, the most healthful and the most fascinating kind of literature for the young, gives a review of Roman history from Romulus to Augustus. The deeds, adventures, vicissitudes, and virtues of Rome's greatest men, told in classic phrase, are sure to create a lively interest, and to give to the student an introduction to Roman history and to Roman life and custom, such as will be of great benefit to him when he comes to read the authors that follow.

The text of the selections contained in this volume has been taken, with but little variation, from C. Holzer's tenth edition (Stuttgart, 1889). What changes have been made are mainly in orthography and punctuation. Holzer's revision of Lhomond's text consisted in following the original authors more closely, in omitting some selections, and in adding interesting anecdotes to others.

The quantity of all long vowels has been marked to assist beginners in forming correct habits of pronunciation. The authority for these has been Lewis's Elementary Latin Dictionary, 1895 edition, as being the latest and most widely followed.

Thanks are due for assistance and suggestions to Mr. Wm. C. Collar, headmaster of the Roxbury Latin School,

PREFACE.

and to Mr. John Tetlow, headmaster of the Boston Girls' High and Latin Schools, general editors of this series. The editor is under obligations also to Miss Helen B. Muir, assistant in Ancient Languages in this institution, and to Mr. C. D. Crittenden of the Central High School, Grand Rapids, Mich., for reading proof and for work on the vocabulary.

B. L. D'OOGE,

Sept. 2, 1895. *Mich. State Normal School.*

CONTENTS.

SELECTIONS	PAGE
Hints to Teachers	vii
I. Romani imperi exordium	1
II. Romulus, Romanorum rex primus	3
III. Numa Pompilius, Romanorum rex secundus	5
IV. Tullus Hostilius, Romanorum rex tertius	6
V. Ancus Marcius, Romanorum rex quartus	9
VI. Lucius Tarquinius Priscus, Romanorum rex quintus	10
VII. Servius Tullius, Romanorum rex sextus	12
VIII. Tarquinius Superbus, Romanorum rex septimus et ultimus	14
IX. Horatius Cocles	16
X. Menenius Agrippa	16
XI. Lucius Virginius centurio	17
XII. Marcus Furius Camillus	19
XIII. Spurius Postumius	22
XIV. Publius Valerius Laevinus et Pyrrhus, rex Epiri	25
XV. Gaius Fabricius	28
XVI. Gaius Duilius	30
XVII. Gaius Lutatius Catulus	31
XVIII. Quintus Fabius Maximus	32
XIX. Aemilius Paulus et Terentius Varro	37

CONTENTS.

SELECTIONS	PAGE
XX. TIBERIUS GRACCHUS ET GAIUS GRACCHUS	39
XXI. GNAEUS POMPEIUS MAGNUS	42
XXII. GAIUS IULIUS CAESAR	48
XXIII. MARCUS TULLIUS CICERO	57
XXIV. CAESAR OCTAVIANUS AUGUSTUS	63
REFERENCE BOOKS AND BOOKS FOR COLLATERAL READING	72, 73
NOTES	75
SUGGESTIONS TO STUDENTS	139
EXERCISES IN LATIN COMPOSITION	141
WORD-GROUPS	183
VOCABULARY	197

LIST OF COLORED MAPS.

URBS ROMA ANTIQUA	*Frontispiece.*
ITALIA SUPERIOR	16
ITALIA INFERIOR	17
IMPERIUM ROMANUM AUGUSTO MORTUO XIV A.D.	72

FULL-PAGE ILLUSTRATIONS.

THE BRONZE WOLF OF THE CAPITOL	1
NUMA POMPILIUS	5
TRIUMPHAL CHARIOT	19
GNAEUS POMPEIUS MAGNUS	42
GAIUS JULIUS CAESAR	48
MARCUS TULLIUS CICERO	57
CAESAR OCTAVIANUS AUGUSTUS	63

HINTS TO TEACHERS.

1. How to Read Latin. — As this is the first continuous reading in Latin that many students using this book will do, it is very important that the right method of reading be adopted from the outset. First, and most important, the text should be read and understood in the order in which it stands. Any rearrangement of the order of the words and thought destroys that apprehension of Latin idiom and style which should be most carefully cultivated. As each word is met it should be disposed of as far as may be. If it should prove impossible to settle all points definitely, keep the mind expectant until the progress of the sentence settles all that was doubtful. It is thus that the Romans read and understood their language, and we must learn to do likewise if we would master it and partake of its spirit. Prof. W. G. Hale's pamphlet on the 'Art of Reading Latin' (Ginn & Co.), gives a clear exposition of this method.

2. Reading at Sight. — No discipline is more useful for inspiring confidence in pupils than frequent practice in sight reading. Much of the *Viri Romae* is peculiarly adapted to this purpose, and though no pages of the text have been especially set apart and annotated for it, still, with such help as the teacher may deem necessary, almost any passage may be so studied, and the effect is sure to be beneficial and inspiring to the class.

3. The Translation of Latin. — To read Latin is one thing; to translate it is quite another. To read Latin is to get

the thought without a conscious appeal to the English equivalent; the translator will clothe this thought in English thoroughly idiomatic and as good as his command of English makes possible. The so-called 'literal translation' has no place in scholarly work. It is but seldom that the Latin idiom and the English idiom are so far identical as to make a literal translation tolerable. Students that are allowed to translate literally, are in danger of doing more to ruin their English than they will ever gain from the study of Latin. On the contrary, there can be no doubt of the excellent training in the mother tongue that a good translation affords. Students should be asked at frequent intervals to hand in such translations.

4. THE PRONOUNCING OF LATIN. — Students should be taught to distinguish carefully between the long and the short vowel sounds. To this end the quantity of all vowels long by nature has been marked. Many students do not have their attention called to this important point until they begin to scan verse, or perhaps not until they enter college. For one to reform who has been careless in his Latin speech for many years, is a most discouraging task. Accuracy should be insisted upon from the outset, and no faulty pronunciation should ever be heard in the class-room. Quantities may be learned gradually by marking them in all written work during the first and second years. This will insure care and accuracy in the years to come without further formal instruction. During the second year Latin should always be pronounced before translation. Often it is useful to read the review lesson without a translation; seeking, so far as possible, to convey the meaning by proper expression in pronunciation. Anecdotes and striking passages should often be learned as a memory exercise, and spoken before the class. Sometimes the teacher should read the review, and the class translate with books closed. It is important that the ear and the eye should be alike trained.

HINTS TO TEACHERS.

5. THE NOTES. — The notes to the text have not been made chiefly grammatical. References are usually given but once, and similar constructions are referred to the first instance of each for comparison and explanation. This method of teaching syntax has proved more effective than repeated reference to the same principle without comparison. Such further drill as is necessary is left to the teacher. It is well to bear in mind that too much attention to syntax is an absolute hindrance to idiomatic and appreciative translation.

On the other hand, the aim of the notes has been to interest the student in ancient life and custom, and to create about him that classic atmosphere without which all our teaching is vain. Modern life is so far removed from ancient life, that the beginner in Latin finds himself even more strange to his environment than to the language. He needs an interpreter to the former quite as much as to the latter. The difficulties that students find with the ancient languages and their lack of enthusiasm for them are often due to their living in an unfamiliar world without guide to its mysteries and beauties. It is to satisfy this larger need that the text has been supplied with maps, illustrations, copious references to collateral reading, and with such concise information as seemed most helpful. It is in directing the collateral reading of his pupils that a teacher can be of perhaps the largest service, and he can accomplish this best by having in the reference library of his school such books as have been recommended (see pp. 72, 73).

6. LATIN COMPOSITION. — It is the unanimous testimony of teachers that nothing can take the place of frequent practice in speaking and in writing idiomatic Latin. In no other way can a knowledge of words, forms, constructions, and idioms be so easily acquired. Prose exercises for oral and written translation have been added to this book, based upon the text, and accompanied by appropriate grammatical refer-

ences. These exercises have been carefully graded and adapted to a systematic development of syntactical principles. It is hoped that they will be found to combine the advantages of both of the methods of teaching Latin composition most in vogue ; that of using short sentences to illustrate grammatical principles, and that of using continuous English with no systematic instruction in syntax. The editor has found that each method has its advantages and its disadvantages. Perhaps he has been so fortunate as to solve the problem by combining the advantages of both. Teachers will of course use their own judgment in determining the amount and frequency of work in Latin composition. Many find it most useful to have some oral and written work every day. Such will be able to complete these exercises in twenty weeks or less. Others, that proceed more slowly, may find it advantageous to continue with them even after the text has been finished and some other author begun, in order that the systematic study of syntax may not be interrupted and prematurely abandoned. In oral translation, quick, sharp, accurate work should be insisted upon. A minute on each sentence is sufficient. For obvious reasons many more lessons have been devoted to the constructions of the moods than to those of the cases; but all that is most essential to a sound knowledge of syntax will be found fully illustrated.

7. WORD-GROUPS. — Immediately preceding the vocabulary, some pages will be found containing groups of words selected from the text and based on the commonest Latin roots. It is suggested that students be given a few lessons on the formation of Latin words, and the meanings of the most frequently recurring prefixes and suffixes, and that then a systematic study of these groups be made. Want of a vocabulary is a fatal obstruction to the easy reading of Latin, and there is no easier way of building one up than by

HINTS TO TEACHERS. xiii

memorizing lists of words fundamentally connected by a common root. A thorough knowledge of even the few roots contained in this list may form the basis for a vocabulary surprisingly large.

8. THE VOCABULARY. — The vocabulary has been constructed not merely for help in translating, but to afford abundant opportunity for etymological and comparative word study. Primary derivations have been given only when the roots are included in the list forming the basis for the Word-Groups; secondary etymologies are given in all cases. In addition, every word is referred to the text for illustrations of its use and range of meaning.

THE BRONZE WOLF OF THE CAPITOL.

URBIS ROMAE VIRI INLUSTRES.

I. Romani imperi exordium.

Proca, rēx Albānōrum, Numitōrem et Amūlium fīliōs habuit. Numitōrī, quī nātū māior erat, rēgnum relīquit; sed Amūlius pulsō frātre rēgnāvit et, ut eum subole prīvāret, Rhēam Silviam, ēius fīliam, Vestae sacerdōtem fēcit, quae tamen Rōmulum et Remum 5 geminōs ēdidit. Eā rē cōgnitā Amūlius ipsam in vincula coniēcit, parvulōs alveō impositōs abiēcit in Tiberim, quī tunc forte super rīpās erat effūsus; sed relābente flūmine eōs aqua in siccō relīquit. Vāstae tum in eīs locīs sōlitūdinēs erant. Lupa, ut fāmā trā- 10 ditum est, ad vāgītum accurrit, īnfantēs linguā lambit, ūbera eōrum ōrī admōvit mātremque sē gessit.

Cum lupa saepius ad parvulōs velutī ad catulōs reverterētur, Faustulus, pāstor rēgius, rē animadversā eōs tulit in casam et Accae Lārentiae coniugī dedit 15 ēducandōs. Adultī deinde hī inter pāstōrēs prīmō lūdicrīs certāminibus vīrēs auxēre, deinde vēnandō saltūs peragrāre et latrōnēs ā rapīnā pecorum arcēre coepērunt. Quā rē cum eīs īnsidiātī essent latrōnēs, Remus captus est, Rōmulus vī sē dēfendit. Tum 20 Faustulus necessitāte compulsus indicāvit Rōmulō quis esset eōrum avus, quae māter. Rōmulus statim armātīs pāstōribus Albam properāvit.

Intereā Remum latrōnēs ad Amūlium rēgem perdūxērunt, eum accūsantēs quasi Numitōris agrōs īnfestāre solitus esset; itaque Remus ā rēge Numitōrī ad supplicium trāditus est; at cum Numitor, adulēscentis voltum cōnsīderāns, aetātem minimēque servīlem indolem comparāret, haud procul erat quīn nepōtem āgnōsceret. Nam Remus ōris lineāmentīs erat mātrī simillimus aetāsque expositiōnis temporibus congruēbat. Ea rēs dum Numitōris animum anxium tenet, repente Rōmulus supervenit, frātrem līberat, interēmptō Amūliō avum Numitōrem in rēgnum restituit.

Deinde Rōmulus et Remus urbem, in eīsdem locīs ubi expositī ubique ēducātī erant, condidērunt; sed ortā inter eōs contentiōne uter nōmen novae urbī daret eamque imperiō regeret, auspicia dēcrēvērunt adhibēre. Remus prior sex voltūrēs, Rōmulus posteā duodecim vīdit. Sīc Rōmulus, victor auguriō, urbem Rōmam vocāvit. Ad novae urbis tūtēlam sufficere vāllum vidēbātur. Cūius angustiās inrīdēns cum Remus saltū id trāiēcisset, eum īrātus Rōmulus interfēcit hīs increpāns verbīs: "Sīc deinde, quīcumque alius trānsiliet moenia mea." Ita sōlus potītus est imperiō Rōmulus.

II. Romulus, Romanorum rex primus.

753–715 B.C.

Rōmulus imāginem urbis magis quam urbem fēcerat; incolae deerant. Erat in proximō lūcus; hunc asȳlum fēcit. Et statim eō mīra vīs latrōnum pāstōrumque cōnfūgit. Cum vērō uxōrēs ipse populusque nōn habērent, lēgātōs circā vīcīnās gentēs mīsit, quī societātem cōnūbiumque novō populō peterent. Nusquam benīgnē audīta lēgātiō est; lūdibrium etiam additum: "Cūr nōn fēminīs quoque asȳlum aperuistis? Id enim compār foret cōnūbium." Rōmulus aegritūdinem animī dissimulāns lūdōs parat; indīcī deinde fīnitimīs spectāculum iubet. Multī convēnēre studiō etiam videndae novae urbis, māximē Sabīnī cum līberīs et coniugibus. Ubi spectāculī tempus vēnit eōque conversae mentēs cum oculīs erant, tum sīgnō datō iuvenēs Rōmānī discurrunt, virginēs rapiunt.

Haec fuit statim causa bellī. Sabīnī enim ob virginēs raptās bellum adversus Rōmānōs sūmpsērunt et, cum Rōmae appropinquārent, Tarpēiam virginem nactī sunt, quae aquam forte extrā moenia petītum ierat. Hūius pater Rōmānae praeerat arcī. Titus Tatius, Sabīnōrum dux, Tarpēiae optiōnem mūneris dedit, sī exercitum suum in Capitōlium perdūxisset. Illa petiit quod Sabīnī in sinistrīs manibus gererent, vidēlicet et ānulōs et armillās. Quibus dolōsē prōmissīs Tarpēia Sabīnōs in arcem perdūxit, ubi Tatius scūtīs eam obruī iussit; nam et ea in laevīs habuerant. Sīc impia prōditiō celerī poenā vindicāta est.

Deinde Rōmulus ad certāmen prōcessit et in eō locō ubi nunc Rōmānum Forum est, pūgnam cōnseruit. Prīmō impetū vir inter Rōmānōs īnsīgnis, nōmine Hostīlius, fortissimē dīmicāns cecidit; cūius 5 interitū cōnsternātī Rōmānī fugere coepērunt. Iam Sabīnī clāmitābant: "Vīcimus perfidōs hospitēs, imbellēs hostēs. Nunc sciunt longē aliud esse virginēs rapere, aliud pūgnāre cum virīs." Tunc Rōmulus arma ad caelum tollēns Iovī aedem vōvit, et exercitus 10 seu forte seu dīvīnitus restitit. Itaque proelium redintegrātur; sed raptae mulierēs crīnibus passīs ausae sunt sē inter tēla volantia īnferre et hinc patrēs, hinc virōs ōrantēs, pācem conciliārunt.

Rōmulus foedere cum Tatiō ictō et Sabīnōs in 15 urbem recēpit et rēgnum cum Tatiō sociāvit. Vērum nōn ita multō post occīsō Tatiō ad Rōmulum potentātus omnis recidit. Centum deinde ex seniōribus ēlēgit, quōrum cōnsiliō omnia ageret, quōs senātōrēs nōmināvit propter senectūtem. Trēs equitum cen- 20 turiās cōnstituit, populum in trīgintā cūriās distribuit. Hīs ita ōrdinātīs cum ad exercitum lūstrandum cōntiōnem in campō ad Caprae palūdem habēret, subitō coorta est tempestās cum māgnō fragōre tonitribusque et Rōmulus ē cōnspectū ablātus est. Ad deōs trāns- 25 īsse volgō crēditus est; cui reī fidem fēcit Iūlius Proculus, vir nōbilis. Ortā enim inter patrēs et plēbem sēditiōne, in cōntiōnem prōcessit iūreiūrandō adfīrmāns vīsum ā sē Rōmulum augustiōre fōrmā, eundemque praecipere ut sēditiōnibus abstinērent et rem 30 militārem colerent; futūrum ut omnium gentium domi-

NUMA POMPILIUS.

nī exsisterent. Aedēs in colle Quirīnālī Rōmulō cōnstitūta, ipse prō deō cultus et Quirīnus est appellātus.

III. **Numa Pompilius, Romanorum rex secundus.**

715–673 B.C.

Successit Rōmulō Numa Pompilius, vir inclutā iūstitiā et religiōne. Is Curibus, ex oppidō Sabīnōrum, accītus est. Quī cum Rōmam vēnisset, ut populum ferum religiōne mītigāret, sacra plūrima īnstituit. Āram Vestae cōnsecrāvit et īgnem in ārā perpetuō alendum virginibus dedit. Flāminem Iovis sacerdōtem creāvit eumque īnsīgnī veste et curūlī sellā adōrnāvit. Dīcitur quondam ipsum Iovem ē caelō ēlicuisse. Hīc ingentibus fulminibus in urbem dēmissīs dēscendit in nemus Aventīnum, ubi Numam docuit quibus sacrīs fulmina essent prōcūranda, et praetereā imperī certa pīgnora populō Rōmānō datūrum sē esse prōmīsit. Numa laetus rem populō nūntiāvit. Postrīdiē omnēs ad aedēs rēgiās convēnērunt silentēsque exspectābant quid futūrum esset. Atque sōle ortō dēlābitur ē caelō scissō scūtum, quod ancīle appellāvit Numa. Id nē fūrtō auferrī posset, Māmurium fabrum ūndecim scūta eādem fōrmā fabricāre iussit. Duodecim autem Saliōs Mārtis sacerdōtēs lēgit, quī ancīlia, sēcrēta illa imperī pīgnora, custōdīrent et Kalendīs Mārtiīs per urbem canentēs et rīte saltantēs ferrent.

Annum in duodecim mēnsēs ad cursum lūnae dēscrīpsit; nefāstōs fāstōsque diēs fēcit; portās Iānō geminō aedificāvit, ut esset index pācis et bellī; nam apertus, in armīs esse cīvitātem, clausus, pācātōs circā omnēs populōs, sīgnificābat.

Lēgēs quoque plūrimās et ūtilēs tulit Numa. Ut vērō māiōrem īnstitūtīs suīs auctōritātem conciliāret, simulāvit sibi cum deā Ēgeriā esse conloquia nocturna, ēiusque monitū sē omnia quae ageret facere. Lūcus erat, quem medium fōns perennī rigābat aquā; eō saepe Numa sine arbitrīs sē īnferēbat, velut ad congressum deae: ita omnium animōs eā pietāte imbuit ut fidēs āc iūsiūrandum nōn minus quam lēgum et poenārum metus cīvēs continēret. Bellum quidem nūllum gessit, sed nōn minus cīvitātī prōfuit quam Rōmulus. Morbō exstīnctus in Iāniculō mōnte sepultus est. Ita duo deinceps rēgēs, ille bellō, hīc pāce, cīvitātem auxērunt. Rōmulus septem et trīgintā rēgnāvit annōs, Numa trēs et quadrāgintā.

IV. Tullus Hostīlius, Rōmānōrum rēx tertius.

673–641 B.C.

Mortuō Numā Tullus Hostīlius rēx creātus est. Hīc nōn sōlum proximō rēgī dissimilis, sed ferōcior etiam Rōmulō fuit. Eō rēgnante bellum inter Albānōs et Rōmānōs exortum est. Ducibus Hostīliō et Fūfetiō placuit rem paucōrum certāmine fīnīrī. Erant apud Rōmānōs trigeminī frātrēs Horātiī, trēs apud Albānōs Cūriātiī. Cum eīs agunt rēgēs, ut prō suā quisque patriā dīmicent ferrō. Foedus ictum est eā lēge, ut unde victōria ibi imperium esset.

Ictō foedere trigeminī arma capiunt et in medium

LUCIUS TARQUINIUS PRISCUS.

comparātō Tarquinius pecūniā et industriā dīgnitātem atque etiam Ancī rēgis familiāritātem cōnsecūtus est; ā quō tūtor līberīs relictus rēgnum intercēpit et ita administrāvit, quasi iūre adeptus esset.

Tarquinius Prīscus Latīnōs bellō domuit; Circum Māximum aedificāvit; dē Sabīnīs triumphāvit; mūrum lapideum urbī circumdedit. Equitum centuriās duplicāvit, nōmina mūtāre nōn potuit, dēterritus, ut ferunt, Attī Nāvī auctōritāte. Attus enim, eā tempestāte augur inclutus, id fierī posse negābat; nisi avēs addīxissent; īrātus rēx in experīmentum artis eum interrogāvit fierīne posset quod ipse mente concēpisset; Attus auguriō āctō fierī posse respondit. "Atquī hōc," inquit rēx, "agitābam, num cōtem illam secāre novāculā possem." "Potes ergō," inquit augur, et rēx secuisse dīcitur. Tarquinius fīlium tredecim annōrum, quod in proeliō hostem percussisset, praetextā bullāque dōnāvit; unde haec ingenuōrum puerōrum insignia esse coepērunt.

Supererant duo Ancī fīliī, quī aegrē ferentēs sē paternō rēgnō fraudātōs esse rēgī īnsidiās parāvērunt. Ex pāstōribus duōs ferōcissimōs dēligunt ad patrandum facinus. Eī simulātā rixā in vestibulō rēgiae tumultuantur. Quōrum clāmor cum penitus in rēgiam pervēnisset, vocātī ad rēgem pergunt. Prīmō uterque vōciferārī coepit et certātim alter alterī obstrepere. Cum vērō iūssī essent invicem dīcere, ūnus ex compositō rem ōrditur; dumque intentus in eum sē rēx tōtus āvertit, alter ēlātam secūrim in ēius caput dēiēcit, et relictō in volnere tēlō ambō forās sē prōripiunt.

VII. Servius Tullius, Romanorum rex sextus.

578-534 B.C.

Post hunc Servius Tullius suscēpit imperium genitus ex nōbilī fēminā, captīvā tamen et famulā. Quī cum in domō Tarquinī Prīscī ēducārētur, ferunt prōdigium vīsū ēventūque mīrābile accidisse. Flammae speciēs pueri dormientis caput amplexa est. Hōc vīsū Tanaquil summam eī dīgnitātem portendī intellēxit coniugīque suāsit ut eum haud secus āc suōs līberōs ēducāret. Is postquam adolēvit, et fortitūdine et cōnsiliō īnsīgnis fuit. In proeliō quōdam, in quō rēx Tarquinius adversus Sabīnōs cōnflīxit, mīlitibus sēgnius dīmicantibus, raptum sīgnum in hostem mīsit. Cūius recipiendī grātiā Rōmānī tam ācriter pūgnāvērunt ut et sīgnum et vīctōriam referrent. Quā rē ā Tarquiniō gener adsūmptus est; et cum Tarquinius occīsus esset, Tanaquil, Tarquinī uxor, mortem ēius cēlāvit populumque ex superiōre parte aedium adlocūta, ait rēgem grave quidem, sed nōn lētāle volnus accēpisse eumque petere ut interim, dum convalēsceret, Serviō Tulliō dictō audientēs essent. Sīc Servius Tullius rēgnāre coepit, sed rēctē imperium administrāvit. Sabīnōs subēgit; montēs trēs, Quirīnālem, Vīminālem, Esquilīnum urbī adiūnxit; fossās circā mūrum dūxit. Īdem cēnsum ōrdināvit et populum in classēs et centuriās distribuit.

Servius Tullius aliquod urbī decus addere volēbat. Iam tum inclutum erat Diānae Ephesiae fānum. Id commūniter ā cīvitātibus Asiae factum fāma ferēbat. Itaque Latīnōrum populīs suāsit ut et ipsī fānum

SERVIUS TULLIUS.

Diānae cum populō Rōmānō Rōmae in Aventīnō mōnte aedificārent. Quō factō bōs mīrae māgnitūdinis cuidam Latīnō nāta dīcitur et respōnsum somniō datum eum populum summam imperī habitūrum cūius cīvis bovem illam Diānae immolāsset. Latīnus bovem ad fānum Diānae ēgit et causam sacerdōtī Rōmānō exposuit. Ille callidus dīxit prius eum vīvō flūmine manūs abluere dēbēre. Latīnus dum ad Tiberim dēscendit, sacerdōs bovem immolāvit. Ita imperium cīvibus sibique glōriam adquīsīvit.

Servius Tullius fīliam alteram ferōcem, mītem alteram habēns, cum Tarquinī fīliōs parī esse animō vidēret, ferōcem mītī, mītem ferōcī in mātrimōnium dedit, nē duo violenta ingenia mātrimōniō iungerentur. Sed mitēs seu forte seu fraude periērunt; ferōcēs mōrum similitūdō coniūnxit. Statim Tarquinius ā Tulliā incitātus advocātō senātū rēgnum paternum repetere coepit. Quā rē audītā Servius dum ad cūriam contendit, iūssū Tarquinī per gradūs dēiectus et domum refugiēns intérfectus est. Tullia carpentō vecta in Forum properāvit et coniugem ē cūriā ēvocātum prīma rēgem salūtāvit; cūius iūssū cum ē turbā āc tumultū dēcessisset domumque redīret, vīsō patris corpore mūliōnem cunctantem et frēna inhibentem super ipsum corpus carpentum agere iussit. Unde vīcus ille scelerātus dictus est. Servius Tullius rēgnāvit annōs quattuor et quadrāgintā.

VIII. Tarquinius Superbus, Romanorum rex septimus et ultimus.

534-510 B.C.

Tarquinius Superbus regnum sceleste occupavit. Tamen bello strenuus Latinos Sabinosque domuit. Urbem Gabios in potestatem redegit fraude Sexti fili. Is cum indigne ferret eam urbem a patre expugnari
5 non posse, ad Gabinos se contulit, patris saevitiam in se conquerens: Benigne a Gabinis exceptus paulatim eorum benevolentiam consequitur, fictis blanditiis ita eos adliciens ut apud omnes plurimum posset et ad postremum dux belli eligeretur. Tum e suis unum ad
10 patrem mittit sciscitatum quidnam se facere vellet. Pater nuntio fili nihil respondit, sed velut deliberabundus in hortum transiit ibique inambulans sequente nuntio altissima papaverum capita baculo decussit. Nuntius fessus exspectando rediit Gabios. Sextus
15 cognito silentio patris et facto intellexit quid vellet pater. Primores civitatis interemit patrique urbem sine ulla dimicatione tradidit.

Postea rex Ardeam urbem obsidebat. Ibi cum in castris essent, Tarquinius Collatinus, sorore regis
20 natus, forte cenabat apud Sextum Tarquinium cum iuvenibus regiis. Incidit de uxoribus mentio: cum suam unus quisque laudaret, placuit experiri. Itaque citatis equis Romam avolant; regias nurus in convivio et luxu deprehendunt. Pergunt inde Collatiam; Lu-
25 cretiam, Collatini uxorem, inter ancillas lanae deditam inveniunt. Ea ergo ceteris praestare iudicatur. Paucis

TARQUINIUS SUPERBUS.

interiectīs diēbus Sextus Collātiam rediit et Lucrētiae vim attulit. Illa posterō diē advocātīs patre et coniuge rem exposuit et sē cultrō, quem sub veste abditum habēbat, occīdit. Conclāmant vir paterque et in exitium rēgum coniūrant. Tarquiniō Rōmam redeuntī clausae sunt urbis portae et exsilium indictum.

In antīquīs annālibus memoriae haec sunt prōdita. Anus hospita atque incōgnita ad Tarquinium quondam Superbum rēgem adiit, novem librōs ferēns, quōs esse dīcēbat dīvīna ōrācula : eōs sē velle vēnum dare. Tarquinius pretium percontātus est : mulier nimium atque immēnsum poposcit. Rēx, quasi anus aetāte dēsiperet, dērīsit. Tum illa foculum cum īgnī appōnit et trēs librōs ex novem deūrit; et, ecquid reliquōs sex eōdem pretiō emere vellet, rēgem interrogāvit. Sed Tarquinius id multō rīsit magis dīxitque anum iam procul dubiō dēlīrāre. Mulier ibīdem statim trēs aliōs librōs exussit; atque id ipsum dēnuō placidē rogat, ut trēs reliquōs eōdem illō pretiō emat. Tarquinius ōre iam sēriō atque attentiōre animō fit; eam cōnstantiam cōnfīdentiamque nōn neglegendam intellegit ; librōs trēs reliquōs mercātur nihilō minōre pretiō quam quod erat petītum prō omnibus. Sed eam mulierem tunc ā Tarquiniō dīgressam posteā nusquam locī vīsam cōnstitit. Librī trēs in sacrāriō conditī Sibyllīnīque appellātī. Ad eōs, quasi ad ōrāculum, Quīndecim virī adeunt, cum diī immortālēs pūblicē cōnsulendī sunt.

IX. Horatius Cocles.

507 B.C.

Porsena, rēx Etruscōrum, ad restituendōs in rēgnum Tarquiniōs īnfestō exercitū Rōmam vēnit. Prīmō impetū Iāniculum cēpit. Nōn umquam aliās ante tantus terror Rōmānōs invāsit; adeō valida rēs tum Clūsīna erat māgnumque Porsenae nōmen. Ex agrīs in urbem dēmigrant : urbem ipsam saepiunt praesidiīs. Alia urbis pars mūrīs, alia Tiberī obiectō tūta vidēbātur. Pōns sublicius iter paene hostibus dedit, nisi ūnus vir fuisset Horātius Coclēs, illō cōgnōmine appellātus, quod in aliō proeliō oculum āmīserat. Is extrēmā pontis parte occupātā aciem hostium sōlus sustinuit dōnec pōns ā tergō interrumperētur. Ipsa audācia obstupefēcit hostēs; ponte rescissō armātus in Tiberim dēsiluit et multīs superincidentibus tēlīs incolumis ad suōs trānāvit. Grāta ergā tantam virtūtem cīvitās fuit; eī tantum agrī pūblicē datum est quantum ūnō diē circumarāvit. Statua quoque eī in Comitiō posita.

X. Menenius Agrippa.

494 B.C.

Menēnius Agrippa concordiam inter patrēs plēbemque restituit. Nam cum plēbs ā patribus in mōntem sacrum sēcessisset, quod tribūta simul et mīlitiam nōn tolerāret, Agrippa, vir fācundus, ad plēbem missus est. Quī intrōmissus in castra nihil aliud nisi hōc nārrāsse fertur. "Ōlim hūmānī artūs, cum ventrem ōtiōsum

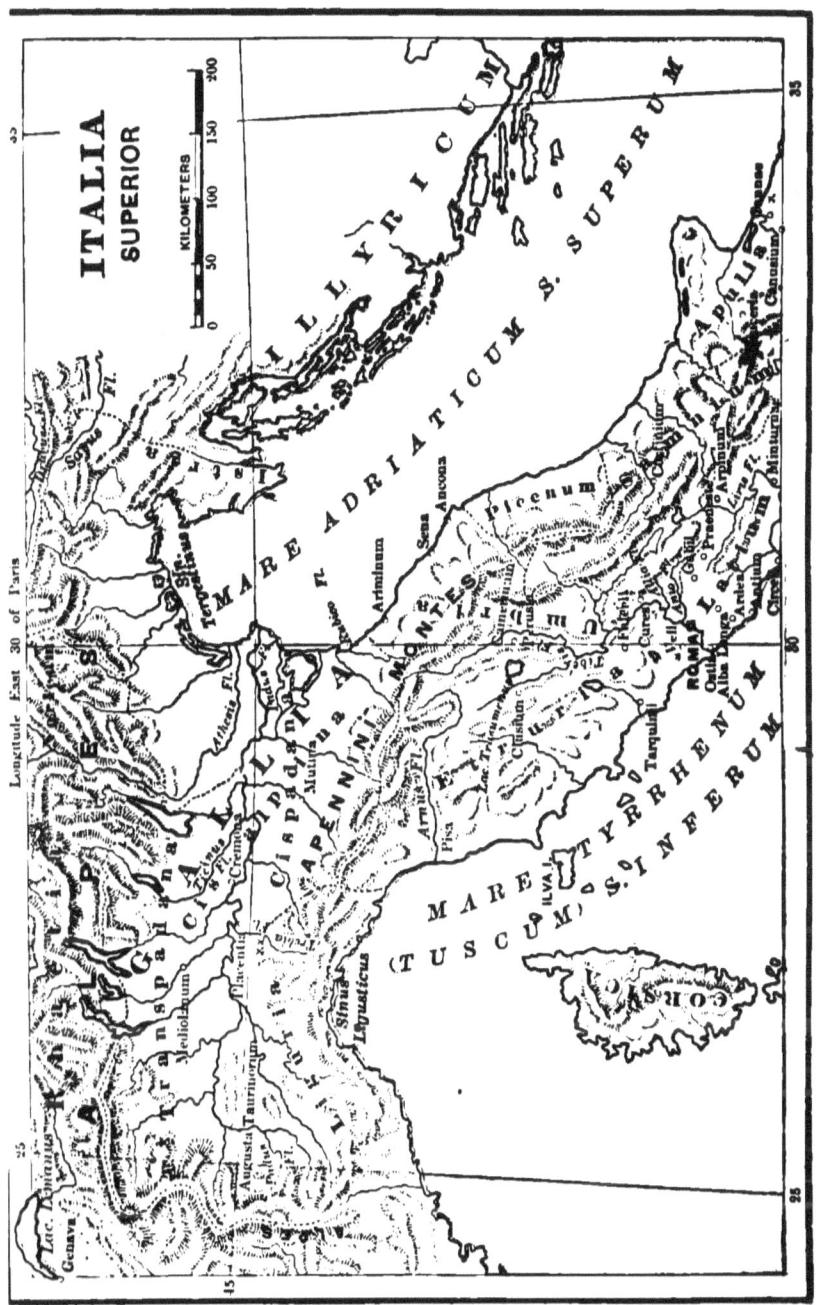

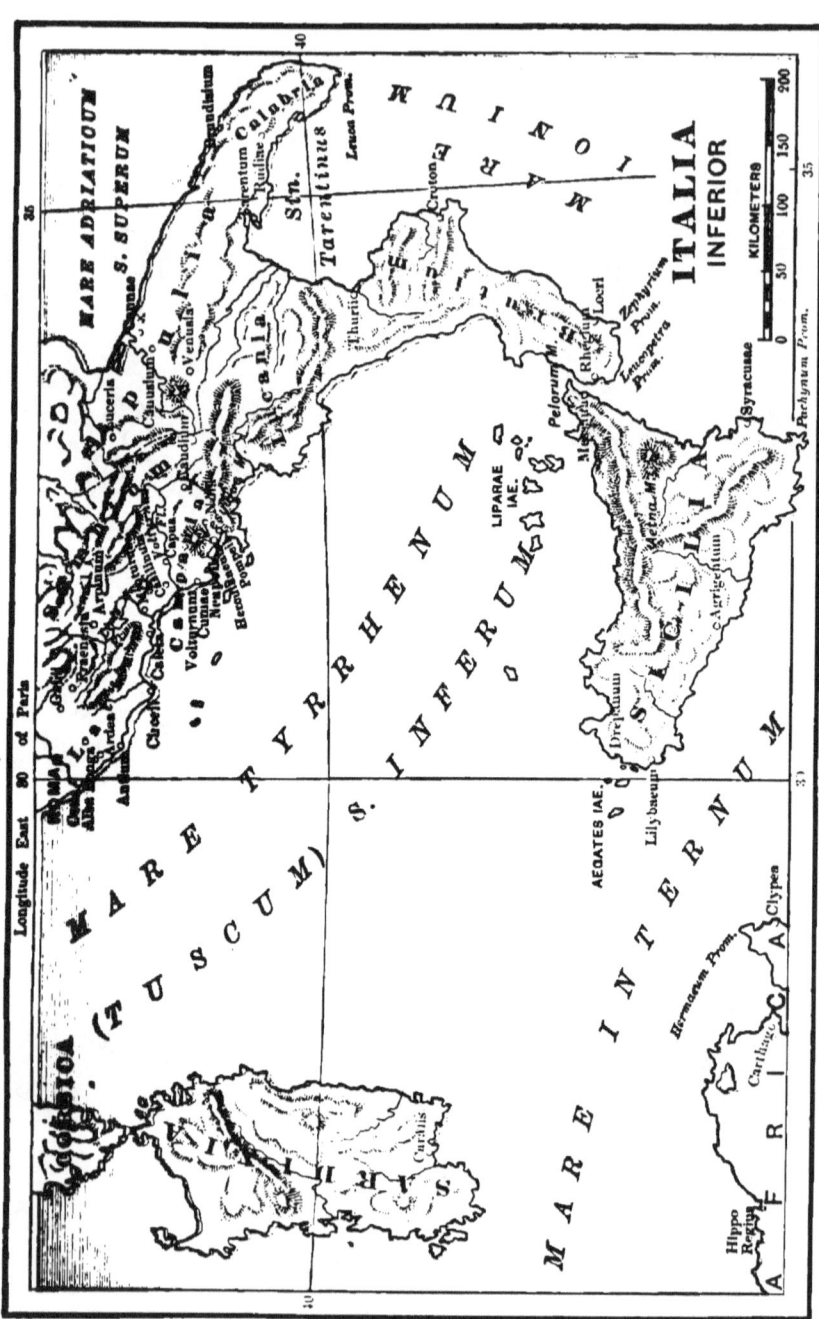

cernerent, ab eō discordārunt, cōnspīrāruntque nē
manūs ad ōs cibum ferrent nēve ōs acciperet datum
nēve dentēs cōnficerent. At dum ventrem domāre
volunt, ipsī quoque defēcērunt, tōtumque corpus ad
extrēmam tābem vēnit ; inde intellēxērunt ventris 5
quoque haud sēgne ministerium esse eumque acceptōs
cibōs concoquere et per omnia membra dīgerere, et cum
eō in grātiam rediērunt. Sīc senātus et plēbēs, quasi
ūnum corpus, discordiā pereunt, concordiā valent."
Hāc fābulā Menēnius flēxit hominum mentēs : plēbs 10
in urbem regressa est. Creāvit tamen tribūnōs, quī
lībertātem suam ā nōbilitātis superbiā dēfenderent.
Paulō post mortuus est Menēnius, vir omnī vītā pariter
patribus āc plēbī cārus. Is tamen in tantā paupertāte
dēcessit ut eum plēbs conlātīs sextantibus sepelīret, 15
locum sepulcrō senātus pūblicē daret. Potest cōn-
sōlārī pauperēs Menēnius, sed multō magis docēre
locuplētēs quam nōn sit necessāria solidam laudem
cupientī nimis anxia dīvitiārum comparātiō.

XI. **Lucius Virginius Centurio.**

451 B.C.

Annō trecentēsimō ab urbe conditā prō duōbus cōn- 20
sulibus decem virī creātī sunt, quī adlātās ē Graeciā
lēgēs populō prōpōnerent. Duodecim tabulīs eae sunt
perscrīptae. Cēterum decem virī suā ipsōrum īnsolen-
tiā in exitium āctī sunt. Nam ūnus ex eīs Appius
Claudius virginem plēbēiam adamāvit. Quam cum 25
Appius nōn posset pretiō āc spē pellicere, ūnum ē

clientibus subōrnāvit, quī eam in servitūtem dēposceret, facile victūrum sē spērāns, cum ipse esset et accūsātor et iūdex. Lūcius Virgīnius, puellae pater, tunc aberat mīlitiae causā. Cliēns igitur virginī venientī in
5 Forum (namque ibi in tabernīs litterārum lūdī erant) iniēcit manum, adfirmāns suam esse servam; eam sequī sē iubet; nī faciat, minātur sē vī abstractūrum. Pavidā puellā stupente, ad clāmōrem nūtrīcis fit concursus. Itaque cum ille puellam vī nōn posset ab-
10 dūcere, eam vocat in iūs ipsō Appiō iūdice.

Intereā missī nūntiī ad Virgīnium properant. Is, commeātū sūmptō, ā castrīs profectus prīmā lūce Rōmam advēnit, cum iam cīvitās in Forō exspectātiōne ērēcta stābat. Virgīnius statim in Forum lacrimābun-
15 dus et cīvium opem implōrāns fīliam suam dēdūcit. Neque eō sētius Appius, cum in tribūnal ēscendisset, Virgīniam clientī suō addīxit. Tum pater, ubi nihil usquam auxilī vīdit, "Quaesō," inquit, "Appī, īgnōsce patriō dolōrī; sine mē fīliam ūltimum adloquī." Datā
20 veniā pater cum fīliam sēdūxisset, ab laniō cultrō adreptō pectus puellae trānsfīgit. Tum vērō sibi viam facit et respersus cruōre ad exercitum profūgit et mīlitēs ad vindicandum facinus accendit. Concitātus exercitus montem Aventīnum īnsēdit; decem tribūnōs
25 mīlitum creāvit; decem virōs magistrātū sē abdicāre coēgit eōsque omnēs aut morte aut exsiliō multāvit; ipse Appius Claudius in carcerem coniectus mortem sibi cōnscīvit.

TRIUMPHAL CHARIOT.

XII. Marcus Furius Camillus.

390 B.C.

Cum Mārcus Fūrius Camillus urbem Falēriōs obsidēret, lūdī magister plūrimōs et nōbilissimōs inde puerōs, velut ambulandī grātiā ēductōs, in castra Rōmānōrum perdūxit. Quibus Camillō trāditīs nōn erat dubium quīn Faliscī dēpositō bellō sēsē Rōmānīs dēditūrī essent. Sed Camillus perfidiam prōditōris dētestātus, "Nōn ad similem tuī," inquit, "vēnistī: sunt et bellī sīcut pācis iūra; arma habēmus nōn adversus eam aetātem cui etiam captīs urbibus parcitur, sed adversus armātōs, quī nec laesī nec lacessītī ā nōbīs castra Rōmāna ad Vēiōs oppūgnāvērunt." Dēnūdārī deinde magistrum iussit, eumque manibus post tergum inligātīs in urbem redūcendum puerīs trādidit virgāsque eīs dedit, quibus prōditōrem agerent in urbem verberantēs. Statim Faliscī, beneficiō magis quam armīs victī, portās Rōmānīs aperuērunt.

Vēientēs etiam illō tempore rebellāvērunt. Quōrum quanta rēs fuerit, indicat decennis obsidiō. Tunc prīmum hībernācula mīlitibus facta hiemātumque sub pellibus, tum prīmum stīpendium ex aerāriō mīlitibus datum adāctusque mīles iūreiūrandō, nisi captā urbe, sē nōn esse discessūrum. Dēnique nōn scālīs neque inruptiōne sed cunīculō et subterrāneīs dolīs perāctum urbis excidium.

Postmodum Camillō est crīminī datum, quod albīs equīs triumphāsset et praedam inīquē dīvīsisset; diē dictā ab L. Appulēiō tribūnō plēbis damnātus Ardeam

concessit. Urbe ēgrediēns ā diīs precātus esse dīcitur, ut, sī innoxiō sibi ea iniūria fieret, prīmō quōque tempore dēsīderium suī cīvitātī ingrātae facerent. Neque multō post Gallī Senonēs Clūsium, Etrūriae
5 oppidum, obsēdērunt. Clūsīnī novō bellō exterritī ab Rōmānīs auxilium petiērunt. Missī sunt Rōmā trēs lēgātī, quī Gallōs monērent ut ab oppūgnātiōne dēsisterent. Ex hīs lēgātīs ūnus contrā iūs gentium in aciem prōcessit et ducem Senonum interfēcit. Quā
10 rē commōtī Gallī, petītīs in dēditiōnem lēgātīs neque impetrātīs, Rōmam petiērunt et exercitum Rōmānum apud Alliam fluvium cecīdērunt ante diem quīntum decimum Kalendās Sextīlēs: quī diēs inter nefāstōs relātus Alliēnsis dictus est.
15 Gallī vīctōrēs haud multō ante sōlis occāsum ad urbem Rōmam perveniunt. Postquam hostēs adesse nūntiātum est, reliqua iuventūs Rōmāna cum Manliō in arcem fūgit; seniōrēs vērō domōs regressī adventum Gallōrum obstinātō ad mortem animō exspectābant.
20 Quī eōrum curūlēs magistrātūs gesserant, ōrnātī honōrum īnsīgnibus in vestibulīs aedium eburneīs sellīs īnsēdērunt, ut, cum vēnisset hostis, in suā dīgnitāte morerentur. Interim Gallī domōs patentēs ingressī vident praetextātōs senēs, virōs ōrnātū et voltūs māie-
25 stāte diīs simillimōs. Ad quōs cum Gallī velutī ad simulācra conversī stārent, ūnus ex hīs senibus dīcitur Gallō barbam suam permulcentī scīpiōnem eburneum in caput incussisse. Īrātus Gallus eum occīdit; ab eō initium caedis ortum est. Cēterī omnēs in sēdibus
30 suīs trucīdātī sunt.

MARCUS FURIUS CAMILLUS.

Gallī deinde impetum facere in arcem statuunt. Prīmō mīlitem, quī temptāret viam, praemīsērunt. Tum nocte sublūstrī, sublevantēs invicem et trahentēs aliī aliōs, in summum saxum ēvāsērunt tantō silentiō ut nōn custōdēs sōlum fallerent, sed nē canēs quidem, sollicitum animal ad nocturnōs strepitūs, excitārent. Ānserēs nŏn fefellēre, quibus in summā inopiā Rōmānī abstinuerant, quia avēs erant Iūnōnis sacrae: quae rēs Rōmānīs salūtī fuit. Namque clangōre eārum ālārumque crepitū excītus Mānlius, vir bellō ēgregius, cēterōs ad arma vocat et, dum cēterī trepidant, armīs adreptīs Gallum quī iam in summō cōnstiterat umbōne ictum dēturbaṭ. Cūius cāsus cum proximōs sterneret, omnēs Gallī ascendentēs facile dēiciuntur.

Tunc cōnsēnsū omnium placuit ab exsiliō Camillum accīrī. Missī igitur ad eum lēgātī ipseque dictātor absēns dictus est. Interim famēs utrumque exercitum urguēbat; sed nē Gallī putārent Rōmānōs eā necessitāte ad dēditiōnem cōgī, multīs locīs dē Capitōliō pānis iactātus est in hostium statiōnēs. Ad postrēmum Gallī quoque, obsidiōne fatīgātī, pretiō mīlle pondō aurī addūcuntur ut obsidiōnem relinquerent. Cum autem inīqua pondera essent adlāta et Gallōrum dux gladiō per īnsolentiam additō vae victīs increpāret, Camillus dictātor intervēnit, conlēctīs Rōmānī exercitūs reliquiīs; auferrī aurum dē mediō iubet dēnūntiatque Gallīs ut sē ad proelium expediant. Īnstruit deinde aciem et Gallōs dēvīcit. Nē nūntius quidem clādis relictus est. Dictātor recuperātā ex hostibus patriā triumphāns urbem ingressus et ā mīlitibus parēns patriae conditorque alter urbis appellātus est. Sed ut oppidum cīvibus, ita cīvēs oppidō reddidit. Agitābant enim tribūnī plēbem ut relictīs ruīnīs in urbem parātam Vēiōs trānsmigrārent ; quod quidem cōnsilium gravissimā Camillī ōrātiōne discussum est. Mōvit populum vōcis quoque ōmen ex centuriōne audītae, quī, cum in Forum vēnisset, manipulāribus suīs dīxerat: "Sīgnifer, statue signum, hīc manēbimus optimē." Quā vōce audītā et senātus accipere sē ōmen conclāmāvit et plēbs circumfūsa approbāvit.

M. Mānlius, quī Capitōlium ā Gallīs dēfenderat, cum obstrictōs aere aliēnō līberāret, nexōs exsolveret, crīmine adfectātī rēgnī damnātus dē saxō Tarpēiō dēiectus est.

XIII. Spurius Postumius.
321 B.C.

Iam Rōmānī bellum contrā Samnītēs suscēpērunt, ā Campānīs in auxilium vocātī. Omnium nōn modo Ītaliae sed tōtō orbe terrārum pulcherrima Campāniae plaga est. Nihil mollius caelō, nihil ūberius solō: bis flōribus vernat. Ideō Līberī Cererisque certāmen dīcitur. Nihil hospitālius marī. Hīc illī nōbilēs portūs, Cāiēta, Mīsēnum et tepentēs fontibus Bāiae ; hīc Lucrīnus et Avernus lacus; hīc amictī vītibus montēs Gaurus, Falernus, Massicus, et pulcherrimus omnium Vesuvius, Aetnaeī īgnis imitātor. Urbēs ad mare Formiae, Cūmae, Puteolī, Neāpolis, Herculāneum, Pompeii et ipsa, caput urbium, Capua quondam inter trēs māximās cum Rōmā et Carthāgine numerāta. Prō hāc

SPURIUS POSTUMIUS.

urbe, prō his regiōnibus populus Rōmānus Samnītēs invāsit. Per quīnquāgintā ferē annōs cum Samnītibus pūgnātum saepeque in extrēma perīcula ventum est.

Spurius Postumius cōnsul cum bellum adversus Samnītēs gereret, ā Gāiō Pontiō, hostium duce, in insidiās inductus est : namque is simulātōs trānsfugās mīsit, quī Rōmānīs dīcerent Lūceriam, Āpūliae urbem, ā Samnītibus obsidērī. Nōn erat dubium quīn Rōmānī Lūcerīnīs, bonīs āc fidēlibus sociīs, opem ferrent. Duae ad Lūceriam ferēbant viae, altera longior et tūtior, altera brevior et perīculōsior; festīnātiō breviōrem ēlēgit. Itaque cum in īnsidiās vēnissent, quī locus Furculae Caudīnae vocābātur, et fraus hostīlis appāruisset, retrō viam, quā vēnerant, repetunt, at eam quoque hostium praesidiō clausam inveniunt. Sistunt igitur gradum et, omnī spē ēvādendī adēmptā, intuentēs aliī aliōs diū immōbilēs silent; deinde ērumpunt in querellās adversus ducēs, quōrum temeritāte in eum locum erant adductī. Ita noctem tum cibī tum quiētis immemorēs trādūxērunt.

Nec Samnītēs ipsī, quid sibi faciendum esset in rē tam laetā, sciēbant. Pontius accītum patrem Hērennium rogāvit quid fierī placēret. Is ubi audīvit inter duōs saltūs clausum esse exercitum Rōmānum, dīxit aut omnēs esse occīdendōs, ut vīrēs frangerentur, aut omnēs dīmittendōs esse incolumēs, ut beneficiō obligārentur. Neutra sententia accepta est. Intereā Rōmānī necessitāte vīctī lēgātōs mittunt, quī pācem petant ; pāx concessa est eā lēge, ut omnēs sub iugum trādūcerentur. Itaque palūdāmenta cōnsulibus dē-

tracta, ipsīque prīmī sub iugum missī, deinde singulae legiōnēs. Circumstābant armātī hostēs exprobrantēs inlūdentēsque. Rōmānīs ē saltū ēgressīs lūx ipsa omnī morte trīstior fuit; ubi Capuam vēnērunt, pudor fugere
5 conloquia et coetūs hominum cōgēbat. Sērō Rōmam ingressī sē in suās quisque aedēs abdidērunt.
Dēlīberante senātū dē pāce Caudīnā Postumius sententiam dīcere iūssus, "Turpī spōnsiōne," inquit, "quā mē obstrinxī, nōn tenētur populus Rōmānus, quoniam
10 ēius iniūssū facta est; nec quidquam ex eā praeter corpus meum dēbētur Samnītibus. Eīs dēdite mē nūdum vinctumque; in mē ūnum saeviant; exsolvam religiōne populum." Senātus, hanc animī māgnitūdinem admīrātus, Postumium laudāvit ēiusque sententiam
15 secūtus est. Trāditus est igitur Postumius fētiālibus, quī eum ad Samnītēs dūcerent. Vestis eī dētracta, manūs post tergum vinctae sunt, cumque appāritor, verēcundiā māiestātis, Postumium laxē vincīret, "Quīn tū," inquit ipse Postumius, "addūcis lōrum, ut iūsta
20 fīat dēditiō?" Tum ubi in coetum Samnītium vēnit, factā dēditiōne, Postumius fētiālis femur genū, quantā potuit vī, perculit et clārā vōce ait sē Samnītem cīvem esse, illum lēgātum fētiālem ā sē contrā iūs gentium violātum; eō iūstius bellum adversus Samnītēs fore.
25 Accepta nōn est ā Samnītibus illa dēditiō Postumiusque in castra Rōmāna inviolātus rediit.

XIV. Publius Valerius Laevinus et Pyrrhus, rex Epiri.

281 B.C.

Tarentīnīs, quod Rōmānōrum lēgātīs iniūriam fēcissent, bellum indictum est. Hī Pyrrhum, Ēpīrī rēgem, contrā Rōmānōs auxilium poposcērunt, quī ex genere Achillis originem trahēbat. Is paulō post in Ītaliam vēnit tumque prīmum Rōmānī cum trānsmarīnō hoste dīmicāvērunt. Missus est contrā eum cōnsul Pūblius Valerius Laevīnus, quī cum explōrātōrēs Pyrrhī cēpisset, iussit eōs per castra dūcī, ostendī omnem exercitum tumque dīmittī, ut renūntiārent Pyrrhō quaecumque ā Rōmānīs agerentur. Commissā mox pūgnā cum iam Pyrrhī exercitus pedem referret, rēx elephantōs in Rōmānōrum aciem agī iussit; tumque mūtāta est proelī fortūna. Rōmānōs vāstōrum corporum mōlēs terribilisque superadstantium armātōrum speciēs turbāvit. Equī etiam, cōnspectū et odōre bēluārum exterritī, sessōrēs vel excutiēbant vel sēcum in fugam abripiēbant. Nox proeliō fīnem dedit.

Pyrrhus captīvōs Rōmānōs summō honōre habuit; occīsōs sepelīvit. Quōs cum adversō volnere et trucī voltū etiam mortuōs iacentēs vīdisset, tulisse ad caelum manūs dīcitur cum hāc vōce: sē tōtīus orbis dominum esse potuisse, sī tālēs sibi mīlitēs contigissent. Amīcīs grātulantibus, "Quid mihi cum tālī victōriā," inquit, "ubi exercitūs rōbur āmittam? Sī iterum eōdem modō vīcerō, sine ūllō mīlite in Ēpīrum revertar." Deinde ad urbem Rōmam māgnīs itineribus contendit; omnia ferrō īgnīque vāstāvit; ad vīcēsimum ab urbe lapidem castra posuit. Pyrrhō obviam vēnit Laevīnus cum novō exercitū. Quō vīsō rēx ait sibi eandem adversus Rōmānōs esse fortūnam quam Herculī adversus hydram, cui tot capita renāscēbantur quot praecīsa erant; 5 deinde in Campāniam sē recēpit. Missōs ā senātū dē redimendīs captīvīs lēgātōs honōrificē excēpit; captīvōs sine pretiō reddidit ut Rōmānī, cōgnitā iam virtūte suā, cōgnōscerent etiam līberālitātem.

Erat Pyrrhus mītī āc plācābilī animō; solet enim 10 māgnī animī comes esse clēmentia. Eius hūmānitātem expertī sunt Tarentīnī. Quī cum sērō intellēxissent sē prō sociō dominum accēpisse, sortem suam miserābantur idque aliquantō līberius ubi vīnō incaluerant. Neque deerant quī ad Pyrrhum dēferrent; arcessītīque 15 nōnnūllī, quod inter convīvium parum honōrificē dē rēge locūtī essent; sed perīculum simplex cōnfessiō culpae discussit. Nam cum rēx percontātus esset num ea quae pervēnissent ad aurēs suās dīxissent "Et haec dīximus," inquiunt, "rēx, et nisi vīnum 20 dēfēcisset, multō plūra et graviōra dictūrī fuimus." Pyrrhus, quī mālēbat vīnī quam hominum eam culpam vidērī, subrīdēns eōs dīmisit.

Pyrrhus igitur cum putāret sibi glōriōsum fore pācem et foedus cum Rōmānīs post victōriam facere, 25 Rōmam mīsit lēgātum Cīneam, quī pācem aequīs condiciōnibus prōpōneret. Erat is rēgī familiāris multumque apud eum grātiā valēbat. Dīcere solēbat Pyrrhus sē plūrēs urbēs Cīneae ēloquentiā quam vī et armīs expūgnāsse. Cīneās tamen rēgis cupiditātem nōn 30 adūlābātur; nam cum in sermōne Pyrrhus eī cōnsilia

LAEVINUS ET PYRRHUS.

sua aperīret dīxissetque sē velle Ītaliam diciōnī suae subicere, Cīneās, "Superātīs Rōmānīs," inquit, "quid agere dēstinās, ō rēx?" "Ītaliae vīcīna est Sicilia," inquit Pyrrhus, "nec difficile erit eam armīs occupāre." Tunc Cīneās: "Occupātā Siciliā quid posteā āctūrus es?" Rēx, quī nōndum Cīneae mentem perspiciēbat, "In Āfricam," inquit, "trāicere mihi in animō est." Cui ille: "Quid deinde, ō rēx?" "Tum dēnique, mī Cīneās," inquit Pyrrhus, "nōs quiētī dabimus dulcīque ōtiō fruēmur." Tum Cīneās: "At quid impedit quōminus istō ōtiō iam nunc fruāris?"

Rōmam cum vēnisset Cīneās, domōs prīncipum cum ingentibus dōnīs circumībat. Nusquam vērō receptus est. Nōn ā virīs sōlum sed etiam ā mulieribus sprēta ēius mūnera. Intrōductus deinde in cūriam cum rēgis virtūtem prōpēnsumque in Rōmānōs animum verbīs extolleret et dē condiciōnum aequitāte dissereret et sententia senātūs ad pācem et foedus faciendum inclināre vidērētur, tum Appius Claudius, ob senectūtem et caecitātem abstinēre cūriā ōlim solitus, cōnfestim in senātum lectīcā dēferrī sē iussit ibique gravissimā ōrātiōne pācem dissuāsit, itaque respōnsum Pyrrhō ā senātū est eum, dōnec Ītaliā excessisset, pācem cum Rōmānīs habēre nōn posse. Praetereā Rōmānī captīvōs omnēs quōs Pyrrhus reddiderat, īnfāmēs habērī iussērunt, quod armātī capī potuissent, neque ante eōs ad veterem statum revertī quam sī bīnūm hostium occīsōrum spolia rettulissent. Ita lēgātus ad rēgem revertit: ā quō cum Pyrrhus quaereret quālem Rōmam comperisset, Cīneās respondit urbem sibi templum, senātum vērō cōnsessum rēgum esse vīsum.

XV. Gaius Fabricius.

278 B.C.

Ex lēgātīs quī ād Pyrrhum dē captīvīs redimendīs vēnerant, fuit C. Fabricius. Cūius postquam aūdīvit Pyrrhus māgnum esse apud Rōmānōs nōmen, ut virī bonī et bellō ēgregiī, sed admodum pauperis, eum prae
5 cēterīs honōrificē āc līberāliter habuit eīque mūnera atque aurum obtulit, quae omnia repudiāvit Fabricius. Posterō diē cum illum Pyrrhus vellet exterrēre cōnspectū subitō elephantī, imperāvit suīs ut, Fabriciō sēcum conloquente, bēlua post aulaeum admovērētur.
10 Quod ubi factum est, sīgnō datō remōtōque aulaeō, repente bēlua strīdōrem horrendum ēmīsit et proboscidem super Fabricī caput dēmīsit. Sed ille subrīdēns: "Neque herī mē aurum tuum pellēxit, neque hodiē perterrefēcit bēlua."
15 Fabricī admīrātus virtūtem Pyrrhus illum sēcrētō invītāvit ut patriam dēsereret sēcumque vellet vīvere, quārtā etiam rēgnī suī parte oblātā; cui Fabricius ita respondit: "Sī mē virum bonum iūdicās, cūr mē vīs corrumpere? sīn vērō malum, cūr mē ambīs?" Annō
20 interiectō, omnī spē pācis inter Pyrrhum et Rōmānōs conciliandae ablātā, Fabricius cōnsul factus contrā eum missus est. Cumque vīcīna castra ipse et rēx habērent, medicus rēgis nocte ad Fabricium vēnit eīque pollicitus est, sī praemium sibi prōposuisset, sē
25 Pyrrhum venēnō necātūrum. Hunc Fabricius vinctum redūcī iussit ad dominum et Pyrrhō dīcī quae contrā caput ēius medicus spopondisset. Tunc rēx admīrātus

GAIUS FABRICIUS.

eum dixisse fertur: "Ille est Fabricius, qui difficilius ab honestāte quam sōl ā suō cursū potest āvertī."

Fabricius cum apud Pyrrhum rēgem lēgātus esset, Cineam audīvit nārrantem esse quendam Athēnīs quī sē sapientem profitērētur, eumque dīcere omnia quae facerēmus ad voluptātem esse referenda. Tunc Fabricium exclāmāsse ferunt: "Utinam id hostibus nostrīs persuādeātur, quō facilius vincī possint cum sē voluptātibus dederint!" Nihil magis ab ēius vītā aliēnum erat quam voluptās et lūxus. Tōta ēius supellex argentea salīnō ūnō cōnstābat et patellā ad ūsum sacrōrum, quae corneō pediculō sustinēbātur. Cēnābat ad focum rādīcēs et herbās, cum lēgātī Samnītium ad eum vēnērunt māgnamque eī pecūniam obtulērunt; quibus sīc respondit: "Quam diū cupiditātibus imperāre poterō, nihil mihi deerit; vōs autem pecūniam ad eōs quī hāc indigent reportāte."

Gāius Fabricius cum Rūfīnō, virō nōbilī, simultātem gerēbat ob mōrum dissimilitūdinem, cum ipse pecūniae contemptor esset, hīc avārus et fūrāx exīstimārētur. Quia tamen Rūfīnus industrius āc bonus imperātor erat, māgnumque et grave bellum imminēre vidēbātur, Fabricius auctor fuit ut Rūfīnus cōnsul creārētur, cumque is deinde Fabriciō grātiās ageret, quod sē homō inimīcus cōnsulem fēcisset, hīc respondit nōn esse mīrandum sī compīlārī quam vēnīre māluisset. Eundem posteā Fabricius cēnsor factus senātū mōvit, quod argentī factī decem pondō habēret. Fabricius omnem vītam in glōriōsā paupertāte exēgit adeōque inops dēcessit ut, unde dōs fīliārum expedīrētur, nōn relinqueret. Senātus patris sibi partēs dēsūmpsit et, datīs ex aerāriō dōtibus, fīliās conlocāvit.

Pyrrhus cum adversus Rōmānōs parum prōfectūrum sē intellegeret, Siciliam diciōnis suae facere statuit. Inde rediēns cum Locrōs classe praeterveherētur, thēsaurōs fānī Prōserpinae intāctōs ad eam diem spoliāvit; atque ita, pecūniā in nāvēs impositā, ipse terrā est profectus. Quid ergō ēvēnit? Classis posterō diē foedissimā tempestāte lacerāta omnēsque nāvēs quae sacram pecūniam habēbant in lītora Locrōrum ēiectae sunt. Quā tantā clāde ēdoctus tandem deōs esse, superbissimus rēx pecūniam omnem conquīsītam in fānum Prōserpinae referrī iussit. Nec tamen illī umquam prōsperī quidquam ēvēnit, pulsusque Italiā ignōbilī morte occubuit, cum temere noctū ingressus esset Argos.

XVI. Gaius Duilius.

260 B.C.

Gāius Duīlius Poenōs nāvālī proeliō prīmus dēvīcit. Quī cum vidēret nāvēs Rōmānās ā Pūnicīs vēlōcitāte superārī, manūs ferreās sīve corvōs, māchinam ad comprehendendās hostium nāvēs tenendāsque ūtilem, excōgitāvit. Quae manūs ubi hostīlem apprehenderant nāvem, superiectō ponte trānsgrediēbātur Rōmānus et in ipsōrum ratibus comminus dīmicābant, unde Rōmānīs, quī rōbore praestābant, facilis vīctōria fuit. Celeriter sunt expūgnātae nāvēs Pūnicae trīgintā, in quibus etiam praetōria septirēmis capta est, mersae tredecim.

Duilius victor, Romam reversus, primus navalem triumphum egit. Nulla victoria Romanis gratior fuit, quod invicti terra iam etiam mari plurimum possent. Itaque Duilio concessum est ut per omnem vitam praelucente funali et praecinente tibicine a cena rediret.

Hannibal, dux classis Punicae, e navi quae iam capiebatur, in scapham saltu se demittens Romanorum manus effugit. Veritus autem ne in patria classis amissae poenas daret, civium odium astutia avertit; nam ex illa infelici pugna, priusquam cladis nuntius domum perveniret, quendam ex amicis Carthaginem misit. Qui postquam curiam intravit, "Consulit," inquit, "vos Hannibal, cum dux Romanorum magnis copiis maritimis instructis advenerit, num cum eo confligere debeat." Acclamavit universus senatus non esse dubium quin confligi oporteret. Tum ille "Conflixit," inquit, "et superatus est." Ita non potuerunt factum damnare quod ipsi fieri debuisse iudicaverant. Sic Hannibal victus crucis supplicium effugit; nam eo poenae genere dux, re male gesta, apud Poenos adficiebatur.

XVII. Gaius Lutatius Catulus.
241 B.C.

Gaius Lutatius Catulus consul finem primo Punico bello imposuit. Cum classe trecentarum navium in Siciliam transvectus, dum Drepanum oppugnat et inter primos strenue dimicat, grave volnus in femore accepit. Nondum convaluerat, cum maxima Poenorum classis

adesse nūntiātur. Nāvēs erant quadringentae commeātū onustae, quem ad exercitum portābant, cōpiīs
praetereā mīlitum permāgnīs armōrumque et pecūniae
amplissimō numerō. Summae rērum Hannō praeerat,
5 nōbilis Poenus. Hīc māgnō studiō id agēbat, ut nāvēs
onere levāret et strēnuīs virīs ab Hamilcare acceptīs
complēret atque sīc deinde cum Rōmānā classe cōnflīgeret. At Lutātius, ut cōnsilia Poenōrum praevenīret
et potius cum classe gravī suīsque oneribus impedītā
10 cōnflīgeret, statim ad Aegātēs īnsulās cursum intendit
hostiumque classem aggreditur. Nec longa fuit vīctōriae mora, nam brevissimō tempore omnēs Carthāginiēnsium nāvēs aut captae aut dēpressae sunt. Ingēns
fuit praeda. Poenī victī pācem postulārunt; quae eīs
15 hāc condiciōne concessa est, ut omnibus īnsulīs quae
sunt inter Ītaliam et Āfricam dēcēderent et certum
populō Rōmānō vectīgal per vīgintī annōs penderent.

XVIII. Quintus Fabius Maximus.

218–203 B.C.

Hannibal, Hamilcaris fīlius, novem annōs nātus, ā
patre ārīs admōtus odium in Rōmānōs perenne iūrāvit.
20 Quae rēs māximē vidētur concitāsse secundum Pūnicum bellum. Nam mortuō Hamilcare Hannibal, causam bellī quaerēns, Saguntum, cīvitātem Hispāniae
Rōmānīs foederātam, ēvertit. Quāpropter Rōmā missī
sunt Carthāginem lēgātī, quī Hannibalem, malī auctō-
25 rem, exposcerent. Tergiversantibus Poenīs Quīntus
Fabius, lēgātiōnis prīnceps, sinū ex togā factō, "Hīc,"

inquit, "vōbīs bellum et pācem portāmus; utrum placeat, sūmite." Poenīs "Bellum" succlāmantibus, Fabius excussā togā bellum sē dare dīcit. Poenī accipere sē respondērunt et, quibus acciperent animīs, eīsdem sē gestūrōs.

Hannibal superātīs Pȳrēnaeī et Alpium iugīs in Ītaliam vēnit. Pūblium Scīpiōnem apud Tīcinum amnem, Semprōnium apud Trebiam, Flāminium apud Trasumēnum prōflīgāvit.

Adversus hostem totiēns vīctōrem missus Quīntus Fabius dictātor Hannibalis impetum morā frēgit; namque priōrum ducum clādibus ēdoctus, bellī ratiōnem mūtāre et adversus Hannibalem, successibus proeliōrum īnsolentem, recēdere ab ancipitī discrīmine et tuērī tantum modo Ītaliam cōnstituit, Cunctātōrisque nōmen et laudem summī ducis meruit. Per loca alta āgmen dūcēbat modicō ab hoste intervāllō, ut neque omitteret eum neque cum eō congrederētur; castrīs, nisi quantum necessitās cōgeret, mīles tenēbātur. Dux neque occāsiōnī reī bene gerendae deerat, sī qua ab hoste darētur, neque ūllam ipse hostī dabat. Itaque cum ex levibus proeliīs superior discēderet, mīlitem minus iam coepit aut virtūtis suae aut fortūnae paenitēre.

Hīs artibus cum Hannibalem Fabius in agrō Falernō locōrum angustiīs clausisset, ille sine ūllō exercitūs dētrīmentō sē expedīvit. Namque ārida sarmenta in boum cornibus dēligāta prīncipiō noctis incendī bovēsque ad mōntēs, quōs Rōmānī īnsēderant, agī iussit. Quī cum accēnsīs cornibus per mōntēs, per silvās hūc illūc discurrerent, Rōmānī mirāculō attonitī cōnstitērunt; ipse Fabius īnsidiās esse ratus mīlitem extrā vāllum ēgredī vetuit. Intereā Hannibal ex angustiīs ēvāsit.

5 Dein Hannibal, ut Fabiō apud suōs cōnflāret invidiam, agrum ēius, omnibus circā vāstātīs, intāctum relīquit. At Fabius missō Rōmam Quīntō filiō inviolātum ab hoste agrum vēndidit ēiusque pretiō captīvōs Rōmānōs redēmit.

10 Haud grāta tamen Rōmānīs erat Fabī cūnctātiō: eumque prō cautō timidum, prō cūnctātōre sēgnem vocitābant. Augēbat invidiam Minucius, magister equitum, dictātōrem crīminandō; illum in dūcendō bellō sēdulō tempus terere, quō diūtius in magistrātū 15 esset sōlusque et Rōmae et in exercitū imperium habēret. Hīs sermōnibus accēnsa plēbs dictātōrī magistrum equitum imperiō aequāvit. Hanc iniūriam aequō animō tulit Fabius exercitumque suum cum Minuciō dīvīsit. Cum autem Minucius temerē proelium com20 mīsisset, eī perīclitantī auxiliō vēnit Fabius. Cūius subitō adventū repressus Hannibal receptuī cecinit, palam cōnfessus ab sē Minucium, sē ā Fabiō victum esse. Redeuntem ex aciē dīxisse eum ferunt tandem eam nūbem quae sedēre in iugīs mōntium solita esset, 25 cum procellā imbrem dedisse. Minucius autem perīculō līberātus castra cum Fabiō iūnxit et patrem eum appellāvit idemque facere mīlitēs iussit.

Posteā Hannibal Tarentō per prōditiōnem potītus est. Hanc urbem ut Poenīs trāderent, tredecim ferē 30 nōbilēs iuvenēs Tarentīnī coniūrāverant. Hī nocte per speciem vēnandī urbe ēgressī ad Hannibalem, quī haud procul castra habēbat, vēnērunt. Cui cum, quid parārent, exposuissent, conlaudāvit eōs Hannibal monuitque ut redeuntēs pecora Carthāginiēnsium quae pāstum prōpulsa essent ad urbem agerent, et velutī praedam 5 ex hoste factam aut praefectō aut custōdibus portārum dōnārent. Id iterum āc saepius ab eīs factum eōque cōnsuētūdinis adducta rēs est ut, quōcumque noctis tempore sībilō dedissent sīgnum, porta urbis aperīrētur. Tunc Hannibal eōs nocte mediā cum decem mīlibus 10 hominum dēlēctōrum secūtus est. Ubi portae appropinquārunt, nōta iuvenum vōx et familiāre sīgnum vigilem excitāvit. Duo prīmī īnferēbant aprum vāstī corporis. Vigil incautus, dum bēluae māgnitūdinem mīrātur, vēnābulō occīsus est. Ingressī prōditōrēs cē- 15 terōs vigilēs sōpītōs obtruncant. Tum Hannibal cum suō āgmine ingreditur; Rōmānī passim trucīdantur. Livius Salīnātor, Rōmānōrum praefectus, cum eīs quī caedī superfuērunt, in arcem cōnfūgit.

Profectus igitur Fabius ad recipiendum Tarentum 20 urbem obsidiōne cinxit. Leve dictū mōmentum ad rem ingentem perficiendam eum adiūvit. Praefectus praesidī Tarentīnī dēperībat amōre mulierculae, cūius frāter in exercitū Fabī erat. Miles iūssus ā Fabiō prō perfugā Tarentum trānsiit āc per sorōrem praefectum 25 ad trādendam urbem perpulit. Fabius vigiliā prīmā accessit ad eam partem mūrī quam praefectus custōdiēbat. Adiuvantibus recipientibusque ēius mīlitibus Rōmānī in urbem trānscendērunt. Inde, proximā portā refrāctā, Fabius cum exercitū intrāvit. Hannibal 30

nūntiātā Tarentī oppūgnātiōne cum ad opem ferendam festīnāns captam urbem esse audīvisset, "Et Rōmānī," inquit, "suum Hannibalem habent; eādem quā cēperāmus arte Tarentum āmīsimus."
5 Cum posteā Līvius Salīnātor cōram Fabiō glōriārētur, quod arcem Tarentīnam retinuisset, dīxissetque eum suā operā Tarentum recēpisse, "Certē," inquit Fabius rīdēns, "nam nisi tū āmīsissēs, ego numquam recēpissem."
10 Quīntus Fabius iam senex fīliō suō cōnsulī lēgātus fuit; cumque in ēius castra venīret, fīlius obviam patrī prōgressus est, duodecim līctōribus prō mōre antecēdentibus. Equō vehēbātur senex neque appropinquante cōnsule dēscendit. Iam ex līctōribus ūndecim
15 verēcundiā paternae māiestātis tacitī praeterierant. Quod cum cōnsul animadvertisset, proximum līctōrem iussit inclāmāre Fabiō patrī ut ex equō dēscenderet. Pater tum dēsiliēns, "Nōn ego, fīlī," inquit, "tuum imperium contempsī, sed experīrī voluī num scīrēs
20 cōnsulem tē esse." Ad summam senectūtem vīxit Fabius Māximus, dignus tantō cōgnōmine. Cautior quam prōmptior habitus est, sed īnsita ēius ingeniō prūdentia eī bellō quod tum gerēbātur propriē apta erat. Nēminī dubium est quīn rem Rōmānam cunc-
25 tandō restituerit. Ut Scīpiō pūgnandō, ita hīc nōn dīmicandō māximē cīvitātī Rōmānae succurrisse vīsus est. Alter enim celeritāte suā Carthāginem oppressit, alter cunctātiōne id ēgit, nē Rōma opprimī posset.

XIX. Aemilius Paulus et Terentius Varro.

216 B.C.

Hannibal in Āpūliam pervēnerat. Adversus eum
Rōmā profectī sunt duo cōnsulēs, Aemilius Paulus et
Terentius Varrō. Paulō Fabī cunctātiō magis placē-
bat; Varrō autem, ferōx et temerārius, ācriōra sequē-
bātur cōnsilia. Ambō cōnsulēs ad vīcum quī Cannae
appellābātur castra commūnīvērunt. Ibi deinde Varrō,
invītō conlēgā, aciem īnstrūxit et signum pūgnae dedit.
Hannibal autem ita cōnstituerat aciem ut Rōmānīs et
sōlis radiī et ventus ab oriente pulverem adflāns adversī essent. Victus caesusque est Rōmānus exercitus;
nusquam graviōre volnere adflīcta est rēs pūblica.
Aemilius Paulus tēlīs obrutus cecidit; quem cum mediā in pūgnā sedentem in saxō opplētum cruōre cōn-
spēxisset quīdam tribūnus mīlitum, "Cape," inquit,
"hunc equum et fuge, Aemilī. Etiam sine tuā morte
lacrimārum satis lūctūsque est." Ad ea cōnsul: "Tū
quidem macte virtūte estō! Sed cavē exiguum tempus
ē manibus hostium ēvādendī perdās! Abī, nūntiā
patribus ut urbem mūniant āc, priusquam hostis victor
adveniat, praesidiīs firment. Mē in hāc strāge meōrum mīlitum patere exspīrāre." Alter cōnsul cum
paucīs equitibus Venusiam perfūgit. Cōnsulārēs aut
praetōriī occidērunt vīgintī, senātōrēs captī aut occīsī
trīgintā, nōbilēs virī trecentī, mīlitum quadrāgintā mīlia,
equitum tria mīlia et quīngentī. Hannibal in testimōnium victōriae suae trēs modiōs aureōrum ānulōrum
Carthāginem mīsit, quōs dē manibus equitum Rōmānōrum et senātōrum dētrāxerat.

Hannibalī victōrī cum cēterī grātulārentur suādērentque ut quiētem iam ipse sūmeret et fessīs mīlitibus daret, ūnus ex ēius praefectīs, Maharbal, minimē cessandum ratus, Hannibalem hortābātur ut statim
5 Rōmam pergeret. "Diē quīntō," inquit, "victor in Capitōliō epulāberis." Cumque Hannibal illud nōn probāsset, Maharbal, "Nōn omnia nīmīrum," inquit, "eīdem diī dedēre. Vincere scīs, Hannibal; victōriā ūtī nēscīs." Mora hūius diēī satis crēditur salūtī fuisse
10 urbī et imperiō. Hannibal cum victōriā posset ūtī, fruī māluit, relictāque Rōmā in Campāniam dēvertit, cūius dēliciīs mox exercitūs ārdor ēlanguit; adeō ut vērē dictum sit Capuam Hannibalī Cannās fuisse.

Numquam tantum pavōris Rōmae fuit quantum ubi
15 acceptae clādis nūntius advēnit. Neque tamen ūlla pācis mentiō facta est; quin etiam animō cīvitās adeō māgnō fuit ut Varrōnī ex tantā clāde redeuntī obviam īrent et grātiās agerent, quod dē rē pūblicā nōn dēspērāsset; quī, sī Poenōrum dux fuisset, temeritātis
20 poenās omnī suppliciō dedisset. Nōn autem vītae cupiditāte, sed reī pūblicae amōre sē superfuisse, reliquō aetātis suae tempore approbāvit. Nam et barbam capillumque submīsit, et posteā numquam recubāns cibum cēpit. Honōribus quoque, cum eī dēferrentur
25 ā populō, renūntiāvit dīcēns fēliciōribus magistrātibus reī pūblicae opus esse. Dum igitur Hannibal sēgniter et ōtiōsē agēbat, Rōmānī interim respīrāre coepērunt. Arma nōn erant; dētracta sunt templīs vetera hostium spolia. Deerat iuventūs; servī manūmissī et armātī
30 sunt. Egēbat aerārium; opēs suās libēns senātus in

medium prōtulit, nec praeter quod in bullīs singulīsque ānulīs erat, quidquam sibi aurī relīquērunt. Patrum exemplum secūtī sunt equitēs imitātaeque equitēs omnēs tribūs. Dēnique vix suffēcēre tabulae, vix scrībārum manūs, cum omnēs prīvātae opēs in pūblicum dēferrentur.

Cum Hannibal redimendī suī cōpiam captivīs Rōmānīs fēcisset, decem ex ipsīs Rōmam eā dē rē missī sunt; nec pīgnus aliud fideī ab eīs postulātum est quam ut iūrārent sē, sī nōn impetrāssent, in castra esse reditūrōs. Eōs senātus nōn redimendōs cēnsuit responditque, eōs cīvēs nōn esse necessāriōs, quī, cum armātī essent, capī potuissent. Ūnus ex eīs lēgātīs ē castrīs Poenōrum ēgressus, velutī aliquid oblītus, paulō post in castra erat regressus, deinde comitēs ante noctem adsecūtus erat. Is ergō, rē nōn impetrātā, domum abiit. Reditū enim in castra sē līberātum esse iūreiūrandō interpretābātur. Quod ubi innōtuit, iussit senātus illum comprehendī et vinctum dūcī ad Hannibalem. Ea rēs Hannibalis audāciam māximē frēgit, quod senātus populusque Rōmānus rēbus adflīctīs tam excelsō esset animō.

XX. Tiberius Gracchus et Gaius Gracchus.

170–121 B.C.

Tiberius et Gāius Gracchī Scīpiōnis Āfricānī ex fīliā nepōtēs erant. Hōrum adulēscentia bonīs artibus et māgnā omnium spē exācta est: ad ēgregiam enim indolem optima accēdēbat ēducātiō. Erant enim dīligen-

tiā Cornēliae mātris ā puerīs doctī et Graecīs litterīs ērudītī. Māximum mātrōnīs ōrnāmentum esse liberōs bene īnstitūtōs meritō putābat māter illa sapientissima. Cum Campāna mātrōna, apud illam hospita, ōrnāmenta
5 sua, illō saeculō pulcherrima, ostentāret eī muliebriter, Cornēlia trāxit eam sermōne quousque ē scholā redīrent līberī. Quōs reversōs hospitae ostendēns, "Haec," inquit, "mea ōrnāmenta sunt." Nihil quidem hīs adulēscentibus neque ā nātūrā neque ā doctrīnā dēfuit;
10 sed ambō rem pūblicam, quam tuērī poterant, perturbāre māluērunt.

Tiberius Gracchus, tribūnus plēbis creātus, ā senātū dēscīvit: populī favōrem profūsīs largītiōnibus sibi conciliāvit; agrōs plēbī dīvidēbat; prōvinciās novīs
15 colōniīs replēbat. Cum autem tribūnīciam potestātem sibi prōrogārī vellet et palam dictitāsset interēmptō senātū omnia per plēbem agī dēbēre, viam sibi ad rēgnum parāre vidēbātur. Quā rē cum convocātī patrēs dēlīberārent quidnam faciendum esset, statim
20 Tiberius Capitōlium petit, manum ad caput referēns, quō signō salūtem suam populō commendābat. Hōc nōbilitās ita accēpit quasi diadēma posceret, sēgniterque cessante cōnsule, Scīpiō Nāsīca, cum esset cōnsōbrīnus Tiberī Gracchī, patriam cōgnātiōnī praeferēns
25 sublātā dextrā prōclāmāvit: "Quī rem pūblicam salvam esse volunt, mē sequantur!" Dein optimātēs, senātus atque equestris ōrdinis pars māior in Gracchum inruunt, quī fugiēns dēcurrēnsque clīvō Capitōlīnō frāgmentō subselliī ictus, vītam quam glōriōsissimē dēgere potue-
30 rat, immātūrā morte fīnīvit. Mortuī Tiberī corpus in flūmen prōiectum est.

TIBERIUS GRACCHUS ET GAIUS GRACCHUS. 41

Gāium Gracchum īdem furor quī frātrem Tiberium occupāvit. Tribūnātum enim adeptus, seu vindicandae frāternae necis, seu comparandae rēgiae potentiae causā, pessima coepit inīre cōnsilia: māximās largītiōnēs fēcit; aerārium effūdit; lēgem dē frūmentō plēbī dīvidendō tulit; cīvitātem omnibus Ītalicīs dabat. Hīs Gracchī cōnsiliīs quantā poterant contentiōne obsistēbant omnēs bonī, in quibus māximē Pīsō, vir cōnsulāris. Is cum multa contrā lēgem frūmentāriam dīxisset, lēge tamen lātā ad frūmentum cum cēterīs accipiendum vēnit. Gracchus ubi animadvertit in cōntiōne Pīsōnem stantem, eum sīc compellāvit audiente populō Rōmānō: "Quī tibi cōnstās, Pīsō, cum eā lēge frūmentum petās quam dissuāsistī?" Cui Pīsō: "Nōlim quidem, Gracche," inquit, "mea bona tibi virītim dīvidere liceat; sed sī faciēs, partem petam." Quō respōnsō apertē dēclārāvit vir gravis et sapiēns, lēge quam tulerat Gracchus, patrimōnium pūblicum dissipārī.

Dēcrētum ā senātū est, ut vidēret cōnsul Opīmius nē quid dētrīmentī rēs pūblica caperet: quod nisi in māximō discrīmine dēcernī nōn solēbat. Gāius Gracchus, armātā familiā, Aventīnum occupāvit. Cōnsul, vocātō ad arma populō, Gāium aggressus est, quī pulsus profūgit et, cum iam comprehenderētur, iugulum servō praebuit, quī dominum et mox sēmet ipsum super dominī corpus interēmit. Ut Tiberī Gracchī anteā corpus, ita Gāī, mīrā crūdēlitāte victōrum, in Tiberim dēiectum est; caput autem ā Septimulēiō, amīcō Gracchī, ad Opīmium relātum aurō repēnsum fertur. Sunt quī trādant infūsō plumbō, eum partem capitis, quō gravius efficerētur, explēsse.

Occīsō Tiberiō Gracchō, cum senātus cōnsulibus mandāsset ut in eōs quī cum Gracchō cōnsēnserant animadverterētur, Blosius quīdam, Tiberī amīcus, prō sē dēprecātum vēnit, hanc, ut sibi īgnōscerētur, causam adferēns, quod tantī Gracchum fēcisset ut, quidquid ille vellet, sibi faciendum putāret. Tum cōnsul, "Quid?" inquit, "sī tē Gracchus templō Iovis in Capitōliō facēs subdere iussisset, obsecūtūrusne voluntātī illīus fuistī propter istam quam iactās familiāritātem?" "Numquam," inquit Blosius, "voluisset id quidem, sed sī voluisset, pāruissem." Nefāria est ea vōx: nūlla enim est excūsātiō peccātī, sī amīcī causā peccāveris.

Exstat Gāī Gracchī ē Sardiniā Rōmam reversī ōrātiō, in quā cum alia tum haec dē sē nārrat. "Versātus sum in prōvinciā quō modo ex ūsū vestrō exīstimābam esse, nōn quō modo ambitiōnī meae condūcere arbitrābar. Nēmō possit vērē dīcere, assem aut eō plūs in mūneribus mē accēpisse aut meā causā quemquam sūmptum fēcisse. Zōnās quās Rōmā proficīscēns plēnās argentī extulī, eās ex prōvinciā inānēs rettulī. Aliī amphorās quās vīnī plēnās extulērunt, eās argentō replētās domum reportārunt."

XXI. Gnaeus Pompeius Magnus.
106–48 B.C.

Gnaeus Pompēius, stirpis senātōriae, bellō cīvīlī sē et patrem cōnsiliō servāvit. Cum enim Pompēī pater exercituī suō ob avāritiam esset invīsus, factā in eum coniūrātiōne Terentius quīdam, Gnaeī Pompēī fīlī

GNAEUS POMPEIUS MAGNUS

GNAEUS POMPEIUS MAGNUS. 43

contubernālis, hunc occīdendum suscēpit dum aliī tabernāculum patris incenderent. Quae rēs cum iuvenī Pompēiō cēnantī nūntiāta esset, nihil perīculō mōtus, solitō hilarius bibit et cum Terentiō eādem quā anteā cōmitāte ūsus est. Deinde cubiculum ingressus clam 5 subdūxit sē tentōriō et firmam patrī circumdedit custōdiam. Terentius tum dēstrictō ēnse ad lectum Pompēī accessit multīsque ictibus strāgula percussit. Ortā mox sēditiōne Pompēius sē in media coniēcit āgmina, militēsque tumultuantēs precibus et lacrimīs plācāvit 10 āc ducī reconciliāvit.

Eōdem bellō Pompēius partēs Sullae secūtus ita sē gessit ut ab eō māximē dīligerētur. Annōs trēs et vīgintī nātus, ut Sullae auxiliō venīret, paternī exercitūs reliquiās conlēgit, statimque dux perītus exstitit. 15 Māgnus illīus apud mīlitem amor, māgna apud omnēs admīrātiō fuit; nūllus eī labor taediō, nūlla dēfatīgātiō molestiae erat. Cibī vīnīque temperāns, somnī parcus; inter mīlitēs corpus exercēns cum alacribus saltū, cum vēlōcibus cursū, cum validīs lūctandō certābat. Tum 20 ad Sullam iter intendit et in eō itinere trēs hostium exercitūs aut fūdit aut sibi adiūnxit. Quem ubi Sulla ad sē accēdere audīvit ēgregiamque sub sīgnīs iuventūtem aspēxit, dēsiluit ex equō Pompēiumque salūtāvit imperātōrem et posteā eī venientī solēbat sellā adsur- 25 gere et caput aperīre et equō dēscendere, quem honōrem nēminī nisi Pompēiō tribuēbat.

Posteā Pompēius in Siciliam profectus est, ut eam ā Carbōne, Sullae inimīcō, occupātam reciperet. Carbō comprehēnsus et ad Pompēium ductus est : quem Pom- 30 pēius, etsī Carbō muliebriter mortem extimēscēns dēmissē et flēbiliter mortem dēprecābātur, ad supplicium dūcī iussit. Longē moderātior fuit Pompēius ergā Sthenium, Siciliae cūiusdam cīvitātis principem. Cum enim in eam cīvitātem animadvertere dēcrēvisset, quae sibi adversāta fuisset, inīquē eum factūrum Sthenius exclāmāvit, sī ob ūnīus culpam omnēs pūnīret. Interrogantī Pompēiō quisnam ille ūnus esset, "Ego," inquit Sthenius, "quī cīvēs meōs ad id indūxī." Tam līberā vōce dēlectātus Pompēius omnibus et Stheniō ipsī pepercit.

Trānsgressus inde in Āfricam Iarbam, Numidiae rēgem, quī Marī partibus favēbat, bellō persecūtus intrā diēs quadrāgintā oppressit et Āfricam subēgit adulēscēns quattuor et vīgintī annōrum. Deinde cum litterae eī ā Sullā redditae essent, quibus exercitū dīmissō cum ūnā legiōne successōrem exspectāre iubēbātur, Pompēius, quamquam aegrē id ferēbat, tamen pāruit et Rōmam revertit. Revertentī incrēdibilis hominum multitūdō obviam īvit; Sulla quoque laetus eum excēpit et Māgnī cōgnōmine cōnsalūtāvit. Nihilō minus Pompēiō triumphum petentī restitit; neque vērō eā rē ā prōpositō dēterritus est Pompēius aususque dīcere plūrēs adōrāre sōlem orientem quam occidentem; quō dictō innuēbat Sullae potentiam minuī, suam crēscere. Eā vōce audītā Sulla, cōnfidentiā adulēscentis perculsus: "Triumphet! triumphet!" exclāmāvit.

Metellō iam senī et bellum in Hispāniā sēgnius gerentī conlēga datus Pompēius adversus Sertōrium variō ēventū dīmicāvit. Māximum ibi in proeliō quōdam

GNAEUS POMPEIUS MAGNUS.   45

perīculum subiit; cum enim vir vāstā cǫrporis māgnitūdine impetum in eum fēcisset, Pompēius manum amputāvit; sed multīs in eum concurrentibus volnus in femore accēpit et ā suīs fugientibus dēsertus in hostium potestāte erat. At praeter spem ēvāsit; barbarī enim 5 equum ēius aurō phalerīsque eximiīs īnstrūctum cēperant. Dum igitur praedam inter sē altercantēs partiuntur, Pompēius eōrum manūs effūgit. Alterō proeliō cum Metellus Pompēiō labōrantī auxiliō vēnisset, Sertōrius recēdere coāctus dīxisse fertur. "Nisi anus illa 10 supervēnisset, ego hunc puerum verberibus castīgātum Rōmam dīmīsissem." Metellum anum appellābat, quia is, iam senex, ad mollem et effēminātam vītam dēflēxerat. Sertōriō interfectō Pompēius Hispāniam recēpit.

Cum pīrātae illā tempestāte maria omnia īnfestārent 15 et quāsdam etiam Ītaliae urbēs dīripuissent, ad eōs opprimendōs cum imperiō extraōrdināriō missus est Pompēius. Nimiae virī potentiae obsistēbant quīdam ex optimātibus et imprīmīs Quīntus Catulus. Quī cum in cōntiōne dīxisset esse quidem praeclārum virum 20 Cn. Pompēium, sed nōn esse ūnī omnia tribuenda, adiēgissetque, "Sī quid huic acciderit, quem in ēius locum substituētis?" summō cōnsēnsū succlāmāvit ūniversa cōntio: "Tē, Quīnte Catule." Tam honōrificō cīvium testimōniō vīctus Catulus ē cōntiōne dis- 25 cessit. Pompēius, dispositīs per omnēs maris recessūs nāvibus, brevī terrārum orbem illā peste līberāvit; praedōnēs multīs locīs vīctōs fūdit; eōsdem in dēditiōnem acceptōs in urbibus et agrīs procul ā marī conlocāvit. Nihil hāc vīctōriā celerius; nam intrā 30 quadrāgēsimum diem pīrātās tōtō marī expulit.

Cōnfectō bellō pīrāticō Gnaeus Pompēius contrā Mithridātem profectus in Asiam māgnā celeritāte contendit. Proelium cum rēge cōnserere cupiēbat, neque opportūna dabātur pūgnandī facultās, quia Mithridātēs
5 interdiū castrīs sē continēbat, noctū vērō haud tūtum erat congredī cum hoste in locīs īgnōtīs. Nocte tamen aliquandō cum Pompēius Mithridātem aggressus esset, lūna māgnō fuit Rōmānīs adiūmentō. Quam cum Rōmānī ā tergō habērent, umbrae corporum longius prō-
10 iectae ad prīmōs usque hostium ōrdinēs pertinēbant; unde dēceptī rēgiī mīlitēs in umbrās, tamquam in propinquum hostem, tēla mittēbant. Victus Mithridātēs in Pontum profūgit. Pharnacēs fīlius bellum eī intulit, quī, occīsīs ā patre frātribus, vītae suae ipse
15 timēbat. Mithridātēs ā fīliō obsessus venēnum sūmpsit; quod cum tardius subīret, quia adversus venēna multīs anteā medicāmentīs corpus firmāverat, ā mīlite Gallō, ā quō ut adiuvāret sē petierat, interfectus est.

Tigrānī deinde, Armeniae rēgī, quī Mithridātis partēs
20 secūtus erat, Pompēius bellum intulit eumque ad dēditiōnem compulit. Quī cum prōcubuisset ad genua Pompēī, eum ērēxit, et benīgnīs verbīs recreātum diadēma, quod abiēcerat, capitī repōnere iussit, aequē pulchrum esse iūdicāns et vincere rēgēs et facere.
25 Inde in Iūdaeam profectus Rōmānōrum prīmus Iūdaeōs domuit, Hierosolyma, caput gentis, cēpit, templumque iūre vīctōriae ingressus est. Rēbus Asiae compositīs in Italiam versus ad urbem vēnit, nōn, ut plērīque timuerant, armātus, sed dīmissō exercitū, et
30 tertium triumphum bīduō dūxit. Īnsīgnis fuit multīs

GNAEUS POMPEIUS MAGNUS.

novīs inūsitātīsque ōrnāmentīs hīc triumphus; sed nihil inlūstrius vīsum quam quod tribus triumphīs trēs orbis partēs dēvictae causam praebuerant; Pompēius enim, quod anteā contigerat nēminī, prīmum ex Āfricā, iterum ex Eurōpā, tertiō ex Asiā triumphāvit, fēlīx opīniōne hominum futūrus, sī, quem glōriae, eundem vītae fīnem habuisset neque adversam fōrtūnam esset expertus iam senex.

Posteriōre enim tempore ortā inter Pompēium et Caesarem gravī dissēnsiōne, quod hīc superiōrem, ille parem ferre nōn posset, bellum cīvīle exārsit. Caesar īnfestō exercitū in Ītaliam vēnit. Pompēius, relictā urbe āc deinde Ītaliā ipsā, Thessaliam petit et cum eō cōnsulēs senātusque omnis; quem īnsecūtus Caesar apud Pharsālum aciē fūdit. Victus Pompēius ad Ptolemaeum, Aegyptī rēgem, cui tūtor ā senātū datus erat, profūgit, quī Pompēium interficī iussit. Latus Pompēī sub oculīs uxōris et līberōrum mucrōne cōnfossum est, caput praecīsum, truncus in Nīlum coniectus. Deinde caput cum ānulō ad Caesarem dēlātum est, quī eō vīsō lacrimās nōn continēns illud multīs pretiōsissimīsque odōribus cremandum cūrāvit.

Is fuit Pompēī post trēs cōnsulātūs et totidem triumphōs vītae exitus. Erant in Pompēiō multae et māgnae virtūtēs āc praecipuē admīranda frūgālitās. Cum eī aegrōtantī praecēpisset medicus ut turdum ederet, negārent autem servī eam avem usquam aestīvō tempore posse reperīrī nisi apud Lūcullum, quī turdōs domī sagīnāret, vetuit Pompēius turdum inde petī, medicōque dīxit: "Ergō, nisi Lūcullus perditus dēliciis esset, nōn vīveret Pompēius?" Aliam avem, quae parābilis esset, sibi iussit appōnī.

Virīs doctīs māgnum honōrem habēbat Pompēius. Ex Syriā dēcēdēns, cōnfectō bellō Mithridāticō, cum Rhodum vēnisset, Posīdōnium cupiit audīre; sed cum audīvisset eum graviter esse aegrum, quod vehementer ēius artūs labōrārent, voluit tamen nōbilissimum philosophum vīsere. Mōs erat ut, cōnsule aedēs aliquās ingressūrō, līctor forēs percuteret, admonēns cōnsulem adesse; at Pompēius forēs Posīdōnī percutī honōris causā vetuit. Quem ut vīdit et salūtāvit, molestē sē dīxit ferre, quod eum nōn posset audīre. At ille, "Tū vērō," inquit, "potes, nec committam ut dolor corporis efficiat ut frūstrā tantus vir ad mē vēnerit." Itaque cubāns graviter et cōpiōsē dē hōc ipsō disputāvit: nihil esse bonum nisi quod honestum esset, nihil malum dīcī posse quod turpe nōn esset. Cum vērō dolōrēs ācriter eum pungerent, saepe, "Nihil agis," inquit, "dolor! quamvīs sīs molestus, numquam tē esse malum cōnfitēbor."

XXII. Gaius Iulius Caesar.

100–44 B.C.

C. Iūlius Caesar, nōbilissimā Iūliōrum genitus familiā, annum agēns sextum et decimum patrem āmīsit. Cornēliam, Cinnae fīliam, dūxit uxōrem; cūius pater cum esset Sullae inimīcissimus, is Caesarem voluit compellere ut eam repudiāret; neque id potuit efficere. Quā rē Caesar bonīs spoliātus cum etiam ad

GAIUS JULIUS CAESAR.

GAIUS IULIUS CAESAR.

necem quaererētur, mūtātā veste, nocte urbe ēlapsus est et, quamquam tunc quartānae morbō labōrābat, prope per singulās noctēs latebrās commūtāre cōgēbātur; et comprehēnsus ā Sullae lībertō, nē ad Sullam perdūcerētur, vix datā pecūniā ēvāsit. Postrēmō per 5 propinquōs et adfīnēs suōs veniam impetrāvit. Satis cōnstat Sullam, cum dēprecantibus amīcissimīs et ōrnātissimīs virīs aliquamdiū dēnegāsset atque illī pertināciter contenderent, expūgnātum tandem prōclāmāsse vincerent, dummodo scīrent eum quem incolumem 10 tantopere cuperent, aliquandō optimātium partibus, quās sēcum simul dēfendissent, exitiō futūrum; nam Caesarī multōs Mariōs inesse.

Stīpendia prīma in Asiā fēcit. In expūgnātiōne Mitylēnārum corōnā cīvicā dōnātus est. Mortuō Sullā 15 Rhodum sēcēdere statuit, ut per ōtium Apollōniō Molōnī, tunc clārissimō dīcendī magistrō, operam daret. Hūc dum trāicit, ā praedōnibus captus est mānsitque apud eōs prope quadrāgintā diēs. Per omne autem illud spatium ita sē gessit ut pīrātīs pariter terrōrī 20 venerātiōnique esset. Comitēs interim servōsque ad expediendās pecūniās quibus redimerētur, dīmīsit. Vīgintī talenta pīrātae postulāverant: ille quīnquāgintā datūrum sē spopondit. Quibus numerātīs cum expositus esset in lītore, cōnfestim Mīlētum, quae urbs proximē 25 aberat, properāvit ibique contractā classe invectus in eum locum in quō ipsī praedōnēs erant, partem classis fugāvit, partem mersit, aliquot nāvēs cēpit pīrātāsque in potestātem redāctōs eō suppliciō quod illīs saepe minātus inter iocum erat, adfēcit crucīque suffīxit. 30

Quaestōrī ulterior Hispānia obvēnit. Quō profectus cum Alpēs trānsīret et ad cōnspectum pauperis cūiusdam vīcī comitēs per iocum inter sē disputārent num illīc etiam esset ambitiōnī locus, sēriō dīxit Caesar
5 mālle sē ibi prīmum esse quam Rōmae secundum. Dominātiōnis avidus ā prīmā aetāte rēgnum concupīscēbat semperque in ōre habēbat hōs Eurīpidis, Graecī poētae, versūs :

> Nam sī violándum est iūs, rēgnándī grātiā
> Violándum est, áliīs rēbus pietátém colās.

10

Cumque Gādēs, quod est Hispāniae oppidum, vēnisset, animadversā apud Herculis templum māgnī Alexandrī imāgine ingemuit et quasi pertaesus īgnāviam suam, quod nihildum ā sē memorābile āctum esset
15 in eā aetāte quā iam Alexander orbem terrārum subēgisset, missiōnem continuō efflāgitāvit ad captandās quam prīmum māiōrum rērum occāsiōnēs in urbe.

Aedīlis praeter Comitium āc Forum etiam Capitōlium ōrnāvit porticibus. Vēnātiōnēs autem lūdōsque
20 et cum conlēgā M. Bibulō et sēparātim ēdidit ; quō factum est ut commūnium quoque impēnsārum sōlus grātiam caperet. Hīs autem rēbus patrimōnium effūdit tantumque cōnflāvit aes aliēnum ut ipse dīceret sibi opus esse mīliēns sēstertiūm ut habēret nihil.

25 Cōnsul deinde creātus cum M. Bibulō societātem cum Gnaeō Pompēiō et Mārcō Crassō iūnxit Caesar, nē quid agerētur in rē pūblicā quod displicuisset ūllī ex tribus. Deinde lēgem tulit ut ager Campānus plēbī dīviderētur. Cui lēgī cum senātus repūgnāret,

rem ad populum dētulit. Bibulus conlēga in Forum vēnit, ut lēgī obsisteret, sed tanta in eum commōta est sēditiō ut in caput ēius cophinus stercore plēnus effunderētur fascēsque eī frangerentur atque adeō ipse armīs Forō expellerētur. Quā rē cum Bibulus per reliquum annī tempus domō abditus cūriā abstinēret, ūnus ex eō tempore Caesar omnia in rē pūblicā ad arbitrium administrābat, ut nōnnūllī urbānōrum, sī quid testandī grātiā sīgnārent, per iocum nōn, ut mōs erat, cōnsulibus Caesare et Bibulō āctum scrīberent, sed Iūliō et Caesare, ūnum cōnsulem nōmine et cōgnōmine prō duōbus appellantēs.

Fūnctus cōnsulātū Caesar Galliam prōvinciam accēpit. Gessit autem novem annīs quibus in imperiō fuit haec ferē: Galliam in prōvinciae fōrmam redēgit; Germānōs, quī trāns Rhēnum incolunt, prīmus Rōmānōrum ponte fabricātō aggressus māximīs adfēcit clādibus. Aggressus est Britannōs, īgnōtōs anteā, superātīsque pecūniās et obsidēs imperāvit. Hīc cum multa Rōmānōrum mīlitum īnsīgnia nārrantur, tum illud ēgregium ipsīus Caesaris, quod nūtante in fugam exercitū, raptō fugientis ē manū scūtō, in prīmam volitāns aciem proelium restituit. Īdem aliō proeliō legiōnis aquiliferum, ineundae fugae causā iam conversum, faucibus comprehēnsum in contrāriam partem dētrāxit dextramque ad hostem tendēns, "Quōrsum tū," inquit, "abīs? Illīc sunt cum quibus dīmicāmus." Quā adhortātiōne omnium legiōnum trepidātiōnem corrēxit, vincīque parātās vincere docuit.

Interfectō intereā apud Parthōs Crassō et dēfūnctā

Iūliā, Caesaris filiā, quae, nūpta Pompēiō, generī socerīque concordiam tenēbat, statim aemulātiō ērūpit. Iam prīdem Pompēiō suspectae Caesaris opēs et Caesarī Pompēiāna dīgnitās gravis, nec hīc ferēbat parem,
5 nec ille superiōrem. Itaque cum Caesar in Galliā dētinērētur, et, nē imperfectō bellō discēderet, postulāsset ut sibi licēret, quamvīs absentī, alterum cōnsulātum petere, ā senātū suādentibus Pompēiō ēiusque amīcīs negātum eī est. Hanc iniūriam acceptam vin-
10 dicātūrus in Ītaliam rediit et, bellandum ratus, cum exercitū Rubicōnem flūmen, quī prōvinciae ēius fīnis erat, trānsiit. Hōc ad flūmen paulum cōnstitisse fertur āc reputāns quantum mōlīrētur, conversus ad proximōs, "Etiam nunc," inquit, "regredī possumus; quod
15 sī ponticulum trānsierimus, omnia armīs agenda erunt." Postrēmō autem, "Iacta ālea estō!" exclāmāns exercitum trāicī iussit plūrimīsque urbibus occupātīs Brundisium contendit, quō Pompēius cōnsulēsque cōnfūgerant.

20 Quī cum inde in Ēpīrum trāiēcissent, Caesar eōs secūtus ā Brundisiō Dyrrhachium inter oppositās classēs gravissimā hieme trānsmīsit; cōpiīsque, quās subsequī iusserat, diūtius cessantibus cum ad eās arcessendās frūstrā mīsisset, mīrae audāciae facinus
25 ēdidit. Morae enim impatiēns castrīs noctū ēgreditur, clam nāviculam cōnscendit, obvolūtō capite nē āgnōscerētur et, quamquam mare saevā tempestāte intumēscēbat, in altum tamen prōtinus dīrigī nāvigium iubet et gubernātōre trepidante, "Quid timēs?" inquit,
30 "Caesarem vehis!" neque prius gubernātōrem cēdere

adversae tempestāti passus est quam paene obrutus esset fluctibus.

Deinde Caesar in Ēpīrum profectus Pompēium Pharsālicō proeliō fūdit, et fugientem persecūtus, ut occīsum cōgnōvit, Ptolemaeō rēgī, Pompēī interfectōrī, ā quō sibi quoque īnsidiās tendī vidēret, bellum intulit ; quō victō in Pontum trānsiit Pharnacemque, Mithridātis fīlium, rebellantem et multiplicī successū praeferōcem intrā quīntum ab adventū diem, quattuor, quibus in cōnspectum vēnit, hōrīs ūnā prōflīgāvit aciē mōre fulminis quod ūnō eōdemque mōmentō vēnit, percussit, abscessit. Nec vāna dē sē praedicātiō est Caesaris, ante victum hostem esse quam vīsum. Ponticō posteā triumphō trium verbōrum praetulit titulum : " Vēnī, vīdī, vīcī." Deinde Scīpiōnem et Iubam, Numidiae rēgem, reliquiās Pompēiānārum partium in Āfricā refoventēs, dēvīcit.

Victōrem Āfricānī bellī Gāium Caesarem gravius excēpit Hispāniēnse, quod Cn. Pompēius, Māgnī fīlius, adulēscēns fortissimus, ingēns āc terribile cōnflāverat, undique ad eum auxiliīs paternī nōminis māgnitūdinem sequentium ex tōtō orbe cōnfluentibus. Sua Caesarem in Hispāniam comitāta fortūna est ; sed nūllum umquam atrōcius perīculōsiusque ab eō initum proelium, adeō ut, plūs quam dubiō Mārte, dēscenderet equō cōnsistēnsque ante recēdentem suōrum aciem, increpāns Fortūnam, quod sē in eum servāsset exitum, dēnūntiāret mīlitibus vestīgiō sē nōn recessūrum ; proinde vidērent quem et quō locō imperātōrem dēsertūrī essent. Verēcundiā magis quam virtūte aciēs restitūta est. Cn. Pompēius vīctus et interēmptus est. Caesar, omnium victor, regressus in urbem, omnibus quī contrā sē arma tulerant īgnōvit, et quīnquiēns triumphāvit.

5 Bellis cīvīlibus confectīs conversus iam ad ōrdinandum reī pūblicae statum, fāstōs corrēxit annumque ad cursum sōlis accommodāvit, ut trecentōrum sexāgintā quīnque diērum esset et intercalāriō mēnse sublātō ūnus diēs quartō quōque annō intercalārētur. Iūs
10 labōriōsissimē āc sevērissimē dīxit. Repetundārum convictōs etiam ōrdine senātōriō mōvit. Peregrīnārum mercium portōria īnstituit; lēgem praecipuē sūmptuāriam exercuit. Dē ōrnandā instruendāque urbe, item dē tuendō ampliandōque imperiō plūra āc māiōra in
15 diēs dēstinābat; imprīmīs iūs cīvīle ad certum modum redigere atque ex immēnsā lēgum cōpiā optima quaeque et necessāria in paucissimōs cōnferre librōs; bibliothēcās Graecās et Latīnās quās māximās posset pūblicāre; siccāre Pomptīnās palūdēs; viam mūnīre
20 ā Marī Superō per Appennīnī dorsum ad Tiberim usque; Dācōs quī sē in Pontum effūderant, coërcēre; mox Parthīs bellum īnferre per Armeniam.

Haec et alia agentem et meditantem mors praevēnit. Dictātor enim in perpetuum creātus agere īnsolentius
25 coepit; senātum ad sē venientem sedēns excēpit et quendam, ut adsurgeret, monentem īrātō voltū respēxit. Cum Antōnius, Caesaris in omnibus bellīs comes et tunc cōnsulātūs conlēga, capitī ēius in sellā aūreā sedentis prō rōstrīs diadēma, īnsīgne rēgium, imposu-
30 isset, id ita ab eō est repulsum ut nōn offēnsus vidē-

rētur. Quā rē coniūrātum in eum est ā sexāgintā amplius virīs, Cassiō et Brūtō ducibus, dēcrētumque eum Īdibus Mārtiīs in senātū cōnfodere.

Plūrima indicia futūrī perīculī obtulerant diī immortālēs. Uxor Calpurnia territa nocturnō vīsū, ut Īdibus Mārtiīs domī subsisteret ōrābat, et Spūrinna haruspex praedīxerat ut proximōs diēs trīgintā quasi fātālēs cavēret, quōrum ūltimus erat Īdūs Mārtiae. Hōc igitur diē Caesar Spūrinnae, "Ecquid scīs," inquit, "Īdūs Mārtiās iam vēnisse?" et is, "Ecquid scīs illās nōndum praeterīsse?" Atque cum Caesar eō diē in senātum vēnisset, adsidentem coniūrātī speciē officī circumstetērunt īlicōque ūnus, quasi aliquid rogātūrus, propius accessit renuentīque ab utrōque umerō togam apprehendit. Deinde clāmantem, "Ista quidem vīs est," Casca, ūnus ē coniūrātīs, adversum volnerat paulum īnfrā iugulum. Caesar Cascae bracchium adreptum graphiō trāiēcit cōnātusque prōsilīre aliō volnere tardātus est. Dein ut animadvertit undique sē strictīs pugiōnibus petī, togā caput obvolvit et ita tribus et vīgintī plāgīs cōnfossus est. Cum Mārcum Brūtum, quem fīlī locō habēbat, in sē inruentem vīdisset, dīxisse fertur: "Tū quoque, mī fīlī!"

Illud inter omnēs ferē cōnstitit, tālem eī mortem paene ex sententiā obtigisse. Nam et quondam cum apud Xenophōntem lēgisset Cȳrum ūltimā valētūdine mandāsse quaedam dē fūnere suō, āspernātus tam lentum mortis genus, subitam sibi celeremque optāverat, et prīdiē quam occīderētur, in sermōne nātō super cēnam quisnam esset fīnis vītae commodissimus,

repentīnum inopīnātumque praetulerat. Percussōrum autem neque trienniō quisquam amplius supervīxit neque suā morte dēfūnctus est. Damnātī omnēs alius aliō cāsū periērunt, pars naufragiō, pars proeliō; nōn-
5 nūllī sēmet eōdem illō pugiōne quō Caesarem violāverant, interēmērunt.

Quō rārior in rēgibus et prīncipibus virīs moderātiō, hōc laudanda magis est. C. Iūlius Caesar vīctōriā cīvīlī clēmentissimē ūsus est; cum enim scrīnia dē-
10 prehendisset epistulārum ad Pompēium missārum ab eīs quī vidēbantur aut in dīversīs aut in neutrīs fuisse partibus, legere nōluit, sed combūssit, nē forte in multōs gravius cōnsulendī locum darent. Cicerō hanc laudem eximiam Caesarī tribuit, quod nihil oblīvīscī
15 solēret nisi iniūriās. Simultātēs omnēs occāsiōne oblātā libēns dēposuit. Ūltrō āc prior scrīpsit C. Calvō post fāmōsa ēius adversum sē epigrammata. Valerium Catullum, cūius versiculīs fāmam suam lacerātam nōn īgnōrābat, adhibuit cēnae. C. Memmī
20 suffrāgātor in petītiōne cōnsulātūs fuit, etsī asperrimās fuisse ēius in sē ōrātiōnēs sciēbat.

Fuisse trāditur excelsā statūrā, ōre paulō plēniōre, nigrīs vegetīsque oculīs, capite calvo; quam calvitī dēfōrmitātem, quod saepe obtrectātōrum iocīs obnoxia
25 erat, aegrē ferēbat. Ideō ex omnibus dēcrētīs sibi ā senātū populōque honōribus nōn alium aut recēpit aut ūsūrpāvit libentius quam iūs laureae perpetuō gestandae. Vīnī parcissimum eum fuisse nē inimīcī quidem negāvērunt. Verbum Catōnis est, ūnum ex
30 omnibus Caesarem ad ēvertendam rem pūblicam sō-

MARCUS TULLIUS CICERO.

brium accessisse. Armōrum et equitandī perītissimus, labōris ūltrā fidem patiēns; in āgmine nōnnumquam equō, saepius pedibus anteībat, capite dētēctō, seu sōl, seu imber erat. Longissimās viās incrēdibilī celeritāte cōnficiēbat, ut persaepe nūntiōs dē sē praevenī- 5 ret; neque eum morābantur flūmina, quae vel nandō vel innīxus īnflātīs ūtribus trāiciēbat.

XXIII. Marcus Tullius Cicero.

106-43 B.C.

Mārcus Tullius Cicerō, equestrī genere, Arpīnī, quod est Volscōrum oppidum, nātus est. Ex ēius avīs ūnus verrūcam in extrēmō nāsō sitam habuit, ciceris grānō 10 similem; inde cōgnōmen Cicerōnis gentī inditum. Suādentibus quibusdam ut id nōmen mūtāret: " Dabō operam," inquit, "ut istud cōgnōmen nōbilissimōrum nōminum splendōrem vincat." Cum ā patre Rōmam missus, ubi celeberrimōrum magistrōrum scholīs in- 15 teresset, eās artēs discerет quibus aetās puerīlis ad hūmānitātem solet īnfōrmārī, tantō successū tantāque cum praeceptōrum tum cēterōrum discipulōrum admīrātiōne id fēcit ut, cum fāma dē Cicerōnis ingeniō et doctrīnā ad aliōs mānāsset, nōn paucī, quī ēius videndī 20 et audiendī grātiā scholās adīrent, repertī esse dīcantur.

Cum nūllā rē magis ad summōs in rē pūblicā honōrēs viam mūnīrī posse intellegeret quam arte dīcendī et ēloquentiā, tōtō animō in ēius studium incubuit; in quō quidem ita versātus est ut nōn sōlum eōs, quī 25

in Forō et iūdiciīs causās perōrārent, studiōsē sectārētur, sed prīvātim quoque dīligentissimē sē exercēret.
Prīmum ēloquentiam et lībertātem adversus Sullānōs
ostendit. Nam cum Rōscium quendam, parricīdī ac-
5 cūsatum, ob Chrȳsogonī, Sullae libertī, quī in ēius
adversāriīs erat, potentiam nēmō dēfendere audēret,
tantā ēloquentiae vī eum dēfendit Cicerō ut iam tum
in arte dīcendī nūllus eī pār esse vidērētur. Ex quō
invidiam veritus Athēnās studiōrum grātiā petiit, ubi
10 Antiochum philosophum studiōsē audīvit. Inde ēloquentiae causā Rhodum sē contulit, ubi Molōnem,
Graecum rhētorem tum disertissimum, magistrum
habuit. Quī cum Cicerōnem dīcentem audīvisset,
flēvisse dīcitur, quod per hunc Graecia ēloquentiae
15 laude prīvārētur.

Rōmam reversus quaestor Siciliam habuit. Nūllīus
vērō quaestūra aut grātior aut clārior fuit; cum māgna
tum esset annōnae difficultās, initiō molestus erat
Siculīs, quōs cōgeret frūmenta in urbem mittere;
20 posteā vērō, dīligentiam et iūstitiam et cōmitātem ēius
expertī, māiōrēs quaestōrī suō honōrēs quam ūllī umquam praetōrī dētulērunt. E Siciliā reversus Rōmam
in causīs dīcendīs ita flōruit ut inter omnēs causārum
patrōnōs et esset et habērētur prīnceps.

25 Cōnsul deinde factus L. Sergī Catilīnae coniūrā-
tiōnem singulārī virtūte, cōnstantiā, cūrā compressit.
Catilīnae proavum, M. Sergium, incrēdibilī fortitūdine
fuisse Plīnius refert. Stīpendia is fēcit secundō bellō
Pūnicō. Secundō stīpendiō dextram manum perdidit;
30 stīpendiīs duōbus ter et vīciēns volnerātus est; ob id

neutrā manū, neutrō pede satis ūtilis, plūrimīsque posteā stīpendiīs dēbilis, mīles erat. Bis ab Hannibale captus, bis vinculōrum ēius profugus, vīgintī mēnsibus nūllō nōn diē in catēnīs aut compedibus custōdītus. Sinistrā manū sōlā quater pūgnāvit, duōbus equīs īnsidente eō suffossīs. Dextram sibi ferream fēcit eāque religātā proeliātus Cremōnam obsidiōne exēmit, Placentiam tūtātus est, duodēna castra hostium in Galliā cēpit. "Cēterī profectō," Plīnius addit, "vīctōrēs hominum fuēre, Sergius vīcit etiam fortūnam."

Singulārem hūius virī glōriam foedē dehonestāvit pronepōtis scelus. Hīc enim reī familiāris, quam profūderat, inopiā multōrumque scelerum cōnscientiā in furōrem āctus et dominandī cupiditāte incēnsus, indīgnātusque quod in petītiōne cōnsulātūs repulsam passus esset, coniūrātiōne factā, senātum cōnfodere, cōnsulēs trucīdāre, urbem incendere, dīripere aerārium cōnstituerat. Āctum erat dē pulcherrimō imperiō, nisi illa coniūrātiō in Cicerōnem et Antōnium cōnsulēs incidisset, quōrum alter industriā rem patefēcit, alter manū oppressit. Cum Cicerō habitō senātū in praesentem reum perōrāsset, Catilīna, incendium suum ruīnā sē restīnctūrum esse minitāns, Rōmā profugit et ad exercitum quem parāverat, proficīscitur, sīgna inlātūrus urbī. Sed sociī ēius, quī in urbe remānserant, comprehēnsī in carcere necātī sunt. A. Fulvius, vir senātōriī ōrdinis, fīlium, iuvenem et ingeniō et fōrmā inter aequālēs nitentem, prāvō cōnsiliō Catilīnae amīcitiam secūtum inque castra ēius ruentem, ex mediō itinere retractum suppliciō mortis adfēcit, praefātus nōn sē

Catilīnae illum adversus patriam, sed patriae adversus Catilīnam genuisse.

Neque eō magis ab inceptō Catilīna dēstitit, sed īnfestīs signīs Rōmam petēns Antōnī exercitū opprimitur. Quam atrōciter dīmicātum sit, exitus docuit; nēmō hostium bellō superfuit; quem quisque in pūgnandō cēperat locum, eum āmissā animā tegēbat. Catilīna longē ā suīs inter hostium cadāvera repertus est: pulcherrimā morte, sī prō patriā sīc concidisset! Senātus populusque Rōmānus Cicerōnem patrem patriae appellāvit. Cicerō ipse in ōrātiōne prō Sullā palam praedicat cōnsilium patriae servandae fuisse iniectum sibi ā diīs, cum Catilīna coniūrāsset adversus eam. "Ō diī immortālēs," inquit, "vōs profectō incendistis tum animum meum cupiditāte cōnservandae patriae. Vōs āvocāstis mē ā cōgitātiōnibus omnibus cēterīs et convertistis ad salūtem ūnam patriae. Vōs dēnique praetulistis mentī meae clārissimum lūmen in tenebrīs tantīs errōris et īnscientiae. Tribuam enim vōbīs quae sunt vestra. Nec vērō possum tantum dare ingeniō meō ut dispēxerim sponte meā, in tempestāte illā turbulentissimā reī pūblicae, quid esset optimum factū."

Paucīs post annīs Cicerōnī diem dīxit Clōdius tribūnus plēbis, quod cīvēs Rōmānōs indictā causā necāvisset. Senātus maestus, tamquam in pūblicō lūctū, veste mūtātā prō eō dēprecābātur. Cicerō, cum posset armīs salūtem suam dēfendere, māluit urbe cēdere quam suā causā caedem fierī. Proficīscentem omnēs bonī flentēs prōsecūtī sunt. Dein Clōdius ēdictum prōposuit ut Mārcō Tulliō īgnī et aquā interdīcerētur; illīus domum et vīllās incendit. Sed vīs illa nōn diūturna fuit; mox enim tōtus ferē populus Rōmānus ingentī dēsīderiō Cicerōnis reditum flāgitāre coepit et māximō omnium ōrdinum studiō Cicerō in patriam revocātus est. Nihil per tōtam vītam Cicerōnī itinere quō in patriam rediit, accidit iūcundius. Obviam eī redeuntī ab ūniversīs itum est; domus ēius pūblicā pecūniā restitūta est.

Gravissimae illā tempestāte inter Caesarem et Pompēium ortae sunt inimīcitiae, ut rēs nisi bellō dirimī nōn posse vidērētur. Cicerō quidem summō studiō ēnītēbātur ut eōs inter sē reconciliāret et ā bellī cīvīlis calamitātibus dēterrēret, sed cum neutrum ad pācem ineundam permovēre posset, Pompēium secūtus est. Sed victō Pompēiō, ā Caesare victōre veniam ūltrō accēpit. Quō interfectō Octāviānum, Caesaris hērēdem, fōvit, Antōnium impūgnāvit effēcitque ut ā senātū hostis iūdicārētur.

Sed Antōnius, initā cum Octāviānō societāte, Cicerōnem iam diū sibi inimīcum prōscrīpsit. Quā rē audītā Cicerō trānsversīs itineribus in vīllam, quae ā marī proximē aberat, fūgit indeque nāvem cōnscendit in Macedoniam trānsitūrus. Unde aliquotiēns in altum prōvectum cum modo ventī adversī rettulissent, modo ipse iactātiōnem maris patī nōn posset, taedium tandem eum et fugae et vītae cēpit regressusque ad villam, "Moriar," inquit, "in patriā saepe servātā." Satis cōnstat, adventantibus percussōribus servōs fortiter fidēliterque parātōs fuisse ad dimicandum, ipsum dē-

pōnī lectīcam et quiētōs patī quod sors inīqua cōgeret, iussisse. Prōminentī ex lecticā et immōtam cervīcem praebentī caput praecīsum est. Manūs quoque abscīsae; caput relātum est ad Antōnium ēiusque iūssū
5 cum dextrā manū in rōstrīs positum.

Quam diū rēs pūblica Rōmāna per eōs gerēbātuı quibus sē ipsa commīserat, in eam cūrās cōgitātiōnēsque ferē omnēs suās cōnferēbat Cicerō et plūs operae pōnēbat in agendō quam in scrībendō. Cum autem
10 dominātū ūnius C. Iūlī Caesaris omnia tenērentur, nōn sē angōribus dēdidit nec indignīs homine doctō voluptātibus. Fugiēns cōnspectum Forī urbisque rūra peragrābat abdēbatque sē, quantum licēbat, et sōlus erat. Nihil agere autem cum animus nōn posset, ex-
15 istimāvit honestissimē molestiās posse dēpōnī, sī sē ad philosophiam rettulisset, cui adulēscēns multum temporis tribuerat, et omne studium cūramque convertit ad scrībendum; atque ut cīvibus etiam ōtiōsus aliquid prōdesse posset, ēlabōrāvit ut doctiōrēs fierent
20 et sapientiōrēs, plūraque brevī tempore ēversā rē pūblicā scrīpsit quam multīs annīs eā stante scrīpserat. Sīc fācundiae et Latīnārum litterārum parēns ēvāsit pāruitque virōrum sapientium praeceptō, quī docent nōn sōlum ex malīs ēligere minima oportēre,
25 sed etiam excerpere ex hīs ipsīs, sī quid īnsit bonī.

Multa exstant facētē ab eō dicta. Cum Lentulum, generum suum, exiguae statūrae hominem, vīdisset longō gladiō accīnctum, "Quis," inquit, "generum meum ad gladium adligāvit?"—Mātrōna quaedam
30 iūniōrem sē quam erat simulāns dictitābat sē trīgintā

CAESAR OCTAVIANUS AUGUSTUS.

tantum annōs habēre; cui Cicerō, "Vērum est," inquit, "nam hōc vīgintī annōs audiō."—Caesar, alterō cōnsule mortuō diē Decembris ūltimā, Caninium cōnsulem hōrā septimā in reliquam diēī partem renūntiāverat, quem cum plērique īrent salūtātum dē mōre, "Festinēmus," inquit Cicerō, "priusquam abeat magistrātū." Dē eōdem Caniniō scrīpsit Cicerō: "Fuit mīrificā vigilantiā Caninius, quī tōtō suō cōnsulātū somnum nōn vīderit."

XXIV. Caesar Octavianus Augustus.

63 B.C.–14 A.D.

Octāviānus, Iūliae, Gāī Caesaris sorōris, nepōs, quartum annum agēns patrem āmīsit. Ab avunculō adoptātus profectum eum in Hispāniās adversus Gnaeī Pompēī līberōs secūtus est. Deinde ab eō Apollōniam missus studiīs vacāvit. Utque prīmum occīsum Caesarem hērēdemque sē comperit, in urbem regressus hērēditātem adiit, nōmen Caesaris sūmpsit conlēctōque veterānōrum exercitū opem Decimō Brūtō tulit, quī ab Antōniō Mutinae obsidēbātur. Cum autem urbis aditū prohibērētur, ut Brūtum dē omnibus rēbus certiōrem faceret, prīmō litterās mīsit plumbeīs lāminīs īnscrīptās, quās ad bracchium religātās ūrīnātōrēs Scultennam amnem trānantēs ad Brūtum dēferēbant. Quīn et avibus internūntiīs ūtēbātur. Columbīs enim, quās inclūsās ante famē adfēcerat, epistulās ad collum religābat eāsque ā proximō moenibus locō ēmittēbat.

Illae, lūcis cibīque avidae, altissima aedificiōrum petentēs excipiēbantur ā Decimō Brūtō; quī eō modō dē omnibus rēbus certior fīēbat, utique postquam dispositō quibusdam locīs cibō columbās illūc dēvolāre
5 īnstituerat.

Bellum Mutinēnse Octāviānus duōbus proeliīs cōnfēcit; quōrum in alterō nōn ducis modo, sed mīlitis etiam fūnctus est officiō atque in mediā dīmicātiōne, aquiliferō legiōnis suae graviter sauciō, aquilam umerīs
10 subīsse diūque fertur portāsse. Posteā reconciliātā cum Antōniō grātiā iūnctīsque cum eō cōpiīs, ut Gāī Caesaris necem ulcīscerētur, ad urbem hostīliter accessit mīsitque quī nōmine exercitūs sibi cōnsulātum dēposcerent. Cunctante senātū centuriō, prīnceps
15 lēgātiōnis, rēiectō sagulō, ostendēns gladī capulum nōn dubitāvit in cūriā dīcere: " Hīc faciet, sī vōs nōn fēceritis."

Ita cum Octāviānus vīcēsimō aetātis annō cōnsulātum invāsisset, pācem fēcit cum Antōniō et Lepidō
20 ita ut triumvirī reī pūblicae cōnstituendae per quīnquennium essent ipse et Lepidus et Antōnius, et ut suōs quisque inimīcōs prōscrīberent. Quae prōscrīptiō Sullānā longē crūdēlior fuit. Exstant autem ex eā multa vel extrēmae impietātis vel mīrae fideī āc cōn-
25 stantiae exempla. T. Tōranius, triumvirōrum partēs secūtus, prōscrīptī patris suī, praetōriī et ōrnātī virī, latebrās, aetātem, notāsque corporis quibus āgnōscī posset, centuriōnibus ēdidit, quī eum persecūtī sunt.

Alius quīdam cum prōscrīptum sē cōgnōvisset, ad
30 clientem suum cōnfūgit; sed fīlius ēius, per ipsa

vestīgia patris militibus ductīs, occīdendum eum in cōnspectū suō obiēcit.

Cum C. Plōtius Plancus ā triumvirīs prōscrīptus in regiōne Salernitānā latēret, servī ēius comprehēnsī multumque āc diū tortī negābant sē scīre ubi dominus esset. Nōn sustinuit deinde Plancus tam fidēlēs tamque bonī exemplī servōs ūlterius cruciārī; sed prōcessit in medium iugulumque gladiīs mīlitum obiēcit.

Senātōris cūiusdam servus cum ad dominum prōscrīptum occīdendum mīlitēs advēnisse cōgnōsset, commūtātā cum eō veste, permūtātō etiam ānulō, illum posticō clam ēmīsit, sē autem in cubiculum ad lectulum recēpit et sē prō dominō occīdī passus est. "Quantī virī est," addit Seneca, "cum praemia prōditiōnis ingentia ostendantur, praemium fideī mortem concupiscere!"

Octāviānus deinde M. Brūtum, interfectōrem Caesaris, bellō persecūtus id bellum, quamquam invalidus atque aeger, duplicī proeliō trānsēgit; quōrum priōre castrīs exūtus vix fugā ēvāsit. Victor acerbissimē sē gessit; in nōbilissimum quemque captīvum nōn sine verbōrum contumēliā saeviit. Ūnī suppliciter sepultūram precantī respondisse dīcitur iam istam in volucrum fore potestāte. Aliōs, patrem et fīlium, prō vītā rogantēs, sortīrī fertur iussisse, ut alterutrī concēderētur, āc cum patre, quia sē obtulerat, occīsō fīlius quoque voluntāriā occubuisset nece, spectāsse utrumque morientem. Orāre veniam vel excūsāre sē cōnantibus ūnā vōce occurrēbat, moriendum esse. Scrībunt quīdam trecentōs ex dēditīciīs ēlēctōs ad āram dīvō Iūliō exstrūctam Īdibus Mārtiīs hostiārum mōre mactātōs.

Abaliēnātus posteā est ab Antōniō, quod is repudiātā Octāviā sorōre Cleopatram, Aegyptī rēgīnam, dūxisset uxōrem; quae quidem mulier cum Antōniō lūxū et dēliciīs certābat. Ūnā sē cēnā centiēns sēstertium absūmptūram aliquandō dīxerat. Cupiēbat discere Antōnius, sed fierī posse nōn arbitrābātur. Posterō igitur diē māgnificam aliās cēnam, sed cottīdiānam Antōniō apposuit inrīdentī quod prōmissō stāre nōn potuisset. At illa īnferrī mēnsam secundam iussit. Ex praeceptō ministrī ūnum tantum vās ante eam posuēre acētī, cūius asperitās vīsque margarītās resolvit. Exspectante igitur Antōniō quidnam esset āctūra, margarītam, quam auribus gerēbat, dētrāxit et acētō liquefactum absorbuit. Victum Antōnium omnēs, quī aderant, prōnūntiāvērunt.

Octāviānus cum Antōniō apud Actium, quī locus est in Epīrō, nāvālī proeliō dīmicāvit. Victum et fugientem persecūtus Aegyptum petiit, et Alexandrēam, quō Antōnius cum Cleopatrā cōnfūgerat, obsēdit. Antōnius in ūltimā rērum dēspērātiōne, cum habitū rēgis in soliō rēgālī sēdisset, mortem sibi ipse cōnscīvit. Cleopatra, quam Octāviānus, Alexandrēā in potestātem redāctā, māgnopere cupiēbat vīvam comprehendī triumphōque servārī, aspidem sibi adferendam cūrāvit ēiusque morsū periit. Cleopatrae mortuae commūnem cum Antōniō sepultūram tribuit.

Tandem Octāviānus, hostibus victīs, sōlus imperiō potītus, clēmentem sē exhibuit. Omnia posteā in eō plēna mānsuētūdinis et hūmānitātis. Multis īgnōvit vel eīs quī saepe graviter eum offenderant. **Reversus**

CAESAR OCTAVIANUS AUGUSTUS.

in Italiam triumphāns Rōmam ingressus est. Tum bellīs tōtō orbe compositīs Iānī geminī portās suā manū clausit, quae bis tantum anteā clausae fuerant, prīmum sub Numā rēge, iterum post prīmum Pūnicum bellum. Tunc omnēs praeteritōrum malōrum oblīviō cēpit populusque Rōmānus praesentis ōtī laetitiā perfruēbātur. Octāviānō māximī honōrēs ā senātū dēlātī sunt. Ipse Augustus cōgnōminātus et in honōrem ēius mēnsis Sextīlis eōdem nōmine appellātus est, quod illō mēnse bellīs cīvīlibus fīnis esset impositus. Patris patriae cōgnōmen ūniversī māximō cōnsēnsū dētulērunt eī. Dēferentibus lacrimāns respondit Augustus hīs verbīs: " Compos factus vōtōrum meōrum, patrēs cōnscrīptī, quid habeō aliud quod deōs immortālēs precer, quam ut hunc cōnsēnsum vestrum ad ūltimum vītae fīnem mihi perferre liceat!"

Dictātūram māgnā vī offerente populō dēprecātus est. Dominī appellātiōnem semper exhorruit eamque sibi tribuī ēdictō vetuit. Immō dē restituendā rē pūblicā nōn semel cōgitāvit, sed reputāns et sē prīvātum nōn sine perīculō fore, et rem pūblicam plūrium arbitriō commissum īrī, summam retinuit potestātem, id vērō studuit, nē quem novī status paenitēret. Bene dē eīs etiam quōs adversāriōs expertus erat, et sentiēbat et loquēbātur. Legentem aliquandō ūnum ē nepōtibus invēnit; cumque puer territus volūmen Cicerōnis, quod manū tenēbat, veste tegeret, Augustus librum cēpit eōque statim redditō: " Hīc vir," inquit, " fīlī mī, doctus fuit et patriae amāns."

Pedibus saepe per urbem incēdēbat summāque cōmi-

tāte adeuntēs excipiēbat. Convēnit aliquandō eum
veterānus mīles, quī vocātus in iūs perīclitābātur,
rogāvitque ut sibi adesset; statim Augustus ūnum ē
comitātū suō ēlēgit advocātum, quī lītigātōrem com-
5 mendāret. Tum veterānus exclāmāvit, "At nōn ego,
tē perīclitante bellō Actiacō, vicārium quaesīvī, sed
ipse prō tē pūgnāvī," simulque dētēxit cicātricēs.
Erubuit Augustus atque ipse vēnit in advocātiōnem.

Cum post Actiacam victōriam Octāviānus Rōmam
10 reverterētur, occurrit eī inter grātulantēs opifex quīdam
corvum tenēns, quem īnstituerat haec dīcere: "Avē,
Caesar, victor, imperātor!" Mīrātus Caesar officiōsam
avem vīgintī mīlibus nummōrum ēmit. Socius opificis,
ad quem nihil ex illā līberālitāte pervēnerat, adfīrmāvit
15 Caesarī habēre illum et alium corvum, quem ut adferre
cōgerētur rogāvit. Adlātus verba quae didicerat, ex-
pressit: "Avē, Antōnī, victor, imperātor!" Nihil
exasperātus Caesar satis dūxit iubēre illum dīvidere
dōnātīvum cum contubernālī. Salūtātus similiter ā
20 psittacō emī eum iussit.

Exemplum sūtōrem pauperem sollicitāvit ut corvum īnstitueret ad parem salūtātiōnem. Quī impendiō
exhaustus saepe ad avem nōn respondentem dīcere
solēbat: "Opera et impēnsa periit!" Aliquandō
25 tamen corvus coepit dīcere dictam salūtātiōnem. Hāc
audītā, dum trānsit, Augustus respondit: "Satis domī
tālium salūtātōrum habeō." Superfuit corvō memoria,
ut et illa, quibus dominum querentem solēbat audīre,
subtexeret, "Opera et impēnsa periit." Ad quod Caesar
30 rīsit emīque avem iussit quantī nūllam ante ēmerat.

CAESAR OCTAVIANUS AUGUSTUS.

Solēbat Graeculus quīdam dēscendentī ē palātiō Caesarī honōrificum aliquod epigramma porrigere. Id cum frūstrā saepe fēcisset et tamen rūrsus eum idem factūrum dūxisset Augustus, breve suā manū in chartā exarāvit Graecum epigramma et Graeculō advenientī 5 obviam mīsit. Ille inter legendum laudāre mīrārīque tam vōce quam voltū gestūque. Deinde cum accessisset ad sellam quā Caesar vehēbātur, dēmissā in pauperem crumēnam manū paucōs dēnāriōs prōtulit, quōs prīncipī daret dīxitque sē plūs datūrum fuisse, 10 sī plūs habuisset. Secūtō omnium rīsū dispēnsātōrem Caesar vocāvit et satis grandem pecūniae summam numerārī Graeculō iussit.

Augustus ferē nūllī sē invītantī negābat. Exceptus igitur ā quōdam cēnā satis parcā et paene cottīdiānā, 15 hōc .tantum īnsusurrāvit, "Nōn putābam mē tibi esse tam familiārem." Cum aliquandō apud Pōlliōnem quendam cēnāret frēgissetque ūnus ē servīs vās crystallinum, rapī eum ad mortem Pōlliō iussit et obicī mūraenīs quās ingēns piscīna continēbat. Ēvāsit ē 20 manibus puer et ad pedēs Caesaris cōnfūgit nihil aliud petītūrus quam ut aliter perīret nec ēsca piscium fieret. Mōtus est novō crūdēlitātis genere Caesar et illum quidem mittī, crystallina autem omnia cōram sē frangī iussit complērīque piscīnam. 25

Augustus in quādam vīllā aegrōtāns noctēs inquiētās agēbat, rumpente somnum ēius crēbrō noctuae cantū. Quā molestiā cum līberārī sē vehementer cupere significāsset, mīles quīdam, aucupī perītus, noctuam prehendendam cūrāvit, vīvamque Augustō attulit spē 30

ingentis praemī. Cui cum Augustus mīlle nummōs darī iussisset, ille minus dīgnum praemium exīstimāns dīcere ausus est, "Mālō ut vīvat," et avem dimīsit. Imperātōrī nec ad īrāscendum causa deerat nec ad
5 ulcīscendum potestās; hanc tamen iniūriam aequō animō tulit Augustus hominemque impūnītum abīre passus est.

Augustus amīcitiās neque facile admīsit et cōnstantissimē retinuit. Imprīmīs familiārem habuit Mae-
10 cēnātem, equitem Rōmānum; quī eā quā apud prīncipem valēbat grātiā ita semper ūsus est ut prōdesset omnibus quibus posset, nocēret nēminī. Iūs aliquandō dīcēbat Augustus et multōs capite damnātūrus vidēbātur. Aderat tum Maecēnās, quī per circumstantium
15 turbam perrumpere et ad tribūnal propius accēdere cōnābātur. Quod cum frūstrā temptāsset, haec verba in tabellā scrīpsit, "Surge tandem, carnifex!" eamque tabellam ad Augustum. prōiēcit. Quā lēctā is statim surrēxit neque quisquam est morte multātus.

20 Habitāvit Augustus in aedibus modicīs, neque laxitāte neque cultū cōnspicuīs, āc per annōs amplius quadrāgintā in eōdem cubiculō hieme et aestāte mānsit. Supellex quoque ēius vix prīvātae ēlegantiae erat. Rārō veste aliā ūsus est quam cōnfectā ab
25 uxōre, sorōre, fīliā neptibusque. Item tamen Rōmam, quam prō māiestāte imperī nōn satis ōrnātam invēnerat, adeō excoluit ut iūre glōriārētur marmoream sē relinquere quam latericiam accēpisset.

Fōrmā fuit Augustus eximiā et per omnēs aetātis
30 gradūs venustissimā. Erat tamen omnis lēnōcinī

CAESAR OCTAVIANUS AUGUSTUS.

neglegēns et in capite cōmendō tam incūriōsus ut eō ipsō tempore quō illud tōnsōribus committeret, aut legeret aliquid aut etiam scrīberet.

Paucīs annīs ante quam morerētur, gravissimam in Germāniā accēpit clādem, tribus legiōnibus cum duce Vārō lēgātīsque et auxiliīs omnibus caesīs. Hāc nūntiātā excubiās per urbem indīxit, nē quis tumultus exsisteret, et māgnōs lūdōs Iovī optimō māximō vōvit, sī rēs pūblica in meliōrem statum vertisset. Adeō dēnique cōnsternātum ferunt ut, per continuōs mēnsēs barbā capillōque submissō, caput interdum foribus inlīderet, vōciferāns: "Quīnctilī Vāre, legiōnēs redde!" diemque clādis quotannīs maestum habuerit āc lūgubrem.

Tandem adflictā valētūdine in Campāniam concessit, ubi, remissō ad ōtium animō, nūllō hilaritātis genere abstinuit. Suprēmō vītae diē petītō speculō capillum sibi cōmī iussit et amīcōs circumstantēs percontātus ecquid eīs vidērētur mīmum vītae commodē trānsēgisse, adiēcit solitam clausulam: "Ēdite strepitum vōsque omnēs cum gaudiō applaudite." Obiit Nōlae sextum et septuāgēsimum annum agēns.

ESSENTIAL BOOKS FOR REFERENCE.

Classic Myths. — *Gayley.*
History of Classical Greek Literature, 2 vols. — *Mahaffy.*
Elementary Latin Dictionary. — *Lewis.*
Latin Grammar. — *Madvig.*
Students' Classical Dictionary. — *Smith.*
History of Roman Literature. — *Cruttwell.*
Dictionary of Greek and Roman Antiquities. — *Rich.*
Atlas Antiquus. — *Kiepert.*
Atlas of Classical Antiquities. — *Schreiber.*
History of Rome. — *Liddell.*
History of Greece. — *Smith.*
History of Ancient Art. — *von Reber.*
A Companion to School Classics. — *Gow.*

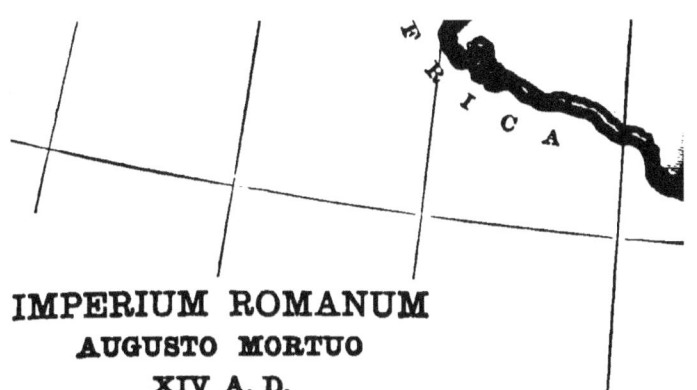

IMPERIUM ROMANUM
AUGUSTO MORTUO
XIV A. D.

BOOKS FOR COLLATERAL READING.

History of Rome, 3 vols. — *Niebuhr.*
*History of Rome. — *Liddell.*
History of Rome, 5 vols. — *Duruy.*
History of Rome, 4 vols. — *Mommsen.*
*Early Rome. — *Ihne.*
*Lives of Illustrious Men. — *Plutarch* (Clough's Translation)
*Stories from Livy. — *A. J. Church.*
*Roman Life in the Days of Cicero. — *A. J. Church.*
*Two Thousand Years Ago. — *A. J. Church.*
*The Story of the Nations, Carthage. — *A. J. Church.*
*Pictures from Roman Life and Story. — *A. J. Church.*
*The Story of the Nations, Rome. — *Gilman.*
*Last Days of Pompeii. — *Bulwer.*
*Ben-Hur. — *Wallace.*
Zenobia. — *Ware.*
*Lays of Ancient Rome. — *Macaulay.*
*Virginius. — *James Sheridan Knowles.*
*Rome and Carthage. — *Smith.*
*Life of Hannibal. — *Arnold.*
*History of Julius Caesar. — *Abbott.*
The Roman Triumvirates. — *Merivale.*
Life of Caesar. — *Froude.*
Caesar, Great Captains' Series. — *Dodge.*
*Julius Caesar. — *Shakespeare.*
*Life of Cicero. — *Forsyth.*
The Students' Cicero. — *Fausset.*
Catiline, Clodius, and Tiberius. — *E. S. Beesly.*
*The Roman Traitor. — *H. W. Herbert.*
The Gracchi, Marius, and Sulla. — *A. H. Beesly.*

*Books thus marked are such as are particularly adapted to interest and profit youthful readers.

ABBREVIATIONS USED IN THE NOTES.

A. = Allen and Greenough.
abl. = ablative.
abs. = absolute.
adj. = adjective.
acc. = accusative.
app. = apposition, or appositive.
cf. = *cōnfer* = compare.
cl. = clause.
conj. = conjunction.
cons. = construction.
dat. = dative.
decl. = declension.
dir. disc. = direct discourse.
f. n. = footnote.
fig. = figure.
fr. = from.
gen. = genitive.
ger. = gerund, or gerundive.
H. = Harkness.
id. = idiom.
ind. = indicative.

ind. disc. = indirect discourse.
l. = line, or lines.
Lat. = Latin.
lit. = literally.
n. = note.
nom. = nominative.
p. = page.
part. = participle.
perf. = perfect.
poss. = possessive.
pred. = predicate.
prep. = preposition.
pro. = pronoun.
R. = remark.
rel. = relative.
s. t. = see text.
sc. = *scīlicet*, = supply, namely.
subj. = subject, or subjunctive.
tr. = translate, or translation.
v. = *vidē* = see.
voc. = vocabulary.

Notes to words separated by a dash (*armātīs — properāvit*), refer to them and all intervening words.

Notes to words separated by dots (*daret . . . regeret*), refer only to the words named.

NOTES.

I. Romani imperi exordium.

The beginnings of Rome, like those of other powers of old, are shrouded in much doubt and uncertainty. That some truth lies hid in the mass of fables that Fabius, Piso, Tubero, Livy, and other Latin historians have left us, cannot be questioned; but where fiction ends and fact begins, is the question that has been troubling scholars ever since the middle of the 18th century, when the credibility of early Roman history first began to be suspected. The Romans themselves believed the stories as they came down to them, and they were accepted as trustworthy for many centuries. The first volume of Niebuhr's great work, which appeared in 1811, first brought before the world the results of a scientific investigation of the subject. It was made clear that many of the traditions were manufactured to explain facts and institutions already existing at the beginning of authentic history, that much was derived from Greek sources; that the Alban kings and the seven kings of Rome were mythical; that, in short, nothing prior to the destruction of the city by the Gauls in 390 B.C. could be received unchallenged.

The student is referred for a full discussion of this subject to the following books:

>Niebuhr's History of Rome, Vol. I.
>Liddell's History of Rome, Bk. I., Chap. V.
>Duruy's History of Rome, Vol. I., Chaps. I. and II.
>Ihne's Early Rome, Chaps. II. and IV.
>Mommsen's History of Rome, Vol. I.

Page 1. 1. **Proca**: the twelfth of the mythical kings of Alba. For gender see A. 35, Exc.; H. 48, 5, 1. — **Albānōrum**: the people of Alba, a city in Latium, S. E. of Rome. It stretched along a narrow ridge of land and from this fact is often called *Alba Longa*.

2. **Numitōrī**: put first for emphasis, to contrast with *Amūlius* in the next clause. — **nātū**: v. A. 253; II. 424.

3. **pulsō frātre**: *after he had expelled his brother.* A. 255, d. and note; H. 431, 1, 2. Avoid a literal translation of the ablative absolute.

4. **subole**: cons. A. 243, a; H. 414, I. — **filiam**: decl. A. 36, e; H. 49, 4. — **Vestae**: the goddess of the home and the fireside. She was worshiped in every house; and, in addition, had public sacred worship in a temple. There the Vestal virgins kept the fire forever burning upon her altar.

5. **sacerdōtem**: cons. A. 239, 1, a; H. 373, 1.

6. **Eā rē cōgnitā**: cf. *frātre*, l. 3. — **ipsam** = *the mother;* lit. *herself.*

7. **alveō**: cons. A. 228; H. 386. — **Tiberim**: for form v. A. 56, a, 1; H. 62, II, 2, (1). The Tiber is the largest river in Latium. At Rome it is some four hundred feet wide and from twelve to eighteen feet deep. After heavy rains it overflows its banks even as in ancient days.

9. **relābente flūmine**: cf. *Eā rē cognitā*, l. 6. — **eōs**: by being put before the subject *aqua*, the object is made emphatic and is strongly contrasted with it, — THEM *the water left on the shore.*

9. **Vāstae**: note the emphatic position.

10. **locīs**: v. A. 78, 2, b; H. 141. — **ut** = *as. Ut* with an indicative is translated by *as, how,* or *when;* with a subjunctive by *in order that, in order to, for the purpose of, in order that not* (after verbs of fearing), *so that,* or *though.*

12. **ōrī**: cons. cf. *alveō*, l. 7. — **sē gessit**: *sē gerere* = *to conduct oneself, act as.*

13. **Cum** is either a preposition or a conjunction. If it be a preposition that fact will be determined by the ablative following it; if it be a conjunction it may mean *when, since,* or *although.* In the sense of *when* it will take the indicative when used with a present or a future tense, or with a past tense when defining or fixing the time of the main action; otherwise the subjunctive is used. Practically the instances of *cum* with a past indicative are not very common. In the sense of *since* or of *although, cum* is followed by the subjunctive. — **saepius**: *again and again.*

14. **reverterētur**: see note on *cum* above, also A. 323, 325; H.

521, II, 2. — **pāstor rēgius** = *the king's shepherd.* A. 214, a, 2; H. 395, n. 2.

16. **ēducandōs** agrees with *eōs.* A. 294, d; H. 544, 2, n. 2, — **prīmō**: beginning a series is followed by *deinde* meaning *next,* or *in the second place.*

18. **rapīnā**: A. 243; H. 413, n. 3.

19. **Quā rē**: A. 245; H. 416. — **eīs**: cf. *ōrī* p. 1. l. 12. — **īnsidiātī essent**: cf. *reverterētur* l. 14.

Page 2. 1. **esset**: an indirect question is a question used as *subject,* as *object,* or as *appositive.* How is it used here? — **māter**: sc. *fuisset.*

2. **armātīs properāvit**: *armed the shepherds* AND *hastened,* etc. It is often best to translate a verb and participle by *two* verbs connected by *and.* Latin prefers the subordinate, English the coördinate construction. — **Albam**: why no preposition? A. 258, b; H. 380, II.

4. **solitus esset**: cons. A. 312; H. 513, II, n. 1.

5. **ā rēge**: the ablative of the agent, as distinguished from the ablative of the means, takes the preposition *ā,* or *ab.*

8. **haud procul erat quīn**: *he lacked little of . . .,* on cons. of *āgnōsceret,* v. A. 319, d; H. 504, 4.

9. **līneāmentīs**: for cons. cf. *nātū,* p. 1. l. 2. — **mātrī**: what would MĀTRIS *simillimus* mean?

10. **Ea rēs**: words in a subordinate clause that are specially emphatic are often put before the conjunction.

11. **dum** in temporal clauses means either *while* or *until.* If the former, it is followed by the indicative, if the latter, usually by the subjunctive. — **tenet**: for tense v. A. 328, a; H. 467, 4.

12. **supervenit**: what tense? A. 276, d; H. 467, III, 1.

16. **uter**: distinguish between *uter, uterque; quis,* and *quisque.*

17. **daret . . . regeret**: v. *esset,* above. — **auspicia**: this word (v. voc. for etymology) and *augurium* are terms used to refer to the will of the gods as interpreted by the flight of birds. A college of priests known as *augurs,* founded by Romulus, had this for its special business. Nothing of importance was undertaken at Rome without first taking the auspices.

19. **augurĭō**: abl. of cause, or means.
21. **vāllum**: this was a mere earth-work.
23. **sīc deinde**: sc. *pereat.*
24. **sōlus**: note emphasis of position. — **imperĭō**: cons. A. 249 ; H. 421, I, and f. n. 1.

II. Romulus, Romanorum rex primus.

Read Plutarch's Life of Romulus, also Church's Stories from Livy, Chap. I.

Page 3. 1. **Rōmulus**: though Romulus is a mythical character, the political institutions attributed to him are authentic in that they had their origin in the earliest times.

2. **asȳlum**: for cons. v. *sacerdōtem*, p. 1, l. 5. This *asylum* was a grove of oak-trees lying between the two summits of the Capitoline hill.

4. **uxōrēs**: note the emphatic position. — **ipse** refers to Romulus. — **habērent**: see n. on *cum*, p. 1, l. 13.

5. **quī . . . peterent**: A. 317, 2, n.; 318, (2), a ; H. 497, I.

8. **quoque** always follows the emphatic word.

9. **foret**: a rare form for *esset*, A. 119, b, n.; H. 204, 2. For the construction v. A. 308, a ; 311, I, R.; H. 486, n. 2 ; 510, n. 2.

11. **convēnēre**: not an infinitive.

12. **videndae novae urbis**: distinguish from *videndī novam urbem*. Remember that the gerund with a direct object is regularly used only in the genitive case and in the ablative case without a preposition. — **Sabīnī**: one of the early native peoples of Italy. Their principal city was Cures.

13. **vēnit**: A. 324; H. 518, n. 1. — **conversae**: pred. adj. — **eō**: not a pronoun.

14. **sīgnō datō**: v. n. on *pulsō frātre*, p. 1, l. 3.

16. **ob virginēs raptās**: *on account of the seizure of the maidens.* This use of the perf. part. is a very common idiom, v. A. 292, a ; H. 549, n. 2.

18. **Rōmae**: cf. *alveō*, p. 1, l. 7. — **adpropinquārent**: cons. ?

19. **petītum**: v. A. 302, R.; H. 546.

20. **Hūius pater**: *Her father.* Remember that the Latin demonstrative pronouns are often best translated in English by the possessives and the personals. — **arcī**: cf. *Rōmae* above.

22. **perdūxisset**: *if she would lead,* not *had led.* This word and *gererent,* in the next sentence, illustrate a very common use of the subjunctive known as implied or informal ind. disc. Tatius' words to Tarpeia are: "*Tibi optiōnem mūneris dabō, sī exercitum meum in Capitōlium perdūxeris.*" She replies, "*Date id quod in sinistrīs manibus geritis.*" Now this conversation is reported without a formal introduction of indirect discourse; but the mood and tense of the verbs in the subordinate clauses are the same as if we had placed "*Dīxit,*" "*He said,*" before the first sentence; and "*Respondit,*" "*She replied,*" before the second, v. A. 341, c; 336, 2; H. 525, 2; 528, 1.

24. **Quibus**: a relative is often used in Latin where good English requires a demonstrative or a personal pronoun; tr. *after these had been treacherously promised.*

26. **prōditiō**: the Capitoline hill has two summits, upon one of which stood the Capitol, upon the other the citadel. The steep wall of rock on the west side was known as the "*saxum Tarpēium.*" From it traitors were hurled to death.

27. **poenā**: "Their heavy shields upon the maid they threw,
And with their splendid gifts entombed at once and slew."

Page 4. 2. **Rōmānum Forum**: this was a large open square between the Capitoline and Palatine hills. It was surrounded by temples, porticoes, and shops; and was used for holding courts, and public meetings of all kinds.

6. **clāmitābant**: bring out the force of this tense.

7. **longē aliud . . . aliud**: tr. *one thing . . . quite another.*

9. **Iovī**: decl. A. 60, b; H. 66, 3. — **aedem**: this was the temple of Jupiter Stator (the flight-stayer). It stood on the slope of the Palatine next to the arch of Titus. Its site has been recently laid bare, but of the temple itself not a vestige remains.

11. **passīs**: perf. part. from *pandō,* in abl. abs. with *crīnibus.* Wearing the hair disheveled was one of the commonest ways of expressing sorrow.

NOTES.

13. **conciliārunt** = *conciliāvērunt*.

14. **foedere ictō** = *after making* (lit. *striking*) *a treaty*. The making of a treaty was accompanied by a sacrifice. The verb *to strike* in the above phrase is a reminder of the ancient custom, referring to the striking of the victim.

16. **multō**: A. 250; H. 423.

18. **ageret**: cf. *peterent*, p. 3, l. 6. — **senātōrēs**: the senate was an advisory body under the kings, but at an early period of the republic it became the ruling power of the state. Its numbers, too, were largely increased, and it was known collectively as "*Patrēs (et) Cōnscrīptī*," in which some say that *Patrēs* stands for the original number, and *Cōnscrīptī* for those that were added. See Ihne's Early Rome, Chap. VIII.

19. **equitum**: the order of Knights, who were originally the cavalry of the state, was based upon a property qualification of 400,000 sesterces (about $17,000). In later times the cavalry consisted almost entirely of foreigners.

20. **cūriās**: the people were made up of three tribes, the Ramnes, Tities, and Luceres; and each tribe was divided into ten *cūriae*.

22. **campō**: the Campus Martius, a large plain lying outside the city walls in the bend of the Tiber, north-west of the Capitoline. It was used for large assemblies, and for all kinds of warlike and gymnastic exercises. It is now a part of the city thickly covered with buildings.

24. **ablātus est**: v. *auferō*.

25. **crēditus est**: personal use, A. 330, b; H. 534, 1, n. 1. — **fidem fēcit**: *strengthened belief*. For the following dative v. A. 227, n. 2.

28. **vīsum**: sc. *esse*. — **fōrmā**: A. 251, a; H. 419, II, and 2, 1) — 4).

Page 5. 1. **exsisterent**: A. 332, 2; H. 501, I, 1. Why is the circumlocution *futūrum — exsisterent* used? v. A. 288, f; H. 537. 3, n. 1.

2. **Quirīnus**: This is a Sabine word, and the name of the Sabine god of war. Romulus was known by this name after his death and deification.

III. Numa Pompilius, Romanorum rex secundus.

Read Plutarch's Life of Numa Pompilius.

3. **Successit Rōmulō Numa**: note the order. The fact of the succession is more important than the person who succeeds. To Numa was ascribed much of the religion of the early Romans. — **iūstitiā**: cf. *fōrmā*, p. 4, l. 28.

4. **Curibus**: cf. n. on *Sabīnī*, p. 3, l. 12.

5. **Quī cum**: *When he.* An emphatic word or phrase in a subordinate clause is often put before the conjunction. *Do not translate in that order.* — **Rōmam**: cf. *Albam*, p. 2, l. 2. — **vēnisset**: cf. n. on *reverterētur*, p. 1, l. 14.

7. **Vestae**: cf. n. p. 1, l. 4. The worship of Vesta goes back to the very earliest times.

8. **alendum**: A. 294, d; 318, b; H. 544, n. 2. — **virginibus**: indirect object. — **Flāminem**: these were priests devoted to a particular deity. There were 15 of them, and each was distinguished by the name of the deity he served.

9. **īnsīgnī veste**: the *flamen* was dressed in a woollen robe folded double, and wore upon his head a cap called *apex*, which had a pointed piece of olive wood, set in a flock of wool, on its crown. — **curūlī sellā**: seats of this kind were originally used exclusively by the kings at Rome, but were subsequently granted as a privilege to the flamens and the curule magistrates, (consuls, censors, praetors, curule aediles, dictators, and the *magister equitum*). The chair could be folded like a modern camp-stool. See fig. 1, which shows how the legs were hinged for folding, and also the *sella* complete.

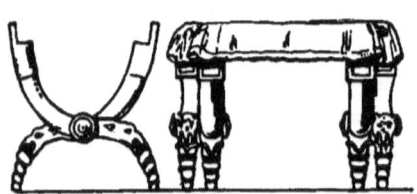

FIG. 1.

10. **dīcitur**: he is said.

13. **fulmina**: the falling of a thunderbolt was always regarded by the Romans as an omen calling for a propitiatory sacrifice. — **essent prōcūranda**: v. n. on *esset*, p. 2, l. 1.

NOTES.

16. **aedēs**: A. 79, a; H. 132.
17. **futūrum esset**: v. *essent prōcūranda* above.
18. **ancīle**: this was made of bronze. Upon its safety the welfare of the state was supposed to depend. — **Id nē**: v. n. on *Quī cum*, p. 5, l. 5.

Fig. 2.

20. **Saliōs**: (cf. *salīre* to leap). This college of priests consisted of twelve eminent men, who yearly, in the month of March, went through the city singing and dancing. In their right hands they carried spears with which they struck the *ancilia*, which were suspended on a pole and carried on the shoulders of the priests' ministers. See fig. 2.

21. **quī . . . custodīrent**: *to guard*. But what literally?

24. **duodecim mēnsēs**: the year of Romulus had but ten months and 304 days. For this, Numa substituted a year of 12 months and 355 days. The agreement between this and the solar year was made by inserting an intercalary month every two years. This arrangement continued until the reform of the calendar by Julius Caesar in 46 B.C.

25. **nefāstōs**: these were days of ill-omen upon which legal business could not be done, nor public assemblies held. — **Iānō**: originally worshiped as the sun-god; one of the oldest and most important of the Italian deities. Later he is generally viewed as god of gates, doors, and of all beginnings. He is represented with two faces, looking in opposite directions, to symbolize that the beginning or the present has to do both with the past and the future. The covered passage-way known as the temple of Janus, built near the Forum by Numa, was not closed after his time until the end of the first Punic war, 241 B.C.

Page 6. 5. **sibi**: A. 231; H. 387.
6. **monitū**: A. 245; H. 416. — **ageret**: cons. A. 336, 2; H. 524.
7. **quem medium**: *the middle of which*, v. A. 193; H. 440, 2, notes 1 and 2. — **perennī rigābat aquā**: note the order. It will often be met with in Nepos.

NOTES. 83

8. **inferēbat**: the imperfect indicative is used in descriptions, and to denote continued, customary, or repeated action; cf. *rigābat* and *erat* above.

9. **ita**: what construction does this word suggest for the subordinate clause that is to follow? A. 319, R.; H. 500, II, n. 1. — **eā** = *tāli*.

11. **quidem** never stands first in a sentence. It makes the preceding word emphatic. Tr. *to be sure*.

12. **cīvitātī**: all the prepositional compounds of *sum*, excepting *absum*, take the dative.

IV. Tullus Hostilius, Romanorum rex tertius.

17. **Mortuō Numā**: an expression of time. — Tullus Hostilius reminds us most of Romulus. See Ihne's Early Rome, p. 77. See also Church's Stories from Livy, Chap. II.

20. **Ducibus — fīnīrī**: *rem — fīnīrī* is the subject of *placuit; ducibus* is the dative after a verb of *pleasing;* tr. *the commanders Hostilius and Fufetius determined that*, etc.

21. **Erant**: when a form of *esse* stands first, it usually means that the verb is not used as a copula, but to express *being* or *existence*.

23. **quisque**: note the order of the clause.

24. **ictum est**: cf. n. on *foedere ictō*, p. 4, l. 14. — **eā lēge**: cf. n. on *quā rē*, p. 1, l. 19. — **ut — esset**: in apposition with *lēge*.

Page 7. 2. **ternī**: distinguish from *trēs* and *tertius*.

4. **increpuēre**: A. 324; H. 518, n. 1. This word probably refers to the dashing of the spears against the shields. This was followed by the drawing of the swords for the hand-to-hand combat.

7. **cecidērunt**: distinguish from *cecīdērunt*.

11. **erat**: *quia* states a *fact* as a cause, and for that reason regularly takes the indicative.

12. **singulōs**: distinguish from *ūnus* and *prīmus*.

13. **ratus**: tr. *thinking*. — **aliquantum spatī**: *a considerable distance*.

14. **pūgnātum est**: do not translate literally.

15. **videt**: v. n. on *cum*, p. 1, l. 13. — **ē Cūriātiīs**: the partitive gen., which might have been used, does not distinguish sharply from the rest as this does.

17. **inclāmat**: v. n. on *tenet*, p. 2, l. 11.
18. **alterum**: in an enumeration, this word is used oftener than *secundus*.
20. **singulī**: *one on each side.*
21. **alter ... alter**: distinguish between this and *alius ... alius*, v. voc. — **ferōx**: not *fierce.*
26. **domum**: cf. *Albam*, p. 2, l. 2. — **Prīnceps**: *at the head.*
27. **obvia**: v. voc.
29. **palūdāmentō**: a military cloak worn by generals and superior officers over their armor. It was wide, of fine texture, and white, scarlet, or purple. It was fastened by a brooch upon the shoulder.
30. **crīnēs solvere**: v. n. on *passīs*, p. 4, l. 11. — **ferōcis**: cf. *ferōx* above. Is the meaning the same?

Page 8. 4. **oblīta**: v. A. 219; H. 406, II. — **Sīc — Rōmāna**: tr. *thus perish every Roman woman who*, etc. On *eat* v. A. 267; H. 484, I.
6. **Atrōx**: note its emphatic position.
7. **in iūs**: *to court* — **iūdicēs**: this was the council of two (*Duūmvirī perduelliōnis*) appointed to try persons accused of the murder of a Roman.
8. **līctor**: a public officer attached to the service of certain Roman magistrates, whom he preceded whenever they went abroad. The king had twelve of these, who carried out his judicial decrees. See fig. 3.
9. **prōvocāvit**: the right of appeal to the people from the decision of a magistrate was an ancient right belonging to Roman citizens. This right continued, with few interruptions, until the time of the empire.
12. **nē — faceret**: in direct disc. = *nōlīte mē, quem paulō ante cum ēgregiā stirpe cōnspēxistis, orbum līberīs facere.* Note carefully the changes in construction.
13. **līberīs**: A. 243, d; H. 414, III.
14. **Nōn tulit**: *could not resist.*

FIG. 3.

18. **quod**: *and this.* Latin often uses a relative where English requires a conjunction and a demonstrative, or a conjunction and a personal pronoun.
19. **tigillum sorōrium**: with reference to this Livy, the historian,

says, "*Id hodiē quoque pūblicē semper refectum manet,*" and the venerable relic was pointed out in his day, in the first century A.D.

22. **fīnīsset**: A. 321; H. 516.
23. **Vēientēs**: Veii was 12 miles north of Rome. — **Fīdēnātēs**: Fīdēna was on the left bank of the Tiber about a mile N.E. of Rome.
26. **Quā rē Tullus intellēctā**: tr. *when Tullus perceived this;* v. n. on *quod* above, l. 18.
27. **suō**: emphatic position.
28. **Quō audītō**: cf. *Quā rē*, etc. above, l. 26.
29. **Posterō diē Mettius**: v. n. on *Ea rēs*, p. 2, l. 10.
30. **iūssū**: cf. *monitū*, p. 6, l. 6. — **quadrīgīs**: abl. of means. — **in dīversa** = *in dīversās partēs*.

Page 9. 4. **quō**: this conj. is used with a comparative to express purpose.
9. **mīlitiae quam domī**: A. 258, 4, 2, d; H. 426, 2.
11. **frāctī**: with *sunt*.
12. **ut**: v. n. on *ut*, p. 1, l. 10.
13. **Memorant**, etc.: Livy (Bk. I, 31, § 8) says that this was done by Jupiter, angry because Tullus improperly tried to imitate Numa in performing sacred rites.

V. Ancus Marcius, Romanorum rex quartus.

" The similarity apparent between Romulus and Tullus Hostilius has its counterpart in the stories of Numa and Ancus. The latter is evidently the shadow of the former." Ihne's Early Rome, p. 77.

19. **sustulerant**: v. *tollō*.
21. **indīceret**: in reference to an anticipated or intended action *antequam* and *priusquam* are always followed by the subjunctive.
22. **quī rēs repeteret**: *to demand satisfaction.* — **lēgātum**: this was the *fētiālis*, one of a college of priests instituted by Numa, who acted as heralds to hostile states in carrying declarations of war and in concluding treaties of peace. They hurled a bloody spear across the hostile frontier when declaring war.
24. **capite vēlātō**: the Roman always veiled his head in making prayer or sacrifice.

> " Ere yet you light your altars, spread
> A purple covering o'er your head,
> Lest sudden bursting on your sight
> Some hostile presence mar the rite.
> Thus worship you, and thus your train,
> And sons unborn the rite retain."
>
> VERGIL, *Aen.* iii. 405-9. Conington's Translation.

Page 10. 2. **ēmittit**: this spear was tipped with iron or charred at the end and smeared with blood, emblematic of fire and slaughter.

4. **bellī indīcendī**: would *bellum indīcendī* be good Latin? — **iūs fētiāle**: of interest as a beginning of international law.

5. **Lēgātō** has *repetentī* in agreement with it and depends on *respōnsum est.* — **superbē respōnsum est**: *a haughty reply was given.*

6. **hōc**: this refers to what precedes. Usually it refers to what follows.

8. **cīvēs**: some historians believe that these were the original Roman plebeians or common people.

9. **autem**: remember that this word has no strong adversative force, and often merely continues the narrative. — **tantā hominum multitūdine**: notice the order, which is very common in Latin.

10. **fierent**: v. n. on *cum*, p. 1, l. 13. — **carcerem**: this is situated on the slope of the Capitoline and overlooks the Forum. The dungeon below was used for executions and was called the *Tulliānum*. It is still in a good state of preservation. See fig. 4.

11. **audāciae**: the objective genitive is often best translated by *for*. A. 217; H. 396, III.

12. **urbī**: A. 228, 225, d; H. 384, II, 2, n. — **ponte sublicio**: the oldest and most famous bridge at Rome. Many noteworthy events are connected with it, and it was so sacred that no repairs could be made to it without

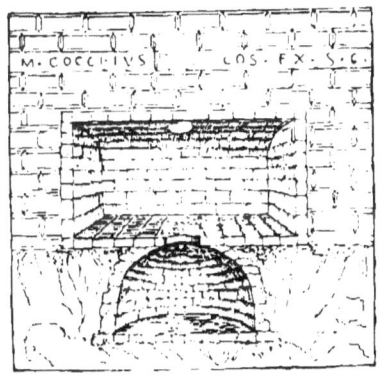

FIG. 4.

previous sacrifice. It was several times rebuilt, and was still in existence in our era.

13. **Tiberī**: decl. v. A. 56, a, 1; 57, a, 1; H. 62, II, 2. — **urbī**: A. 248, a, R.; H. 385, II, 4, 3).

14. **Ōstiam**: 16 mi. fr. Rome. At one time it was an important and flourishing seaport. After the time of Trajan (98–117 A.D.) it was gradually abandoned for a better harbor on the right arm of the Tiber. The ruins of Ostia are between two and three miles from the coast, owing to the accumulation of sand brought down by the river.

VI. Lucius Tarquinius Priscus, Romanorum rex quintus.

The latter part of the history of the kings is as fabulous as the first. The stories of the Tarquins and of Servius Tullius are full of arbitrary fiction. They seem, however, to point to an Etruscan dominion over Latium. See Church's Stories from Livy, Chap. III, Ihne's Early Rome, p. 79.

19. **haec**: cf. n. on *hōc*, l. 6.
20. **advenientī**: sc. *eī*. — **carpentum**: v. fig. 7.
21. **cui**: cf. *alveō*, p. 1, l. 7.
23. **perīta**: what adjectives take the gen.? A. 218, a, b; H. 399, I, 1, 2, 3, II.
24. **virum**: *her husband*. — **excelsa et alta**: the neuter of adjectives is often used substantively.

Page 11. 3. **relictus**: *i.e.* by will. — **ita**: omit in translation.

4. **adeptus esset**: the object is understood from *rēgnum*. For cons. v. A. 312; H. 513, II, and n. 1.

5. **Circum Māximum**: between the Palatine and Aventine hills. Scarcely a vestige now remains. Its length was 1800 ft., its breadth 350 ft., and its seating capacity 150,000. For vivid description of the ancient circus read Bulwer's Last Days of Pompeii, Bk. V, Chaps. II, IV; Wallace's Ben-Hur, Chaps. XII–XIV.

6. **triumphāvit**: a grand military procession in which a victorious general rode through the city in a four-horse chariot, followed by his troops and the spoils of war. Read Macaulay's Lays of Ancient

Rome, Prophecy of Capys, XXVII–XXX; also Ware's Zenobia, pp. 276-280.

8. ut ferunt: *as they say.* A common phrase.

10. id fierī, etc.: in dir. disc. *id fierī nōn potest, nisi avēs addīxerint.* Account for changes in mode and tense.

11. in experimentum: *to make a trial.*

12. posset: cf. n. on *esset*, p. 2, l. 1. So also **possem** below, l. 15. — **concēpisset**: cf. n. on *perdūxisset*, p. 3, l. 22.

16. secuisse: sc. *eam.* This stone was kept as a relic. A veiled statue of Accius stood in the Comitium.

17. percussisset: cf. n. on *erat*, p. 7, l. 11. — **praetexta**: the *toga praetexta*, a white garment derived from the Etruscans, ornamented with a wide purple border, and worn with the *bulla* by free-born children of both sexes, and by the chief magistrates. It was laid aside at the age of sixteen.

18. bullā: an ornament usually of gold, of globular shape, containing an amulet. It was worn about the neck by Roman children of noble family and laid aside with the *praetexta*. It was then consecrated to the household gods and hung up over the hearth. See fig. 5. — **dōnāvit**: as in English we can say either "to present some one with something" or "to present something to some one," so Latin says, "*aliquem aliquō dōnāre*" or "*aliquid alicui dōnāre*," cf. n. on *urbī*, p. 10, l. 12.

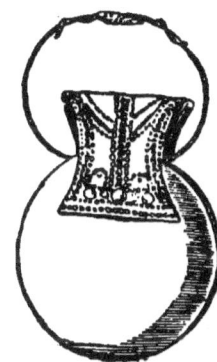

FIG. 5.

22. Ex pāstōribus: the usual construction with numerals instead of the partitive genitive.

24. Quōrum clāmor: v. n. on *quī cum*, p. 5, l. 5.

29. ēlātam ... dēiēcit: v. n. on *armātīs ... properāvit*, p. 2, l. 2.

VII. Servius Tullius, Romanorum rex sextus.

See Church's Stories from Livy, Chap. IV.

The reign of Servius Tullius is as full of marvels as that of his predecessors. His birth is as miraculous as that of Romulus. He is the author of social order like Numa, but he also introduces a military organization, wherein he reminds us of Romulus. His constitution, adapted to the changing conditions of the times, lasted to the end of the republic. See Ihne's Early Rome, pp. 78–80.

Page 12. 2. **Quī cum**: v. n. on same, p. 5, l. 5.

4. **vīsū ēventūque**: lit. *in respect to the seeing and the outcoming*, tr. *in its appearance and its consequences*, A. 303; H. 547.

7. **haud secus āc**: *just like* (lit. *not otherwise than*). To deny something instead of affirming its opposite is called *litotes*.

8. **Is postquam**: cf. *Quī cum* above, l. 2.—**adolēvit**: cf. *vēnit*, p. 3, l. 13.

9. **quŏdam**: *quīdam* is the nearest approach in Latin to the English indefinite article.

10. **sēgnius**: *with too little spirit.*

11. **sīgnum**: *i.e.* the *eagle*, the principal standard of the legion. See fig. 6. To lose it was considered a great disgrace.

16. **aedium**: cf. *aedēs*, p. 5, l. 16.

18. **dictō audientēs**: this, being an expression meaning to *obey*, is followed by the *dative.*

22. **mūrum**: the wall of Servius can still be traced.—**cēnsum**: this refers to the registration of all Roman citizens in six classes for civil and military purposes. These classes were based upon a property qualification and contained altogether 193 centuries. Each century had one vote, the classes voting in order beginning with the first, or

FIG. 6.

wealthiest. The number of centuries was so divided among the classes as to give the political control to the rich. See article *Comitia*, Smith's Dict. of Antiquities and Gow's Companion to School Classics, pp. 200–202.

24. **aliquod urbī decus**: notice the order and cf. *summam eī dignitātem*, l. 6.

25. **Ephesiae**: Ephesus is in Asia Minor on the coast of Ionia. Its Diana temple was one of the seven wonders of the world, v. Acts xix. 24, etc.

Page 13. 2. **bōs**: decl. v. A. 60, b; 61; H. 66.—**māgnitūdinis**: cons. A. 215 and n.; H. 396, V; 419, 2. Cf. *augustiōre fōrmā*, p. 4, l. 28, and see note.

3. **nāta**: sc. *esse.*—**datum**: sc. *esse.*

5. **immolāsset**: in dir. disc. *is populus summam imperī habēbit cūius cīvis bovem illam Diānae immolāverit.* Explain modes.

7. **eum**: does this word refer to the Latin or to the priest?

8. **Latīnus dum**: cf. *quī cum*, p. 5, l. 5.—**dēscendit**: cf. n. on *tenet*, p. 2, l. 11.

11. **Servius Tullius**: subject of what verb?—**alteram ferōcem, mītem alteram**: and ferōcem mītī, mītem ferōcī. Note the order and see A. 344, f. and n.; H. 562.

15. **seu . . . seu**: *whether . . . or* allows a choice between alternatives.

18. **contendit**: cf. *dēscendit* above, l. 8.

Fig. 7.

20. **carpentō**: a two-wheeled carriage with an awning over it, and curtains in front of it, usually drawn by mules, and used from remote antiquity by women of distinction. See fig. 7.

21. **prīma salūtāvit**: *was the first to salute.*

24. **super ipsum corpus**: *right over the body.*

VIII. Tarquinius Superbus, Romanorum rex septimus et ultimus.

See Church's Stories from Livy, Chap. V; Macaulay's Lays of Ancient Rome, The Battle of Lake Regillus.

Page 14. 3. **Gabiōs**: an ancient city in Latium. The story of the reduction of Gabii may have been borrowed from Greek sources. Herodotus (III, 153-160) tells the same story of Zopyrus, a noble Persian by whose artifice Darius took Babylon. — **in potestātem**: *to a state of subjection.*

10. **sciscitātum**: cf. *petītum*, p. 3, l. 19. — **quidnam**: *-nam* adds emphasis, e.g. *quid = what, quidnam = what in the world;* so *ubi* and *ubinam*, etc. — **vellet**: cf. *esset*, p. 2, l. 1, and note.

11. **dēlīberābundus**: A. 164, p; H. 333, 1.

14. **exspectandō**: abl. of ger. expressing cause. — **Gabiōs**: cf. n. on *Albam*, p. 2, l. 2.

18. **Ardeam**: the ancient capital of the Rutuli, 18 miles from Rome.

20. **apud** followed by a pronoun or a proper name means '*at the house of,*' '*with*'; with names of authors, '*in the works of.*'

22. **placuit**: this verb is often used impersonally with an infinitive for subject in the sense of to *resolve* or *determine*; tr. *they determined to try the matter*; lit. *to try was pleasing (to them).*

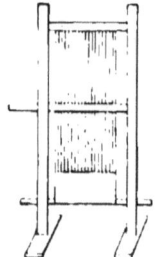

Fig. 8.

25. **lānae dēditam**:

"They at a task eternal their hands religiously plying,
Held in the left on high, with wool enfolded, a distaff,
Delicate fibres wherefrom, drawn down, were shaped by the right hand,
Shaped by fingers up-turned — but the down-turned thumb set a-whirling,
Poised with perfected whorl, the industrious shaft of the spindle.
Still, as they span, as they span, was the tooth kept nipping and smoothing,
Close at their feet, meanwhile, were woven baskets of wicker,
Guarding the soft white balls of the wool resplendent within them."

This excellent description of ancient weaving is taken from the Latin poet Catullus (87–47 B.C.). For a picture of the ancient loom, see fig. 8.

Page 15. 3. **abditum habēbat**: *kept hidden.*
4. **occīdit**: distinguish from *occidit.* — **in** expresses purpose, *to bring about, for.*
5. **rēgum**: plural because referring to the whole royal family.
7. **annālibus**: the oldest historical records among the Romans were called *annālēs librī = year books*. They were written on white boards.
9. **rēgem**: cons. A. 237, d; H. 372.
10. **ōrācula**: these were the revelations made by the gods to men.
11. **nimium atque immēnsum**: sc. *pretium*, tr. *the woman asked an excessive and in fact (atque) enormous price.*
12. **quasi**, etc.: *as if the old woman were in her dotage.*
15. **pretiō**: A. 252; H. 422.
17. **dubiō**: A. 261, b, n.; H. 437, 2.
18. **ut — emat**: in apposition with *id.*
21. **neglegendam**: sc. *esse.*
23. **Sed eam mulierem**: emphatic, to change the thought from the *books* to the *woman;* tr. freely, *but as for that woman, it is certain*, etc.
24. **locī**: A. 216, 4; H. 397, 4.
25. **Sibyllīnī**: these prophecies were probably written in Greek verse. Niebuhr supposes them to have come from Ionia, but they were more probably derived from the Greek city Cumae in Campania. The palm leaves, upon which the prophecies were written, were kept in a stone chest, and one was drawn out at random for guidance in case of prodigies or calamities. When the temple of Jupiter Capitolinus was destroyed by fire, B.C. 82, the Sibylline books perished; but a fresh collection was made by sending ambassadors to various towns in Italy, Greece, and Asia Minor. The early Christian writers frequently appeal to them as prophesying the Messiah.
26. **Quīndecim virī**: at first there were but two, next ten, finally fifteen.

IX. Horatius Cocles.

Read Church's Stories from Livy, Chap. VI; Macaulay's Lays of Ancient Rome, Horatius.

Page 16. 1. **Etruscōrum**: little is known of the Etruscans save that they are foreign in origin and language to the other peoples of Italy. They were a highly civilized and powerful nation when Rome was still in its infancy. The Romans borrowed many of their religious and political institutions from them. The last three Roman kings seem to have been Etruscans. — **ad restituendōs . . . Tarquiniōs**: a gerundive construction expressing purpose. This very common construction is usual only in short phrases.

2. **exercitū**: cons. A. 248, a, n.; H. 419, 1, 1), (1).

3. **Iāniculum**: one of the hills of Rome, connected with the city by the famous sublician or pile bridge (v. note p. 10, l. 12). Ancus Marcius built a fort upon it. — **Nōn umquam aliās ante**: these are all adverbs, tr. *never before.*

4. **rēs**: the translation of this word must always be determined by the context. Here it = *the state.* — **Clūsīna**: adj. fr. *Clūsium*, Porsenna's capital.

7. **Tiberī obiectō**: v. n. on *ob virginēs raptās*, p. 3, l. 16.

9. **fuisset**: what form of condition? A. 308; H. 510. The conclusion *paene dedit* is elliptical; sc. *et dedisset* v. A. 308, b, n.; H. 511, 1, n. 4. — **Coclēs** = one-eyed. Personal defects or peculiarities suggest surnames among all peoples, cf. Short, Strong, Green, etc.

11. **sōlus**: according to Livy he had two companions.

12. **dōnec**: the subj. is used with this conjunction to express purpose, doubt, or futurity. Which here?

13. **ponte rescissō . . . multīs superincidentibus tēlīs**: the first abl. abs. expresses time, the second concession. Translate accordingly.

16. **agrī**: A. 216, 3; H. 397, 3.

17. **eī**: *in his honor.* — **Comitiō**: an open space adjoining the Forum.

X. Menenius Agrippa.

19. **patrēs plēbemque**: the struggle for power between the patricians and the plebeians dates from the earliest times. In the beginning the plebeians had no political or religious power whatever; but by a continual and noble struggle for five hundred years against fraud and tyranny, they finally raised themselves to an equality with the patrician classes.

20. **mōntem sacrum**: a solitary hill on the right bank of the Arno, three miles from Rome. It was not called *sacer* until later.

21. **quod — tolerāret**: tr. *because they would not bear at the same time taxation and military service.* On the use of the subjunctive cf. *fīnīsset*, p. 8, l. 22.

Page 17. 1. **discordārunt** = *discordāvērunt*. So too **cōnspīrārunt**.

2. **nēve**: the regular connective for negative purpose clauses. — **datum**: sc. *cibum*.

4. **volunt**: how translated? cf. *tenet*, p. 2, l. 4.

6. **haud sēgne** = *ācre*, v. p. 12, l. 7.

9. **discordiā . . . concordiā**: etymology?

11. **Creāvit**: sc. *plēbs*. — **tribūnōs**: the tribunes of the plebs were inviolable in person. At first clothed with scant powers, it was through them that the plebeians finally triumphed. — **quī . . . dēfenderent**: would *ut . . . dēfenderent* mean the same? A. 318, a.

15. **conlātīs sextantibus**: *by collecting coppers.* The *sextāns* was worth about ⅕ of a cent.

18. **quam nōn**, etc.: this clause is secondary object after *docēre* (A. 239, 2, c; H. 374, 2); its subject is *comparātiō*. — **sit**: cons. cf. *esset*, p. 2, l. 1, and note.

19. **cupientī**: dative after *necessāria*.

XI. Lucius Virginius Centurio.

Read Macaulay's Lays of Ancient Rome, Virginia; Church's Stories from Livy, Chap. X; James Sheridan Knowles' Virginius, a Tragedy.

20. **ab urbe conditā**: cf. *ob virginēs raptās*, p. 3, l. 16.

21. **decem virī**: these, known as *decem virī lēgibus scrībendīs*, were a board of ten patricians who were appointed to draw up a code of laws. To them the whole government of the state was intrusted.— **Graeciā**: Livy says that an embassy was sent to Athens for the purpose of studying the famous laws of Solon.

22. **Duodecim tabulīs**: these were the laws of the Twelve Tables. "Unfortunately only fragments of them have come down to us. Yet these fragments are of invaluable service in the study of Roman life and manners. The documentary history of Rome may be said to begin with these laws." Ihne, Early Rome, p. 169.

23. **ipsōrum**: A. 197, e; H. 398, 3; 452, 4.

24. **Appius Claudius**: the leading man among the *decem virī*.

26. **pretiō āc spē**: tr. *by the hope of reward*. See n. p. 26, l. 28.

Page 18. 1. **clientibus**: these were a distinct class, consisting of such plebeians as appear to have been attached as hereditary dependents to certain patrician families. Each patrician had a number of these clients who looked to him for aid and protection, for which they paid in fixed dues and services. — **in servitūtem**: tr. *as his slave*, lit. *for servitude*.

2. **victūrum sē** = *sē victūrum esse*.

4. **virginī**: dat. after *iniēcit*.

5. **tabernīs**: the Roman shop usually consisted of a single room, entirely open in front, with the exception of a low wall forming a counter, and was closed at night by wooden shutters. — **litterārum lūdī**: schools were early established by the Romans. To these children of both sexes and of all classes were admitted.

6. **esse**: sc. *eam*. Also below after *abstractūrum*.

7. **nī faciat**, etc.: cf. note on *perdūxisset*, p. 3, l. 22.

8. **Pavidā — concursus**: tr. *though the maid is dumb with terror, her servant's cries quickly cause a crowd to gather.* — **nūtrīcis**: Roman

boys and girls, when going abroad, were usually accompanied by a servant, slave, or teacher.

12. **commeātū sūmptō**: *being granted a leave of absence.*
13. **cīvitās** = *cīvēs.* — **cum**: *at which time.*
14. **lacrimābundus**: cf. *dēlīberābundus*, p. 14, l. 11.
16. **Neque eō sētius**: *nevertheless.*
18. **Appī**: A. 40, c; H. 51, 5.
19. **dolōrī**: A. 227; H. 385, II. — **sine**: not a preposition. — **ūltimum**: the acc. of *ūltimus* used adverbially, cf. n. p. 15, l. 11.
20. **cultrō**: the illustration (fig. 9) is from an original discovered in a kitchen at Pompeii.
21. **Tum vērō**: commonly used to introduce the climax of a story.
24. **tribūnōs**: there had been no tribunes during the power of the *decem virī.*
25. **sē abdicāre**: a common idiom, followed by the abl. of separation.
27. **mortem sibi cōnscīvit**: tr. *committed suicide.* Appius was being reserved in prison for a more severe punishment than that inflicted on the rest.

FIG. 9.

XII. Marcus Furius Camillus.

Read Plutarch's life of Camillus, also Church's Stories from Livy, Chaps. XI-XIV; Ihne's Early Rome, Chap. XXI.

Page 19. 1. **Faleriōs**: a city in Etruria.
3. **ambulandī grātiā**: cf. *mīlitiae causā*, p. 18, l. 4.
6. **dēditūrī essent**: A. 319, d; H. 504, 3, 2).
7. **dētestātus**: tr. as a present participle. The perfect participle of deponent verbs is often so used. — **similem tuī**: *like yourself in character*, cf. p. 2, l. 9.
9. **cui ... parcitur**: verbs that take the dative in the active, are used impersonally in the passive and retain the dative, e.g. *He spares me* = *mihi parcit*; *I am spared* = *mihi parcitur.* — **captīs urbibus**: *when cities are taken.*

11. **Vēiōs**: v. n. p. 8, l. 23.
13. **redūcendum**: v. A. 294, d; H. 544, n. 2.
14. **quibus** = *ut hīs*, cf. *quī . . . peterent*, p. 3, l. 5.
15. **Statim aperuērunt**: "This story is condemned as a silly fiction, not only by its intrinsic improbability, but by the undoubted fact that Falerii continued for a long time afterwards to be an independent town." Ihne's Early Rome, p. 201. — **magis quam** = *potius quam*, rather than.

18. **quanta fuerit**: the object of *indicat*. — **Tunc prīmum**, etc.: the importance of these reforms in the military system of the Romans can hardly be overestimated. As regards the siege of Veii nothing can be surely ascertained beyond the bare fact that it fell into the hands of the Romans in 396 B.C. The mode of its conquest is hidden in a cloud of fables.

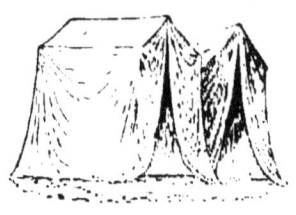

FIG. 10.

19. **facta**: sc. *sunt*. — **hiemātum**: sc. *est*. The verb is impersonal. — **sub pellibus** = *in tents*, so called because in the winter the canvas was covered with skins. See fig. 10.

21. **datum**: sc. *est;* so with *adāctus*, and *perāctum* below. — **nisi captā urbe**: the abl. abs. is sometimes used with *nisi*, when a negative precedes, to point out an exception.

25. **Postmodum datum**: tr. *afterwards a charge was brought against Camillus*. But what literally? A. 233, a; H. 390, I.
26. **triumphāsset**: cf. *fīnīsset*, p. 8, l. 22. Also n. p. 11, l. 6. — **diē**: on gender v. A. 73; H. 123.
27. **Ardeam**: cf. n. p. 14, l. 18.

Page 20. 2. **sibi**: ind. obj. of *fieret*. — **prīmō quōque tempore**: *at the very first opportunity*.

3. **suī**: an objective gen. modifying *dēsīderium;* tr. *for him* — **facerent**: sc. *diī*.

4. **Senonēs**: this tribe settled in northern Italy about 400 B.C.

8. **Ex hīs lēgātīs ūnus**: cf. n. p. 11, l. 22. — **contrā iūs gentium**: international law began with the Romans, cf. n. p. 10, l. 4.

12. **Alliam**: now a nameless brook running into the Tiber, about eleven miles from Rome. — **ante** — **Sextīlēs** = *July 18*. A. 376, a–e; H. 641-644. The year was 390.

13. **nefāstōs**: sc. *diēs*. The Romans numbered 40,000; the Gauls 70,000. The wild and furious onslaught of the Gauls dismayed the Romans, who fled in a panic and were slain by the thousand. The Romans never forgot the Allia, and thenceforth forever the Gaul was the most dreaded foe.

19. **obstinātō ad mortem animō**: tr. *determined to die.* — **exspectābant**: note how finely the continuance of a past action is brought out by the imperfect tense.

21. **sellīs**: v. fig. 1, and note. The dat. is due to *in* in composition.

24. **praetextātōs**: v. note on *praetexta*, p. 11, l. 17. — **ōrnātū**: abl. of specification; so *māiestāte*.

25. **Ad quōs cum**: cf. n. on *Quī cum*, p. 5, l. 5; tr. with *conversī*.

27. **Gallō**: tr. as if a gen. The Latin idiom, however, requires the acc. and *dat.* after *incussisse.* — **barbam** is the object of *permulcentī*, which agrees with *Gallō*.

Page 21. 3. **nocte sublūstrī**: abl. absolute. — **sublevantēs** — **aliōs**: tr. *helping each other in turn by pushing and pulling;* tr. also literally.

5. **canēs**: note the order. An emphatic word or a phrase is placed between *nē* and *quidem*.

7. **quibus**: abl. of separation. The preposition *ā, ab* is generally found after *abstineō*.

8. **erant**: we expect to find the indicative after *quia*, because its clause assigns a *fact* as a cause. How is it with *quod?* — **quae rēs**: *rēs* is the antecedent of *quae*, and in apposition with the previous sentence. In such a case the antecedent is regularly incorporated within the relative clause; tr. *a circumstance which*.

10. **Mānlius**: from this heroic deed he received the surname *Capitōlīnus*.

12. **umbōne**: the projecting knob in the center of a shield, v. fig. 11. — **ictum dēturbat** = *īcit et dēturbat*, cf. p. 2, l. 2.

Fig. 11.

NOTES.

13. cūius cāsus cum: cf. *ad quōs cum* above. The watchfulness of the goose was proverbial among the Romans. One was often kept to guard the house, and it was believed to be more vigilant than a dog.

> . . . . . nec vóce siléntia rúmpunt
> Sóllicitíve canés, canibúsve sagácior ánser.
>
> <div align="right">Ovid, <i>Met.</i> xi. 598–9.</div>

15. placuit: cf. n. p. 14, l. 22.

21. pretiō: abl. of means. — **mīlle**: sc. *librīs* = *pounds*, in apposition with *pretiō*.

23. inīqua: *excessive, i.e.* more than 1000.

25. Rōmānī exercitūs: the one which had been defeated at the Allia.

28. nūntius: cf. n. p. 21, l. 5, *canēs*.

29. triumphāns: cf. n. on *triumphāvit*, p. 11, l. 6.

30. ingressus: sc. *est*.

Page 22. **1. alter**: v. n. on *alterum*, p. 7, l. 18.

3. Vēiōs: cf. p. 8, l. 23.

6. ōmen: subj. of *mōvit*.

7. manipulāribus: a legion consisted of thirty maniples; a maniple of two centuries; each century was led by a centurion. The number of men in a legion varied at different periods from four to six thousand. — **sīgnifer**: the annexed illustration is from Trajan's column in Rome. See also fig. 6.

8. Quā vōce audītā: tr. *on hearing these words.*

9. ōmen: it was not at all unusual for the Romans to attach a peculiar and oracular significance to a chance remark, as in this case. To *accept* an omen was to consider it favorable; tr. in this order: *et senātus conclāmāvit sē accipere ōmen.*

12. obstrictōs: sc. *eōs*. Tr. *obstrictōs aere aliēnō, debtors.* — **crīmine — damnātus**: *convicted on the charge of aspiring to the throne.* To secure his conviction it is said that he had to be tried in a spot whence the Capitol, the scene of his heroism, could not be seen.

13. Tarpēiō: v. n. on *prōditiō*, p. 3, l. 26.

Fig. 12.

XIII. Spurius Postumius.

Read Church's Stories from Livy, Chap. XVII.

15. **Samnītēs**: they lived to the east and south of Latium and Campania, and were distinguished for their bravery and their love of freedom. The Romans found them the most formidable enemies whom they had yet encountered in Italy. The war, begun in 343 B.C., was continued with but few interruptions for fifty-three years.

16. **in auxilium vocātī**: *called upon for assistance.*

17. **orbe**: cons? — **Campāniae**: appositional gen., so we say 'the state of New York.'

18. **Nihil**: sc. *est.* Forms of *sum* are often omitted.

19. **certāmen**: *the scene of the contest.*

21. **Cāiēta**: on the coast of Latium, near Campania. It is one of the oldest cities in Italy. Its modern name is Gaeta, and it is an important fortification. — **Mīsēnum**: formerly the station of the Roman fleet. — **Bāiae**: between Misenum and Puteoli; a famous and much-visited watering-place. —

> "Your grace, sweet Muses, shields me still
> On Sabine heights, or lets me range
> Where cool Praeneste, Tibur's hill,
> Or liquid Baiae proffers change."
>
> HOR. *Od.* iii. 4.

Lucrīnus: a lake near to Baiae, celebrated for its oyster beds.

22. **Avernus**: a lake near Naples filling the crater of an extinct volcano. It was supposed to communicate with the lower world. — **vītibus**: the wines of Campania were famous, especially the Falernian, Massic, and Formian.

> "—— these cups of mine
> Falernum's bounty ne'er has blessed,
> Nor Formian vine.
>
> HOR. *Od.* i. 20.

24. **ad**: *near.*

25. **Pompēii**: read Bulwer's Last Days of Pompeii.

NOTES.

26. Capua: consult the map for the localities above mentioned. The author has not exaggerated the beauties of Campania.

27. Carthāgine: the largest city in northern Africa, and for many years the rival of Rome for the mastery of the world.

Page 23. 3. **pūgnātum est**: cf. n. p. 7, l. 14. So *ventum est*.

4. **Spurius Postumius cōnsul**: of what is it the subject? cf. n. p. 2, l. 10.

7. **quī dīcerent**: v. n. p. 20, l. 7.

9. **ferrent**: cf. *dēditūrī essent,* p. 19, l. 6.

10. **altera**: distinguish between *alter* and *alius* in meaning.

11. **breviōrem**: sc. *viam*.

12. **quī locus**: tr. *in a place which*.

13. **Furculae Caudīnae**: the Caudine Forks, a narrow ravine near Caudium, a city in Samnium.

16. **intuentēs aliī aliōs**: *looking at one another*.

19. **tum . . . tum**: *at one time . . . at another*.

21. **faciendum esset**: v. n. p. 2, l. 1. So *placēret* below, l. 23.

22. **accītum**: *who had been sent for*.

29. **iugum**: this was formed by two spears stuck in the ground, with another fastened transversely over their tops. To pass under the yoke was a disgrace worse than death.

30. **palūdāmenta**: v. n. p. 7, l. 29. — **cōnsulibus**: the dat., A. 229; H. 385, 2. — **dētracta**: sc. *sunt*, so too with *missī*.

Page 24. 1. **prīmī . . . missī**: *were the first to be sent*. Distinguish this use of the adj. *prīmus* from that of the adv. *prīmum*, and *prīmō*.

3. **Rōmānīs**: dat. with adj. *trīstior*. — **ipsa**: tr. *very*.

4. **fugere**: here transitive = *to shun*.

6. **quisque**: in partitive app. with the subj. of *abdidērunt*. Note its position. In this idiom it regularly follows the poss. pro. referring to the subj. — **aedēs**: cf. n. p. 5, l. 16.

7. **sententiam dīcere**: any magistrate, except aedile or quaestor, might summon the senate. The presiding officer was the magistrate who called the meeting. After the president had stated the matter

of business, he might call for an immediate vote, or he might invite discussion. In the latter case he called upon the members to speak (*sententiam dīcere*) in order of precedence, beginning with the *prīnceps senātūs*.

10. **ēius iniūssū**: *without its authority.* — **facta est**: subject *spōnsiō.* — **ex eā**: sc. *spōnsiōne;* tr. *by that agreement.*

12. **saeviant**: do not translate as if it were *saeviunt.*

13. **animī**: not *mind.*

15. **fētiālibus**: v. n. on *lēgātum*, p. 9, l. 22.

16. **eī**: cf. *cōnsulibus* above. — **dētracta**: sc. *est.*

18. **māiestātis**: v. n. on *audāciae*, p. 10, l. 11. — **quīn**: learn the following principal uses: —

$$\text{quīn}\begin{cases} \text{I. Principal Clauses.} \begin{cases} \text{a. Interrog.} = why\ not? \\ \text{b. Corroborative} = indeed, \\ \quad nay,\ verily,\ \text{etc.} \end{cases} \\ \text{II. Subordinate Clauses — used after negative sentences to express result.} \end{cases}$$

21. **fētiālis**: gen.

24. **violātum**: sc. *esse.* It is connected with *esse* in the preceding line by *et* understood. To do violence to a fetial legate was sure to lead to war. — **eō**: abl. of degree.

25. **Accepta — rediit**: note the chiastic order, and how well the emphasis is brought out.

Pontius, the noble Samnite, continued to fight the battles of his country for yet many years. Often victorious, he was finally defeated and taken prisoner. He was led in chains in the triumph of his victor, and was then beheaded; an act which Niebuhr characterizes as "the greatest stain in the Roman annals."

XIV. Publius Valerius Laevinus, et Pyrrhus, rex Epiri.

Read Plutarch's Life of Pyrrhus.

Page 25. 1. **Tarentīnis**: Tarentum was a large city in souther Italy on a gulf of the same name, now Taranto. — **iniūriam**: v. n.

on *violātum*, p. 24, l. 24.— **fēcissent**: subj. because assigned as the reason of the Romans, not that of the author.

2. **Pyrrhum**: a noble king, and one of the greatest generals of antiquity. — **Ēpīrī**: a district in northern Greece, on the west coast.

3. **auxilium**: cons. A. 239, 2, c; H. 374.— **quī**: refers to *Pyrrhum*.

4. **Achillis**: many Greek and some Roman families traced their ancestry back to the heroes of the Trojan war, of all of whom Achilles was the most glorious.

5. **prīmum**: v. n. on *prīmī*, p. 24, l. 1.

7. **quī cum**: v. n. p. 5, l. 5.

8. **exercitum**: subj. of *ostendī*, after which sc. *eīs*.

9. **dīmittī**: sc. *eōs* as subject. — **quaecumque**: an indefinite relative = *omnia quae*.

10. **agerentur**: v. n. on *perdūxisset*, p. 3, l. 22. — **commissā pūgnā**: for tr. v. n. on *pulsō frātre*, p. 1, l. 3.

11. **elephantōs**: elephants frequently figure in the history of the wars of the Persians, Greeks, and Romans, though at this time the Romans were unacquainted with them.

12. **aciem**: distinguish from *exercitus*, and *āgmen*.

16. **sēcum** — abripiēbant: give an idiomatic translation.

19. **occīsōs**: sc. *Rōmānōs*. — **adversō volnere**: *with wounds in front*.

22. **potuisse** = *potuī* of dir. disc. A. 308, c; H. 511, 1, n. 3.

23. **Quid mihi cum tālī vīctōriā**: *of what advantage is such a victory to me?* sc. *est*, which is often omitted in colloquial questions and in exclamations.

24. **ubi** = *when (the result is that)* v. A. 319, 2; H. 500, I.

27. **ferrō ignīque**: *with fire and sword*. The Latin inverts the English order, cf. *caede atque incendiīs*, Cic. Cat. I, § 3. — **lapidem**: C. Gracchus (died 121 B.C.) introduced the practice of marking the distance from Rome on the great highways by means of mile-stones (*milliaria*) at intervals of 1000 Roman paces. Of course there were none at the time of Pyrrhus. See fig. 13.

FIG. 13.

Page 26. 1. obviam vēnit: *came to meet*, an expression followed by the dat.

2. Quō vīsō: *at the sight of this.* — sibi . . . Herculī: datives of possessor with *esse*, of which *fortūnam* is the subj. — quam: *as*.

3. hydram: one of the twelve labors of the Greek hero Hercules was to kill the dragon or hydra which dwelt in the marshes of Lerna near Argos. It had nine heads, and as often as one was cut off, two new ones grew in its stead. Hercules finally killed it by burning the stumps where the heads had been.

8. cōgnōscerent: this verb means to *learn* in the present system and to *know*, i.e. *to have learned*, in the perfect.

10. clēmentia: subj. of *solet*.

12. dominum: the Tarentines found to their sorrow that, if they would have the help of Pyrrhus, they must give up their idle and luxurious living, and conform to the strictness of military discipline.

14. Neque deerant: v. n. on *haud secus āc*, p. 12, l. 7. — arcessītī: sc. *sunt*.

15. quod — locūtī essent: observe that the charge was true, but, as it is given on the authority of the accusers, and not on that of the author, the subj. is used.

16. perīculum: observe the emphasis from its position.

18. pervēnissent: v. n. on *perdūxisset*, p. 3, l. 22.

20. dictūrī fuimus: we might have expected *dīxissēmus*, but bear in mind that the periphrastic forms are regularly in the ind. in the conclusion of conditional sentences.

21. vīnī: pred. gen. of possession after *vidērī*.

24. pācem — facere: this infinitive clause is the subj. of *fore* (*futūrum esse*), and *glōriōsum* is pred. adj. agreeing with it.

25. Cīneam: nom. *Cineās*; for decl. v. A. 37; H. 50.

27. valēbat: *multum valēre* is an idiom = *to be very influential;* cf. *plūrimum posse*.

28. vī et armīs: tr. *by force of arms*. The use of two nouns and a conjunction instead of a noun with a gen. or with an adj. is known as hendiadys. Cf. *pretiō āc spē*, p. 17, l. 26.

29. tamen: *i.e.* though a courtier, he was not a flatterer.

NOTES.   105

Page 27. 5. āctūrus es: about equivalent to *agere dēstinds* above.

7. mihi: dat. of possessor.

8. ille: sc. *inquit*. Verbs of saying are often omitted when they can be readily supplied from the context. — Quid deinde: sc. *āctūrus es*.

9. nōs: obj. of *dabimus*.

10. ōtiō: cons. A. 249; H. 421, I.— quōminus: regularly introduces a subj. clause of purpose after verbs of hindering.

11. istō: to what person does *istō* refer as distinguished from *hīc* and *ille?* Make the person clear in translating.

12. Rōmam: note the order.

17. condiciōnum: sc. *pācis*.

18. sententia: v. n. *sententiam dīcere*, p. 24, l. 7.

19. Appius Claudius: one of the greatest of the noble Claudian gens. He built the great Appian aqueduct, and began the famous Appian Way, which runs from Rome to Capua; he was no less distinguished as a soldier, and was the earliest Roman writer in prose and verse whose name has come down to us. — ob — solitus: tr. by a rel. cl.

21. lectīcā: a *palanquin* introduced into Italy from the East. It was made in various sizes and styles and carried by from two to eight slaves. At first it was used only by the sick and by women, but later it was a common vehicle for pleasure, business, or travel. See fig. 14.

22. itaque — est: *and so the senate replied to Pyrrhus.* What is the subject of *respōnsum est?*

FIG. 14.

23. excessisset: what in dir. disc.?

26. potuissent: why subjunctive? cf. *pervēnissent*, p. 26, l. 18.— ante . . . quam sī: *unless*, or *until;* but what literally taking *ante* as an adverb? v. A. 262; H. 520, f. n. 1.

27. **revertī** depends on *iussērunt*. — **bīnūm** = *bīnōrum*. How different in sense from *duōrum* ?

29. **quālem Rōmam comperīsset**: tr. *what kind of city he had found Rome to be*.

31. **vērō**: used to bring in something additional, of more weight and importance than what precedes. — **vīsum**: agrees with *senātum* and is understood with *urbem*.

XV. Gaius Fabricius.

Page 28. 1. **Ex lēgātīs**: *among the ambassadors*.

2. **C. Fabricius**: a typical Roman of the old style. He is often referred to by later writers as a model citizen. — **Cūius**: *his*. It modifies *nōmen*.

3. **ut**: tr. *as*, and sc. *that* referring to *nōmen*. The English redundant 'that' in the phrase 'that of' is never expressed in Latin.

5. **cēterīs**: distinguish between *cēterī* and *aliī*.

6. **quae omnia**: *all of which*. Would *omnia quōrum* be good Latin? A. 216, e; H. 397, 2, n.

16. **vellet** = *be willing*.

17. **etiam**: usually precedes the emphatic word.

18. **vīs**: fr. *volō*.

19. **sīn vērō malum**: sc. *virum mē iūdicās*.

21. **ablātā**: v. *auferō*.

24. **sī — necātūrum**: what form of condition? Put into dir. disc.

25. **vinctum redūcī**: cf. n. on *armātīs* . . . *properāvit*, p. 2, l. 2; *vinctum* not fr. *vincō*.

27. **spopondisset**: subordinate clause, ind. disc.

Page 29. 2. **honestāte**: not *honesty*. Make it a general rule not to translate a Latin word by the English word it most resembles.

3. **apud Pyrrhum**: v. n. on *apud*, p. 14, l. 20.

4. **quendam**: this word always signifies that the author has some particular person or thing in mind which he may not choose to name. In this case it was Epicurus (died 270 B.C.), the founder of the school of philosophy bearing his name. He was a great man, and of

blameless and simple life. Perhaps no one has been more violently attacked by rival philosophers, and by those who had but a superficial knowledge of his doctrines.

7. **hostibus**: cf. n. on *cui* . . . *parcitur*, p. 19, l. 9.
8. **quō**: v. n. p. 9, l. 4.
9. **dederint**: v. n. on *cum*, p. 1, l. 13. This is the fut. perf. ind. — **ab — aliēnum**: Eng. says 'foreign to.' What does Lat. say?
11. **salīnō**: the abl. of material usually has *ē, ex*, but sometimes omits it. Salt was much used in sacrifice, hence the salt-cellar was an object of veneration, and was usually of silver even among the poorer citizens. Often it was a much-valued heirloom. —

> "More happy he whose modest board
> His father's well-worn silver brightens."
>
> Hor. *Od.* ii. 16.

patellā: a small bowl or basin in which solid viands were offered to the gods.
14. **vēnērunt**: why ind.?
16. **mihi**: v. n. on *cīvitātī*, p. 6, l. 12.
17. **hāc**: v. n. on *subole*, p. 1, l. 4.
18. **simultātem gerēbat**: *was on bad terms with*. For force of tense v. n. on *inferēbat*, p. 6, l. 8.
19. **ipse**: *i.e.* Fabricius.
21. **Quia . . . erat**: v. n. on *erant*, p. 21, l. 8.
22. **bellum**: what war?
23. **auctor fuit** = *studuit*.
25. **homō inimīcus**: in app. with the subj. of *fēcisset*; translate by a concessive clause. *Sē* refers to Rufinus.
26. **vēnīre**: used for the passive of *vēndō*. Distinguish from *venīre*. The point is that Fabricius feared the approaching war more than he did the thieving of the consul; especially since the latter, with all his faults, was still '*industrius āc bonus imperātor.*'
27. **posteā**: not *post* nor *postquam*. Distinguish carefully among these three words. — **cēnsor**: the censorship, instituted B.C. 443, discharged three chief duties : (1) to assess the property of each

citizen; (2) to prepare the list of the senate; (3) to manage the finances of the republic. Censors were elected about every five years, and held office eighteen months.

28. **quod — habēret**: tr. *because he had ten pounds of silver plate.*
30. **unde**: a relative adv. introducing a result clause.

Page 30. 2. **cōnlocāvit**: i.e. *in mātrimōnium.*
4. **diciōnis**: cons. A. 214, c; H. 403.
7. **ita** means 'with this guilt on his shoulders.'
9. **lacerāta**: sc. *est.*
11. **Quā**: tr. *this.*
14. **prōsperī**: cons. A. 216, 3; H. 397, 3. — **Italiā**: a prep. would have been regular here.
15. **ignōbilī morte**: he was struck by a heavy tile which an Argive woman threw from the house-top.

XVI. Gaius Duilius.

17. **Gāius Duīlius**: his brilliant victory over the Carthaginians near Mylae, off the northern coast of Sicily, led the way to the successful conclusion of the first Punic war. The memory of it was perpetuated by a column which stood in the Forum, and which was adorned with the beaks of the captured ships (*Columna Rōstrāta*). See fig. 15. — **prīmus**: cf. n. on *prīmī*, p. 24, l. 1.

18. **ā Pūnicīs**: the Phoenicians excelled all other ancient peoples as mariners. Their commercial spirit carried their ships to every sea. They colonized northern Africa and Spain and, going beyond the straits, they traded north and south along the coasts of Africa and Europe. The Romans were an agricultural people and had no fondness for sea-faring.

FIG. 15.

20. **excōgitāvit**: note the etymology.
21. **quae manūs ubi**: tr. *when these hooks.*
22. **trānsgrediēbātur**: mark the force of the imperfect: also in **dīmicābant**, l. 23.

23. **ipsōrum**: refers to the enemy. — **comminus**: see Word-Groups under MA-. — **Rōmānīs**: cf. *mihi*, p. 27, l. 7.

25. **expūgnātae**: distinguish between *expūgnō* and *oppūgnō*.

26. **septirēmis**: *i.e.* a ship having seven banks of oars. The rest had probably five banks of oars (*quīnquerēmēs*), as these were commonly used for war at that period. Before the first Punic war, the Romans had only triremes (see fig. 16), and not many of them. — **mersae**: sc. *sunt*.

FIG 16.

Page 31. 2. **triumphum**: v. n. on *triumphāvit*, p. 11, l. 6.

3. **terrā**: why no prep.? A. 258, f, 1; H. 425, 2. — **etiam**: v. n. p. 28, l. 17. — **marī**: v. *terrā*, above.

5. **fūnālī**: a torch made of plant fibres twisted into a rope (*fūnis*) and smeared with pitch. — **tībīcine**: see fig. 17. It is taken from a painting at Herculaneum. — **cēnā**: the principal meal of the day taken in the afternoon or early evening.

6. **Hannibal**: not the great general of the second Punic war.

7. **capiēbātur**: *was on the point of being taken*.

8. **Veritus**: *fearing*, cf. *ratus*, p. 7, l. 13; *dētestātus*, p. 19, l. 7. — **classis āmissae**: for tr. cf. *ob virginēs raptās*, p. 3, l. 16; see

FIG. 17.

also n. on *audāciae*, p. 10, l. 11.

10. **ex**: *directly after*.

11. **perveniret**: cons. v. n. on *indūceret*, p. 9, l. 21. — **quendam**: v. n. p. 29, l. 4.
12. **Cōnsulit** . . . **vōs**: *asks your advice.* What would *cōnsulit vōbīs* mean? v. A. 227, c; H. 385, 1.
15. **dēbeat**: v. n. on *esset*, p. 2, l. 1.
16. **quīn**: v. n. p. 24, l. 18.
19. **victus**: part. expressing concession.
20. **rē male gestā**: tr. *when he had met defeat.*
21. **adficiēbātur**: cf. n. on *īnferēbat*, p. 6, l. 8.

XVII. Gaius Lutatius Catulus.

Catulus and Duilius were the naval heroes of the first Punic war (264-241 B.C.).

24. **dum**: for cons. and tense with this conjunction v. n. on p. 2, l. 11; and the note on *tenet* in the same line. — **Drepanum**: city and harbor on the north-west side of Sicily.

Page 32. 1. **nūntiātur**: why indicative?
2. **ad exercitum**: the land force which, under the great Hamilcar, was holding Sicily. — **cōpiīs**: sc. *onustae* with this and the following ablatives.
3. **et pecūniae amplissimō numerō**: tr. *with a very large sum of money.*
4. **summae rērum**: tr. *the whole expedition.* Cons. of *summae*?
5. **Hīc — agēbat**: tr. *He was making great exertions with this in view.*
6. **levāret . . . complēret**: what case follows verbs of plenty and want?
7. **sīc**: *thus prepared.*
8. **At**: this word serves to recall our attention emphatically to the consul.
9. **potius**: distinguish between this word and *amplius* and *magis.*
10. **Aegātēs īnsulās**: off the western coast of Sicily. This battle, both for the numbers engaged and for its consequences, is to be remembered as one of the great naval engagements of history.
15. **hāc condiciōne**: abl. of cause.

XVIII. Quintus Fabius Maximus.

Read Plutarch's Life of Fabius; Arnold's Life of Hannibal.

Quintus Fabius Maximus was one of the most distinguished members of that famous Fabian gens whose history goes back to the very beginning of Rome. The most important period of his life is embraced within the years included between the dates placed at the head of this passage, though he had already been consul twice before this. In 217, in the second year of the second Punic war (218–202 B.C.), immediately after the Roman defeat at Trasumenus, he was appointed dictator against Hannibal; and for many years he was a conspicuous figure in that great struggle. He died in 203: too soon to witness Hannibal's final overthrow.

18. **Hannibal**: he and his father Hamilcar are among the very greatest generals of all time. — **novem annōs nātus**: *at the age of nine years*. What literally?

20. **rēs**: v. n. p. 16, l. 4; **Quae rēs maximē**: *this incident more than anything else*.

22. **Saguntum**: a city on the east coast of Spain, south of the Ebro river. Its site is covered with interesting ruins.

23. **foederātam**: such states were independent, but could look to Rome for help in time of need and were expected to furnish in return troops and supplies. They did not possess Roman citizenship.

26. **togā**: the principal outer garment of the Romans, derived from the Etruscans. It was usually of white wool. The *sinus* of the toga was the fold on the breast. In this articles were often carried. A Roman had no pocket. A second *sinus* appears farther down (v. fig. 18).

FIG. 18.

Page 33. 1. **utrum**: distinguish from *quis*.

4. **eīsdem**: sc. *animīs*.

6. **superātīs — iugīs**: his march across the Alps filled the Romans with astonishment and dismay. It is one of the great events

in military history. What general in modern times did the same?

7. **Pūblium Scīpiōnem**: father of the great Africānus. — **Tīcīnum**: this and the Trebia are tributaries of the Po. The greatest of these victories was that over Flaminius at lake Trasumenus in north-eastern Etruria, 217 B.C.

11. **dictātor**: an officer having autocratic power who was appointed whenever great and unusual danger threatened the state. He held office for but six months. — **mora**: the Fabian tactics were to avoid a decisive engagement and to weaken Hannibal by cutting off his supplies and harassing his rear and outposts.

14. **recēdere ab ancipitī discrīmine**: tr. *to decline a hazardous engagement.*

15. **tuērī**: note the emphasis.

16. **laudem**: many writers glorify the deeds of Fabius. Ennius (239 B.C.), the father of Latin poetry, says of him:

> "'T was one man's courage saved the state,
> By wise delay. The people's frown
> He scorned, for safety dared to wait. .
> The years still glorify his crown."

18. **castrīs**: the locative abl. is often used without a preposition, when the idea of cause, manner, or means is combined with that of place.

19. **quantum**: adverbial acc. — **cōgeret**: informal ind. disc., v. n. p. 3, l. 22.

20. **occāsiōnī**: v. n. p. 6, l. 12. — **reī bene gerendae**: cf. *rē male gestā*, p. 31, l. 20. — **qua**: A. 105, d; H. 190, 1; sc. *occāsiō*.

22. **mīlitem . . . virtūtis . . . paenitēre**: cons. v. A. 221, b; H. 409, III.

Page 34. 2. **ratus**: v. n. on *dētestātus*, p. 19, l. 7.

5. **ut — invidiam**: *that he might make Fabius unpopular among his countrymen.*

12. **vocitābant**: fr. *vocitō*, the intensive or iterative form of *vocō*, expressing emphasis and repetition, v. Word-Groups under VOC-. — **magister equitum**: this was an officer appointed by the dictator to

NOTES. 113

act as his lieutenant. He represented the dictator in his absence and had command of the cavalry in battle.

13. **illum, etc.** : ind. disc. depending upon the idea of saying in *crīminandō*.

14. **quō**: cf. n. p. 9, l. 4.

16. **dictātōrī** : ind. object of *aequāvit*.

17. **imperiō** : abl. of specification.

20. **eī . . . auxiliō** : cons. A. 233, a ; H. 390, I.

25. **autem** : cf. n. p. 10, l. 9.

26. **cum Fabiō** : i.e. *cum castrīs Fabī*.

28. **posteā** : v. n. p. 29, l. 27. — **Tarentō** : a large city of Greek origin on the western coast of Calabria. Up to this time it had been the most important city in Magna Graecia. (See also n. p. 25, l. 1.) For cons. v. A. 249; H. 421, I.

30. **per speciem vēnandī** : *on the pretence that they were going hunting.*

Page 35.

4. **pāstum** : A. 302 ; H. 546.

7. **iterum āc saepius,** *again and again.* — **factum** : sc. *est*.

8. **cōnsuētūdinis** : partitive gen. with the adv. *eō*. Tr. the phrase: *became such a regular custom.*

9. **dedissent** : why subjunctive? A. 342 ; H. 529, II.

11. **appropinquārunt** = *appropinquāvērunt;* often used with the dat.

14. **corporis** : cf. *māgnitūdinis*, p. 13, l. 2.

15. **mīrātur** : v. n. on *dum*, p. 2, l. 11.

18. **Līvius Salīnātor** : Cicero tells this anecdote of him in his "*Dē Senectūte*," but he is mistaken in the man. It was M. Livius Macatus that lost Tarentum, and gave efficient service from the citadel in its recovery.

19. **caedī** : cons. ?

21. **Leve dictū** : *trifling*. A. 303 ; H. 547, 1, 2.

23. **mulierculae** : what kind of a gen. ? Mark the force of the suffix.

26. **vigiliā** : the night was divided into four watches of three hours each from sunset to sunrise.

Page 36. 2. **et Rōmānī**, etc.: tr. *the Romans also have a Hannibal of their own.*

3. **eādem**: with *arte.*

6. **retinuisset**: why subjunctive? Bring out the force of the mood in your translation.

8. **nisi — recēpissem**: form of condition? Sc. *eam arcem* for obj. of the verbs.

10. **lēgātus**: a general officer attached to the army and to the governors of provinces, who acted both in a military and civil capacity; his duty being to advise and assist his superiors in their plans and operations, as well as to act in their stead whenever occasion required. A general could nominate his *lēgātus*, but the choice had to be ratified by the senate.

12. **lictōribus**: v. n. p. 8, l. 8.

16. **proximum lictōrem**: the lictors walked in single file and the one nearest the magistrate was called *proximus lictor.*

19. **num** in indirect questions means *whether* and does not imply a negative answer.

21. **dīgnus**: the Romans honored Fabius till the last, and each citizen contributed something to his funeral as a farewell offering of gratitude. The fame of his last years was obscured by the rising glory of Scipio, who was the exact opposite of Fabius in disposition. Fabius never ceased to warn the Romans against the aggressive policy of his rival, and appears to have been very jealous of him. — **cautior quam prōmptior**: *more wary than quick.* The Latin uses the comparative in both adjectives.

23. **eī bellō**: dat. with *apta.*

24. **quīn**: v. n. p. 24, l. 18.

25. **ut**: v. n. p. 1, l. 10.

28. **nē — posset**: substantive clause of negative purpose in apposition with *id.*

XIX. Aemilius Paulus et Terentius Varro.

The events of the second Punic war, up to the time that Fabius was made dictator (217 B.C.), have been briefly summarized in the preceding selection (p. 33, l. 6–9). After the Roman defeat at Lake Trasumenus, Hannibal made his way into southern Italy, passing through Umbria and Picenum into Campania, and thence into Apulia. In this neighborhood he spent the summer and the following winter, the tactics of Fabius preventing any decisive action. The Romans made great preparations for the year 216. They raised a splendid army; but the consuls, Paulus the patrician and Varro the plebeian, represented opposing factions and held opposing views as to the conduct of the war. Their differences foreshadowed defeat.

Page 37. 5. **Cannae**: near the eastern coast of Apulia.
8. **autem**: v. n. p. 10, l. 9.
12. **quem cum**: v. n. p. 5, l. 5.
14. **quīdam**: v. n. on *quōdam*, p. 12, l. 9. — **tribūnus**: the *tribūnī mīlitārēs* ranked below the *lēgātī*, but above the *centuriōnēs*. The number attached to each legion varied at different times. At this time there were six.
16. **Ad ea**: sc. *respondit*.
17. **macte**: v. A. 241, d, and n.; H. 369, 3.
18. **perdās**: A. 269, a, 3; H. 489, 2); 499, 2.
19. **patribus** = *senātuī*.
20. **adveniat**: v. n. on *indūceret*, p. 9, l. 21.
23. **occidērunt**: not *occīdērunt*.
25. **quīngentī**: i.e. *equitēs*. — **in testimōnium**: *as evidence*.
26. **modiōs**: a grain measure holding about a peck. — **aureōrum ānulōrum**: signet-rings were originally of iron. Golden rings could be worn only by senators, knights, and the chief magistrates. See fig. 19.

FIG. 19.

Page 38. 1. **Hannibalī**: *grātulor* takes the dat.
3. **ex . . . praefectīs**: v. *ex pāstōribus*, p. 11, l. 22.
4. **cessandum**: sc. *esse*. Impersonal because intransitive. Do not translate literally. — **ratus**: cf. n. on *veritus*, p. 31, l. 8.
5. **diē quīntō**: *in five days*.

116   NOTES.

6. Capitōliō: the Capitoline hill has two summits; on one of them stood the *Arx*, or citadel, upon the other the famous temple constructed by the last Tarquin in honor of Jupiter, Juno, and Minerva. To the Romans it was the symbol of the strength and stability of the state. When Horace wished to declare his immortality he said:

> " Ever new
> My after fame shall grow while pontiffs climb,
> With silent maids, the Capitolian height."

8. eīdem: ind. obj. of *dedēre*. — **vīctōriā**: cons.?

9. Mora: what Hannibal might have gained by an immediate advance upon Rome has always been an interesting but fruitless field for speculation. — **diēī**: duration of time is expressed by the gen. with nouns, by the acc. with verbs. — **salūtī , . . urbī**: cf. p. 34, l. 20.

13. Capuam Hannibalī Cannās: in judging of the truth of this statement we must not forget that Hannibal's army remained superior in the field, and that he did not leave Italy until twelve years after.

16. quīn: v. n. p. 24, l. 18.

17. obviam īrent: cf. *obviam vēnit*, p. 26, l. 1.

18. dēspērāssent: why subj.? Cf. *fēcissent*, p. 25, l. 1.

19. quī: v. n. on *quod*, p. 8, l. 18. — **sī . . . fuisset, . . . dedisset**: note the form of condition.

20. nōn — approbāvit: *moreover he showed by the rest of his life that he had survived the battle, not from love of life, but from love of his country.*

22. barbam — submīsit: the ancient Romans used to wear the hair and beard long, but after 300 B.C. adults wore the hair short and the face smooth except when in mourning or deep trouble.

23. recubāns: the Romans usually reclined at their meals. (v. fig. 20.)

25. magistrātibus: A. 243, e; H. 414, IV.

FIG. 20.

NOTES. 117

26. igitur: used, as often, to resume the narrative, after the digression about Varro.

27. agēbat: the present tense would have been regular here; the past makes the time emphatic by contrast. A. 276, e, n.

28. erant: sc. *eīs*, dat. of possessor. — **templīs**: dat., cf. *alveō*, p. 1, l. 7. The ancients used to hang the spoils of war upon the walls of the temples.

29. manūmissī: i.e. *ē manū missī*.

Page 39. 1. **bullīs**: v. n. p. 11, l. 18. — **singulīs ānulīs**: tr. *a ring apiece*.

2. **patrum**: cf. *patribus*, p. 37, l. 19.

3. **equitēs**: object of *imitātae*, which agrees with *tribūs*.

4. **tabulae**: these were thin pieces of wood smeared with wax on one side, which were written upon by a sharp instrument called a *stilus*. Usually two were hinged together to close like a double slate. The waxed side had a raised edge of wood to keep the writing from rubbing. Erasures were made by smoothing over the wax with the broad end of the stilus. See fig. 21.

FIG. 21.

7. **redimendī suī**: cons. A. 298, a; H. 542, I, n. 1.

10. **iūrārent**: cons. A. 320, c; H. 503, II, 3. — **impetrāssent**: not *imperāssent*. What form of condition? Put into dir. disc.

14. **velutī aliquid oblītus**: tr. *pretending that he had forgotten something*. For **aliquid** v. A. 219; H. 407.

18. **iūreiūrandō**: viz. the oath that he would return if allowed to go. Of course it was a palpable evasion of his promise.

20. **Ea — frēgit**: *that event, more than anything else* (*māximē*), *checked Hannibal's presumption*.

21. **rēbus adflīctīs**: tr. by a concessive clause.

22. **esset**: why subj.?

XX. Tiberius Gracchus et Gaius Gracchus.

Read Plutarch's Life of Tiberius Gracchus, and of Gaius Gracchus; A. H. Beesley's The Gracchi, Marius, and Sulla.

23. **Gracchī**: plural because two members of the family are named. — **Scīpiōnis Āfricānī**: the great general who conquered Hannibal in the battle of Zama, 202 B.C. The sister of the Gracchi was married to Scipio Africanus the younger, who destroyed Carthage in 146 B.C.

24. **bonīs artibus**: *liberal studies* or *arts.*

39. **et — est**: *and all had great hopes of them.*

Page 40. 1. **Graecīs litterīs**: before this time the average education of the Roman youth was confined mainly to reading, writing, arithmetic, and the laws of the Twelve Tables (see p. 17, l. 22). It was rudimentary and intensely practical. After about 100 B.C. Greek letters, in all departments of learning, became paramount in Roman education.

2. **Māximum — sapientissima**: note the chiastic order of this sentence and its emphasis. Imitate the order in translation.

4. **apud**: cf. n. p. 14, l. 20.

6. **redīrent**: subj. because purpose is expressed as well as time.

10. **poterant**: the pluperfect subjunctive might be expected, but see A. 308, c.; H. 511, 1, n. 3. — **perturbāre**: the story of the Gracchi is here told from the standpoint of the aristocratic party, which was hostile to them. They were noble men, who sacrificed their lives for the welfare of the common people.

12. **tribūnus plēbis**: v. p. 17, l. 11. — **creātus**: 133 B.C.

14. **agrōs**: by the Licinian laws, passed 367 B.C., no one was to hold more than 320 acres of land. These laws had become a dead letter, and Tiberius Gracchus wished to revive them, with some changes of his own. The land of Italy and Sicily had been absorbed by a few rich men, who worked their estates with slaves; while Rome was filled with a landless, famishing crowd. — **dīvidēbat . . . replēbat**: what is the force of this tense here?

NOTES.

16. **prōrogārī**: the tribunate could not be held for two successive years by the same person.— **interēmptō senātū**: no doubt an invention of his accusers, as well as the statement that follows.

19. **quidnam**: v. n. p. 14, l. 10.
20. **Capitōlium**: v. n. p. 38, l. 6.
21. **quō sīgnō**: cf. n. on *quae rēs*, p. 21, l. 8.
22. **diadēma**: a royal crown, for which *corōna* is never used.
23. **cum**: concessive, *though*.
26. **sequantur**: not *sequuntur*.
29. **subsellī**: a movable bench without any back, and long enough to accommodate several persons. The illustration (fig. 22) is from an original found at Pompeii. The mob of aristocrats killed three hundred with the fragments of the benches. — **potuerat**: cf. *poterat* above.

FIG. 22.

Page 41. 2. **Tribūnātum**: 123 B.C. Gāius went somewhat farther in his reforms than Tiberius. He was of charming personality and of irresistible eloquence.

3. **necis**: depends on *causā*.
6. **dabat**: make clear the force of the tense.
7. **quantā ... contentiōne**: *with all their might.*
8. **bonī**: i.e. the aristocrats.
13. **quī**: adv.
14. **nōlim quidem ... tibi ... liceat** = *I should be quite unwilling to let you; nōlim* is the potential subjunctive or the subjunctive in apodosis with omitted protasis, and is made emphatic by *quidem*. With *liceat* sc. *ut*.
16. **partem petam**: *I shall ask for my share.* — **quō**: v. n. p. 3, l. 24.
19. **ut vidēret**, etc.: the regular formula by which dictatorial power was conferred upon the consul, cf. Cic. Cat. I, § 4.
22. **familiā**: *not* family; v. voc.
27. **Gāī**: sc. *corpus.*
29. **aurō repēnsum**: tr. *and sold for its weight in gold.* But what literally? v. voc.

30. **īnfūsō plumbō**: *by pouring in lead.* — **eum**: i.e. Septimuleius.
31. **quō**, etc.: a purpose clause.

Page 42. 2. **ut ... animadverterētur**: *that punishment be inflicted.*
4. **dēprecātum**: supine. — **īgnōscerētur**: v. n. p. 19, l. 9.
5. **tantī**: A. 252 a ; H. 403, 404.
12. **sī ... peccāveris**: the indefinite second person singular with the subjunctive — *you = any one.* This kind of protasis is usually followed by an indicative in the conclusion stating a general truth, as here by *est.*
17. **possit**: cf. *nōlim* above, p. 41, l. 14. — **eō plūs**: *more than that.*

FIG. 23.

19. **zōnās**: broad double belts for carrying money about the person.
20. **eās** simply repeats *sōnās*, which is placed first for emphasis. So *eās* below repeats *amphorās.*
21. **amphorās**: a large earthenware vessel, terminating in a point at the bottom, so that it would stand upright in the ground, or remain stationary if leaned against a wall. The illustration (fig. 23) is taken from a wine shop's sign found at Pompeii.

XXI. Gnaeus Pompeius Magnus.

Read Plutarch's Life of Pompey, Church's Two Thousand Years Ago, and his Roman Life in the Days of Cicero, Chap. IX.

23. **bellō cīvīlī**: the civil war between Marius and Sulla, 88–82 B.C. Marius died in 86 B.C., but the war was carried on by his party after his death.
26. **fīlī**: he was at this time but nineteen.

NOTES.

Page 43. 1. **hunc occīdendum suscēpit**: *undertook to kill him*. The gerundive is here used as a participle to express purpose, cf. *alendum*, p. 5, l. 8.

2. **incenderent**: implied ind. disc.

3. **nihil**: *not at all*.

4. **cum — ūsus est**: *treated Terentius with the same good-fellowship as before*.

6. **tentōriō**: dat. with *sub-*.

11. **ducī**: soon after this the elder Pompey was killed by a stroke of lightning. He was so hated that his corpse was snatched from the funeral bier, dragged through the streets of Rome, and thrown into the Tiber.

12. **Sullae**: 138–78 B.C. He served with distinction in Africa as quaestor under Marius in 107 against Jugurtha; took part in the campaigns against the Cimbri and Teutones, 102; conquered Mithridates king of Pontus, 88–84; and, after a struggle of many years, completely vanquished the Marian party and became dictator of Rome and Italy in 82. Though preëminently a military man, he was finely educated and took a great interest in literature. His great abilities were marred by monstrous cruelty and licentiousness. (Read Plutarch's Life of Sulla.)

13. **annōs — nātus**: *when he was twenty-three years old*. Note the idiom.

14. **ut — venīret**: *in order to render aid to Sulla*, i.e. against the Marian party. This was in 83 B.C., just after Sulla's return from the first Mithridatic war. (See note p. 46, l. 2.)

15. **perītus**: Pompey's natural military skill was phenomenal.

25. **posteā**: cf. p. 29, l. 27.

26. **honōrem**: the antecedent of *quem*. Cp. p. 21, l. 8, and see note.

Page 44. 2. **dēprecābātur**: tr. *tried to avert*.

4. **cūiusdam**: v. n. p. 12, l. 9; p. 29, l. 4.

6. **fuisset**: cons. A. 320, e; H. 517.

8. **quisnam**: cf. *quidnam*, p. 14, l. 10, and see note. — **esset**: v. n. p. 2, l. 1.

NOTES.

9. **Tam līberā vōce**: *by so frank a speech.*
15. **adulēscēns**, etc.: in app. with the subj., tr. by a concessive clause, v. H. 363, 3, 2).
18. **aegrē id ferēbat**: tr. *he felt hurt.*
19. **revertentī**: sc. *eī* dependent on **obviam īvit**. Cf. p. 38, l. 17.—**laetus eum excēpit**: *received him with joy.*
21. **Nihilō**: A. 250; H. 423.
22. **triumphum**: v. n. p. 11, l. 6.
23. **rē**: cf. n. p. 16, l. 4.
25. **suam**: sc. *potentiam.*
26. **Eā vōce audītā**: *on hearing that remark*, v. n. p. 1, l. 3.
28. **Metellō**: one of the most successful of Sulla's generals against the Marian party. In 80 B.C. Metellus was consul with Sulla himself; and in the following year he went as proconsul into Spain, in order to prosecute the war against Sertorius, who adhered to the Marian party. For eight years he contended against Sertorius, but with so little success that the senate sent Pompey to his assistance.
29. **Sertōrium**: one of the greatest generals that ever lived, considering his scanty resources. He was more than a match for both Metellus and Pompey, but was assassinated 72 B.C. Read Plutarch's Life of Sertorius.

Page 45. 7. **partiuntur**: to be translated by what tense?
8. **Alterō**: here = *aliō.*
11. **castīgātum ... dīmīsissem**: translate by two verbs.
12. **Metellum anum**: v. n. on *sacerdōtem*, p. 1, l. 5.
13. **dēflēxerant**: v. n. on *erant*, p. 21, l. 8.
15. **pīrātae**: these pirates, having their hiding-places along the southern coast of Cilicia, were masters of the entire Mediterranean. No sea-port nor vessel was safe from their attack. With a thousand swift ships they swept the seas.
20 **esse**: note the emphatic position, so *nōn esse.*
21. **nōn — tribuenda**: *unlimited power ought not to be bestowed on one man.*
23. **summō cōnsēnsū**: *with the greatest unanimity.*

NOTES. 123

26. **dispositis — nāvibus:** *by stationing his ships here and there, in all the nooks and corners of the sea.*

27. **brevī:** an adv., v. voc.

28. **locīs:** why no prep.? Cf. *terrā*, p. 31, l. 3. — **victōs fūdit:** tr. by two verbs.

30. **Nihil:** sc. *est*.

Page 46. 2. **Mithridātem:** a most remarkable man and a great military genius. He was the most formidable of all the enemies that Rome had to meet in the East. This was his third and last struggle against Rome, 74–63 B.C. Pompey went against him in 66 B.C. Cicero calls him the greatest of all kings after Alexander. (Read Plutarch's Life of Lucullus.)

11. **unde** = *quā rē*.

13. **Pontum:** an almost inaccessible and strongly fortified district of Asia Minor, south of the Black Sea.

16. **quod — subīret:** *when this acted too slowly.*

17. **corpus firmāverat:** it was no unusual thing thus to protect one's self against possible assassination by poison.

19. **Armeniae:** a country of Asia lying between Asia Minor and the Caspian. Tigranes, the king, was son-in-law to Mithridates.

22. **recreātum** agrees with **eum**, subject of *repōnere*.

25. **Iūdaeam:** this name was applied by Greeks and Romans to the whole of Palestine. The country was subject to Rome from this time on (63 B.C.). — **prīmus:** cf. p. 13, l. 21.

26. **templum:** Pompey touched none of the treasures. These were plundered nine years later by Crassus.

30. **bīduō:** *lasting two days.* The abl. not infrequently expresses duration of time.

Page 47. 2. **quam quod:** *than the fact that.* — **triumphīs:** dative.

4. **quod:** rel. pron.; its antecedent is the cl. following, *prīmum — triumphāvit*.

5. **tertiō:** an adv. — **fēlīx:** means *blessed of heaven, always successful, always fortunate, lucky.* Translate the sentence as if it read

NOTES.

'*et fēlīx opīniōne hominum futūrus esset, sī quem fīnem glōriae habuit, eundem vītae fīnem habuisset neque*, etc.'; the thought being that it would have been better for Pompey had he died at this the zenith of his glory.

10. **Caesarem**: the great Gaius Julius Caesar. — **hīc . . . ille**: *the former . . . the latter*, A. 102, a, b; H. 450, 2.

13. **Thessaliam**: a province in northern Greece.

14. **quem**: tr. *et eum*.

15. **Pharsālum**: the battle of Pharsālus, fought B.C. 48, which made Caesar master of the Roman world.

16. **tūtor**: the father of this Ptolemy had left the execution of his will to the Roman senate, and the senate appointed Pompey guardian of the young king.

17. **Latus — coniectus**: note the absence of conjunctions, and observe how this adds to the vividness of the description. Omission of conjunctions is called *asyndeton*.

20. **ānulō**: v. n. p. 37, l. 26.

21. **eō vīsō**: *at the sight of it.* — **illud . . . cremandum cūrāvit**: cf. *hunc occīdendum suscēpit*, p. 43, l. 1.

24. **multae et māgnae**: two adjectives belonging to the same noun are regularly connected by a conjunction. — **Erant in Pompēiō**: *Pompey had*. The Romans often said qualities were in a person, where we should say a person had qualities.

27. **negārent**: subj. with *cum*.

28. **apud Lūcullum**: v. n. p. 14, l. 20.

30. **perditus dēliciīs**: *spoiled by high living*. The thought is: "*Must Pompey owe his life to the ruinous extravagance of Lucullus?*" Lucullus was enormously rich and prodigal. He preceded Pompey in the conduct of the third Mithridatic war.

Page 48. 5. **Rhodum**: a large island in the eastern Aegean Sea, celebrated for Greek art, oratory, and learning. Cons.?

6. **quod . . . labōrārent**: tr. *because he was suffering severely from the gout*. How lit.?

9. **līctor**: v. p. 8, l. 8.

11. **ut vīdit**: v. n. on *ut*, p. 1, l. 10. — **molestē sē dīxit ferre**: *he said that he was disappointed*.

12. **Tū vērō ... potes**: *indeed you can.*
14. **frūstrā**: note the emphatic position.
16. **honestum**: not *honest.* Cf. n. p. 29, l. 2.
19. **quamvīs sīs molestus**: *however annoying you may be.*

XXII. Gaius Iulius Caesar.

Read Abbott's History of Julius Caesar; Plutarch's Life of Caesar; Church's Roman Life in the Days of Cicero, Chap. VIII.; Froude's Life of Caesar; Dodge's Caesar, Great Captains Series; Shakespeare's Julius Caesar.

21. **Iūliōrum**: the Julian gens is one of the oldest, and goes back to the very beginning of Rome. Its members enjoyed distinction from the earliest times. — **genitus**: past part. expressing parentage or birth are followed by the abl. without a prep.

22. **annum — decimum**: *when he was in his sixteenth year.* How else could this be expressed? Cf. id. p. 43, l. 13.

23. **Cinnae**: the colleague of Marius in his seventh consulship, 86 B.C., and a prominent democratic leader. — **dūxit**: sc. *in mātrimōnium.*

24. **is**: i.e. Sulla.

25. **neque efficere**: *but he could not accomplish it.* Caesar, by defying the merciless dictator at seventeen, showed the mettle that was in him.

Page 49. 2. **quartānae morbō**: sc. *febris,* an intermittent fever that returns every fourth day.

3. **prope per singulās noctēs**: *almost every night.*

6. **veniam**: a noun.

7. **dēprecantibus**: tr. by a rel. cl.

10. **vincerent** = *vincite* of dir. disc. A. 339; H. 523, III.

13. **Caesarī**: v. n. p. 6, l. 12.

15. **corōnā cīvicā**: a chaplet of oak leaves with the acorns, presented to the Roman soldier who had saved the life of a comrade in battle and slain his opponent. The illustration (fig. 24) is from a painting at Pompeii.

FIG. 24.

NOTES.

16. **Rhodum**: v. n. p. 48, l. 5.
20. **pīrātīs ... terrōrī**: for cons. cf. *partibus ... exitio*, l. 11.
22. **quibus** = *ut eis*.
23. **talenta**: the value of a talent varied in different states and at different times. The Attic talent, which was that adopted by many states, was worth about $1080.
26. **ibique**: *-que* connects *properāvit* and *fugāvit*.
27. **partem classis**, etc.: v. n. p. 47, l. 17.
29. **illīs**: dat. Why?

Page 50. 1. **Quaestōrī**: i.e. *quaestor prōvinciālis*, an officer appointed as assistant to a consul or praetor in charge of a province, v. voc. — **ūlterior Hispānia**: the southern part of Spain. The northern two-thirds was *Citerior Hispānia*. — **Quō profectus**: *on his way thither*.

2. **cūiusdam**: v. n. p. 12, l. 9.
3. **num**: v. n. p. 36, l. 19.
4. **sēriō**: an adv.
10. **rēbus**: A. 253; H. 424. **colās**: subj. of desire in a weak command.
11. **Gādēs**: why no prep.?
15. **Alexander**: he had conquered the East at the age of thirty-two.
18. **Aedīlis**: the aediles had charge of the public buildings and public works, and general police control over the city. They also superintended all public games and spectacles, and were expected to entertain the people by magnificent shows at their own expense. It was thus that they won support and favor for the higher offices of the state. — **Comitium**: v. n. p. 16, l. 17. — **Forum**: v. n. p. 4, l. 2. — **Capitōlium**: v. n. p. 38, l. 6.
19. **porticibus**: long, narrow walks, covered by a roof supported upon columns, affording protection from snow and rain. They were often constructed with great magnificence and were decorated with statues and paintings. They served as places for public resort. — **Vēnātiōnēs**: i.e. in the amphitheatre. Caesar surpassed all before him in the splendor of his displays.

NOTES. 127

24. **mīliēns sēstertiūm**: a contracted expression for *mīliēns centēna mīlia sēstertiūm* = *a hundred million sesterces*, about $4,100,000. The meaning is that Caesar needed that sum to pay his debts.

25. **societātem**: the First Triumvirate, 60 B.C.

28. **ager Campānus**: this was public domain.

Page 51. 5. **fascēsque**: a bundle of rods, sometimes with an axe, carried by each lictor preceding a Roman magistrate. These were symbols of magisterial power; the rods of scourging, which preceded execution, the axe of beheading. See fig. 25. — **eī**: cons. A. 235, and n.; H. 384, 4, n. 3.

8. **sī — sīgnārent**: *whenever they signed anything as witnesses; sīgnārent* is the imperf. subj. in a general condition denoting repeated action in past time.

FIG. 25.

10. **āctum**: sc. *esse*. — **Iūliō et Caesare**: sc. *cōnsulibus*.

11. **nōmine**: Romans regularly had three names, e.g. Gāius (*praenōmen*) Iūlius (*nōmen*) Caesar (*cōgnōmen*).

12. **duōbus**: i.e. *cōnsulibus*.

13. **cōnsulātū**: cons.?

14. **novem annīs**: abl. of time within which.

16. **prīmus**: v. n. p. 24, l. 1.

17. **ponte fabricātō**: *by building a bridge*.

18. **Britannōs**: Caesar invaded only the southern part of England. It was a century later before the Romans became masters of this land. — **superātīs**: sc. *eīs*, ind. obj. of *imperāvit*.

19. **cum ... tum**: v. voc.

20. **īnsīgnia**: tr. *remarkable deeds of valor*.

21. **quod** = *in that*, introducing a substantive clause.

22. **scūtō**: the large oblong shield used by the Roman infantry, 4 ft. long by 2½ wide. See fig. 26.

23. **aquiliferum**: v. figs. 6 and 12, with notes.

25. **comprehēnsum**: tr. as if *comprehendit et*.

FIG. 26.

28. **vincīque ... docuit**: *and taught those how to conquer*

who were ready to be conquered. — **Parātās** agrees with *legiōnēs* understood.

30. **Crassō**: p. 50, l. 26.

Page 52. 3. **Pompēiō**: dat. of agent. — **suspectae**: sc. *sunt.*
4. **ferēbat**: *could endure.* — **hīc** . . . **ille**: v. n. p. 47, l. 10.
7. **altĕrum**: v. n. p. 7, l. 18.
8. **suādentibus Pompēiō ēiusque amīcīs**: *through the influence of Pompey and his friends.*
9. **eī**: ind. obj. of *negātum est.* What is its subj.? — **vindicātūrus**: cons. A. 293, b, 2; H. 549, 3.
11. **Rubicōnem**: crossing this stream at the head of an army was equivalent to a declaration of war, inasmuch as it was the boundary of his province.
16. **Iacta ālea estō**: *let the die be cast.*
17. **Brundisium**: now Brindisi, and, as in ancient times, the most important seaport for all traffic to the East.
23. **diūtius**: *too long.*
26. **nāviculam**: cf. *ponticulum*, l. 15. Note the force of the suffix.
30. **prius . . . quam** = *priusquam*, to be translated here, as always, with the last clause. The separation of the parts of a compound word is called tmē′sis.

Page 53. 3. **Pharsālicō proeliō**: on this and events immediately following see p. 47, ll. 12–22, and notes.
4. **occīsum** = *eum occīsum esse.*
7. **Pontum**: v. n. p. 46, l. 13. — **Mithridātis**: v. n. p. 46, l. 2.
9. **quattuor**: limits *hōrīs*, abl. of time within which; cf. p. 51, l. 14. — **quibus in cōnspectum vēnit**: *from the time that he had come in sight.*
13. **ante . . . quam** = *sooner than*, cf. n. p. 52, l. 30.
15. **Scīpiōnem**: Metellus Scipio, Pompey's father-in-law.
17. **dēvīcit**: the battle of Thapsus, 46 B.C.
19. **excēpit**: what is the subject?
21. **auxiliīs . . . cōnfluentibus**: abl. abs.

22. **sequentium**: sc. *eōrum*, limiting *auxiliīs*. — **Sua . . . fortūna**: *His peculiar good fortune.* A. 196, g; H. 449, 2.

24. **initum**: sc. *est.*

25. **proelium**: the battle of Munda, 45 B.C. — **dubiō Mārte**: abl. abs. *Mārte* is here put by metonymy for *proeliō.*

27. **servāsset**: why subj.?

29. **proinde vidērent**: *that they should therefore consider.* For *vidērent* cf. *vincerent*, p. 49, l. 10. — **quem . . . imperātōrem** = *what kind of general.* — **locō**: why no prep.? — **dēsertūrī essent**: cons.?

30. **magis**: cf. *potius*, p. 32, l. 9.

Page 54. 2. **omnibus**: cf. *dolōrī*, p. 18, l. 19.

6. **annum**: v. n. on *duodecim mēnsēs*, p. 5, l. 24.

11. **etiam**: v. n. p. 28, l. 17. — **cōnvictōs**: sc. *eōs*, object of *mōvit.*

12. **lēgem . . . sūmptuāriam**: *law against extravagance.* There were many such laws enacted, the first of any importance being in 215 B.C. As might be supposed, they failed of accomplishing their purpose.

15. **iūs cīvīle**: Caesar's death postponed the important work of making a digest of Roman law for more than 500 years. — **optima quaeque**: tr. *all the best.* A. 93, c; H. 458, 1.

19. **Pomptīnās palūdēs**: a marshy district extending southward along the coast of Latium for about 25 miles and of varying width. It is still almost entirely waste land, although millions have been spent since Caesar's time in efforts to reclaim it.

22. **Parthīs**: a nomadic people living south of the Caspian sea. They were very warlike and formidable in war, and had at times inflicted severe defeats upon the Roman arms. — **Armeniam**: v. n. p. 46, l. 19.

23. **agentem**: sc. *eum.*

29. **rōstrīs**: the speaker's stand in the Forum, so called because adorned with the beaks (*rōstra*) of

FIG. 27.

captured ships. It was circular, raised on arches, with a parapet and platform at the top, on which an elevated stand was placed. The illustration (fig. 27) is from a Roman coin.

Page 55. 10. **is**: sc. *respondit*.

14. **rogātūrus**: cf. *vindicātūrus*, p. 52, l. 9. — **renuentī**: sc. *eī*; for cons. v. n. p. 51, l. 5. — **ab**: *on*.

15. **togam**: v. fig. 18. — **clāmantem**: sc. *eum*.

16. **adversum**: *in front*, an adj. used for an adv.

18. **adreptum**: cf. tr. of *comprehēnsum*, p. 51, l. 25. — **graphiō**: usually called *stilus*; v. fig. 21.

21. **cōnfossus est**:

"Then burst his mighty heart;
And in his mantle muffling up his face,
Even at the base of Pompey's statua,
Which all the while ran blood, Great Caesar fell."

22. **quem fīlī locō habēbat**: tr. *whom he used to regard as a son;* v. n. on *inferēbat*, p. 6, l. 8.

25. **et**: correlative with *et* in l. 29.

26. **Xenophōntem**: the well-known Athenian general and historian (400 B.C.), author of many works, among them a history of Cyrus the Great. — **ūltimā valētūdine**: tr. *in his last sickness*.

28. **subitam**: sc. *mortem*.

29. **prīdiē quam**: A. 262, n. 1; H. 520, n. 2.

30. **quisnam**: v. n. p. 14, l. 10. — **esset**: subj. ind. question. — **suā morte dēfūnctus est**: *died a natural death*.

FIG. 28.

Page 56. 3. **alius aliō cāsū**: *one by one fate, another by another;* note the idiom.

7. **Quō ... hōc**: abl. degree of difference; tr. *the ... the*.

8. **vīctōriā**: cons. cf. *morte*, l. 3, and *imperiō*, p. 2, l. 24.

9. **scrīnia**: a circular box in which books, letters, papers, etc., were kept. The illustration (fig. 28) is from a Pompeian painting.

14. **quod**: *that*, introduces a substantive clause in apposition with *laudem*, cf. p. 51, l. 21. For the mood of the verb v. n. on *perdūxisset*, p. 3, l. 22.

19. **cēnae**: v. n. p. 31, l. 5.

Page 57. 1. **Armōrum . . . equitandī . . . labōris**: cf. *cibī*, p. 23, l. 19.

2. **ūltrā fidem**: *incredibly*.

3. **anteībat**: note the use of the imperfect tense here and in the following clauses.—**seu . . . seu**: v. n. p. 13, l. 15.

XXIII. Marcus Tullius Cicero.

Read Plutarch's Life of Cicero; A. J. Church's Two Thousand Years Ago, and Roman Life in the Days of Cicero; Forsyth's Life of Cicero; Fausset's Cicero; Beesly's Catiline, Clodius, and Tiberius, first part; H. W. Herbert's The Roman Traitor.

8. **equestrī genere**: ranking next to the senators, the moneyed aristocracy, v. n. on *equitum*, p. 4, l. 19. For cons. cf. *familiā*, p. 48, l. 21.—**Arpīnī**: the locative case.

11. **cōgnōmen**: v. n. on *nōmine*, p. 51, l. 11.

15. **ubi** = *ut ibi*, hence the subj.

21. **scholās**: A. 237, d; H. 372.—**adīrent**: cons.?

Page 58. 1. **sectārētur**: intensive form of *sequor*, v. n. on *vocitābant*, p. 34, l. 12.

4. **Rōscium**: obj. of *dēfendere*.—**parricīdī**: cons. A. 220; H. 409, II, N. 2.

5. **Chrȳsogonī** depends on *potentiam*.

8. **nūllus**: used substantively. The defence of Roscius was, under the circumstances, an act of great courage that reflects high credit upon the youthful advocate.

11. **Rhodum**: v. n. p. 48, l. 5.

13. **Quī cum**: v. n. p. 5, l. 5.

15. **laude**: for cons. cf. *līberīs*, p. 8, l. 13.—**prīvārētur**: why subj.?

16. **quaestor**: v. n. p. 50, l. 1.
17. **māgna**: note emphatic position.
19. **cōgeret**: cons. A. 321, b; H. 517.
22. **praetōrī**: the praetors were the judges of Rome. After their year of office, they were sent out to the provinces as propraetors or governors.

Page 59. 1. **neutra — ūtilis**: *maimed in both hands and both feet.* — **-que**: connects *ūtilis* and *dēbilis.*
2. **mīles erat**: *he continued to serve as a soldier.* — **Hannibale**: the hero of the second Punic war (218–202). Note the absence of connectives in this passage and cf. p. 47, ll. 17–20, and note.
3. **ēius**: to whom does it refer?
4. **nūllō nōn diē**: *every day.*
5. **sinistrā — suffossīs**: *he engaged in combat four times with only his left hand, and two horses were stabbed from below while he was mounted on them.*
8. **duodēna**: A. 95, b; H. 174, 2, 3).
9. **victōrēs**: pred. nom. after *fuēre* of which *Cēterī* is the subj.
10. **etiam**: v. n. p. 28, l. 17.
14. **dominandī**: v. n. on *audāciae*, p. 10, l. 11.
16. **senātum cōnfodere**, etc.: note the asyndeton.
18. **Āctum erat**: tr. *it would have been all over with;* for the mood v. A. 308, b, R.; H. 511, 1.
19. **in Cicerōnem — incidisset**: *had happened when Cicero and Antonius were consuls.*
24. **inlātūrus**: cf. *vindicātūrus*, p. 52, l. 9.
26. **carcere**: v. fig. 4, and note.
28. **nitentem**: this and the following participles afford a good illustration of the various relations that may be expressed by them; *nitentem* should be translated by a concessive clause, *secūtum* and *ruentem* by causal clauses, and *retractum* by a principal clause coördinate with *adfēcit.*
30. **suppliciō mortis adfēcit**: *punished with death.* The Roman father had absolute power over his children, even to killing them. — **sē**: subj. of *genuisse.*

NOTES.   133

Page 60. 1. illum: i.e. *filium.*

5. Quam atrōciter dīmicātum sit: tr. *how desperate the conflict was,* v. n. on *pūgnātum est,* p. 7, l. 14.

6. quem: an emphatic relative clause sometimes stands first, and often contains the antecedent noun. So here, the relative comes first, the antecedent noun is *locum,* which has been taken into the relative clause and is repeated by *eum*; tr. in the order *locum quem,* etc.

9. pulcherrimā morte: how may this abl. abs. be expanded?

20. quae: sc. *ea.*

23. factū: cf. *leve dictū,* p. 35, l. 21.

24. Paucīs post annīs: cons. A. 259, d; H. 430, n. 1, 2). — diem dīxit: tr. *made an accusation against,* followed by the dat. of the person accused. — Clōdius: the notorious enemy of Cicero and one of the most profligate characters of a profligate age. — tribūnus: v. n. p. 17, l. 11.

27. veste mūtātā = *in mourning.*

29. suā causā: with *causā* the poss. adj. is regularly used instead of the gen. of the personal pronoun. — Proficīscentem: sc. *eum.*

30. ipsum: *but that he.*

Page 61. 1. Mārcō Tulliō — interdīcerētur: to interdict fire and water was a formula that was used in pronouncing a decree of banishment upon a citizen.

6. itinere depends on *iūcundius.*

7. Obviam — itum est: tr. as if we had *Obviam eī redeuntī ūniversī iērunt.* The impersonal cons. emphasizes the verb; the personal, the subj. On the use of *obviam* see notes p. 38, l. 17, and p. 26, l. 1.

16. veniam: in spite of this pardon, Cicero continued to regard Caesar as an enemy to his country, and he greatly rejoiced at Caesar's death.

17. Octāviānum: afterwards known as the emperor Augustus Caesar.

18. Antōnium: the famous triumvir who divided the world with Octavianus and Lepidus, and whose life was ruined by Cleopatra, the 'serpent of the Nile.'

24. trānsitūrus : cf. *vindicātūrus*, p. 52, l. 9.
25. prōvectum : sc. *eum* obj. of *rettulissent*.

Page 62. 1. lectīcam : v. fig. 14 and note. — quiētōs : sc. *eōs* subj. of *patī* and referring back to *servōs*, tr. as an adv. — quod : sc. *id*.

2. Prōminentī : sc. *eī* dat. of the person after *praecīsum est ;* so, too, with *praebentī*.

5. rōstrīs : v. fig. 27 and note.

* 8. plūs operae pōnēbat : *he gave more of his attention.*

20. brevī tempore : cf. *novem annīs*, p. 51, l. 14.

30. sē : subj. of *esse* understood. — dictitābat : cf. *vocitābant*, p. 34, l. 12.

Page 63. 2. audiō = *I have heard.* A. 276, a ; H. 467, 2. — alterō — ūltimā : *upon the death of the other consul on the last day of December.* The new consuls would enter office the following day.

4. hōrā septimā : i.e. about 1 P.M. The Romans numbered the hours of the day consecutively from sunrise till sunset, when the official day closed. The night was divided into four watches of three hours each.

5. salūtātum : cf. *pāstum*, p. 35, l. 4.
6. abeat : v. n. p. 9, l. 21.
9. vīderit : subj. of cause, or of characteristic.

XXIV. Caesar Octaviānus Augustus.

Read Church's Pictures from Roman Life and Story, Chaps. I–IV ; Plutarch's Life of Antony.

11. quārtum annum agēns : cf. n. p. 48, l. 22.

13. Apollōniam : a city in Illyria famed for its learning and commerce.

15. hērēdemque sē : *and that he was his heir.*

17. Brūtō : D. Junius Brutus Albinus, one of the conspirators against Julius Caesar, but not to be confused with Marcus Brutus (v. p. 55, l. 22). At this time (43 B.C.) he was fighting with Antony

for the possession of Cisalpine Gaul. Octavianus was appointed by
the senate to assist Brutus in crushing Antony.

23. **Quīn**: v. n. p. 24, l. 18. — **Columbīs**: a dat. where our idiom
would lead us to expect a gen. modifying *collum*.

Page 64. 1. **altissima**: *the tops*, cf. n. p. 10, l. 24.

3. **utique**: adv.

9. **aquiliferō**: v. fig. 12. — **legiōnis**: v. n. p. 22, l. 7. — **aquilam**:
v. fig. 6. — **umerīs subīsse**: *to have taken upon his shoulders.*

10. **Posteā**: v. n. p. 29, l. 27.

13. **quī**: sc. *eōs* as antecedent.

15. **cǎpulum**: the hilt of a sword was made of wood,
bone, ivory, silver, or gold, and was sometimes inlaid with
precious stones. The illustration (fig. 29) is from an
original found at Pompeii.

20. **triumvirī**: known as the Second Triumvirate, 43
B.C. They took the title *Triumvirī Reī Pūblicae Cōnstituendae.*

22. **quisque**: cf. p. 24, l. 6, and see note. — **quae**: v. n.
on *quibus*, p. 3, l. 24.

23. **Sullānā**: sc. *prōscrīptiōne*. This was in 82 B.C.,
when many thousands were slain; v. n. on *Sulla*, p. 43, l.
12. — **autem**: v. n. p. 10, l. 9.

24. **multa**: mark its separation from *exempla*.

27. **quibus — posset**: a rel. cl. of result.

29. **quīdam**: v. n. p. 12, l. 9; also p. 29, l. 4.

30. **clientem**: v. n. p. 18, l. 1.

FIG. 29.

Page 65. 1. **occīdendum eum ... obiēcet**: cf. p. 43, l. 1,
and n.

5. **tortī**: this was the regular way in which testimony was procured from slaves.

11. **ānulō**: v. fig. 19, and note.

13. **Quantī virī est**: *of how great a man is it a mark.*

16. **M. Brūtum**: v. p. 55, ll. 2 and 22.

20. **quemque**: cf. *optima quaeque*, p. 54, l. 16.

23. **Aliōs**: obj. of *iussisse* and subj. of *sortīrī.*

24. **fertur** = *dīcitur* = *he is said.* — **ut** — **concēderētur** gives the purpose of *sortīrī*.

25. **āc** connects *iussisse* and *spectāsse.* — **cum** : with *occubuisset.*

28. **occurrēbat** : sc. *eīs.* — **quīdam** : cf. previous page, line 29.

29. **dīvō Iūliō** : the Romans deified their good emperors after death. Augustus was worshipped even before death.

Page 66. 1. **Antōniō** : v. n. p. 61, l. 18.

4. **centiēns sēstertiūm** = *centiēns centēna mīlia sēstertiūm*, about $410,000 ; v. n. p. 50, l. 24.

5. **dīxerat** : the subj. is Cleopatra.

8. **inrīdentī** : *who joked her.* — **prōmissō stāre** : tr. *to keep her promise.* How lit.?

12. **quidnam** : v. n. p. 14, l. 10.

14. **vīctum** : sc. *esse.*

16. **Actium** : one of the great naval battles of history, 31 B.C.

18. **persecūtus** : sc. *eum* as object.

21. **ipse** : A. 195, 1 ; H. 452, 1.

24. **aspidem sibi adferendam cūrāvit** : cf. *occīdendum eum ... obiēcit*, p. 65, l. 1.

Page 67. 2. **Iānī** : v. n. p. 5, l. 25.

3. **tantum** : an adv.

6. **laetitiā** : cons. A. 249 ; H. 421, I.

9. **Sextīlis** : the month of August, which had the name *Sextīlis*, or sixth, because the old Roman year began with March. Cf. September (*septem*), the seventh month ; October (*octō*), the eighth, etc.

11. **Patris** : appositional gen.

12. **respondit** : sc. *eīs* with *dēferentibus.*

13. **Compos** — **meōrum** : *should I gain my heart's desire.*

15. **precer** : rel. cl. of characteristic. — **quam ut ... liceat** : A. 320, c ; H. 503, 3.

19. **Immō** : used to correct and strengthen a preceding statement = *nay even.*

20. **nōn semel** = *not once merely.* Litotes.

22. **commissum īrī** : the fut. pass. inf. is quite rare in the best Latin ; instead of it we find *fore* (*futūrum esse*) *ut* with the pres. or

imp. subj. To illustrate by this sentence we should have: *fore ut rēs pūblica plūrium arbitriō committātur.*
23. **quem . . . statūs**: A. 221, b; H. 409, III.
29. **patriae**: cons. A. 218, b; H. 399, II.
30. **Pedibus**: *on foot.*

Page 68. 3. **ut sibi adesset**: *to defend him.*
13. **vīgintī mīlibus nummōrum** = *20,000 sesterces.* A sestertius (*nummus*) was worth about 4.1 cents. What did he pay?
15. **quem**: tr. as if *et rogāvit ut eum* (i.e. *corvum*) *adferre cōgerētur,* and see n. on *quod,* p. 8, l. 18.
24. **periit**: A. 205, b; H. 463, 3.
30. **quantī**: cons. A. 252, a; H. 405.

Page 69. 1. **Graeculus quīdam**=*an insignificant Greek.* Note the force of the diminutive ending *-culus* here. — **palātiō**: this word, originally the name of the Palatine hill, was transferred to the palace of Augustus which was built there.
4. **breve**: with *epigramma.*
6. **laudāre mīrārīque**: historical infinitives. A. 275; H. 536, 1.
12. **satis grandem pecūniae summam**: *a good round sum.*
17. **apud Pōlliōnem**: v. n. on *apud,* p. 14, l. 20.
20. **piscīna**: the cultivation of fish was a favorite pursuit of the rich.
22. **quam ut . . . perīret**: cf. *quam ut . . . liceat,* p. 67, l. 15.
29. **aucupī**: note the etymology.—**noctuam prehendendam cūrāvit**: cf. p. 66, l. 24.

Page 70. 1. **mīlle nummōs** = *mīlle sēstertiōs,* cf. n. p. 68, l. 13.
8. **et**: *but.*
9. **familiārem habuit**: *he was on intimate terms with.* Cf. p. 69, ll. 16 and 17.
10. **eā**: with *grātiā.*
12. **quibus posset**: sc. *prōdesse.*—**nēminī**: cons.?
17. **in tabellā**: v. fig. 21, and note on **tabulae**, p. 39, l. 4.
18. **Quā lēctā**: *after reading this.*
19. **quisquam**: v. A. 202, b; H. 457.

NOTES.

Page 71. 9. sī — vertisset : v. n. on *perdūxisset*, p. 3, l. 22.
  10. cōnsternātum = *eum cōnsternātum esse*.
  11. barbā capillōque submissō : v. n. on *barbam submīsit*, p. 38, l. 22.
  15. adflīctā valētūdine : *in poor health*. How do you say, *in his last illness?* v. p. 55, l. 26.
  17. speculō : Roman mirrors were made of burnished metal.
  20. Ēdite — applaudite : referring to the words spoken by one of the actors to mark the end of a play.
  21. sextum agēns : cf. p. 48, l. 22, for idiom.

The highest claim that the great Augustus has upon the grateful memory of all posterity has scarcely been mentioned by our author. It is his patronage of literature and literary men. Himself a tireless student and keen critic, he surrounded himself with all that was best and brightest in the world of learning. The Augustan Age is the golden age of Latin literature. It gave to the world Vergil, Ovid, Tibullus, Horace, and many others whose inspired words pay immortal homage to the virtues of their distinguished emperor and noble benefactor.

> "Who fears the Parthian or the Scythian horde,
>   Or the rank growth that German forests yield,
> While Caesar lives? Who trembles at the sword
>   The fierce Iberians wield?
> Ah! be it thine long holy days to give
>   To thy Hesperia! thus, dear chief, we pray
> At sober sunrise; thus at mellow eve,
>   When ocean hides the day."
>
> HORACE, *Odes*, iv. 5; Conington's Translation.

SUGGESTIONS TO STUDENTS.[1]

1. In translating these exercises do not use an English-Latin dictionary. None is needed; none will give the words required.

2. Depend upon the text and the notes for idioms and vocabulary.

3. Translate *ideas*, not *words*.

4. Do not render English words by Latin words from which they may be derived unless you are very sure of your ground; honest is not *honestus*, nor secure *sēcūrus*.

5. Avoid the repetition of proper names as much as possible. When necessary refer to them by pronouns.

6. Try to keep the same subject throughout a sentence.

7. English prefers coördinate sentences loosely joined, Latin the periodic structure. (A. 345, Structure of the Period, N., 346; H. 573.)

8. Particular care is necessary in the use of conjunctions and pronouns.

9. In translating such an expression as 'the man I sent,' do not omit the relative which is understood in English, but write '*vir quem misi.*'

10. If the relation between two nouns connected by a preposition cannot be expressed in Latin by the genitive, use a

---

[1] Teachers will find much that is valuable in Abbott's Latin Prose through English Idiom, in Miller's Latin Prose Composition, and in Preble and Parker's Latin Writing, whence some of these suggestions were drawn.

relative clause: *e.g.* 'the love for fatherland' = *amor patriae*, 'the road to Gaul' = *via quae in Galliam dūcit*.

11. Remember that Latin has no perfect active participle, excepting in the case of deponent verbs.

12. The present participle is rarely used as an attributive adjective, *e.g.* 'the running boy,' is not *currēns puer*, but *puer qui currit*.

13. Finally, remember that only by a careful preliminary study of the text can you translate the exercises readily, confidently, and accurately.

LATIN COMPOSITION.

I. Romani imperi exordium.

1.

FOR ORAL TRANSLATION.

Order of Words. — A. & G. 343, N., 344, R., a, 1, 2, b, j, k, N.; H. 559, 560, 561, I–III, 563, 565, 566, 567, 568.

1. Proca, king of the Albans, had two sons. 2. He left the kingdom to Numitor, who was the older. 3. But Amulius, the other[1] son, expelled Numitor from the kingdom. 4. Rhea Silvia, Numitor's daughter, was a priestess of Vesta. 5. She was the mother of Romulus and Remus. 6. Amulius, the king, put her in prison. 7. The little children he put into a trough. 8. Then[2] he threw them into the Tiber.

NOTES: — 1. **alter.** 2. **deinde.**

2.

FOR ORAL TRANSLATION.

Order of Words (continued). — A. & G. 345, a–e, Structure of the Period, N., 346, a–e; H. 569, I–VI, 570, 571, 572, I–III, 573.

1. The Tiber had overflowed its banks. 2. The water flowed back, and left them on dry land. 3. There were then wolves in those places. 4. A wolf heard the wailing of the children, 5. and played the part[1] of mother[2] to them.

6. Faustulus, the shepherd, carried the twins to his cottage. 7. He gave them to his wife to be brought up.

NOTES: — 1. 'to play the part of,' sē gerere. 2. 'of mother,' see text.

3.

For Written Translation.

1. The boys grew up among the shepherds. 2. They used to hunt,[1] and often kept robbers from stealing the flocks. 3. One day[2] Remus was captured by the robbers, and then Faustulus told Romulus who their grandfather was.[3] 4. When Romulus heard this,[4] he armed the shepherds, and[5] hastened to Alba. 5. Meanwhile Remus had been brought before the king by the robbers who had captured him. 6. The king almost[6] recognized him, for Remus looked very much like[7] his mother. 7. Suddenly Romulus appeared on the scene.[8] 8. Amulius was killed, and Numitor was restored to the throne.

NOTES: — 1. Imp. indic. 2. quondam. 3. esset. 4. Lat. 'this having been heard.' 5. Omit. 6. haud procul erat quin. 7. *i.e.* was very similar to. 8. superveniō.

4.

For Oral Translation.

Rules for Agreement.— A. & G. 181, 182, 1–4, a.
Noun in Apposition or as Predicate. — A. & G. 183, 184, a–d, 185, a, b; H. 362, 1, 363, 1, 3, 1), 2), 4, 1), 2), 5, 364.

1. At Alba, a small city, Numitor was king. 2. Romulus and Remus, twin brothers, founded the city of Rome.[1] 3. We all know about their[2] quarrel. 4. Finally[3] Romulus called the city Rome from his own name.[4] 5. There were walls around

the new city. 6. Remus jumped over them in derision. 7. Romulus killed his brother Remus. 8. Romulus thus became[5] king alone.

NOTES:— 1. Lat. 'the city Rome.' 2. eōrum. 3. tandem. 4. dē suō ipsīus nōmine. Cons. of ipsīus ? 5. erat.

II. Romulus Romanorum rex primus.

1.

FOR ORAL TRANSLATION.

Rules for Agreement (continued).
Adjective with its Noun. — A. & G. 186, a, b, d, 187, a, 1, 2, b, N., c; H. 438, 1, 4, 6, 439, 1, 2, N., 3.

1. Romulus, when[1] king of the Romans, prepared games. 2. Many assembled with their wives and children, especially the Sabines. 3. The Roman youth, at a given signal, carried off the maidens. 4. This was straightway a cause for war. 5. When they approached Rome, they met[2] the maid Tarpeia. 6. Titus Tatius was leader of the Sabines. 7. Tarpeia and her father were Romans. 8. Tarpeia asked for the golden[3] rings and bracelets. 9. For the rings and bracelets of the Sabines were golden.

NOTES:— 1. Omit. 2. nanciscor. 3. aureus, -a, -um.

2.

FOR WRITTEN TRANSLATION.

1. Romulus and Remus, brothers, and grandsons of Numitor, built a small city on the banks of the Tiber, in the same place where they had been exposed, and had been found by Faustulus, the king's[1] herdsman. 2. After[2] Romulus had surrounded the new city with a wall, an amazing number of robbers and shep-

herds flocked⁸ thither from every side;⁴ but women were lacking, and the neighboring peoples refused marriage relations.⁵ 3. Romulus, concealing his vexation, gave⁶ orders that the neighbors be invited to games. 4. Many men, women, and children assembled. 5. When⁷ eyes and ears are intent upon⁸ the spectacle, the Roman youths rush in, and carry off the maidens.

NOTES:— 1. Use an adj. 2. **postquam** with the perf. ind. 3. cŏnfugiō. 4. 'from every side,' **undique**. 5. 'marriage relations,' express by one word. 6. 'gave orders, etc.,' Lat. id. 'ordered games to be announced to the neighbors.' 7. See notes p. 1, l. 13. 8. 'intent upon,' **intentus** with the dat. or with **ad** and acc.

III. Numa Pompilius, Romanorum rex secundus.

1.

FOR ORAL TRANSLATION.

Rules for Agreement (continued).
Relative with its Antecedent — A. 198, a, 199; H. 445, 1, 3, N. 1, 4, 7, 8.

1. The king that succeeded Romulus was Numa. 2. He was summoned from Cures, which¹ is a Sabine town. 3. By him many sacred rites were instituted, which tamed the wild people. 4. He consecrated the fire and the altar which are sacred to Vesta. 5. The shield which fell from heaven, Numa called *ancīle*. 6. Mamurius was the smith who made eleven shields of the same shape. 7. Numa chose twelve priests to take care of² the *ancīlia*.

NOTES:— 1. What peculiarity of agreement may be illustrated here? 2. Lat. 'who should guard.'

2.

For Oral Translation.

Rules for Agreement (continued).
Verb with its Subject.—A. 204, a, 205, a, b, c, 1, 2, d; H. 460, 1, 461, 1-3, 462, 463, I, II, 1-4.

1. Both Romulus and Numa were of advantage to the state.[1]
2. You, Numa, and Egeria proposed[2] many useful laws.
3. Before Numa, neither law nor the fear of punishment restrained the citizens.
4. The senate believed that Numa was taught by Jove.
5. Egeria is the goddess who had conversations with the king by night.
6. She increased his[3] authority by her advice.
7. Numa was buried on Mount Janiculum.
8. Romulus reigned thirty-seven years, Numa forty-three.

NOTES:— 1. See p. 6, l. 12. 2. ferō. 3. Not a form of suus.

3.

For Written Translation.

1. Numa, summoned from Cures, a Sabine town, was a man renowned for justice[1] and piety.
2. He taught the Romans many sacred rites, and once Jupiter himself is said to have come down, and to have promised Numa that he would give the Roman people a sure pledge of imperial power.[2]
3. On the next day, at sunrise,[3] a shield fell down from the riven sky.
4. Numa, taking this[4] to Mamurius the smith, said to him, "I, who am your king, order you to make eleven shields of the same shape as this."[5]
5. When the shields were finished, neither Mamurius nor Numa could distinguish[6] the real from the false.

NOTES:— 1. Lat. 'of renowned justice, etc.' 2. 'imperial power,' one word. 3. abl. abs. 4. See n. on quibus, p. 3, l. 24. 5. Omit 'as this.' 6. discernō, — ere, — crēvī, — crētus. Lat. id. discernere vērum et falsa.

IV. Tullus Hostilius, Romanorum rex tertius.

1.

For Oral Translation.

The Subjunctive in Independent Clauses. — A. 265, a, 1, 2, 3, 283.
Hortatory. — A. 266, N. 1, R., b, c; H. 483, 1, 2, 3, 484, II, III, IV.

1. Let Tullus Hostilius be elected king. 2. Let the fate[1] of each people be decided by the contest of a few. 3. Let a treaty be made on this condition. 4. Let the youths fight, three on a side.[2] 5. Do not shout[3] for joy, Albans; all hope has not deserted the Romans. 6. Granted[4] that three Albans are wounded,[5] two Romans have already fallen.

Notes: — 1. Use plural. 2. Lat. 'by threes.' 3. What tense in Lat.? 4. Hortatory subj. expressing concession. 5. Perf. subj.

2.

For Oral Translation.

The Subjunctive in Independent Clauses (continued).
Optative. — A. 267, a, b; H. 483, 1, 2, 3, 484, I.

1. Would that the two Romans had not fallen. 2. I wish that[1] the three Curiatii were not surrounding Horatius alone. 3. Though[2] Horatius is untouched, he is not equal to three. 4. May he take to flight, that[3] he may separate his foes. 5. May Horatius conquer. 6. Let his enemies be slain. 7. Would that the sister of Horatius had received him with joy.

Notes: — 1. 'I wish that,' utinam. 2. Express by the hortatory subj. 3. A purpose clause.

3.

For Written Translation.

1. When, in the reign of Tullus,[1] war had arisen between the Romans and the Albans, the leaders said, "Let us not all fight, but let the fate[2] of each people be decided by the contest[3] of a few; and where[4] victory shall rest,[5] there let the supreme power be." 2. The three Horatii and the three Curiatii fought together on that condition. 3. Already two Romans had been killed, and the three Curiatii had been wounded, when a man[6] called out: "Do not let the Curiatii surround you, Horatius.[7] Take flight, and let the enemy be separated, in order that you may kill them one at a time."[8] 4. In this way he conquered. 5. After his victory, the Romans received Horatius with joy and congratulations;[9] but great horror moved the Albans as they said,[10] "Oh, that the brave Curiatii[11] were still living!"

NOTES: — 1. Lat. 'Tullus reigning.' 2. Use plural. 3. See p. 2, l. 5. 4. Lat. 'whence.' 5. Omit 'shall rest.' 6. quīdam, v. p. 12, l. 9. 7. Where should the voc. stand? 8. singulī. 9. S. T. 10. Use pres. part. 11. 'the brave Curiatii,' Lat. id. 'the Curiatii, the brave heroes (virī).'

V. Ancus Marcius, Romanorum rex quartus.

1.

For Oral Translation.

The Subjunctive in Independent Clauses (continued).
Deliberative. — A. 268; H. 484, V.
Potential. — A. 311, R. a, N. 2, b; H. 485, N. 1, N. 3, 486, I, N. 1, II.

1. Shall the Romans elect Ancus king? 2. Why should he send ambassadors to the Latins? 3. What restitution[1] can

the ambassador demand? 4. You might send the ambassador in the following[2] manner. 5. When he has come to the enemies' country he would say,[3] 6. "Hear me,[4] Jupiter. 7. I am a messenger of the Roman people. 8. Let there be faith[5] in my words." 9. What should the ambassador, who is sent on this business,[6] be called? 10. I am inclined to think[7] that Ancus died a premature death.

NOTES: — 1. 'to demand restitution,' rēs repetere. 2. Use a form of hic. 3. dīcat. 4. Omit. 5. Lat. id. 'faith to.' 6. rēs. 7. Potential subj. in a modest assertion.

VII. Servius Tullius, Romanorum rex sextus.

1.

FOR ORAL TRANSLATION.

Conditional Sentences. — A. 304, a, b, c ; H. 506.
Simple Conditions. — A. 305, a, 1, 2, 306, a; H. 507, I, 508, 1, 4.

1. You might know[1] that Servius Tullius was born of a noble woman. 2. If an appearance of flame surrounded the head, it portended the highest honor. 3. Tanaquil said, "Let us bring him up just as[2] our own children. 4. If the king is dead, Tanaquil has concealed his death. 5. If Servius has begun to reign, let him govern the realm justly. 6. If the Romans built a temple to Diana on the Aventine, the king persuaded them.[3] 7. If the Latin drove the cow to the temple, let the priest sacrifice it.

NOTES: — 1. What subj.? 2. Lat. id. 'not otherwise than.' 3. Not accusative.

2.

FOR ORAL TRANSLATION.

Conditional Sentences (continued).
Future Conditions. — A. 305, b, (α), (β), 2, (α), (β), 307, 1, 2, a, N., b, c, d ; H. 507, I, II, 508 (with the future indicative), 509.

1. Will Servius receive the royal power? 2. Yes, and if he grows up,[1] he will be renowned for his wisdom. 3. If he should throw the standard among[2] the enemy, the Romans would fight more bravely. 4. If the king should not recover, the people would obey[3] Servius Tullius. 5. If the daughter of Servius should marry[4] the son of Tarquin, he would seek the royal power.[5] 6. Servius Tullius reigned forty-four years.

NOTES:— 1. The Eng. present may refer to future or even future perfect time. Latin expresses by the proper tense the time implied. 2. What case should in take here? 3. pāreō. Takes what case? 4. Lat. id. 'should be given in marriage.' 5. 'royal power,' express by one word.

3.

For Written Translation.

1. Servius Tullius received the royal power, though he was born[1] of a woman who was a slave and a captive. 2. Neither Tanaquil nor her husband had perceived[2] that the highest rank was destined[3] for the boy, before they saw[4] an appearance of fire around[5] his head while he was asleep. 3. If Servius was distinguished for wisdom, he was also brave; for, in a[6] battle, when[7] the soldiers were fighting without spirit, he seized a standard and, throwing it among[8] the enemy, called out, "If no one recovers[9] the standard, I myself will die for the sake[10] of recovering it." 4. Then the Romans fought so fiercely, that they won both the standard and the victory.

NOTES:— 1. Express the concession by a participle. 2. What number? 3. 'was destined for,' use passive of dēbeō with the dat. 4. Perf. ind. Cf. n. p. 9, l. 21. 5. Lat. 'embracing the head of him sleeping.' S. T. 6. See n. p. 29, l. 4. 7. Abl. abs. 8. in. 9. Not the present. 10. S. T.

VIII. Tarquinius Superbus, Romanorum rex septimus et ultimus.

1.

For Oral Translation.

Conditional Sentences (continued).
Conditions Contrary to Fact. — A. 305, c, 1, 2, 308, c, d; H. 510, N. 1, 511, N. 3, 2.

1. If Tarquinius Superbus were not wicked, he could[1] not seize the throne.[2]   2. If the king had not been active in war, he would not have subdued the Latins.   3. Shall[3] he reduce Gabii by strategy?   4. If Sextus, the king's son, should go to Gabii, it could be taken by assault.   5. If he had complained of his father's cruelty, they would have received him kindly.   6. If he won their favor, he became very influential.[4]

NOTES: — 1. What mode and tense?   2. rēgnum occupāre.   3. Deliberative question.   4. 'to be very influential' = plūrimum posse.

2.

For Oral Translation.

Conditional Sentences (continued).
Conditional Clauses with dum, modo, āc sī, ut sī, *etc.* — A. 314, a, 312, R.; H. 513, I, II.

1. Provided that Sextus wins the favor of the Gabini, he will be chosen leader.   2. If he sent[1] one of[2] his men to his father, his father would make no reply.[3]   3. The father passed into the garden, as if he were meditating.[4]   4. If the messenger should grow weary of waiting,[5] he would return to Gabii.   5. Sextus will know what his father wishes, provided that he learns of[6] his silence.   6. Sextus will deliver the city to his father, provided he can put the chief men to death.

NOTES: — 1. 'sent' = should send. 2. See n. p. 11, l. 22. 3. Lat. id. 'reply nothing.' 4. Subj. of dēlīberō. 5. Lat. id. 'by waiting.' 6. Omit.

3.

FOR WRITTEN TRANSLATION.

1. During the reign of Tarquin the Proud,¹ an old woman, who was a stranger,² came to the king, carrying nine books; which, she said, would be the king's, provided he wished to buy them. 2. The woman demanded an exorbitant price,³ and the king mocked her, as if she were in her dotage.⁴ 3. The old woman then burned six of⁵ the books. 4. She would have burned them all, if the king had not bought the three remaining. 5. If the king had bought all the books, he could⁶ have bought them at a price no greater than that which was asked for three. 6. Would that he had bought them all!

NOTES: — 1. Abl. abs. 2. Express the rel. cl. by an appositive. 3. S. T., and note p. 15, l. 11. 4. 'to be in one's dotage' = aetāte dēsipere. 5. See n. p. 11, l. 22. 6. Not the subj. Why?

IX. Horatius Cocles.

1.

FOR ORAL TRANSLATION.

Concessive Clauses. — A. 313, a–f, 326, b; H. 514, 515, I, II, 1, 2, 3, I/1, n. 2.

1. Porsenna, king of the Etruscans, was coming to Rome with a hostile army. 2. Though he took Janiculum, yet he did not restore Tarquinius. 3. Though the walls were strong, yet great fear filled the Romans. 4. All feared the mighty name of Porsenna, as if he were present.¹ 5. Though² Horatius was alone, he withstood the enemies' battle-line. 6. Though he was in full armor,³ he leaped into the Tiber. 7.

Though many weapons fell from above, he swam across in safety.[4]

NOTES:— 1. **adsum.** 2. Express as a conceded fact. 3. 'in full armor,' **armātus.** 4. 'in safety' = safe.

2.

FOR ORAL TRANSLATION.

Tenses of the Indicative: Present, Imperfect, and Future.—A. 276, a, 2, d, 3, e, 277, a, b, c, 278; H. 466, 467, I, II, III, 2, 4, 468, 469, I, II, 2, 470.

1. The state of Clusium was strong at that time.[1] 2. If the name of Porsenna were[2] not so great, fear would not possess the Romans. 3. All went from the country into the city. 4. While they were hedging the city about, the bridge almost gave entrance[3] to the enemy. 5. Had it not been for one man, Porsenna would have taken the city. 6. Horatius had for a long time been called[4] Cocles. 7. Even if he should lose[5] the other[6] eye, he would sustain[5] the attack. 8. They were cutting down the bridge behind him.[7] 9. Now he is swimming[8] across the river.

NOTES:— 1. 'at that time' = then. 2. Mood and tense? 3. **iter.** 4. 'had for a long time been called' = **iam diū nōminābātur.** 5. Not imperf. subj. 6. **alter.** 7. 'behind him,' **ā tergō.** 8. Historical present.

X. Menenius Agrippa.

1.

FOR WRITTEN TRANSLATION.

1. The eloquent Agrippa[1] was sent to restore[2] harmony between the senators and the commons. 2. Although he was so eloquent, he said only this to them: 3. "Once[3] the members of the body tried to make[4] a conspiracy[10] against the stomach;

for, while they were toiling,⁵ the stomach seemed to be idle. 4. They therefore⁶ determined to feed⁷ it no longer. 5. But, while they were desiring to conquer the stomach, they themselves also began to fail in strength."⁸ 6. From this story the commons perceived that the senate and themselves, as if a single body, grew weak⁹ through discord.

NOTES : — 1. S. T. 2. A purpose clause. 3. quondam. 4. faciō. What tense? 5. labōrō. 6. itaque. 7. cibum ferre. 8. 'began to fail in strength,' express by one word. 9. Inf. mood. 10. coniūrātiō.

XI. Lucius Virginius Centurio.

1.

FOR ORAL TRANSLATION.

Tenses of the Indicative (continued) :
Perfect, Pluperfect, and Future Perfect. — A. 279, a, e, 280, 281, 307, c ; H. 471, I, II, 4, 472, 473, 2.

1. In 454 B.C.¹ decemviri were elected instead of two consuls. 2. They proposed new laws, which they had brought from Greece. 3. The laws had been recorded on twelve tables. 4. The decemviri were men² of great insolence. 5. One of them was Appius Claudius. 6. Virginia was a beautiful³ plebeian maiden. 7. Appius fell in love with her. 8. Would that he had not seen her! 9. Virginius, the girl's father, was absent on military duty.

NOTES : — 1. Express as in the text. 2. Omit. 3. pulcherrimā formā, abl. of description.

2.

For Oral Translation.

Sequence of Tenses. — A. 284, 285, 1, 2, 286, N., R. (a), (b), 287, a, b, 1, 2, 3, N., c-g ; H. 490-492, 1, 2, 493, 1, 2, N. 2, 494, 495, I-IV, VI, 496, I, II.

1. Decemviri were chosen to submit[1] new laws. 2. But they were of such[2] insolence that they were brought[3] to ruin. 3. Appius instigated one of his dependents to claim Virginia for a slave.[4] 4. Had Virginius not been absent,[5] the client would not have laid his hand upon her. 5. He threatens to take[6] Virginia by force, unless she follows[7] him. 6. Since he cannot[8] lead her away, he summons her to trial. 7. While these things were going on,[9] messengers were sent to summon[1] Virginius.

NOTES: — 1. Purpose clause. 2. **tantus.** 3. Result clause. 4. Lat. 'for slavery.' 5. What form of condition? 6. Fut. inf. 7. Not present indic. 8. cf. '**cum Appius nōn posset.**' 9. **Dum haec geruntur.**

3.

For Written Translation.

1. Though Virginius arrived at Rome at daybreak, the citizens were already standing in the Forum in order to see what would take place.[1] 2. Virginius wept and implored the aid of the citizens, but there was no help anywhere, and Appius adjudged Virginia to his client. 3. Then the centurion asked permission[2] to speak to his daughter for the last time. 4. When he had led her apart, he stabbed her to the heart[3] with a knife, and fled to the army. 5. The army, aroused, compelled the decemviri to resign their office,[4] and threw Appius Claudius into prison, where[5] he committed suicide.

NOTES: — 1. **fīō.** 2. 'asked permission' = **petiit ut sibi licēret.** 3. 'to stab to the heart' = **pectus trānsfīgere.** 4. S. T. 5. **quā.**

XII. Marcus Furius Camillus.

1.

For Oral Translation.

The Subjunctive of Purpose.— A. 317, 1-3, N., b, N. 1, 318, a, b, c, d, 331, a, b, 1, 2, e, 2, f, N., R., h; H. 497, I, II, 1, 2, 498, I-III, N. 1, 2, 499, 2.

1. Camillus went with his army that he might besiege Falerii. 2. The schoolmaster led forth the children to deliver them to the Romans. 3. If Camillus had kept[1] the children as hostages, the Faliscans would have surrendered. 4. But Camillus would despise[2] such[3] treachery. 5. He came to maintain[4] the rights of peace.

NOTES: — 1. **retineō**. 2. Potential subjunctive. 3. **tālis**. 4. **dēfendō**. Express the purpose in six ways.

2.

For Oral Translation.

1. Camillus ordered[1] the hands of the schoolmaster to be bound. 2. At first[2] the schoolmaster feared that he would be thrown into prison. 3. But Camillus gave him over to the children to lead back[3] into the city. 4. He gave them whips to drive[4] him with. 5. He bound the teacher's hands, that[5] they might whip him the more easily. 6. In this way[6] Camillus tried[7] to conquer the Faliscans by kindness. 7. Nothing could prevent[8] them from opening their gates to the Romans.

NOTES: — 1. Express both with **iubeō** and **imperō**. 2. **prīmum**. 3. Follow the idiom of the text and see A. 294, d; H. 544, n. 2. 4. Lat. id. 'by which they might drive.' 5. **quō**. Why? 6. **Ita**. 7. **nītor** with ut and subj. 8. 'to prevent from' = **dēterrēre quōminus**, with subj.

3.

For Written Translation.

1. After the war against Falerii, Camillus besieged Veii, which had revolted at that time. 2. In order that he might take the city, he made winter quarters for his soldiers, gave them wages from the treasury, and[1] bound each[2] soldier by an oath that he would not leave the field[3] until after the city was captured.[4] 3. After the destruction of the city, Camillus withdrew to Ardea, because he had been unjustly condemned[5] by the tribune of the plebs. 4. As he was departing from the city, he prayed that[6] the gods might cause his ungrateful country to long for him.[7]

NOTES: — 1. Omit. 2. quisque. 3. 'leave the field' = discēdō. 4. Follow idiom in the text. 5. cf. quod . . . triumphāsset. 6. S. T. 7. Follow the idiom in the text.

4.

For Oral Translation.

The Subjunctive of Result. — A. 319, 1-3, N., R., a, c, d, R., 332, a, 1, 2, g, R.; H. 500, I, II, 501, I, 1, 2, II, 1, 2, III, 502, 1, 504, 1-3, 1), 2), 4.

1. The ambassadors advised the Gauls to abandon[1] the siege of Clusium. 2. It happened[2] that one of the Roman ambassadors killed the chief of the Senones. 3. The Gauls were so aroused by this,[3] that they attacked Rome. 4. On the 18th of July, the Roman army was slaughtered by the Gauls. 5. The defeat[4] was such that the day was placed among the days of ill-omen. 6. There was no doubt but that[5] the victorious Gauls would reach Rome before sunset. 7. Would that Camillus were there[6] to protect[7] his fatherland.

Notes: — 1. 'to abandon, etc.': is this a purpose or a result cl.? 2. fīēbat, followed by a subject clause of result. 3. Quā rē, etc. S. T. 4. clādēs. 5. quīn. 6. 'to be there' = adesse. 7. quī with subj. of tueor.

5.

For Oral Translation.

The Subjunctive in Relative Clauses of Characteristic. — A. 320. a, b, c, f ; H. 503, I, II, 1, 2, 3.

1. There were some¹ Romans who fled to the citadel. 2. The old men were not the men² to flee. 3. They were the only ones³ to await the approach of the Gauls. 4. Why was it that⁴ the curule magistrates sat in their ivory chairs? 5. So that they might die with the dignity belonging to them.⁵ 6. The men, clad in their robes of office,⁶ were very much like gods. 7. These old men did not deserve⁷ to be put to death. 8. There is no doubt but that Manlius saved the Capitol. 9. There were some who⁸ accused him of aiming at sovereignty.

Notes: — 1. Omit. 2. 'the men to' = eī quī followed by a clause of characteristic. 3. 'only ones to' = ūnī quī. 4. 'Why was it that' = quid erat quod. 5. 'belonging to them' = suus. 6. 'clad in their robes of office,' express by one word. 7. 'did not deserve to be' = dignī nōn erant quī. 8. 'There were some who' = erant quī.

6.

For Written Translation.

1. When the Gauls had made up their minds¹ to attack the citadel, they sent one ahead to try the way. 2. Him² they all followed, one man helping another. 3. They reached the summit in such silence that not even the dogs were aroused. 4. It happened that there were some geese in the temple of Juno. 5. The Romans,³ even in the greatest want, had

spared these because they are sacred birds. 6. These geese were so watchful, that the Gauls did not escape their notice; but, by their screams, they awoke Manlius, a distinguished soldier,[4] who, seizing his arms, easily pushed down the climbing Gauls with the boss of his shield.

NOTES: — 1. **statuō**. 2. Express by a relative. 3. Subordinate this sentence to the previous one by using a relative clause. S. T. 4. S. T.

7.

FOR ORAL TRANSLATION.

Causal Clauses. 1. Clauses with **quod, quia, quoniam,** *and* **quandō**. — A. 321, 1, 2, N. 3; H. 516, I, II.

2. Clauses with **cum** *and* **quī**. — A. 320, e, 321, b, c, 326, N. 1, b; H. 517, 3, 1).

1. Legates were sent to Camillus, because the army was hard pressed by hunger. 2. Since the Gauls thought this, bread was thrown down from the Capitol. 3. The Gauls were induced to abandon[1] the siege, because they were weary. 4. Camillus interposed, because the weights were unjust, 5. and because the Gallic chief was insolent. 6. He commanded the gold to be removed, because he had collected the remnants of the army. 7. He ordered[2] the Gauls to prepare for battle. 8. The victory was so great that not even[3] a messenger was left to tell[4] the disaster.[5]

NOTES: — 1. A result clause. 2. **dēnūntiō**, followed by an object clause of purpose. 3. 'not even,' v. n. p. 21, l. 5. 4. 'to tell,' a relative clause of purpose. 5. **calamitās**.

8.

FOR WRITTEN TRANSLATION.

1. If a false charge had not been brought against[1] Camillus, because he had celebrated his triumph with white horses, he

would not have withdrawn to Ardea. 2. Then, perhaps, the Gauls would not have attacked Rome, since they all feared Camillus, the famous soldier, exceedingly. 3. After his Gallic victory, he entered the city in triumph. 4. Since the city was now in ruins, there were some[2] who urged that[3] Rome be abandoned,[4] and that all move to Veii. 5. This plan was given up,[5] not only because Camillus opposed it strongly,[6] but especially because the people were moved by an omen.

NOTES: — 1. 'bring against' = īnferō. 2. 'there were some who' = erant quī. 3. Object clause of purpose. 4. Use abl. abs. and omit 'and that.' 5. dēpōnō. 6. Follow idiom in the text.

XIII. Spurius Postumius.

1.

FOR ORAL TRANSLATION.

Temporal Clauses. — A. 323, 1, 2.
Clauses with **postquam, ubi,** *etc.* — A. 324, a; H. 518, N. 1.

1. The Romans made war against the Samnites after they[1] had been called[2] by the Campanians. 2. Since the war lasted[3] for nearly fifty years, the dangers were often very great. 3. When Spurius Postumius was consul, he was led into an ambush by Pontius. 4. Pontius sent men to say to the Romans that Luceria was being besieged. 5. As soon as the Romans heard this, they tried to bring[4] aid. 6. They chose the shorter road, although it was the more dangerous. 7. When they had come to the Caudine Forks, the treachery of the enemy became clear.

NOTES: — 1. i.e. the Romans. 2. What tense usually follows **postquam**? 3. S. T. 4. Imperf. ind.

2.

For Oral Translation.

Temporal Clauses (continued).
Clauses with cum. — A. 325, a, c; H. 521, I, II, 1, 2.

1. When the Romans seek the road, they find it closed by a guard of the enemy. 2. When all hope of escape is taken away, they halt.[1] 3. After they had stood in silence for a long time, they broke out into complaints against their leaders. 4. The legions returned to Rome after they had been sent under the yoke. 5. When Postumius gave his opinion[2] in the senate, he said that the Roman people were not bound by the peace. 6. He urged[3] them to surrender him to the Samnites. 7. The senate praised Postumius, because[4] they admired his greatness of soul.

NOTES: — 1. Two words. 2. sententiam dicere. 3. hortor, with ut and subj. 4. Give the reason as if on the authority of the senate.

3.

For Written Translation.

1. When Postumius, the consul, had been led into an ambush by Pontius, the leader of the enemy, the Romans spent the night in silence, looking at one another, and unmindful of food and sleep. 2. Pontius, not knowing what he ought to do,[1] asked his father. 3. When his father had heard that the Romans had given up all hope of escaping, he advised[2] that either all should be put to death, or all should be let go. 4. This advice was not followed,[3] but all the Romans were sent under the yoke. 5. As soon as they reached Rome, they hid themselves through shame,[4] each[5] man in his own house.

NOTES: — 1. 'what ought to be done by him.' 2. moneō, followed by object clause of purpose. 3. Use accipiō. 4. Abl. of cause. 5. Note the order in the text.

XIV. Publius Valerius Laevinus, et Pyrrhus, rex Epiri.

1.

FOR ORAL TRANSLATION.

Temporal Clauses (continued).
Clauses with **antequam**, *and* **priusquam**.—A. 327, a; H. 520, I, 1, 2, II.

1. The Tarentini inflicted injuries upon the Roman ambassadors before war was declared against them. 2. After war had been declared,[1] they asked aid from Pyrrhus. 3. Laevinus was elected consul before Pyrrhus came to Italy. 4. Before Pyrrhus's arrival the Romans had never fought with an enemy from across the sea. 5. When the scouts of Pyrrhus had been captured, they were led through the Roman camp. 6. Laevinus showed them his army before he dismissed them. 7. The scouts reported to Pyrrhus what[2] the Romans were doing.

NOTES:—1. **postquam** with perf. ind. = Eng. pluperf. 2. Indirect question.

2.

FOR ORAL TRANSLATION.

Temporal Clauses (continued).
Clauses with **dum, dōnec,** *and* **quoad**.—A. 328, a; H. 519, I, II, 1, 2.

1. Laevinus said,[1] "Do not[2] dismiss the scouts until they have seen my army." 2. Soon Pyrrhus and Laevinus joined battle. 3. When Pyrrhus was already in retreat, he drove his elephants against the Roman battle line. 4. The Romans withstood the weight of their massive bodies, as long as they could. 5. After the horses had become frightened, they shook off their riders. 6. They fought until night put an end to the conflict. 7. Pyrrhus fought[3] many battles while[4] he was in Italy.

NOTES: — 1. **inquit**; insert in the quotation. 2. **nōlī**, with pres. inf. 3. **faciō.** 4. See n. p. 2, l. 11.

3.

For Written Translation.

1. After the Romans had declared war against the Tarentini because they had inflicted injuries upon their ambassadors, Pyrrhus, a descendant of Achilles,[1] came to assist the Tarentini. 2. Publius Valerius Laevinus, the Roman consul, soon met him in battle,[2] and almost defeated him. 3. When, however, the king drove his elephants against the Roman line, the fortune of the battle was changed. 4. So terrified were the horses by the sight and the smell of the monsters, that they carried their riders away with them in flight. 5. The infantry,[6] too,[3] were thrown into great confusion;[4] but they stood their ground[5] until night put an end to the conflict.

NOTES: — 1. S. T. 2. 'to meet some one in battle' = **proelium cum aliquō committere**. 3. **etiam**, v. n. p. 28, l. 17. 4. 'to throw into great confusion' = **māgnopere turbāre**. 5. 'to stand one's ground,' = **cōnsistere**. 6. **pedes, -itis**, M.

4.

For Oral Translation.

QUESTIONS.

Direct Questions. — A. 210, 1, a–f, 211, a, R., a, b, d, 212; H. 351, 1, Notes 1–3, 2, 352, 353, 1, 2.

Indirect Questions. — A. 210, 2, 334, N., a, f; H. 529, I, 1, N. 1, 3, 1), 2), 4, 5, 1).

1. Did Pyrrhus treat[1] the captive Romans with the greatest honor? 2. Yes,[2] and he buried the slain. 3. What did he say, when he saw the fierce expression on the faces[3] of the dead? 4. "If I had[4] such soldiers, I could[5] become master of

the world." 5. He asked his friends of what advantage⁴ such a victory was to him. 6. Why did he say that? 7. Because he had lost⁶ the flower of his army. 8. Whom did Pyrrhus send to Rome as his ambassador? 9. Was it not Cineas?

NOTES: — 1. **habeō**. 2. Repeat the verb. 3. Tr. 'expression on the faces' by one word. 4. Follow the idiom of the text. 5. A. 308, c; H. 511, N. 3. 6. Express the cause as a fact, v. n. p. 21, l. 8.

5.

FOR ORAL TRANSLATION.

1. Did Pyrrhus defeat the Romans in his first battle?¹ 2. Yes, but the victory cost him dear.² 3. Did he not lose the flower of his army? 4. Who met³ him with a new army? 5. That same Laevinus met him. 6. What did Pyrrhus say? 7. "Is not my fortune against the Romans like that of Hercules against the hydra?" 8. What was the hydra? 9. I don't know what it was.⁴

NOTES: — 1. Abl. of means. Omit 'his.' 2. 'cost him dear' = **māgnō eī stābat**; **māgnō** is abl. of price. 3. S. T. 4. Not indicative.

6.

FOR WRITTEN TRANSLATION.

1. Pyrrhus used to say that he did not know whether his arms, or the eloquence of Cineas, had gained the more cities for him. 2. One day¹ Cineas asked the king what he was planning to do after subduing the Romans.² 3. The king replied that it would not be difficult to seize Sicily and Africa by force of³ arms, and that then⁴ he would give himself up to the pleasures of peace.⁵ 4. "Well," said Cineas, "what prevents your doing⁶ that now?"

NOTES: — 1. **aliquandō**. 2. Abl. abs. 3. Omit 'by force of.' 4. **tum dēmum**. 5. 'the pleasures of peace' = **dulce ōtium**. 6. S. T.

7.

For Oral Translation.

The Gerund and Gerundive. — A. 294, d, 295, 296, N., 297, 298, a–c, 299, 300, N., 301; H. 541, 542, I, N. 1, II, III, N. 1, N. 2, IV, N. 1, 543, 544, 1, 2, N. 1, N. 2.

N. B. — The gerund with a direct object is regular only in the genitive case, and in the ablative case without a preposition.

1. Pyrrhus came to help[1] the Tarentini. 2. He was desirous[2] of conquering the Romans. 3. He understood the art of pleasing, and was of a forgiving disposition;[3] 4. so that he did not surrender the captives to his soldiers to be butchered,[4] 5. but returned them without ransom. 6. The senate had sent ambassadors to confer[5] concerning the ransoming of captives. 7. Often his mildness kept him from punishing.[6] 8. The Tarentini learned by experience[7] that he was their master rather than their ally.

NOTES: — 1. **auxilium ferre** with the dat. Express the purpose by the gen. of the gerund with **causā**. 2. **cupidus**. 3. Abl. of characteristic. 4. **trucīdō**, v. A. 294, d; H. 544, n. 2. 5. Omit 'to confer.' 6. **ā**, with abl. of gerund of **pūniō**. 7. Use abl. of gerund of **experior**.

8.

For Oral Translation.

1. There were some who[1] complained of their lot. 2. These were reported to Pyrrhus for speaking[2] slightingly of him. 3. They were summoned by the king for investigation.[3] 4. They came before[4] him to plead their cause.[5] 5. He first asked them whether those things that had come[6] to his ears were true or not.[7] 6. By confessing their fault,[8] they escaped punishment. 7. They said that too much wine[9] was the cause of their speaking so. 8. Pyrrhus dismissed them with a smile.

LATIN COMPOSITION.

NOTES: — 1. Rel. cl. of characteristic. 2. Dat. of gerund. 3. The gen. of the gerund with causā, or the acc. with ad. 4. apud. 5. causam dīcere. 6. Subj. by attraction. 7. necne or an nōn? 8. cōnfiteor. 9. nimium vīnī.

9.

FOR WRITTEN TRANSLATION.

1. After his victory Pyrrhus sent Cineas to Rome to propose peace[1] on honorable conditions. 2. When he had been introduced to the senate chamber, and there had spoken eloquently[2] concerning the fairness of the conditions, the mind of the senate seemed to be leaning towards making a treaty.[1] 3. But, influenced[3] by the opinion of Appius Claudius, the senate made the following reply to Pyrrhus:[4] "You can have no peace with the Romans until you have left Italy."

NOTES: — 1. 'to propose peace,' ad with gerundive. 2. 'had spoken eloquently,' express by one word. 3. Lat. id. 'led.' 4. S. T.

XV. Gaius Fabricius.

1.

FOR ORAL TRANSLATION.

The Supine. — A. 302, 303, R.; H. 546, 547.

1. Fabricius had come to ransom[1] the captives. 2. It was easy to see[2] that he was a good man. 3. Since he was very poor,[3] Pyrrhus offered him gold and gifts. 4. Fabricius declined everything. 5. The next day an elephant was brought near to frighten Fabricius. 6. The monster was terrible to see. 7. The beast was put behind a curtain. 8. This was easy to do. 9. At a given signal[4] it sent forth a noise dreadful[5] to hear. 10. Strange[6] to say, Fabricius was not frightened.

LATIN COMPOSITION.

NOTES: — 1. Express the purpose in seven ways. 2. Abl. of supine. 3. Express by dat. of adj. agreeing with 'him.' 4. Abl. abs. 5. horribilis. 6. mīrābilis.

2.

FOR WRITTEN TRANSLATION.

The Participle. — A. 289, 290, b, c, d, 1, 2, 291, a, b, 292, a, 293, a-c, 294, b; H. 548, 549, 1-5, N. 2, 550, N. 1, N. 4, N. 5, 438, 1.
See also suggestion 12, p. 139.

1. Pyrrhus admired Fabricius so much that he invited him to leave his fatherland, offering him[1] a fourth of his kingdom. 2. When all hope of establishing peace was at an end,[2] and when Fabricius, who[3] had been elected consul, had pitched his camp near to that of[4] Pyrrhus, the king's physician came to him by night and offered to poison[5] Pyrrhus. 3. After the man had been bound,[6] he was taken back to his master with a letter[7] for[8] Pyrrhus. 4. When he knew all,[9] the king, marveling at him, said that nothing was harder to do[10] than to divert Fabricius from the path of honor.[11]

NOTES: — 1. Turn the phrase into the passive voice, and use the abl. abs. 2. Abl. abs. 3. Use a participle instead of a rel. cl. 4. The redundant 'that,' in the phrase 'that of' is never translated into Latin. 5. Lat. id. = 'kill by poison.' What tense of the infinitive should be used? 6. Use a participle. 7. litterae. 8. ad. 9. Lat. id. = 'all these being known.' 10. Abl. of supine. 11. 'path of honor,' tr. by one word.

3.

FOR ORAL TRANSLATION.

The Infinitive Mode.
Tenses. — A. 288, a; H. 537, 1, 3, N. 1.
Subject of the Infinitive. — A. 240, f; H. 536.
Infinitive with Subject Accusative. — A. 272, R., 330, A, B, 1-3; H. 535, I-III.

Complementary Infinitive. — A. 271, N., a ; H. 533, I, 1, 2.

1. Fabricius heard Cineas telling a story.[1] 2. He said that a certain philosopher lived[2] at Athens. 3. This philosopher used to say[3] that everything must[4] have pleasure for its object. 4. If the enemy should do this, they could be easily conquered. 5. They say[5] that indulgence was foreign to the life of Fabricius. 6. When the Samnite ambassadors offered him money, they could not move[6] him. 7. He could govern his desires. 8. All men cannot be like Fabricius.[7]

NOTES: — 1. 'telling a story,' translate by one word. 2. Pres. inf. 3. 'used to say,' what tense? 4. S. T. 5. **ferunt**. 6. i.e. 'corrupt.' 7. A. 234, 2; H. 391, 4.

4.

FOR ORAL TRANSLATION.

The Infinitive Mode (continued).
The Infinitive as Subject. — A. 270, 1–3, a, b, 330, A.; H. 538, 1.
Personal and Impersonal Construction with the Infinitive. — A. 270, b, 330, a, 1, 2, b, 1, 2, c; H. 534, 1, N. 1, N. 2.
Predicate after Infinitive. — A. 271, c, 272, 2 ; H. 536, 2, 1)–3).
Historical Infinitive. — A. 275 ; H. 536, 1, N.

1. To make headway against[1] the Romans was difficult. 2. Pyrrhus, therefore,[2] determined to bring[3] Sicily beneath his sway. 3. It is said[4] that he plundered the temple of Proserpina. 4. This temple was at Locri.[5] 5. We know that this wealth was placed on ships. 6. The next day a storm arose,[6] the fleet was shattered, the ships cast upon the beach. 7. This disaster taught him that there are gods. 8. He ordered all the sacred treasure to be carried back. 9. It is said that after this[7] nothing succeeded for him, 10. and that he fell by a dishonorable death.

NOTES: — 1. 'To make headway against,' subj. of 'was.' 2. **itaque.** 3. S. T. 4. Remember that the personal construction is preferred. 5. Locative. 6. Hist. infinitives for all the verbs. 'arose' = **coorior.** 7. **posthāc.**

XVI. Gaius Duilius.

1.

FOR WRITTEN TRANSLATION.

1. It is said that Gaius Duilius was the first to conquer the Carthaginians in[1] a naval battle. 2. When he saw that the Carthaginians' ships were the swifter, he made iron grappling-hooks,[2] adapted to seize[3] and hold them. 3. In this way[4] the Romans, who excelled in strength, took[5] thirty ships, captured the admiral's septireme, and[6] sank thirteen others. 4. It is certain[7] that no victory was more welcome to the Romans than this, and that Duilius was the first to celebrate[8] a naval triumph.

NOTES: — 1. Lat. *by*. 2. Lit. 'hands.' 3. 'adapted to' = **ūtilis ad** with gerundive. 4. **ad hunc modum.** 5. Hist. inf. 6. Omit. 7. **cōnstat**, with infinitive. 8. 'was the first to celebrate,' S. T.

2.

FOR ORAL TRANSLATION.

Substantive Clauses introduced by **quod.** — A. 329, N., R., 333, N., a; H. 540, IV, n.

N. B. — Review the other varieties of substantive clauses, viz.: Infinitive, Subjunctive, and Indirect Questions.

1. It is established[1] that Hannibal escaped the hands of the Romans. 2. We know that he let himself down into a skiff. 3. He feared to return to his fatherland. 4. That[2] he escaped punishment for losing his fleet is well known.[3] 5. He sent one of his friends to Carthage. 6. This friend arrived before news

of the disaster reached home. 7. He asked the senate whether Hannibal ought to fight with the Roman fleet. 8. They replied, "There is no doubt but that he ought to fight."[4] 9. He said that Hannibal had fought and had been conquered. 10. Thus he escaped the cross.

NOTES:— 1. cōnstat followed by a quod clause. 2. quod. 3. nōtum est. 4. S. T.

XVII. Gaius Lutatius Catulus.

1.

FOR ORAL TRANSLATION.

The Imperative Mood. — A. 269, f ; H. 487, 1, 2, 1), 2), 488.
Prohibitions. — A. 269, a, 1, 2, 3, b ; H. 489, 1), 2), 3).

1. The consul Catulus shall put an end[1] to the war. 2. Order him to besiege Drepanum with three hundred ships. 3. Announce to him that a very large Carthaginian fleet is at hand. 4. Don't allow[2] Hanno to unload his ships. 5. Don't wait.[3] 6. Straightway lay your course for the Aegatian Islands. 7. Catulus proposed[4] the following conditions of peace: 8. "Vacate all the islands which lie between Italy and Africa. 9. Pay a fixed tribute to the Roman people for twenty years."

NOTES:— 1. Future imperative. 2. permittō. 3. Give this sentence in four ways. 4. adferō.

XVIII. Quintus Fabius Maximus.

1.

FORMAL INDIRECT DISCOURSE.

Definition.— A. 335, 336, 1 ; H. 522, 1, 2.
Declarative Sentences in Indirect Discourse. — A. 336, 2, N. 1, N. 2, a ; H. 523, I.

Subordinate Clauses in Indirect Discourse. — A. 336, 2, b, c ; H. 524, 1, 1), 2, 1).
Tenses of the Infinitive and Subjunctive in Indirect Discourse. — 336, A, 336, B, N. 1, N. 2 ; H. 525, 1, 2.

For Oral or Written Translation.

In this exercise first give the sentences as they stand, then after dīcit, then after dīxit.

1. Hannibal was[1] nine years old. 2. Hannibal swore everlasting hatred against the Romans. 3. The second Punic war was brought on[2] by this circumstance. 4. Hannibal, who was seeking a pretext for war, destroyed Saguntum, 5. because Saguntum was in alliance with the Romans. 6. Therefore ambassadors were sent to demand Hannibal. 7. Fabius was the chief of the embassy. 8. The Carthaginians will not give up[3] Hannibal. 9. They will carry on war with the same courage with which they accept[4] it. 10. Hannibal crossed the Alps.

Notes : — 1. Bear in mind that the infinitive is not subject to the laws of tense sequence. 2. S. T. 3. *i.e.* surrender. 4. Fut. perf.

2.

For Oral or Written Translation.

Formal Indirect Discourse (continued).
Conditions in Indirect Discourse. — A. 337, 1, 2, a, b, 1–3; H. 527, I, II, III, N. 1.
Questions in Indirect Discourse. — A. 338, N. 1, N. 2, a ; H. 523, II, 1, 2, footnote 2.
Commands in Indirect Discourse. — A. 339, R., N. 1, N. 2 ; H. 523, III, N.

Give the first five sentences; first as they stand, then after dīcit, then after dīxit.

1. Take whichever[1] pleases you.[2] 2. Give us whichever[1] you desire. 3. If Fabius should be sent against Hannibal,

he would check his victorious career.⁸ 4. If he protected Italy only, he changed the plan of the war. 5. Had there been a favorable opportunity⁴ for a successful engagement,⁵ the general would not have been wanting. 6. Do not ask whether Fabius deserved his fame. 7. But the delaying policy⁶ of Fabius did not please the Romans. 8. They said, did⁷ not Hannibal escape from the narrow pass?

NOTES: — 1. **utrum** = which of two. 2. Dative. 3. 'victorious career,' one word. 4. 'favorable opportunity,' one word. 5. S. T. 6. 'delaying policy,' one word. 7. How is a fact stated as a question expressed in indirect discourse?

3.

FOR WRITTEN TRANSLATION.

1. After Fabius had shut Hannibal and his army within¹ the narrow pass, he thought that they could never escape. 2. But Hannibal ordered cattle, with blazing fagots fastened to their horns, to be driven towards the mountains. 3. The Romans, astonished at the strange sight,² wondered who were running about through the woods. 4. Fabius, suspecting³ an ambush, kept⁴ his men within their entrenchments. 5. Thus Hannibal escaped.

NOTES: — 1. Lat. id., 'shut in *by*.' 2. 'strange sight,' one word. 3. See notes p. 19, l. 7; p. 31, l. 8. 4. **contineō**.

4.

FOR ORAL OR WRITTEN TRANSLATION.

INFORMAL INDIRECT DISCOURSE.

Definition. — A. 340; H. 528, 1–3.
Implied Indirect Discourse. — A. 341, a–d; H. 528, 1.
Subjunctive of Integral Part (attraction). — A. 342, a, N.; H. 529, II, N. (1, 1), 2).
Alius *and* **alter.** — A. 203, a–c; H. 459, 1.

1. Fabius commanded his son to sell that field which [1] Hannibal had spared. 2. Minucius brought a charge against Fabius, because [2] he was wasting time. 3. For there were two commanders, one Fabius, the other Minucius. 4. Some thought that Fabius was cautious, others that he was afraid. 5. The commons were angered because [3] Fabius desired to have control of the army. 6. Fabius promised [4] his assistance if Minucius should engage in battle. 7. Fabius came to assist Minucius, who [5] had been conquered by Hannibal. 8. Minucius commanded his soldiers to call Fabius, who [5] had delivered him, father.

NOTES: — 1. This rel. cl. is included in what Fabius says. 2. i.e. as Minucius affirmed. 3. cf. n. 2. 4. 'promised' = 'said that he would give,' hence implied indirect discourse. 5. Rel. cl. with subj. by attraction.

5.

For Oral Translation.

EXPRESSIONS OF PLACE.

Place from which. — A. 258, a; H. 412, I, II, 1.
Place to which. — A. 258, b; H. 380, I, II, 1.
Place towards which. — A. 258, b, N. 2, 2, N. 1; H. 380, 1, 412, 3, N.
Place at or in which. — A. 258, c, f; H. 425, I, II, 2.
Place by, through, or over which. — A. 258, g; H. 420, 3).
Words used like names of towns. — A. 258, c, R., d, f, 1, 2; H. 380, II, 2, 1), 2), 412, 1, 426, 1, 2.
Summary. — H. 427, 428.

1. Fabius marched towards Tarentum. 2. When he had come to the city, he invested it by a siege. 3. At Tarentum lived a young woman whose brother was in the army of Fabius, 4. and whose lover [1] was the prefect of the guard. 5. The brother, at the command of Fabius, crossed over to Tarentum, as a deserter. 6. He went to his sister's house. 7. She was

at home. 8. There he persuaded the prefect to betray the city. 9. Then a messenger was sent from the city to Fabius. 10. The Romans entered the city by that part of the wall which the prefect was guarding.

NOTES :— 1. **amāns**.

6.

FOR ORAL TRANSLATION.

EXPRESSIONS OF TIME.

Time when or within which.— A. 256, 259, a, c ; H. 429.
Time how long or during which. — A. 256, 259, c ; H. 379.
Use of prepositions in expressions of time. — A. 256, a, 259, b ; H. 429, 1, 2.
Time before or after an event.— A. 259, d; H. 430, N. 1, 1)-3), N. 3.

1. Livius boasted because he had held the citadel for many months. 2. Many years after, the son of Fabius was consul. 3. Fabius wished to know whether his son knew[1] that he was consul. 4. Within a few days the consul ordered Fabius to dismount from his horse. 5. The son knew who was consul. 6. For many years Fabius upheld the state by a policy of delay.[2] 7. In 216 B.C.[3] Paulus and Varro were consuls. 8. They pitched their camp near Cannae. 9. In a few hours they drew up their battle-line. 10. Their army was cut in pieces. 11. Rome had known[4] no such[5] calamity for two hundred years.

NOTES :— 1. Not indic. 2. 'policy of delay,' one word. 3. Lat. id. 'in the 538th year from the founding of the city.' Cf. p. 17, l. 20. 4. **sentiō**. 5. 'no such ' = ' not so great.'

7.

FOR WRITTEN TRANSLATION.

1. A trivial circumstance[1] assisted Fabius in[2] recovering Tarentum. 2. In that city was a young woman who used to

receive⁸ the prefect of the guard at her house. 3. Though she lived at Tarentum, she was born⁴ at Rome, and had lived there fifteen years before she went to Tarentum. 4. Her brother was in the army of Fabius. 5. Her brother came to her by night,⁵ and there met⁶ the prefect, who promised, before he went forth⁷ from the house, to betray⁸ Tarentum to the Romans. 6. Thus,⁹ within a few hours, Tarentum was recovered.

NOTES:— 1. S. T. 2. ad. 3. What tense? 4. nāscor. 5. noctū. 6. conveniō. 7. ēgredior. 8. Fut. inf. with subj. acc. 9. sīc.

XIX. Aemilius Paulus et Terentius Varro.

1.

FOR ORAL TRANSLATION.

THE ROMAN CALENDAR.

The Year.— A. 259, e, last part; H. 431, 4.

The Month.—A. 376, a–d, 259, e ; H. 641, 642, I, 1–3, II, N., III, 1–4, 644, I, II.

1. Fabius died 203¹ B.C. 2. The consuls entered upon their magistracy on the first of January. 3. King Numa died 673 B.C.² 4. The Salii used to convey the sacred shields through the city on the first of March. 5. The second Punic war began in 218 B.C. 6. Hannibal set out for Italy on the 10th of April.³ 7. He reached the Alps on the 3d of October. 8. He defeated Scipio at⁴ the Ticinus river, on the 14th of November. 9. He defeated Sempronius at the Trebia, on the 20th of December. 10. Some⁵ say that the battle of Cannae⁶ took place on the 2d of August.

NOTES:— 1. Subtract 203 from 754 for the Roman equivalent A.U.C. 2. All dates relating to the Roman kings are mythical. 3. The exact dates of these battles are uncertain. 4. apud. 5. quīdam. 6. proelium Cannēnse.

2.

For Oral Translation.

PRONOUNS.

Personal. — A. 194, a, c ; H. 446.
Demonstrative. — A. 195, d–g, k, l, 102, a–f ; H. 450, 1–4, 451, 3, 452, 2, 3.
Reflexive. — A. 196, a, 1, 2, N., f–i ; H. 448, N., 449, 1, 2, 4.
Possessive. — A. 197, b–e ; H. 447, N. 1, 398, 3.
Relative. — A. 201, a–e ; H. 453.
Indefinite. — A. 202, a–c ; H. 455, 1, 456–458, 1.

1. There were two consuls at Cannae, the one Paulus, the other Varro. 2. The former fell, the latter returned from the great slaughter. 3. Was there any mention of peace at Rome? 4. No; even[1] Varro was thanked because he had not despaired. 5. They took down arms from the very temples. 6. The citizens contributed[2] their private wealth. 7. They left almost no gold for themselves. 8. The tablets[3] in the hands of the clerks were hardly sufficient. 9. Hannibal gave his captives an opportunity of ransoming themselves. 10. Ten of those very[1] ones were sent to Rome. 11. No pledge was asked from any one.[4] 12. Each one swore that he would return. 13. A certain one of the ambassadors returned, as if he had forgotten something.

NOTES : — 1. **ipse.** 2. 'to contribute' = **in medium prōferre.** 3. sc. the omitted relative. 4. **quisquam.**

3.

For Written Translation.

1. Some say that the battle of Cannae, Rome's greatest defeat since[1] the founding of the city, took place on the 2d of August; others, on the 15th of June. 2. So high was the spirit of the state that no one made mention of peace; but

they took the very spoils of war from the temple walls² for arms, and knights and senators, vying with each other,³ contributed their gold. 3. The senate, moreover, refused to ransom some captives taken⁴ by Hannibal, saying that the republic had no need⁵ of citizens who could be taken captive with arms in their hands.

NOTES: — 1. post. 2. pariēs, -etis, m. 3. 'vying with each other,' certātim. 4. Express by a relative clause. 5. S. T.

XX. Tiberius Gracchus et Gaius Gracchus.

1.

FOR ORAL TRANSLATION.

The Genitive Case.
General Rule. — A. 213, 1, 2 ; H. 393, 394, 395.
Quality. — A. 215, N., a, b ; H. 396, V, N. 1.
Partitive. — A. 216, a, 1–4, c, e ; H. 397, 1–3.
Objective. — A. 217 ; H. 396, III.
With Adjectives. — A. 218, a, b ; H. 399, I, 1–3, II.
Predicate Genitive. — A. 214, 2, c, d ; H. 401–404, N. 1, 405.
With Verbs. — A. 219, a, b, 220, 221, a, b, 222, a, b; H. 406, I–III, 407, I, 1, 2, II–IV, 409, I–III.

1. Tiberius Gracchus was the grandson of Scipio Africanus. 2. He was a boy of unusual talent.¹ 3. The mother, Cornelia, was full of wisdom.² 4. She thought that well-trained children were a matron's chief adornment. 5. She considered³ them of more value⁴ than the most beautiful jewels. 6. Her boys were called Cornelia's jewels. 7. Tiberius Gracchus was elected tribune of the people. 8. It was to his interest to win the favor of the people. 9. He did not forget them. 10. Some accused him of aiming⁵ at the royal power.

NOTES: — 1. indolēs. 2. sapientia. 3. habeō. 4. Omit 'value.' 5. Lat. id. 'of preparing a way for himself to.' Use gen. of gerund.

2.

For Written Translation.

1. The Gracchi, sons of Cornelia, the daughter of Scipio Africanus, were boys of unusual talent. 2. Cornelia, who was desirous [1] of educating [2] her children well, called them her jewels and sent them to school from childhood. 3. One [3] of these boys, Tiberius, was so full of love for the people that he won their favor, and was elected tribune. 4. When he desired his power as tribune [4] to be prolonged, the senate suspected [5] that he was seeking [6] the royal power, and he was accused of that crime. 5. He was killed by a mob [7] of senators, and his body was thrown into the Tiber. 6. He was a man [8] of great virtue, and of wonderful eloquence.

NOTES: — 1. **cupidus.** 2. Gen. of gerund. 3. **alter.** 4. 'as tribune,' use an adjective. 5. **suspicor, -ārī, -ātus.** 6. **petō.** 7. **turba.** 8. Omit.

3.

For Oral Translation.

The Dative Case.
General Rule. — A. 224; H. 382, 383.
Indirect Object. — A. 225, d, e, 226; H. 384, I, II, 2, 3, 1), 2).
With Special Verbs. — A. 227, a; H. 385, I, II, N. 1, N. 3.
With Compounds. — A. 228, N. 1, c; H. 386, 1-4.
A Dative rendered from. — A. 229, a; H. 385, 2.

1. Nature gave the same disposition to Gaius Gracchus. 2. He sought the tribunate to avenge his brother's death. 3. He favored [1] the people with lavish grants. 4. He did not spare [2] the treasury. 5. He gave citizenship to all Italians. 6. All good citizens opposed these plans of Gracchus. 7. The common people trusted [3] him. 8. He took corn from [4] the rich and gave it to the poor.

LATIN COMPOSITION.

NOTES: — 1. **faveō**. 2. **parcō**. 3. **cōnfīdō**. 4. **auferō**, followed by accusative of the thing and the dative of the person.

4.

FOR ORAL TRANSLATION.

The Dative Case (continued).
With Passive Intransitives. — A. 230; H. 384, 5.
Possessor. — A. 231; H. 387.
Apparent Agent. — A. 232, a; H. 388, 1, 2.
With Adjectives. — A. 234, a; H. 391, I.

1. The consul Opimius was ordered[1] to see to it that the republic should receive no harm. 2. The people had to be called to arms by the consul. 3. Gaius[2] had the family servants for a guard. 4. Gracchus was defeated[3] and compelled to flee.[4] 5. A slave was persuaded[1] to kill his master. 6. The death of Gaius was like that of[5] Tiberius. 7. Gracchus[6] had many friends. 8. One of[7] them was not faithful[8] to him. 9. He brought the tribune's head to[9] Opimius.

NOTES: — 1. **imperō**, used impersonally, followed by ut and subj. 2. Lat. id. 'The family servants were for a guard to Gaius.' 3. Use perf. part. 4. 2d periphrastic. 5. Omit 'that.' 6. Dat. of possessor. 7. **ex**. 8. **fīdēlis**. 9. When is *to* not a sign of the dative?

5.

FOR WRITTEN TRANSLATION.

1. After the death of Tiberius, Gaius Gracchus, to whom nature had given the same character, was elected[1] tribune. 2. He pleased[2] the commons by many laws relating to[3] the distribution of corn and the giving of the citizenship. 3. But Opimius had to obey[4] the decree of the senate, and so[5] he told the people that they must take up[6] arms against Gracchus. 4. Gracchus seized[7] the Aventine and used his family servants

as a guard, for⁸ he⁹ had no other defenders. 5. He was compelled to flee, however, and, in order that he might not be seized, he persuaded a slave, who was faithful to him, to kill [10] him. 6. His body, like that of his [11] brother, was thrown into the Tiber.

NOTES: — 1. **creō**. 2. **placeō**. 3. **dō**. 4. **pāreō**. Use 2d periphrastic impersonally. 5. **itaque**. 6. **capiō**. 7. Subordinate by using participle. 8. **quod**. 9. Dative of possessor. 10. Object cl. of purpose. 11. Omit 'that of his.'

6.

FOR ORAL TRANSLATION.

The Accusative Case.
Direct Object. — A. 237, a–d; H. 371, III, 372.
Cognate. — A. 238; H. 371. II.
Two Accusatives, same Person. — A. 239, a, 1, a; H. 373, 1, 2.
Two Accusatives, Person and Thing. — A. 239, c, N. 1; H. 374, 1, n. 4, 375, 376.

1. The Romans elected Opimius consul. 2. Tiberius Gracchus was elected tribune. 3. He lived a noble life,¹ and died an undeserved death.¹ 4. After his death the consul inflicted punishment² upon those who had sympathized with Gracchus. 5. Blossius, a friend of Tiberius, asked the senate for pardon.³ 6. He valued Gracchus so highly⁴ that he thought he ought to do whatever Gracchus desired. 7. For⁵ this reason, he thought he ought to be pardoned.

NOTES: — 1. Cognate accusative. 2. 'inflicted punishment,' tr. by one word. 3. **venia**. 4. S. T. 5. Lat. 'because of.'

XXI. Gnaeus Pompeius Magnus.

1.

For Oral Translation.

The Ablative Case.
General Rule. — A. 242, N.; H. 411, I–III.
Separation. — A. 243, a, b, d, e; H. 413, N. 2, N. 3, 414, I–IV.
Source and Material. — A. 244, a; H. 415, I–III.
Cause. — A. 245, a, 1; H. 416, I, 1), 2), 421, III.
Agent. — A. 246; H. 415, I, 1, N. 1, 2.

1. Gnaeus Pompey was born of[1] senatorial stock. 2. Pompey's father was disliked by[2] the army because of his avarice.[3] 3. A plot was made against him by Tarentius. 4. Tarentius[4] was to kill[5] him and others[4] were to set his tent on fire. 5. Pompey, the youth, was informed of the plot. 6. But he was not moved by the peril.[5] 7. He withdrew from the tent secretly, and placed a strong guard about his father. 8. Terentius drew[6] his sword from its scabbard.[7] 9. Pompey threw himself into the midst of the lines. 10. The father was spared[8] on account of the tears of his son.

Notes. — 1. **nāscor**, followed by the abl. of source. 2. 'was disliked by' = 'was hateful to.' 3. Abl. of cause. 4. Dat. of apparent agent. 5. 2d periphrastic. 6. **ēripiō**. 7. **ex vāgīnā**, abl. of separation. 8. Use impersonally.

2.

For Written Translation.

1. The youthful Pompey was greatly beloved by Sulla, because he had followed Sulla's faction, and had gathered the remnants of his father's army that he might go to Sulla's assistance. 2. Among his soldiers, too, because of his many virtues, there was great affection for him. 3. Temperate in

food and drink, unwearied[1] by exertion, he was a skilful commander, and worthy of[2] the highest praise.

NOTES. — 1. Lat. 'wearied by no.' 2. **dignus** with abl. of cause.

3.

FOR ORAL TRANSLATION.

The Ablative Case (continued).
Comparison. — A. 247, a, c; H. 417, 1, N. 1, N. 2.
Manner. — A. 248, N., R.; H. 419, III, N. 1, N. 2.
Accompaniment. — A. 248, a, N.; H. 419, I, 1, 1), 2).
Means. — A. 248, c, 249; H. 420, 1, 3), 421, I.
Degree of Difference. — A. 250, R.; H. 423.

1. Pompey was a more illustrious man than his father. 2. He, together[1] with a band of[2] distinguished youth, joined[3] Sulla. 3. Afterwards he went to Sicily with a fleet. 4. Carbo, an enemy of Sulla, was seized by the soldiers. 5. Though he begged for life with prayers and tears, he was killed. 6. Sthenius, the chief of a Sicilian state, saved[4] his life by a frank speech. 7. "You will act unjustly," said Sthenius, "if you punish all for the guilt[5] of one." 8. "Who, pray,[6] is that one?" asked Pompey. 9. "I," said Sthenius, "who am much more guilty[7] than my fellow-citizens."

NOTES: — 1. Omit. 2. Omit 'band of.' 3. Lat. id. 'joined himself to.' 4. **servō**. 5. 'for the guilt' express in two ways. 6. 'who, pray,' **quisnam**. 7. **nocentior**.

4.

FOR ORAL TRANSLATION.

The Ablative Case (continued).
Quality. — A. 251, a; H. 419, II, 2, 1)–4).
Price. — A. 252, a, c, d; H. 422, N. 1.
Specification. — A. 253, a; H. 424, N. 1.
Absolute. — A. 255, a, d, 1–5, N.; H. 431, 1, 2, 4.

1. Pompey fought against Sertorius with variable success.
2. In a certain battle, a man of immense size made an attack against him. 3. Many rushing upon him at the same time,[1] he was wounded in the thigh. 4. He was deserted by his fleeing men. 5. He escaped from his peril, contrary to his expectations, and at no great price.[2] 6. No one excelled[3] Sertorius in courage. 7. Sertorius called Metellus an old woman, because he was effeminate in his manner of life.[4] 8. After Sertorius was dead, Pompey departed from Spain.

NOTES: — 1. S. T.   2. **pretium.**   3. **praecēdō,** with acc.   4. 'manner of life,' abl. of **cultus.**

5.

FOR WRITTEN TRANSLATION.

1. Pompey was a youth of remarkable talent,[1] and was skilful in war[2] when only twenty-four years of age; but he could not conquer Sertorius, who excelled[3] all his foes in knowledge[4] of military affairs. 2. Spain was finally recovered by the Romans at a great outlay[5] of men and of money. 3. After this war was finished, Pompey was sent with a great fleet to crush the pirates. 4. No victory was more speedy than this, for, by scattering his ships in all the nooks and corners[6] of the sea, he drove them out in less than forty days. 5. The war against Mithridates was then intrusted[7] to him, against whom he set out with the greatest speed.

NOTES: — 1. **ingenium.**   2. Not abl.   3. **praecēdō,** with acc.   4. **scientia.**   5. **sūmptus.**   6. 'nooks and corners,' **recessūs.**   7. **mandō.**

WORD-GROUPS.

Before taking up the study of these groups of kindred words, the student will find it advisable to learn the principal rules for word formation, and the meanings and force of the most important prefixes and suffixes. See A., chap. viii ; H. 313-345.

1. AC-, *sharp, pierce.*

aciēs, edge, battle-line.
ācer, sharp.
acerbus, sharp (to the taste), bitter, cruel.

2. AG-, *drive.*

agō, drive.
adigō, drive to, compel.
cŏgō (co-agō), drive together, assemble.
exigō, drive out, complete.
fatīgō, drive to weariness.
subigō, drive up; subdue.
agitō, keep driving, drive here and there.
āgmen, a thing driven; army; line of march.

3. AL- (AR-), *feed, grow.*

alō, feed.
altus, grown ; high.
altum, the deep.
alacer, well-fed ; quick, lively.

4. AL-, ALI-, *other, strange.*

alius, another.
aliās, another time.
aliēnus, belonging to another.
aliquis, some other, some one.
aliquandō, at some time.
aliquantō, somewhat, rather.
aliquot, some.
aliter, in a different manner.
alter, another, the other (of two).
altercor, quarrel.

5. AM-, *love.*

amīcus, friend.
inimīcus, enemy.
amīcitia, friendship.
amor, love.

6. AN-, *breathe.*

anima, breath ; soul.
animal, a breathing thing; animal.
animus, rational spirit, mind, soul.

7. 1 AR-, *fit.*

arma, arms, implements.
armō, arm, equip.

ars, skill in joining; art, craft.
artūs, joints.

8. 2 AR-, *burn, dry.*
ārdor, heat, fire.
exārdēscō, burst into flames.
āridus, dry.

9. ARC-, *keep off, shut in.*
arceō, keep away.
exerceō, restrain, exercise.
exercitus, trained body, army.
arx, that which shuts in, citadel.

10. 1 AV-, *mark, delight, desire.*
audeō, dare.
audācia, boldness.
avārus, avaricious, desirous.
avāritia, desire, avarice.
avidus, eager.

11. 2 AV-, *notice.*
audiō, hear.
auris, ear.

12. 3 AV-, *blow, waft.*
avis, bird.
aucupium (avis-capiō), bird-catching.
augur, an interpreter of omens, augur.
augurium, interpretation of bird-omens.
auspicium, bird-gazing, auspices.

13. AVG-, *grow.*
augeō, increase.
auctor, author.

auctōritās, rank, power.
auxilium, increasing; assistance.

14. CAD-, *fall.*
cadō (ad-, com-, in-, ob-, re-), fall, befall.
cadāver, dead body.
cāsus (cadtus), falling; event; accident.
occāsiō, opportunity, occasion.

cēdō (ad-, com-, dē-, re-, sub-), give place, go.
recessus, retreat, departure.
successor, one following.
successus, a coming up, advance; success.

15. CAL-, CLA-, *call.*
clāmō, call out.
clāmitō, call often.
conclāmō, call together.
clāmor, a loud call.
praeclārus, very bright, splendid.

16. CAND-, *glow.*
accendō, set fire to, kindle.
incendō, put fire in.
incendium, fire, conflagration.

17. CAP-, *take, hold.*
capiō (ad-, com-, prae-, re-), take, seize; hold.
captīvus, taken, captured.
captō, strive to take; catch.
inceptum, thing begun, undertaking.

praecipuē, taken before; especially.
prīnceps (prīmus–capere), foremost.
prīncipium, beginning.
caput, head.
anceps (ambi-ceps), two-headed, doubtful.

18. CAV-, *watch, ware.*

caveō, beware.
cautus, careful.
causa, cause.
accūsō, call to account.
accūsātor, one who calls to account.
cūra (cavira), care, anxiety.
cūrō, care.
incūriōsus, without care.
prōcūrō, look after, care for.

19. CEL-, CVR-, *strike, drive.*

percellō, strike down; strike with consternation.
procella, driving wind, storm.
celer, swift.
celeritās, swiftness.
celeber, trodden, frequented.
clādēs, destruction, devastation.

procul, at a distance, away.
culter, striking thing; knife.

currō (ad-, com-, dē-, dis-, ob-, sub-), run.
cursus, a running, course.
concursus, a meeting together.
incursiō, a running into, or against.

20. CER-, CRE-, *part, distinguish.*

cernō, separate; perceive.
dēcernō, decide; contend.
sēcrētus, separated; secret.
certus, settled, certain.
certē, certainly.
certō, match; fight.
certāmen, that which decides, contest.
certātim, in rivalry.
crīmen, means of distinguishing, fault.
discrīmen, that which parts, separation.

21. COL-, *till.*

colō, till, inhabit.
excolō, cultivate, improve.
incolō, abide, dwell.
incola, an inhabitant.
cultus, labor; care, culture.
colōnia, settlement.

22. CRV-, *raw.*

cruor, blood.
crūdēlis, cruel.
crūdēlitās, cruelty.

23. CVR-, CIR-, *curve.*

circus, circle, ring.
circum, around.
circā, around.

24. 1 DA-, *give.*

dō, give; grant.
dēdō, give up, surrender.

dēditiō, surrender.
reddō, give back.
trādō, give over, deliver.
dōnum, gift.
dōnō, give.
dōs, thing given; dowry.
sacerdōs, giver of sacrifice, priest.

25. 2 DA-, *put.*

-dō (ab-, ad-, circum-, com-, ē-, per-, prō-, sub-), put, place.
conditor, one who puts together; builder.
prōditor, betrayer.
mandō, put into the hands of, order.
vēndō (vēnum-dō), put for sale, sell.

26. DĪC-, DIC-, *show, point.*

dīcō (ad-, in-, inter-, prae-), show by words; say, speak, tell.
ēdictum, proclamation, edict.
(diciō), saying, authority.
condiciō, agreement, stipulation.
dictitō, say often, maintain.
dictātor, absolute ruler, dictator.
abdicō, disown, disavow.
praedicō, make known.
praedicātiō, a saying forth, public proclamation.
index, one who points out, witness.
indicium, something pointed out; notice, information.
iūdex (iūs-dex), one who speaks the law; judge.
iūdicō, pronounce judgment.

iūdicium, judgment.
discō (di-dec-scō), learn.
discipulus, learner, pupil.
doceō, teach.
doctus, one taught; learned man.
ēdoceō, teach thoroughly.
doctrīna, teaching, learning.

27. DIV-, *bright, shine.*

dīvus, deity, god.
dīvīnus, divine.
dīvīnitus, divinely, from heaven.
deus, god.
dea, goddess.
Iuppiter (Diupiter), Jupiter.
Iānus (Diānus), Janus.
Iāniculum, hill named after Janus.
Diāna (Divāna), shining one; Diana.
Iūnō (Divōna), Juno.

diēs, day, light.
bīduum, a period of two days.
cottīdiānus, daily.
hodiē, to-day.
postrīdiē, the day after.
prīdiē, the day before.

diū, all day; a long time.
diūturnus, of long duration.
interdiū, during the day, by day.
quamdiū, as long as; how long.

dītissimus (sup. of dīs), resplendent; rich.
dīvitiae, riches.
iuvenis, young.
iuventūs, youth.
adiuvō, help, assist.

WORD-GROUPS. 187

adiūmentum (adiuvāmentum), means of helping, aid.
iūcundus, pleasant, agreeable.

28. DVA-, DVI-, *apart, two.*
duo, two.
duodecim, twelve.
duodēnī, twelve each.
dubius, doubtful.
dubitō, go to and fro; hesitate.
duplex, twofold.
duplicō, fold double, duplicate.

bīduum, two days.
bis (dvi-iēs), twice.
bīnī, two apiece, two by two.
bellum (*dvellum), contest between two; war.
bellō, wage war.
rebellō, wage war again, revolt.
bellicōsus, full of war, warlike.
imbellis, unwarlike.

29. DVC-, *lead.*
dūcō (ab-, ad-, com-, dē-, ē-, in-, intro-, per-, re-, sub-, trāns-), lead.
dux, leader.
ēducō, bring up, train.
ēducātiō, bringing up, training.

30. ED-, *eat.*
edō, eat.
ēsca, something to eat, meat; bait.

31. ES-, *be, live.*
sum (esum) (ab-, ad-, dē-, in-, inter-, prae-, prō-, super-), be.

absēns, absent.
possum (pot-sum), be able, can.
praesēns, being before; present.

32. FA-, *shine, show.*
(for), speak, say.
praefor, say beforehand, premise.
īnfāns, that cannot speak; infant.
fābula, thing told, story.
fācundus, that speaks with ease, eloquent.
fācundia, eloquence.
fāma, what people say, report.
īnfāmis, ill spoken of.
fānum, a place dedicated by forms of speech; a temple.
fātum, thing spoken; fate.
fātālis, fateful.
fētiālis, speaking, negotiating (of an embassy).

33. FAC-, *make, put.*
faciō (ad-, com-, dē-, ex-, inter-, sub-), make, build.
fīō, be made, become.
interfector, a slayer.
praefectus, one set over, overseer.
facilis, easy to do.
difficilis, hard to do.
difficiliter, with difficulty.
facultās, ability, power.
difficultās, difficulty, trouble.
facinus, deed, act; crime.
factum, thing done, act.
profectō (prō-factō), for a fact, actually.

adfectō, strive after, aim at.
proficīscor, set out.

patefaciō, lay open, throw open.
aedificō, build, erect a building.
aedificium, building, edifice.
beneficium, good deed, favor, benefit.
carnifex, executioner, hangman.
opifex, worker, workman, artisan.
officium (opificium), service, kindness
pontifex [pōns-faciō, one who makes a bridge (to the gods)], high-priest.
sacrificium, a sacrifice.

faber, maker, workman, smith.
fabricō, make, build, construct.
Fabricius, proper name, cf. English *Smith*.

34. FER-, *bear*.

ferō (ad-, au(ab)-, com-, dē-, ex-, in-, ob-, per-, prae-, prō-, re-), bear, carry; tolerate.
vōciferor, cry out.
sīgnifer, standard bearer.

forte, by chance.
fortūna, chance, hap, luck.

fūrtum, theft.
fūrāx, given to stealing.

35. FĪD-, FID-, *bind, trust*.

fidēs, trust, confidence.
fidēlis, faithful.
perfidus, promise-breaking, faithless.
perfidia, faithlessness.

fidūcia, trust, confidence.
foedus, treaty.

36. FLAG-, FVLG-, *blaze*.

flamma (flagma), blaze.
cōnflagrō, burn, be consumed.
fulgeō, flash, lighten, gleam.
fulmen, lightning flash.

37. FLV-, FLVGV-, *flow*.

fluō, flow.
flūmen, a flowing, river.
fluvius, river.
fluctus, wave.

38. FRAG-, *break*.

frangō, break.
refringō, break up, break open.
fragmentum, piece broken off.
fragor, breaking, crash.
naufragium (navis-frangō), shipwreck.

39. FV-, FVD-, *pour*.

fundō, pour.
effundō, pour out.
īnfundō, pour in, pour upon.
profundō, pour out, pour forth.
profūsus, poured forth, lavish.
fōns (fovōns), that which pours, spring.

40. FVG-, *flee*.

fugiō (au(ab)-, com-, ex-, per-, prō-, re-), flee.
fuga, flight.
fugō, put to flight.
profugus, in flight; exiled.

perfuga, deserter.
trānsfuga, deserter.

41. GEN-, GN-, GNĀ-, *beget.*

gīgnō (reduplicated root), beget.
gēns, begetting; race.
ingēns, misbegotten, unnatural; huge.
genus, birth, race.
gener, son-in-law.
ingènium, inborn nature.
ingenuus, free-born; frank, simple.
benīgnus, kind, good, friendly.
benīgnē, kindly.

nāscor (gnāscor), be born.
nātus (gnātus), born; son.
renāscor, born again, grow again.
cōgnātiō, birth together; blood relationship.

42. GES-, *carry.*

gerō (gesō), carry.
dīgerō, force apart, separate.
gestus, bearing; posture, gesture.

43. GNA-, GNO-, *know.*

īgnōrō, be unacquainted.
nārrō (gnārrō), make known, tell.
nōscō (gnōscō), get knowledge of.
āgnōscō, recognize, identify.
cōgnōscō, become acquainted with.
incōgnitus, not examined, untried.
īgnōscō, not know; pardon, excuse.
nōtus (gnōtus), known.
īgnōtus, unknown, strange.
nōbilis, well known; famous.
nōbilitās, celebrity, fame.
īgnōbilis, unknown, obscure.
nōmen, means of knowing, name.
nōminō, call by name.
cōgnōmen, family name.
nota, means of recognition, sign, mark.

44. GRAD-, *walk.*

gradus, step.
aggredior, walk to, approach.
congredior, come together; meet.
congressus, meeting.
dīgredior, go apart, separate.
ēgredior, go out, come forth.
ingredior, advance, go forward.
prōgredior, go forth.
regredior, go back.
trānsgredior, pass over; desert.

45. HAB-, *have.*

habeō, have, hold.
adhibeō, hold toward; furnish.
exhibeō, hold forth; display.
inhibeō, hold in, restrain.
prohibeō, hold before; debar.
dēbeō (dē-hibeō), keep from; be bound.
praebeō (prae-hibeō), hold forth, give.
habitō, have possession of; dwell.
dēbilis (dē-habilis), lame, feeble.

46. I-, *go.*

eō (stem i) (ab-, ad-, circum-, in-, ob-, per-, praeter-, re-, sub-, trāns-), go.

aditus, a going to, approach.
coetus (com-itus), a coming together; crowd.
comitium, place of assembly.
exitus, going out, departure.
exitium, going out; destruction.
initium, a going in; entrance.
interitus, ruin, destruction.
praetor (prae-itor), leader; praetor.
praetōrius, of the leader.
reditus, a going back, return.
subitus, sudden, unexpected.

ambiō, go around, go about.
ambitiō, going about; searching for favor.
comes, going with, a companion.
comitor, accompany.
iter, going; journey.
sēditiō, going aside, discord.

47. IAC-, *go, send, throw.*

iaciō (ab-, com-, dē-, ē-, in-, inter-, ob-, prō-, re-, sub-, super-), send, hurl.
amiciō, throw about.
iaceō, be thrown; lie.
iactō, keep throwing, shower; toss.
iactātiō, a tossing, shaking; display.

48. IV-, IVG-, *bind, yoke.*

iūs, that which binds; law.
iūstus, in accordance with right, just.
iūstitia, justice.

iniūria, contrary to law; injury.
iūdex, one who administers law, judge.
iūdicō, judge.
iūdicium, judgment; court.
iūrō, bind oneself; swear.
coniūrō, swear together, plot.
coniūrātī, conspirators.
coniūrātiō, conspiracy.
iūsiūrandum, oath.

iungō, join.
adiungō, join to.
coniungō, join together.
coniūnx, one joined; husband, wife.
iugum, yoke.
quadrīgae (quadri-iugae), team of four horses.
iugulum, neck.

49. LAB-, *slide.*

lābor, slide, glide.
dēlābor, glide down.
ēlābor, slip away, escape.
relābor, slide back.

50. LVC-, *shine.*

lūx, light.
praelūceō, shine before; shed light upon.
lūcus, shining place; sacred grove.
lūmen (luc-men), that which shines, light.
lūna (luc-na), shining one; moon.
inlūstris (in-luc-tris), illumined; renowned.
lūstrō, light up; purify.

WORD-GROUPS.

51. MA-, MAN-, *measure.*
manus, that which measures, hand.
comminus (com-manus), hand to hand.
mansuētūdō, being used to the hand, tameness.
mandō (manus-dare), put into the hands of.
commendō, commit to one's care.
manūmittō, set free.

immēnsus, not to be measured, vast.
mēnsis, month.
mōs, measuring rule of life, custom.

52. MAN-, MEN-, *man, mind, stay.*
maneō, stay.
remaneō, stay behind.
mēns, mind.
mentiō, a calling to mind; mention.
moneō, make to think; advise.
admoneō, bring to mind.
monitus, reminding.

53. MIT-, *send, throw.*
mittō (ā-, ad-, com-, dē-, dī-, ē-, intrō-, ob-, prae-, prō-, re-, sub-, trāns-), send.
dēmissē, humbly, abjectly.
missiō, sending; release.

54. MOV-, MV-, *move.*
moveō (ad-, com-, per-, re-), move.

immōtus, unmoved.
immōbilis, immovable.
mōmentum, movement, motion.
mūtō, move, alter.
commūtō, alter wholly.
permūtō, change throughout.

55. MV-, *shut, fasten.*
moenia, walls.
mūniō, fortify.
commūniō, fortify on all sides.
commūnis, bound together; common.
mūrus, wall.

56. OL-, OR-, *grow, rise.*
orior, rise.
coorior, come forth; stand up.
exorior, come out; begin.
orīgō, source, beginning.
ōrdō, weaving; row, series.
ōrdinō, arrange in rows.
ōrdior, begin.
exōrdium, beginning.

adolēscō, grow up; ripen.
adulēscēns, growing, young.
adulēscentia, youth.
indolēs, inborn quality, nature.

57. OS-, *mouth, face.*
ōs, mouth.
Ōstia, sea-port of Rome at the mouth of the Tiber.
ōrō, use the mouth, speak.
adōrō, call upon, entreat; honor.

perōrō, speak at length; close.
ōrāculum, means of speaking; oracle.
ōrātiō, speech.

58. PA-, *feed.*

pater, father.
paternus, of a father, paternal.
patrimōnium, patrimony.
patrius, of a father, ancestral.
patria, land of one's fathers.
patrōnus, protector, defender.
parricīdium, the murder of a father.
pāstor, one that feeds.

59. PAL-, PEL-, PVL-, *drive, scatter.*

pellō, drive, drive out.
appellō, drive to; bring near.
compellō, drive together.
expellō, drive forth.
perpellō, drive, constrain.
prōpellō, drive forward.
repellō, drive back.

60. PARC-, PLEC-, *weave, fold.*

amplector, twine around, encircle.
complector, clasp, embrace.
implicō, enfold, entwine.
duplex, twofold, deceitful.
duplicō, double.
multiplex, with many folds, multiple.
simplex, without a fold; single; simple.
supplex, folded down, kneeling; suppliant.
suppliciter, suppliantly.
supplicium, a kneeling, prayer; punishment (criminals being beheaded kneeling).

61. PED-, *tread.*

pēs, foot.
impediō, entangle, hinder.
impedītus, hindered.
expediō, free the feet; explain.
oppidum (lit. on the plain), town.

62. PLE-, PLO-, PLV-, *fill.*

pleō (com-, ex-, ob-, re-), fill.
plēnus, full.
locuplēs, full of land; rich.
plērīque, very many, most.
plēbs, those that make the mass, common people.
plēbēius, belonging to the common people.
plūs, fuller, more.
complūrēs, several, very many.
plūrimus, fullest, most.
populus (redupl.), the people.
pūblicus (po-pulicus), belonging to the people.
pūblicō, make public.

63. POT-, *master.*

possum (pot-sum), be able.
potior, stronger; better; preferable.
potius, rather, preferable.

compos, having power over.
potentia, power.
potestās, ability.
potior, become master of.

64. RAP-, RUP-, *snatch, break.*

rapiō, snatch.
abripiō, snatch away, carry off.
adripiō, snatch to oneself, seize.
dīripiō, tear in pieces.
praeripiō, take away before another, tear away.
prōripiō, snatch forth.
rapīna, robbery.

rumpō, break.
corrumpō, break to pieces, destroy, ruin.
ērumpō, cause to break forth; break out.
interrumpō, break apart, interrupt.
perrumpō, a breaking.
inruptiō, break through.

65. REG-, RIG-, *stretch, guide.*

regō, keep straight, guide; rule.
corrigō, make straight; reform.
dīrigō, place straight, direct.
ērigō, raise up, raise.
porrigō, stretch forth.
pergō (per-regō), go on, continue.
surgō (sub-regō), raise up, ascend.
adsurgō, rise up.

rēctē, in a straight line.
regiō, direction; region.
rēx, king.

rēgīna, queen.
rēgius, royal.
rēgia, royal palace.
rēgālis, royal.
rēgnum, sovereignty; kingdom.

66. SAC-, SEC-, SCI-, SCID-, *split, divide, distinguish.*

saxum, (broken)stone, rocky fragment.
secō, cut.
secūris, ax.

sciō, know.
nēsciō, not to know.
cōnscīscō, determine in common, decree.
dēscīscō, withdraw, leave.
scīscitor, inform oneself; ask.

excidium, destruction.
rescindō, cut off; abolish.

caedō (scaedō), cut down, slay.
abscīdō, cut off.
occīdō, strike down, kill.
praecīdō, cut off in front, cut off.
trucīdō (trux-cīdō), kill savagely, butcher.
caedēs, slaughter.
parricīdium, the slaying of a father.

67. SED-, SID-, *sit.*

sedeō, sit.
sessor, one who sits.
īnsideō, sit in, sit upon; hold.
īnsidiae, sitting against, snare.

īnsidior, lie in ambush.
obsideō, sit before, be set.
obsidiō, siege.
obses, hostage, pledge.
praesidium, a sitting before; defence.
sēdēs, seat, home.

adsīdō, sit down.
cōnsīdō, sit together, sit.
cōnsessus, assembly.
(In the following *d* is changed to *l*).
sella, chair.
subsellium, low bench, seat.
solium, official seat.

68. SPEC-, *see, spy*.

speciō (ad-, com-, dī-, per-, re-, sub-), look at, behold.
cōnspectus, visible, striking.
cōnspicuus, visible; remarkable.

spectō, look steadfastly at.
spectāculum, sight, spectacle.
exspectō, look out for; await.
exspectātiō, awaiting, expectation.
speciēs, a seeing, sight; appearance.
speculum, looking-glass, mirror.
auspicium (avis-spicium), examination of birds.
haruspex (haru-spex), inspector of entrails, soothsayer.

69. STA-, *stand, set*.

stō (circum-, com-, ex-, prae-), stand.
superadstō, stand over.
cōnstantia, firm standing, constancy.

status, standing, state.
statuō (com-, in-, re-, sub-), make stand, set up; decree.
īnstitūtum, purpose; plan; institution.
statua, image, statue.
statūra, a standing upright; height.
statiō, standing still; station.
statim, firmly; on the spot.

sistō (redupl.) (com-, dē-, ex-, ob-, re-, sub-), cause to stand, station; stand.

dēstinō, make fast; resolve; appoint.
obstinātus, firmly set, resolute.

70. TAG-, *touch, seize*.

contingō, touch on all sides.
intactus, untouched, unbroken.
obtingō, touch, strike; fall to one's lot.
integer, untouched, whole.
redintegrō, make whole again, renew.

71. TEN-, TA-, *stretch*.

tendō (com-, in-, ob-, por-), stretch, tend.
attentus, stretched to, intent upon.

contentiō, straining, exertion.

tentō, handle ; try ; assail.
ostentō (obs-tentō), keep stretching out, show.
tentōrium, thing stretched out, tent.

teneō (ab-, com-, dē-, per-, re-, sub-), hold ; seize; keep.
continuus, joining with something.
continuō, immediately.
pertināciter, obstinately.
prōtinus, right onward.

72. VEH-, VAG-, *move, carry.*

vehō, bear, carry.
vehementer, violently, eagerly.
invehō, carry into, bring in.
prōvehō, carry forward ; transport.
trānsvehō, convey across.

via, way, road.
obvius, in the way, meeting.
obviam, in the way; towards, against.

73. VEN-, VA-, BA-, *go.*

veniō (ad-, circum-, com-, ē-, in-, inter-, ob-, per-, prae-, super-), come ; occur.
adventus, arrival.
adventō, come continually nearer, approach.
cōntiō (conventio), meeting ; discourse before a meeting.

ēventus, that which has come out, event.

arbiter (ad-bater), one that goes to ; spectator ; judge.
arbitror (ad-batror), hear, behold ; think.
arbitrium (ad-batrium), decision, mastery.
ambulō (ambi-balō), go about, walk.
inambulō, walk up and down.

74. VERT-, *turn.*

vertō (ā-, com-, dē-, ē-), turn, change.
adversus, turned towards, opposite.
adversum, opposite, against.
adversārius, one turned against, enemy.
dīversus, turned different ways ; opposite, contrary.
revertor, turn back, return.
trānsversus, turned across, crosswise.

rūrsus (re-versus), turned back ; back ; in return.
rūrsum (re-versum), same as *rūrsus.*
ūniversus, turned into one; whole, entire.
versō, turn about in a place ; dwell, live, be.
adversor, be opposite ; resist, oppose.

versus, furrow; line, verse.
versiculus, little line.

75. VID-, *see*.

videō, see.
invideō, look at askance; envy.
invidia, envy.
invidiōsus, full of envy.
prūdentia (prō-videntia), foreseeing; good sense.
visus, a seeing, sight.
visō, view; go to see.

76. VĪV-, VĪG-, *live*.

vīvō, live.
convīvium, a living together, a feast.
vīvus, alive.
vīta, life.

77. VOC-, VAG-, *call*.

vocō, call.

āvocō, call away.
advocō, call one to a place.
convocō, call together.
ēvocō, call out; summon.
prōvocō, call forth; challenge.
revocō, call back.
vocitō, wont to call.
vōx, voice.
vōciferor, cry out.
vāgītus, crying.

78. VOL-, VOLV-, *roll, twist*.

obvolvō, wrap round.
volūmen, roll of writing, book.
lōrum (vlōrum), thong of leather.

79. VOL-, *wish*.

volō, wish.
nōlō (nōn volō), be unwilling.
mālō (mag-volō), prefer.
benevolentia, well-wishing.
voluntās, will, desire.
voluntārius, willing.
voluptās, enjoyment, pleasure.

VOCABULARY.

ABBREVIATIONS USED IN THE VOCABULARY.

act.	active.		*inf.*	infinitive.
adv.	adverb.		*intens.*	intensive.
comp.	comparative		*interrog.*	interrogative or interrogatively.
dem.	demonstrative.			
dep.	deponent.		*intrans.*	intransitive.
desid.	desiderative.		*M.*	masculine.
esp.	especially.		*N.*	neuter.
dim.	diminutive.		*num.*	numeral.
e.g., exemplī grātiā	for instance.		*obj.*	object.
F.	feminine.		*orig.*	originally.
freq.	frequentative.		*P.*	participle.
fut.	future.		*pass.*	passive.
Gr.	Greek.		*plur.*	plural.
imper.	imperative.		*posit.*	positive.
impers.	impersonal.		*pron.*	pronoun.
inch.	inchoative.		*subst.*	substantive.
indecl.	indeclinable.		*sup.*	superlative.
indef.	indefinite.		*W. G.*	Word-Groups.

* An asterisk before a word means that it is not found in use, but is assumed to account for some derived form.

[ ] Derivations from roots are enclosed in square brackets. Such derivations are given only when the roots are included in the list of roots and word-groups, pp. 183–196.

(...) Secondary etymologies are enclosed in parentheses. Parentheses are also used to indicate such forms in the vocabulary as are incomplete: if substantives, they want the nominative case; if adjectives, the positive degree; if verbs, the present system.

— A dash in place of the genitive of a substantive, or of one of the principal parts of a verb, indicates that this case or this system is not in classical use.

For other abbreviations see page 74.

VOCABULARY.

A

A, abbreviation for *Aulus*, a Roman praenomen, 59, 26.

ā (before consonants), **ab** (before vowels and some consonants), **abs** (before tĕ), prep. with the abl., *away from, from*, 1, 18; 9, 24: to denote the place from which an action proceeds, *at, in, on,* 8, 27: of time, *from, since, after,* 17, 20; 40, 1: of agency, *by*, 2, 5; 4, 28.

ăbăliēnō, 1, -āvī, -ātus (ab, *from;* aliēnō, *estrange*), *alienate, estrange,* 66, 1.

abdĭcō, 1, -āvī, -ātus (ab, *from;* dīcō, *devote*), *disavow, reject:* with sē and abl., *resign, abdicate an office,* 18, 25. (W. G. 26.)

abdō, 3, -idī, -itus [ab, *away;* 2 DA-, *put*], *put away, hide, conceal,* 15, 3; 24, 6. (W. G. 25.)

abdūcō, 3, -dūxī, -ductus (ab, *away;* dūcō, *lead*), *lead away, lead off,* 18, 9. (W. G. 29.)

ăbĕō, -īre, -iī, -itūrus (ab, *away;* eō, *go*), *go from, go away, depart,* 10, 22: *retire from,* 63, 6. (W. G. 46.)

ăbĭcĭō, 3, -iēcī, -iectus (ab, *away;* iacĭō, *throw*), *throw away, cast away,* 1, 7: *give up, resign,* 46, 23. (W. G. 47.)

ablātus, P. of **auferō,** 28, 21.

ăblŭō, 3, -luī, -lūtus (ab, *away;* luō, *wash*), *wash away, remove by washing, wash,* 13, 7.

ăbrĭpĭō, 3, -ripuī, -reptus (ab, *away;* rapĭō, *snatch*), *snatch away, carry off,* 25, 16. (W. G. 64.)

abscēdō, 3, -cessī, -cessus (abs, *away;* cēdō, *go*), *go off, withdraw, depart,* 53, 12.

abscīdō, 3, -cīdī, -cīsus (abs, *off;* caedō, *cut*), *cut off, hew off,* 62, 3. (W. G. 66.)

abscīsus, adj. (P. of **abscīdō**), *cut off, severed,* 62, 3.

absēns, -entis, adj. (P. of **absum**), *absent,* 21, 17; 52, 7. (W. G. 31.)

absolvō, 3, -solvī, -solūtus (ab, *from;* solvō, *loosen*), *set free, release: acquit,* 8, 14.

absorbĕō, 2, -buī, -ptus (ab, *away;* sorbĕō, *swallow*), *swallow down,* 66, 14.

VOCABULARY.

abstineō, 2, -tinuī (**abs**, *away;* **teneō**, *keep*), *keep back, refrain, abstain*, 21, 8 : *absent oneself from*, 27, 20. (W. G. 71.)

abstrahō, 3, -trāxī, -tractus (**abs**, *away;* **trahō**, *drag*), *drag away*, 18, 7.

absum, **abesse**, **āfuī**, **āfutūrus** (**ab**, *away;* **sum**, *be*), *be away from, be absent*, 18, 4: *be far from, be distant*, 7, 15. (W. G. 31.)

absūmō, 3, -sūmpsī, -sūmptus (**ab**, *away;* **sūmō**, *take*), *take away, use up, consume*, 66, 5.

āc, see **atque**.

Acca, -ae, F., *Acca Larentia*, the foster-mother of Romulus and Remus, 1, 15.

accēdō, 3, -cessī, -cessūrus (**ad**, *to;* **cēdō**, *go*), *go to, come to, approach*, 8, 8; 35, 27: *enter upon, undertake*, 57, 1: *be added*, 39, 26. (W. G. 14.)

accendō, 3, -cendī, -cēnsus [**ad**, *to;* CAND-, *glow*], *kindle, set on fire*, 33, 30: *excite, arouse*, 18, 23 ; 34, 16. (W. G. 16.)

accēnsus, P. of **accendō**, 33, 30.

accidō, 3, -cidī (**ad**, *to;* **cadō**, *fall*), *fall to, come to pass, befall, happen*, 12, 4. (W. G. 14.)

accingō, 3, -nxī, -nctus (**ad**, *on;* **cingō**, *gird*), *gird on, bind on*, 62, 28.

acciō, 4, -cīvī, -cītus (**ad**, *to;* **ciō**, *call*), *call to, invite, summon*, 5, 5; 23, 22.

accipiō, 3, -cēpī, -ceptus (**ad**, *to oneself;* **capiō**, *take*), *take to oneself, receive, accept*, 9, 22; 12, 17; 22, 9: *admit, take in*, 17, 2. (W. G. 17.)

acclāmō, 1, -āvī, -ātus (**ad**, *to;* **clāmō**, *call*), *call to, exclaim*, 31, 15.

accommodō, 1, -āvī, -ātus (**ad**, *to;* **commodō**, *fit*), *fit to, adapt, apply*, 54, 7.

accurrō, 3, -cucurrī or -currī, -cursum (**ad**, *to;* **currō**, *run*), *run to, hasten to*, 1, 11. (W. G. 19.)

accūsātor, -ōris, M. (**accūsō**, *accuse*), *accuser, prosecutor, plaintiff*, 18, 2. (W. G. 18.)

accūsō, 1, -āvī, -ātus (orig. = **ad causam prōvocāre**), *call to account, blame, accuse*, 2, 4. (W. G. 18.)

ācer, **ācris**, **ācre**, adj. with comp. and sup. [AC-, *sharp*], *sharp, piercing, active, eager, brave*, 37, 4. (W. G. 1.)

acerbē, adv. with comp. and sup. [**acerbus** (AC-, *sharp*), *bitter*], *bitterly : severely, cruelly*, 65, 19. (W. G. 1.)

acētum, -ī, N. [AC-, *sharp*], *vinegar*, 66, 11.

Achillēs, -is, M., *Achilles*, the hero of Homer's Iliad and of the Trojan War, 25, 4.

aciēs, -ēī, F. [AC-, *sharp*], *sharp edge, point: line of battle*, 7, 1; 8, 24: *battle, engagement*, 47, 15; 53, 10. (W. G. 1.)

ācriter, adv., comp. **ācrius**, sup. **ācerrimē** (**ācer**, *sharp*), *sharply, fiercely*, 12, 12; 48, 18.

VOCABULARY. 201

Actiacus, adj. (**Actium,** *Actium*), of *Actium,* 68, 6.

Actium, -ī, N., *Actium,* a town and promontory of Epirus, 66, 16.

āctus, P. of **agō,** 59, 14.

ad, prep. with acc., *to:* of motion and direction, *to, towards,* 1, 11; 1, 13: of place, *at, beside, near,* 4, 22; 7, 8; 29, 13: of time, *till, until,* 30, 6: of purpose, *for, in order to,* 2, 5; 2, 20; 4, 21; 8, 24: *according to,* 5, 24; 51, 7: **ad postrēmum,** *finally,* 14, 8.

adāctus, P. of **adigō,** 19, 21.

adamō, 1, -āvī, -ātus (**ad,** *intensive;* **amō,** *love*), *fall in love with, desire eagerly,* 17, 25.

addīcō, 3, -dīxī, -dictus (**ad,** *to;* **dīcō,** *speak*), *award, adjudge, give assent,* 18, 17. In augural lang., *be propitious, favor,* 11, 10. (W. G. 26.)

addō, 3, -didī, -ditus [**ad,** *to;* 2 DA-, *put*], *put to, join, add,* 3, 7; 9, 4. (W. G. 25.)

addūcō, 3, -dūxī, -ductus (**ad,** *to;* **dūcō,** *lead*), *lead to, bring to,* 23, 19: *induce, persuade,* 21, 21: *draw, pull,* 24, 19. (W. G. 29.)

adēmptus, P. of **adimō,** 23, 16.

adeō, -īre, -iī, -itus (**ad,** *to;* **eō,** *go*), *go to, come to, draw near,* 15, 9: *enter on,* 63, 16. (W. G. 46.)

adeō, adv. (**ad,** *to;* **eō,** *thither, that point*), *thus far, to such a degree, so far,* 38, 12: *so, so much,* 9, 11; 16, 4: *so very,* 29, 29: *indeed,* 51, 4.

adfectō, 1, -āvī, -ātus (freq. of **adficiō,** *do to*), *strive after, pursue, aim at,* 22, 13. (W. G. 33.)

adferō, adferre, attulī, adlātus (**ad,** *to;* **ferō,** *bring*), *bring, fetch, carry,* 17, 21; 21, 23: **vim adferre,** *offer violence to,* 15, 2. (W. G. 34.)

adficiō, 3, -fēcī, -fectus (**ad,** *to;* **faciō,** *do*), *do to, treat,* 31, 21: *affect, afflict,* 51, 17. (W. G. 33.)

adfīnis, -e, adj. (**ad,** *near to;* **fīnis,** *end*), *adjoining.* As subst., M. and F., *relation* by marriage, 49, 6.

adfīrmō, 1, -āvī, -ātus (**ad,** intensive; **fīrmō,** *strengthen*), *strengthen; assert,* 4, 27.

adflīctus, adj. with comp. (P. of **adflīgō,** *throw down*), *cast down, miserable, wretched,* 39, 21; 71, 15.

adflīgō, 3, -īxī, -īctus (**ad,** *at;* **flīgō,** *strike*), *dash at, overthrow: damage, shatter,* 37, 11.

adflō, 1, -āvī, — (**ad,** *on;* **flō,** *blow*), *blow on: blow towards,* 37, 9.

adhibeō, 2, -uī, -itus (**ad,** *towards;* **habeō,** *hold*), *hold toward: summon, invite,* 56, 19: *consult,* 2, 17. (W. G. 45.)

adhortātiō, -ōnis, F. (**adhortor,** *encourage*), *encouragement, exhortation,* 51, 27.

adiciō, 3, -iēcī, -iectus (**ad,** *to;* **iaciō,** *throw*), *throw to: add,* 45, 22.

VOCABULARY.

adigō, 3, -ēgī, -āctus (ad, *to;* agō, *drive*), *drive, urge: bind by oath,* 19, 21. (W. G. 2.)

adimō, 3, -ēmī, -ēmptus (ad, *to oneself;* emō, *take*), *take away, deprive of,* 23, 16.

adipīscor, 3, adeptus, dep. (ad, *to;* apīscor, *reach*), *arrive, reach: get, obtain,* 11, 4; 41, 2.

aditus, -ūs, M. [ad, *to;* I-, *go*], *going to, approach, access,* 63, 19. (W. G. 46.)

adiūmentum, -ī, N. (for adiuvāmentum; adiuvō, *assist*), *means of helping, aid, assistance,* 46, 8. (W. G. 27.)

adiungō, 3, -ūnxī, -ūnctus (ad, *to;* iungō, *join*), *join to, add, annex,* 12, 21. (W. G. 48.)

adiuvō, 1, -iūvī, -iūtus (ad, without force; iuvō, *help*), *help, aid,* 35, 22. (W. G. 27.)

adlātus, P. of adferō, 68, 16.

adliciō, 3, -lexī, -lectus (ad, *to oneself;* laciō, *draw*), *allure, attract, persuade,* 14, 8.

adligō, 1, -āvī, -ātus (ad, *to;* ligō, *bind*), *bind to,* 62, 29.

adloquor, 3, -cūtus, dep. (ad, *to;* loquor, *speak*), *speak to, address,* 12, 16; 18, 19.

administrō, 1, -āvī, -ātus (ad, *upon;* ministrō, *attend*), *manage, control, rule, direct,* 11, 4.

admīrandus, adj. (P. of admīror), *to be wondered at, admirable, wonderful,* 47, 25.

admīrātiō, -ōnis, F. (admīror, *wonder at*), *admiration,* 8, 15.

admīror, 1, -ātus, dep. (ad, *at;* mīror, *regard with wonder*), *regard with wonder, admire,* 24, 14: *be astonished,* 28, 15.

admittō, 3, -mīsī, -mīssus (ad, *to;* mittō, *send*), *send to, let go: admit,* 70, 8. (W. G. 53.)

admodum, adv. (ad, *up to;* modus, *limit*), *to the proper limit: fully, very,* 28, 4.

admoneō, 2, -uī, -nitus (ad, *to;* moneō, *give warning*), *bring to mind, admonish, warn,* 48, 9. (W. G. 52.)

admoveō, 2, -mōvī, -mōtus (ad, *to;* moveō, *move*), *move to, move towards, bring near,* 28, 9; 32, 19. (W. G. 54.)

adolēscō, 3, -olēvī, -ultus (ad, *up;* olēscō, *grow*), *grow up, come to maturity,* 1, 16. (W. G. 56.)

adoperiō, 4, -eruī, -ertus (ad, *over;* operiō, *cover*), *cover, cover over,* 8, 18.

adoptō, 1, -āvī, -ātus (ad, *to oneself;* optō, *take by choice*), *take by choice, select, adopt,* 63, 12,

adōrnō, 1, -āvī, -ātus (ad, *for;* ōrnō, *prepare*), *provide, furnish, equip,* 5, 9.

adōrō, 1, -āvī, -ātus (ad, *to;* ōrō, *speak*), *entreat, implore, honor, worship,* 44, 24. (W. G. 57.)

adquīrō, 3, -quīsīvī, -quīsītus (ad, *besides;* quaerō, *ask*), *get in addition, obtain besides, acquire,* 13, 10.

adrīpiō, 3, -ipuī, -eptus (ad, to oneself; rapiō, snatch), snatch, grasp, seize, 18, 20. (W. G. 64.)

adsequor, -ī, -secūtus, dep. (ad, up to; sequor, follow), follow up, overtake, 39, 16.

adsīdō, 3, -ēdī, — (ad, upon; sīdō, sit), take a seat, sit down, 55, 12. (W. G. 67.)

adsum, adesse, adfuī (ad, at; sum, be), be at, be near, be present, 20, 16; 32, 1: assist, aid, 68, 3. (W. G. 31.)

adsūmō, 3, -sūmpsī, -sūmptus (ad, to oneself; sūmō, take), take to oneself, receive, 12, 13.

adsurgō, 3, -surrēxī, -surrēctus (ad, up; surgō, rise), rise up, rise, 43, 25. (W. G. 65.)

adulēscēns, -entis, adj. (P. of adolēscō, grow), growing, young. As subst., M. and F., a youth, 2, 6. (W. G. 56.)

adulēscentia, -ae, F. (adulēscēns, young), youth, 39, 24. (W. G. 56.)

adūlor, 1, -ātus, dep., fawn upon, flatter, 26, 30.

adultus, adj. (P. of adolēscō, grow), grown up, mature, 1, 16.

adveniō, 4, -vēnī, -ventus (ad, to; veniō, come), come to, arrive at, 18, 13: draw near, 10, 20; 31, 14. (W. G. 73.)

adventō, 1, —, — (intens. of adveniō), advance, press forward, approach, 61, 29. (W. G. 73.)

adventus, -ūs, M. [ad, to; VEN-, come], coming, approach, 20, 18: arrival, 34, 21. (W. G. 73.)

adversārius, adj. (adversus, opposed), opposite, hostile. As subst., M., an opponent, 58, 6. (W. G. 74.)

adversor, 1, -sātus, dep. (adversus, opposed), resist, withstand, oppose, 44, 6. (W. G. 74.)

adversus, adj. with sup. (P. of advertō, turn to), turned towards, in front, facing, 25, 19; 37, 9: unfavorable, 47, 7. (W. G. 74.)

adversus or **adversum**, adv. and prep. with acc. (ad, towards, against; vertō, turn) opposite: against, 3, 17; 8, 23. (W. G. 74.)

advocātiō, -ōnis, F. (advocō, summon), summoning as counsel: venīre in advocātiōnem, to act as counsel, 68, 8.

advocātus, -ī, M. (advocō, summon), one called to aid, adviser, advocate, 68, 4.

advocō, 1, -āvī, -ātus (ad, to; vocō, call), call, summon, 13, 17; 15, 2. (W. G. 77.)

aedificium, -ī, N. (aedificō, build), building, house, 64, 1. (W. G. 33.)

aedificō, 1, -āvī, -ātus [* aedifex, builder, fr. aedis, dwelling; FAC-, make], build, construct, 10, 11; 11, 6. (W. G. 33.)

aedīlis, -is, M. (aedis, dwelling), commissioner of buildings, aedile, 50, 18.

aedis or **aedēs**, -is, F. [AID-, *burn*, orig. *a hearth*], *dwelling of the gods, temple,* **4,** 9: in plur., *a house,* **5,** 16; **12,** 16.

Aegātēs, -um, F., *the Aegates islands* off the western coast of Sicily, near which the Romans won a great naval battle, 241 B.C., **32,** 10.

aeger, -gra, -grum, adj., *ill, sick, feeble,* **48,** 6.

aegrē, adv. comp. **aegrius**, sup. **aegerrimē**, *painfully, unwillingly,* **44,** 18.

aegritūdō, -dinis, F. (aeger, *sick*), *sickness, vexation,* **3,** 9.

aegrōtō, 1, -āvī, — (aegrōtus, *sick*), *be sick,* **47,** 26.

Aegyptus, -ī, F. *Egypt,* the country about the mouth of the Nile, **66,** 2.

Aemilius, -ī, M., name of a distinguished Roman gens; especially *L. Aemilius Paulus,* consul 216 B.C., **37,** 2.

aemulātiō, -ōnis, F. (aemulor, *rival*), *rivalry, emulation, competition,* **52,** 2.

aequālis, -e, adj. with comp. (aequus, *equal*), *equal, like, even.* As subst. M., *contemporary, comrade,* **59,** 28.

aequē, adv. with comp. and sup. (aequus, *equal*), *equally, in like manner, just as,* **46,** 23.

aequitās, -ātis, F. (aequus, *even*), *uniformity, evenness: fairness, kindness,* **9,** 18; **27,** 17.

aequō, 1, -āvī, -ātus (aequus, *equal*), *make equal, equalize,* **34,** 17.

aequus, adj., *even, level: favorable, kind, fair, reasonable, honorable,* **26,** 25: *undisturbed, calm,* **70,** 5.

aerārium, -ī, N. (aerārius, *of copper*), *part of the temple of Saturn at Rome, in which the public treasure was kept, the treasury,* **19,** 20.

aes, aeris, N. *copper, bronze, money:* **aes aliēnum**, *debt,* **50,** 23.

aestās, -ātis, F. [AID-, *burn*], *summer,* **70,** 22.

aestīvus, adj. (aestās, *summer*), *of summer, summer,* **47,** 27.

aetās, -ātis, F. (for **aevitās** fr. **aevum**, *age*), *life of man, age, old age, life, time of life,* **2,** 7; 15, 12; **38,** 22; **50,** 15.

Aetnaeus, adj., *Aetnaean, of Aetna,* **22,** 24.

Āfrica, -ae, F., *Libya, the Carthaginian territory;* sometimes used of the continent, **32,** 16.

Āfricānus, adj. *African,* **53,** 18. As subst. M. refers to *P. Cornelius Scipio Africanus,* the conqueror of Hannibal, **39,** 23.

ager, agrī, M. [AG-, *drive*], *field, farm, estate, pasture,* **34,** 6; **16,** 16: *territory,* **2,** 4; **9,** 20: *the open country,* **45,** 29.

aggredior, 3, -gressus, dep. (ad, *to;* gradior, *step*), *approach: fall upon, attack,* **32,** 11. (W. G. 44.)

agitō, 1, -āvī, -ātus (freq. of agō, *move*), *set in violent motion, move, urge*, 22, 2: *consider*, 11, 14. (W. G. 2.)

āgmen, -inis, N. [AG-, *drive, lead*], *that which is driven, multitude: army on the march, column*, 35, 17; 43, 9: *march*, 57, 2. (W. G. 2.)

āgnōscō (adgn-), 3, -nōvī, -nitus (ad, *to oneself;* (g)nōscō, *get knowledge of*), *recognize*, 2, 8. (W. G. 43.)

agō, 3, ēgī, āctus [AG-, *drive, lead*], *lead, drive*, 13, 6; 13, 25; 25, 12: *conduct*, 4, 18: *chase, pursue, aim at*, 32, 5: *act, do, perform, manage*, 6, 6: 25, 10; 54, 24: *discuss, speak, treat*, 6, 23: *pass, spend*, 69, 27: **grātiās agere**, *thank*, 29, 24: **nihil agis**, *it is of no use, you cannot succeed*, 48, 18: **āctum est**, *it is all over with, all is lost*, 59, 18. (W. G. 2.)

Agrippa, -ae, M., *Menenius Agrippa*, 16, 19.

āiō, v. defect., *say yes, assent, say*, 12, 16.

āla, -ae, F., *wing*, 21, 9.

alacer, -cris, -cre, adj. [1 AL-, *feed*], *well-fed; lively, quick, nimble*, 43, 19. (W. G. 3.)

Alba, -ae, F. (albus, *white*), *Alba* or *Alba Longa*, 'the long white city,' an ancient city of Latium, 2, 2.

Albānus, adj. (Alba), *Alban, of Alba*, 8, 20. As subst. M., *an inhabitant of Alba*, 1, 1; 6, 19.

albus, adj. *white*, 19, 25.

alea, -ae, F., *game with dice, die*, 52, 16.

Alexander, -drī, M., *Alexander the Great*, the Macedonian king and conqueror, 50, 13.

Alexandrēa, -ae, F., *Alexandria*, the capital of Egypt, founded by Alexander the Great 332 B.C., 66, 18.

aliās, adv. (alius, *other*), *at another time, some other time*, 16, 3; 66, 7. (W. G. 4.)

aliēnus, adj. with comp. and sup. (alius, *other*), *of another, foreign, strange*, 29, 10. (W. G. 4.)

aliquam, adv. [ALI-, *some or other*], *in some degree, somewhat:* **aliquamdiū**, *for a while, for some time*, 49, 8.

aliquamdiū, see aliquam.

aliquandō, adv. [ALI-, *some or other;* quandō, *when*], *at some time or other, once*, 46, 7; 49, 11: *at length, finally*, 68, 24. (W. G. 4.)

aliquantō, adv. (aliquantus, *some, a little*), *by some little, in a degree, somewhat*, 26, 13. (W. G. 4.)

aliquantum, -ī, N. (aliquantus, *some, a little*), *some, a considerable amount*, 7, 13.

aliquī, aliqua, aliquod, pron. adj. indef. [ALI-, *some or other;* quī, *who*], *some, any*, 12, 24; 48, 8.

aliquis, aliqua, aliquid, pron.

VOCABULARY.

subst. indef. [ALI-, *some or other;* quis, *who*], *some one, any one,* 39, 14. (W. G. 4.)

aliquot, indef. num. indecl. [ALI-, *other;* quot, *how many*], *some, several, a number,* 49, 28. (W. G. 4.)

aliquotiēns, adv. [ALI-, *other;* quotiēns, *how often*], *several times,* 61, 24.

aliter, adv. [ALI-, *other*], *in another manner, differently.* — With atque, āc, quam, or ut, *otherwise than,* 69, 22.

alius, -a, -ud, adj. pronoun [AL-, ALI-, *other*], *another, other, different,* 10, 14; 15, 17; 39, 9; 67, 14: alius ... alius, *one ... another,* 4, 7; 7, 7. (W. G. 4.)

Allia, -ae, F., river *Allia*, a small stream near Rome, made famous by the defeat of the Romans by the Gauls 390 B.C., 20, 12.

Alliēnsis, -e, adj. (Allia), *of the Allia,* 20, 14.

alō, 3, aluī, altus, or alitus [1 AL-, *feed*], *feed, support, sustain,* 5, 8. (W. G. 3.)

Alpēs, -ium, F., *the Alps,* 50, 2.

alter, -tera, -terum, gen. alterīus, dat. alterī, pronom. adj. [AL-, ALI-, *other*], *the second, the other,* 7, 18; 11, 29; 22, 1: alter ... alter, *one ... another, the one ... the other* (of two), 7, 21; 11, 26; 13, 11; 23, 10. (W. G. 4.)

altercor, 1, -ātus, dep. (alter, *another,* of two), *dispute, wrangle,* 45, 7. (W. G. 4.)

alteruter, -utra, -utrum, gen. alterutrīus, pronom. adj. [1 AL-, *other*], *one or the other, one of two,* 65, 24.

altum, -ī, N. (altus, *high*), *height, depth: the deep, the sea,* 52, 28. (W. G. 3.)

altus, adj. with comp. and sup. [P. of alō, *feed,* 1 AL-], *nourished: high, lofty,* 10, 25; 14, 13. (W. G. 3.)

alveus, -ī, M., *hollow, cavity: trough, boat,* 1, 7.

amāns, -antis, adj. with comp. and sup. (P. of amō, *love*), *fond, loving,* 67, 29.

ambiō, -īre, -īvī and -iī, -ītus (ambi-, *around;* eō, *go*), *go around, go about: entreat,* 28, 19. (W. G. 46.)

ambitiō, -ōnis, F. (ambiō, *go around*), *going about:* esp. of candidates for office, *the soliciting of votes: ambition,* 42, 16. (W. G. 46.)

ambō, ambae, ambō, num. adj., *both,* 11, 30; 37, 5.

ambulō, 1, -āvī, -ātus [am- (ambi-), *about;* BA-, *go*], *walk, take a walk,* 19, 3. (W. G. 73.)

amiciō, 4, —, -ictus (am- (ambi-), *about;* iaciō, *throw*), *throw around, wrap about: cover,* 22, 22. (W. G. 47.)

amīcitia, -ae, F. (amīcus, *friend*), *friendship, alliance,* 59, 28. (W. G. 5.)

VOCABULARY.

amīcus, adj. with comp. and sup. (amō, *love*), *loving, friendly, kind*, 49, 7. (W. G. 5.)

amīcus, -ī, M. (amīcus, *loving*), *loved one, friend*, 25, 22. (W. G. 5.)

āmittō, 3, -īsī, -issus (ab, *away;* mittō, *send*), *send away: lose*, 16, 10. (W. G. 53.)

amnis, -is, M., *river*, 63, 22.

amor, -ōris, M. (amō, *love*), *love*, 8, 3. (W. G. 5.)

amphora, -ae, F. (Gr., ἀμφορεύς), *amphora*, large oblong vessel for liquids, with a handle on each side, *wine-jar*, 42, 21 (v. notes fig. 23, p. 120).

amplector, 3, -exus, dep. (am-, *on both sides, around;* plectō, *weave*), *twine around, embrace*, 8, 11: *surround*, 12, 5. (W. G. 60.)

ampliō, 1, -āvī, -ātus (amplus, *large*), *widen, extend, enlarge*, 54, 14.

amplius, indecl. adj. and adv. (comp. of amplus and amplē), *more*, 55, 2.

amplus, adj. with comp. and sup. [am- (ambi-), *around;* PLE-, PLV-, *fill*], *large extent, great, ample*, 32, 4.

amputō, 1, -āvī, -ātus [am- (ambi-), *around, off;* putō, *cut*], *cut around, cut away, cut off*, 45, 2.

Amūlius, -ī, M., *Amulius*, son of Proca, king of Alba, grandfather of Romulus and Remus, 1, 1.

anceps, -cipitis, adj. [an- (ambi-) *on both sides;* CAP-, in caput, *head*], *two-headed: double: doubtful, hazardous, uncertain*, 31, 14. (W. G. 17.)

ancīle, -is, N., *small oval shield*, the *sacred shield* that fell from heaven during the reign of Numa, 5, 18 (v. notes, fig. 2, p. 82).

ancilla, -ae, F., *maid-servant, handmaid*, 14, 25.

Ancus, -ī, M., *Ancus Marcius*, the fourth king of Rome, 9, 16.

angor, -ōris, M., *strangling: anguish*, 62, 11.

angustia, -ae (sing. very rare); and **angustiae**, -ārum, F., (angustus, *narrow*), *narrowness*, 2, 21: *narrow pass, defile*, 34, 3: *difficulty*, 33, 26.

anima, -ae, F. [AN-, *breathe;* cf. animus], *air: breath: life*, 60, 7. (W. G. 6.)

animadvertō, 3, -tī, -sus (animus, *attention;* advertō, *turn to*), *give attention to, attend to, consider, observe*, 1, 14; 50, 12: *censure, inflict punishment, punish*, 42, 3; 44, 5.

animal, -ālis, N. [AN-, *breathe*], *living being, animal*, 21, 6. (W. G. 6.)

animus, -ī, M. [AN-, *breathe;* cf. anima], *rational soul: intellect, mind*, 27, 7: *heart, feeling, nature, disposition*, 2, 11; 13, 12; 26, 9: *courage, spirit*, 7, 3; 9, 20; 33, 4: *movēre animum, arouse anger*, 7, 30. (W. G. 6.)

VOCABULARY.

annālis, -is, M. (annālis, *of a year;* sc. liber, *book*), *record of events, annals*, 15, 7.

annōna, -ae, F. (annus, *year*), *year's produce*, 58, 18.

annus, -ī, M., *year*, 5, 24.

ānser, -eris, M., *goose*, 21, 7.

ante, adv. and prep. with acc.: adv., *before*, 8, 12: followed by quam, *sooner than, before*, 53, 13: prep. *before*, 53, 26.

anteā, adv. (ante, *before;* ea, *these things*), *before, previously*, 41, 26.

antecēdō, 3, -cessī, — (ante, *before;* cēdō, *go*), *go before, precede*, 36, 12.

anteeō, -īre, -īvī or iī, — (ante, *before;* eō, *go*), *go before, precede*, 57, 3.

antequam, see ante, 71, 4.

Antiochus, -ī, M., *Antiochus*, a philosopher, Cicero's teacher at Athens, 79 B.C., 58, 10.

antīquus, adj. with comp. and sup. (ante, *before*), *ancient*, 15, 7.

Antōnius, -ī, M., *C. Antonius Hybrida*, Cicero's colleague in his consulship, 63 B.C., 59, 19. *Marcus Antonius*, Mark Antony, one of the second Triumvirate, 43 B.C., 61, 18.

ānulus, -ī, M., *ring, finger-ring*, 3, 24 (v. notes, fig. 19, p. 115).

anus, -ūs, F., *old woman*, 15, 8; 45, 10.

anxius, adj. (cf. angustus), *anxious, troubled*, 2, 11; 17, 19.

aper, aprī, M., *wild boar*, 35, 13.

aperiō, 4, -eruī, -ertus, *open, uncover*, 3, 8; 35, 9; 43, 26: *disclose, reveal*, 27, 1.

apertē, adv. with comp. and sup. (apertus, *uncovered*), *openly, manifestly*, 41, 17.

apertus, adj. with comp. and sup. (P. of aperiō, *uncover*), *uncovered, open*, 6, 1.

Apollōnia, -ae, F., *Apollonia*, an important town in Illyria, 63, 13.

Apollōnius, -ī, M., *Apollonius Molon*, a celebrated rhetorician of Rhodes, 49, 16.

appāreō (adp-), 2, -uī, -itūrus (ad, *to;* pāreō, *be at hand*), *appear, be evident, be apparent*, 23, 14.

appāritor (adp-), -ōris, M. (appāreō, *appear*), *servant, lictor*, 24, 17.

appellātiō (adp-), -ōnis, F. (appellō, *address*), *addressing, name*, 67, 18.

appellō (adp-), 1, -āvī, -ātus [ad, *to;* PEL-, *drive*], *address: call by name, term, name*, 5, 2. (W. G. 59.)

Appennīnus, adj. (sc. mōns), *the Apennines*, the range of mountains running through Italy, 54, 20.

Appius, -ī, M., *Appius*, a Roman praenomen especially common in the Claudian gens, 17, 24; 27, 19.

applaudō (adp-), 3, -sī, -sus (ad, *upon;* plaudō, *strike*), *strike upon, applaud*, 71, 21.

applicō (adp-), 1, -āvī or uī, -ātus (ad, *to;* plicō, *fasten*), *join, connect: apply, direct.*

appōnō (adp-), 3, -posuī, -positus (ad, *near;* pōnō, *put*), *put at, place by, set before,* 15, 13; 66, 8.

apprehendō (adp-), 3, -dī, -hēnsus (ad, *upon;* prehendō, *lay hold*), *seize, take hold of,* 30, 21.

approbō (adp-), 1, -āvī, -ātus (ad, *for;* probō, *test as good*), *assent to, favor,* 22, 10: *make evident, prove,* 38, 22.

appropinquō (adp-), 1, -āvī, -ātus (ad, *to;* propinquō, *draw near*), *come near, approach,* 3, 18; 35, 11.

Appulēius, -ī, M., *L. Appuleius,* tribune of the plebs 391 B.C., 19, 27.

aptē, adv. with sup. (aptus, *fitted*), *closely fitting: suitably, rightly,* 10, 22.

aptus, adj. *fitted: fit, suitable,* 36, 23.

apud, prep. with acc., *with,* 14, 20: *at,* 33, 7: *by, near,* 20, 12: *in the presence of, before,* 8, 7: *among,* 6, 21; 14, 8: *at the house of,* 47, 28: *in the works of,* 55, 26.

Apūlia, -ae, F., *Apulia,* a country in southeastern Italy, 23, 7.

aqua, -ae, F., *water,* 1, 9.

aquila, -ae, F., *eagle,* 10, 20: *standard of a legion,* 64, 9 (v. notes, fig. 6).

aquilifer, -ferī, M. [aquila, *eagle;* FER-, *carry*], *eagle bearer, standard bearer,* 51, 23 (v. notes, fig. 12).

āra, -ae, F., *altar,* 5, 7; 32, 19.

arbiter, -trī, M. [ad, *to;* BA-, *go*], *spectator, hearer, witness,* 6, 8. (W. G. 73.)

arbitrium, -ī, N. (arbiter, *judge*), *judgment, decision: authority, power,* 51, 7: ad arbitrium, *according to one's pleasure,* 51, 7. (W. G. 73.)

arbitror, 1, -ātus, dep. (arbiter, *judge*), *testify, depose: believe, think,* 66, 6. (W. G. 73.)

arceō, 2, -cuī, — [ARC-, *make secure*], *shut up, enclose: keep away,* 1, 18. (W. G. 9.)

arcessō, 3, -īvī, -ītus (intens. of accēdō, *come to*), *cause to come, call, send for, invite,* 8, 24; 26, 14.

Ardea, -ae, F., *Ardea,* an ancient town of Latium, 14, 18.

ārdor, -ōris, M. [2 AR-, *burn*], *burning, fire: ardor, enthusiasm, zeal,* 38, 12. (W. G. 8.)

argenteus, adj. (argentum, *silver*), *silver, made of silver,* 29, 11.

argentum, -ī, N., *silver, silver-plate,* 29, 28.

Argos, N. (only nom. and acc.), usually in the form Argī, -ōrum, M., *Argos,* the capital of Argolis, a district in northeastern Peloponnesus, 30, 16.

āridus, adj. [2 AR-, *dry*], *dry, arid, parched,* 33, 27. (W. G. 8.)

arma, -ōrum, N. [1 AR-, *fit*], *implements, instruments: arms,* *weapons*, 4, 9; 7, 2; 19, 16. (W. G. 7.)

armātus, adj. with sup. (P. of armō, *arm*), *armed, equipped in arms*, 16, 13; 24, 2. As subst. M., *armed men, soldiers*, 19, 10; 25, 14.

Armenia, -ae, F., *Armenia*, 46, 19.

armilla, -ae, F. (armus, *shoulder, arm*), *bracelet, armlet*, 3, 24.

armō, 1, -āvī, -ātus [1 AR-, *fit*], *fit with weapons, arm*, 2, 2. (W. G. 7.)

Arpīnum, -ī, N., *Arpinum*, Cicero's birthplace, about fifty miles southeast of Rome, 57, 8.

ars, artis, F. [1 AR-, *fit*], *practical skill, art*, 11, 11: *learning, studies, accomplishments*, 39, 24: *cunning, stratagem*, 36, 4. (W. G. 7.)

artūs, -uum, M. plur. [1 AR-, *join*], *joints*, 48, 7. (W. G. 7.)

arx, arcis, F. [ARC-, *shut in*], *castle, citadel, fortress*, 3, 20; 20, 18. (W. G. 9.)

ās, assis, M. *one, unity: as*, the unit of money, originally one pound of copper, but gradually reduced to half an ounce, with a value of a little less than one cent, 42, 17.

ascendō (adsc-), 3, -scendī, -scēnsus (ad-, *up to ;* scandō, *climb*), *mount, climb, ascend*, 21, 14.

Asia, -ae, F., *Asia*, usually applies to Asia Minor, sometimes to the continent, 12, 26.

asper, -era, -erum, adj. (ab, *without; spēs, hope*), *without hope: adverse, hostile, cruel*, 56, 20.

asperitās, -ātis, F. (asper, *rough*), *unevenness, roughness: sharpness*, 66, 11.

āspernor, 1, -ātus, dep. (ab, *from;* spernor, *remove*), *disdain, reject, despise*, 55, 27.

aspiciō, (adsp-), 3, -ēxī, -ectus (ad, *at;* speciō, *look*), *look at, look upon: examine, observe*, 43, 24. (W. G. 68.)

aspis, -idis, F., *asp, viper*, 66, 24.

astūtia, -ae, F. (astūtus, *adroit*), *adroitness, shrewdness*, 31, 9.

asȳlum, -ī, N. (Gr., ἄσυλον, *place of refuge*), *place of refuge, asylum*, 3, 8.

at, conj., *but, on the other hand*, 2, 6; 17, 3: *on the contrary*, 32, 8.

Athēnae, -ārum, F., *Athens*, the famous Grecian city, the capital of Attica, 29, 4.

atque or (before consonants) **ăc**, conj. (ad, *in addition to ;* -que, *and*), *and, and what is more, as well as, together with*, 5, 17; 11, 2; 15, 20; 28, 6: with words implying comparison, *as, than*, 12, 7.

atquī, conj., *but somehow, but yet, however, and yet*, 11, 13.

atrōciter, adv. with comp. and sup. (atrōx, *savage*), *fiercely, cruelly*, 60, 5.

atrōx, -ōcis, adj. with comp. and sup., *savage, fierce, wild, cruel*, 8, 6; 53, 24.

attentus (adt-), adj. with comp. and sup. (P. of **attendō,** *attend to*), *attentive, intent,* 15, 20. (W. G. 71.)

attonitus (adt-), adj. (P. of **attonō,** *thunder at*), *thunderstruck, stunned: astounded,* 34, 1.

Attus, -ī, M., praenomen of *Attus Navius,* see **Nāvius,** 11, 9.

auctor, -ōris, M. [AVG-, *grow*], *promoter, producer: author, cause,* 29, 23. (W. G. 13.)

auctōritās, -ātis, F. (auctor, *author*), *origination: authority,* 11, 9. (W. G. 13.)

(auctus), adj. (P. of **augeō,** *increase*), *abundant, ample,* 9, 6.

aucupium, -ī, N. [**auceps,** *bird-catcher*: fr. **avis,** *bird*; CAP-, *take*], *bird catching, fowling,* 69, 29. (W. G. 12.)

audācia, -ae, F. (**audāx,** *bold*), *daring, courage, valor, boldness,* 16, 12 ; *audacity, presumption, insolence,* 10, 11 ; 39, 20. (W. G. 10.)

audeō, 2, ausus [for avideō, 1. AV-, *mark, desire*], *venture, dare,* 4, 11; 44, 23. (W. G. 10.)

audiō, 4, -īvī or -iī, -ītus [2 AV-, *mark; notice*], *hear,* 3, 7 : *assent to,* 12, 18. (W. G. 11.)

audītus, P. of audiō, 22, 6.

auferō, auferre, abstulī, ablātus (ab, *away;* ferō, *carry*), *take away, bear off, remove, carry away,* 4, 24 ; 5, 19 ; 21, 26. (W. G. 34.)

aufugiō, 3, -fūgī, — (ab, *away;* fugiō, *flee*), *flee away, run away,* 7, 14. (W. G. 40.)

augeō, 2, auxī, auctus [AVG-, *increase*], *increase, augment, spread,* 6, 15; 34, 12. (W. G. 13.)

augur, -uris, M. and F., *seer, augur,* 11, 10. (W. G. 12.)

augurium, -ī, M. (augur, *augur*), *observance of omens, divination, augury,* 2, 19: augurium agere, *to try the omens,* 11, 13. (W. G. 12.)

Augustus, -ī, M., *Augustus,* the cognomen given to Octavius Caesar as emperor, 67, 8.

augustus, adj. with comp. and sup. (augeō, *increase*), *consecrated: majestic, noble,* 4, 28.

aulaeum, -ī, N., *curtain,* 28, 10.

Aulus -ī, M., *Aulus,* a Roman praenomen, 59, 26.

aureus, adj. (aurum, *gold*), *of gold, golden,* 37, 26.

auris, -is, F. [2 AV-, *mark, notice*], *ear,* 26, 18. (W. G. 11.)

aurum, -ī, N., *gold,* 21, 21.

auspicium, -ī, N. [**auspex,** *augur;* **avis,** *bird;* SPEC-, *see*], *divination by the flight of birds, augury from birds,* 2, 17. (W. G. 12 and 68.)

ausus, P. of audeō, 44, 23.

aut, conj., *or:* aut . . . aut, *either . . . or,* 23, 25 ; 32, 13.

autem, conj. adversative, postpositive, *but, on the other hand, however,* 29, 16 ; 31, 8 : *more-*

over, in addition, **5,** 20: introductory, *now,* **9,** 23.
auxilium, -ī, N. [AVG-, *grow*], *help, assistance, support,* **8,** 24; **20,** 6: plur. *auxiliary troops,* **53,** 21. (W. G. 13.)
avāritia, -ae, F. (avārus, *covetous*), *inordinate desire, greed, avarice,* **42,** 25. (W. G. 10.)
avārus, adj. with comp. and sup. [1 AV-, *delight, desire*], *grasping, eager, covetous,* **29,** 20. (W. G. 10.)
Aventīnus, -ī, M. (sc. mōns), *the Aventine,* the most southern of the seven hills of Rome, **13,** 1.
Aventīnus, adj., *of the Aventine, on the Aventine,* **13,** 1.
aveō, **2,** —, —, defective; imper. avē, *hail,* in salutation, **68,** 11.
Avernus, adj. (with or without lacus), *Avernus,* a lake near Cumae, **22,** 22.

āvertō, **3,** -tī, -sus (ab, *away;* vertō, *turn*), *turn away, avert,* **11,** 29; **29,** 2; **31,** 9. (W. G. 74.)
avidus, adj. with comp. and sup. [1 AV-, *mark, delight*], *longing eagerly, desirous, eager,* **50,** 6. (W. G. 10.)
avis, -is, F., [3 AV-, *blow, waft*], *bird,* **21,** 8: *omen,* **11,** 10. (W. G. 12.)
āvocō, **1,** -āvī, -ātus (ā, *away;* vocō, *call*), *call off, call away,* **60,** 16. (W. G. 77.)
āvolō, **1,** -āvī, -ātūrus (ā, *away;* volō, *fly*), *fly away: hasten away,* **14,** 23.
avunculus, -ī, M. (dim. of avus), *maternal uncle, uncle,* **63,** 11.
avus, -ī, M. [1 AV-, *mark, delight*], *grandfather, ancestor,* **2,** 1; **57,** 9.

B

baculum, -ī, N. [BA-, *go*], *stick, staff, walking-stick,* **14,** 13.
Bāiae, -ārum, F., *Baiae,* a favorite watering-place of the Romans on the coast of Campania, **22,** 21.
barba, -ae, F., *beard,* **20,** 27.
barbarus, adj. with comp. (Gr., βάρβαρος), *of strange speech: barbarous, savage.* As subst., *the barbarian,* **45,** 5.
bellicōsus, adj. with comp. and sup. (bellicus, *of war*), *warlike, given to fighting,* **9,** 9. (W. G. 28.)
bellō, **1,** -āvī, -ātus (bellum, *war*), *wage war, carry on war,* **52,** 10. (W. G. 28.)
bellum, -ī, N. [old dvellum, DVA-, *apart, two*], *war, conflict,* **3,** 16. (W. G. 28.)
bēlua, -ae, F., *beast, wild beast, monster,* **25,** 15.
bene, adv. with comp. melius,

VOCABULARY. 213

sub. optimē (bonus, *good*), *well*, 22, 8; 67, 23: *successfully*, 33, 20.

beneficium, -ī, N. [bene, *well*; FAC-, *do*], *favor, benefit, kindness, service*, 23, 26. (W. G. 33.)

benevolentia, -ae, F. (benevolus, *friendly*), *good-will, kindness, friendship*, 14, 7. (W. G. 79.)

benīgnē, adv. with comp. and sup. (benignus, *kind*), *in a friendly manner, kindly, courteously*, 14, 6. (W. G. 41.)

benīgnus, adj. [bene, *well*; GEN-, *born*], *well born: kind, pleasing, friendly*, 46, 22. (W. G. 41.)

bibliothēca, -ae, F. (Gr., βιβλιοθήκη), *library, room for books*, 54, 17.

bibō, 3, bibī, —, *drink*, 43, 4.

Bibulus, -ī, M., *L. Calpurnius Bibulus*, consul with Julius Caesar, 59 B.C., 50, 25.

bīduum, -ī, N. (bi-, *two*; diēs, *days*), *period of two days, two days*, 46, 30. (W. G. 27.)

bīnī, -ae, -a, num. distr. [DVI-, *two*], *two by two, two to each*, 27, 27. (W. G. 28.)

bis, adv. num. [DVI-, *two*], *twice*, 59, 2. (W. G. 28.)

blanditia, -ae, F. (blandus, *bland*), *caressing, flattery*, 14, 7.

Blosius, -ī, M., *C. Blosius Cumanus*, a philosopher and friend of Tiberius Gracchus, 42, 3.

bona, -ōrum, N. (bonus, *good*), *goods, property*, 41, 15.

bonus, adj., comp. melior, sup. optimus, *good, morally good*, 23, 9; 28, 18: *brave*, 29, 21. As subst., bonī, M., *the better classes, the aristocracy*, 41, 8.

bōs, bovis, M. and F. (Gr., βοῦς), *ox, bull, cow*, 13, 2.

bracchium, -ī, N. (Gr., βραχίων), *fore-arm, lower arm*, 55, 17.

brevī, adv. (abl. of brevis, *short*), *in a little while, soon*, 45, 27.

brevis, -e, adj. with comp. and sup., *short, brief*, 32, 12.

Britannī, -ōrum, M., *the inhabitants of Britain*, 51, 18.

Brundisium, -ī, N., *Brundisium*, a sea-port in Calabria, in southern Italy, 52, 17.

Brūtus, -ī, M., *Brutus*, a surname of the Junian gens. Mention is made of: 1. *M. Junius Brutus*, who conspired against Caesar, 55, 2; 2. *D. Junius Brutus Albinus*, killed by Antony, 43 B.C., 63, 17.

bulla, -ae, F., *bubble: the bulla*, an amulet worn by free-born children, 11, 18 (v. notes, fig. 5, p. 88).

C

C., abbreviation for *Gaius*, a Roman praenomen, 28, 2.

cadāver, -ēris, N. [CAD-, *fall*],*dead body, corpse, carcass*, 60, 8. (W. G. 14.)

cadō, 3, cecidī, cāsūrus [CAD-,

fall], *fall*, **7, 7**: *die, be slain,* **4, 4**. (W. G. 14.)

caecitās, -ātis, F. (**caecus**, *blind*), *blindness*, **27, 20**.

caedēs, -is, F. [for *scaedēs, SCID-, *split, cut*], *cutting down: killing, murder, slaughter*, **8, 16; 20, 29**. (W. G. 66.)

caedō, 3, cecīdī, caesus [for **scaedō**, SCID-, *split, cut*], *cut, hew: kill*, **8, 10**: *vanquish, cut to pieces, destroy*, **20, 12; 37, 10**. (W. G. 66.)

caelestis, -e, adj. (**caelum**, *sky*), *from heaven, of the heavens, heavenly*, **10, 23**.

Caelius, -ī, M. (sc. mōns), *the Caelian hill*, one of the hills of Rome, **9, 4**.

caelum, -ī, N., *sky, heaven, heavens*, **4, 9**: *air, climate*, **22, 18**.

Caesar, -aris, M., *Caesar*, a family name of the famous Julian gens., e.g., *C. Julius Caesar*, the great dictator, **47, 10**.

Cāiēta, -ae, F., *Caieta*, a town and harbor in Latium, **22, 21**.

calamitās, -ātis, F., *loss, injury, misfortune, calamity, disaster*, **61, 14**.

callidus, adj. with comp. and sup., *practised, expert: crafty, cunning*, **13, 7**.

Calpurnia, -ae, F., *Calpurnia*, wife of Julius Caesar, **55, 5**.

calvitium, -ī, N. (**calvus**, *bald*), *baldness, a bald spot*, **56, 23**.

Calvus, -ī, M., *C. Licinius Macer Calvus*, an orator and poet, who lampooned Julius Caesar, **56, 17**.

calvus, adj., *bald, hairless*, **56, 23**.

Camillus, -ī, M., *Camillus*, family name of the Furian gens, referring especially to *M. Furius Camillus*, the conqueror of Veii, **19, 1**.

Campānī, -ōrum, M., *the inhabitants of Campania*.

Campānia, -ae, F., *Campania*, a district of Italy, **22, 17**.

Campānus, adj., *Campanian, belonging to Campania*, **40, 4**: as subst., *a Campanian*, **22, 16**.

campus, -ī, M., *plain, field*, **4, 22**.

Canīnius, -ī, M., gentile name of *C. Caninius Rebilus*, consul for a few hours in 45 B.C., **63, 3**.

canis, -is, M. and F. [CAV-, *watch*], *dog*, **21, 5**.

Cannae, -ārum, F., *Cannae*, town in Apulia, where Hannibal defeated the Romans in 216 B.C., **37, 5**.

canō, 3, cecinī — [CAN-, *make a musical sound*], *make music, sing*, **5, 23**: **receptuī canere**, *to sound a retreat*, **34, 21**.

cantus, -ūs, M. [CAN-, *make music*], *singing, song: note*, **69, 27**.

capessō, 3, -īvī or -iī, -ītūrus (desid. of **capiō**, *take*), *seize eagerly, lay hold of: strive to reach, resort to, betake oneself to*, **7, 12**.

capillus, -ī, M. (**caput**, *head*), *hair of the head, hair*, **38, 23**.

capiō, 3, cēpī, captus [CAP-, *take*],

take in hand, take up, seize, **6,**
26: *take captive,* **1, 20:** *capture,
occupy, take possession of,* **9, 5;
16, 3:** *suffer, be subjected to,* **41,
20:** *receive,* **50, 22.** (W. G. 17.)

Capitōlīnus, adj., *of the Capitol,
Capitoline,* **40, 28.**

Capitōlium, -ī, N. (caput, *head*),
*the Capitol, temple of Jupiter at
Rome, the hill on which the
Capitol stood,* **3, 22; 21, 19.**

capra, -ae, F., *she-goat :* **Caprae
palūs,** *the Goat's Pool,* the place
in the Campus Martius where
Romulus disappeared, **4, 22.**

captīvus, adj. [CAP-, *take*], *taken
prisoner, captive,* **25, 18.** As
subst. M. and F., *a captive,* **12, 2.**
(W. G. 17.)

captō, 1, -āvī, -ātus (freq. of
capiō), *strive to seize, catch at :
watch for,* **50, 16.** (W. G. 17.)

Capua, -ae, F., *Capua,* a large and
wealthy city of Campania, **22,
26.**

capulus, -ī, M. (capiō, *take*), *that
which is grasped, handle, hilt,*
64, 15 (v. notes, fig. 29).

caput, -itis, N. [CAP-, *take*], *head,*
8, 18: *life,* **28, 27:** *capital,* **22,
26:** *extremity, top,* **14, 13.** (W.
G. 17.)

Carbō, -ōnis, M., family name of
C. Papirius Carbo, **43, 29.**

carcer, -eris, M., *prison, jail,* **10,
10** (v. notes, fig. 4).

carnifex, -ficis, M. [carō, *flesh ;*
FAC-, *make*], *executioner, hangman,* **70, 17.** (W. G. 33.)

carpentum, -ī, N., *carriage, chariot,* **10, 20; 13, 20** (v. notes,
fig. 7, p. 90).

Carthāginiēnsis, -e, adj., *of Carthage, Carthaginian.* As subst.
M., *a Carthaginian,* **32, 12.**

Carthāgō, -inis, F., *Carthage,* a
great city in northern Africa,
22, 27.

cārus, adj. with comp. and sup.
dear, precious, beloved, **17, 14.**

casa, -ae, F., *small house, cottage,
hut,* **1, 15.**

Casca, -ae, M., *C. Servilius Casca,*
one of Caesar's assassins, **55,
16.**

Cassius, -ī, M., gentile name of *C.
Cassius Longinus.* See **Longinus, 55, 2.**

castīgō, 1, -āvī, -ātus [castus,
pure ; AG-, *drive*], *set right,
correct, punish,* **45, 11.**

castrum, -ī, N., *fortified place, castle, fort :* plur. **castra, -ōrum,
N.,** *military camp,* **14, 19.**

cāsus, -ūs, M. [CAD-, *fall*], *fall,*
7, 8 : *misfortune, calamity, fate,
destruction,* **56, 4.** (W. G. 14.)

catēna, -ae, F., *chain, fetter,* **59, 4.**

Catilīna, -ae, M., family name of
L. Sergius Catiline, who made
a dangerous conspiracy against
the Roman government in 63
B.C., **58, 25.**

Catō, -ōnis, M. (catus, *sagacious*),
name of a famous family of the
Porcian gens, e.g., *M. Porcius
Cato Uticensis,* **56, 29.**

Catullus, -i, M., family name of

C. Valerius Catullus, one of the greatest lyric poets of Rome, 56, 18.

catulus, -ī, M. (dim. of **catus,** *cat*), *young animal, whelp, puppy, cub,* 1, 13.

Catulus, -ī, M., family name of Q. *Lutatius Catulus,* political opponent of Pompey, 45, 19. See also **Lutātius,** 31, 22.

Caudīnus, adj., *of Caudium.* **Furculae Caudīnae,** the Caudine Forks, 23, 13.

causa, -ae, F. [CAV-, *watch*], *cause, reason, motive, occasion,* 3, 16; 47, 3: *excuse, pretext,* 32, 21: *lawsuit, case,* 8, 15: *situation, condition,* 13, 6 : abl. **causā** with preceding gen., *for the purpose of, on account of,* 18, 4 ; 41, 4. (W. G. 18.)

cautus, adj. with comp. and sup. (P. of **caveō,** *take care*), *careful, wary, cautious,* 34, 11. (W. G. 18.)

caveō, 2, cāvī, cautus [CAV-, *watch*], *be on one's guard, take care, beware,* 37, 17. (W. G. 18.)

cēdō, 3, cessī, cessus [CAD-, *fall*], *withdraw, retire,* 60, 28 : *submit to, yield,* 52, 30. (W. G. 14.)

celeber, -bris, -bre, adj. with sup. [CEL-, *drive*], *frequented, thronged: renowned, famous,* 57, 15. (W. G. 19.)

celer, -eris, -ere, adj. with comp. and sup. [CEL-, *drive*], *swift, fleet, quick,* 3, 27; 45, 30. (W. G. 19.)

celeritās, -ātis, F. (**celer,** *swift*), *swiftness, speed, quickness,* 36, 27. (W. G. 19.)

celeriter, adv. with comp. and sup. (**celer,** *swift*), *quickly, swiftly, immediately,* 30, 25.

cēlō, 1, -āvī, -ātus, *hide from, conceal, keep secret,* 12, 15.

cēna, -ae, F., *dinner, principal meal,* 55, 30.

cēnō, 1, -āvī, -ātus, (**cēna,** *dinner*), *dine, take a meal,* 14, 20: *eat,* 29, 13.

cēnseō, 2, cēnsuī, cēnsus, *tax, estimate: resolve, decree, decide,* 39, 11.

cēnsor, -ōris, M. (cf. **cēnseō,** *estimate*), *censor,* a Roman magistrate, 29, 27.

cēnsus, -ūs, M. (**cēnseō,** *estimate*), *registering of citizens and property by the censors, census,* 12, 22.

centiēns, num. adv. (**centum,** *hundred*), *hundred times,* 66, 4.

centum, num. adj. indecl., *hundred,* 4, 17.

centuria, -ae, F. (**centum,** *hundred*), *division of a hundred, century,* 4, 19.

centuriō, -ōnis, M. (**centuria,** *century*), *commander of a century, captain, centurion,* 22, 6.

Cerēs, -eris, F., *Ceres,* daughter of Saturn, *goddess of agriculture,* 22, 19.

cernō, 3, crēvī, crētus [CER-, CRE-, *part*], *separate, part: distinguish, see, perceive,* 17, 1. (W. G. 20.)

certāmen, -inis (certō, *contend*), *decisive contest, struggle, battle*, **4**, 1: *contest, match*, 1, 17. (W. G. 20.)

certātim, adv. (certō, *struggle*), *in rivalry, zealously, eagerly*, 11, 26. (W. G. 20.)

certē, adv. with comp. (certus, *assured*), *really, surely, certainly*, 36, 7. (W. G. 20.)

certō, 1, -āvī, -ātus (certus, *assured*), *match, fight: combat, compete, vie*, 43, 20. (W. G. 20.)

certus, adj. with comp. and sup. (P. of cernō), *settled, certain: sure, true, definite, fixed, specified, trustworthy*, 5, 13; 32, 16: with faciō, *informed, assured*, 63, 19. (W. G. 20.)

cervīx, -īcis, F., *neck*, 62, 2.

cessō, 1, -āvī, -ātus (freq. of cēdō, *go away*), *delay, cease from, stop: do nothing, be idle, rest*, 38, 4; 40, 23.

cēterum, adv. (acc. N. sing. of cēterus, *the other*), *for the rest: but*, 17, 23.

(cēterus), adj., *other, remainder*, 35, 15. As subst. M., *the others, all the rest*, 14, 26.

charta, -ae, F., *leaf of the Egyptian papyrus, paper*, 69, 4.

Chrȳsogonus, -ī, M., *L. Cornelius Chrysogonus*, a freedman of Sulla, 58, 5.

cibus, -ī, M., *food, victuals*, 17, 2.

cicātrīx, -īcis, F., *scar, cicatrice*, 68, 7.

cicer, -eris, N., *chick-pea*, 57, 10.

Cicerō, -ōnis, M. (cicer, *chick-pea*), a Roman family name of the Tullian gens, especially *M. Tullius Cicero*, the renowned orator, 106–43 B.C., 56, 13.

Cīneās, -ae, M., *Cineas*, the friend of King Pyrrhus of Epirus, 26, 25.

cingō, 3, -xī, -īnctus, *go around, surround: beset, besiege*, 35, 21.

Cinna, -ae, M., *L. Cornelius Cinna*, consul 86–84 B.C., 48, 23.

circā, adv. and prep., a later form for circum, 6, 1. (W. G. 23.)

circum, adv., and prep. with acc. (acc. of circus), *around, round about, all around*, 6, 1: *near, among*, 3, 5. (W. G. 23.)

circumarō, 1, -āvī, — (circum, *around;* arō, *plough*), *plough around*, 16, 17.

circumdō, 1, -dedī, -datus [circum, *around;* 2 DA-, *put*], *place around, cause to surround: enclose, surround*, 10, 12; 43, 6. (W. G. 25.)

circumeō, -īre, -īvī or -iī, circumitus (circum, *around;* eō, *go*), *go around: visit*, 27, 13. (W. G. 46.)

circumfundō, 3, -fūdī, -fūsus (circum, *around;* fundō, *pour*), *pour around: surround*: pass. *crowd around*, 22, 9.

circumstō, 1, -stetī, — (circum, *around;* stō, *stand*), *stand around*, 24, 2: *surround*, 7, 10. (W. G. 69.)

circumveniō, 4, -vēnī, -ventus (circum, *around;* veniō, *come*), *come around, encircle, surround,* 8, 27. (W. G. 73.)

circus, -ī, M. [CVR-, *curve*], *circle, race-course, circus,* 11, 5. (W. G. 23.)

citātus, adj. with comp. and sup. (P. of citō, *rouse*), *quick, rapid, in haste, at full speed,* 14, 23.

cīvicus, adj. (cīvis, *citizen*), *of citizens, civil, civic,* 49, 15.

cīvīlis, -e, adj. with comp. (cīvis, *citizen*), *of citizens, civil, civic,* 42, 23.

cīvis, -is, M. and F. [CI-, *rest, lie*], *citizen,* 6, 11.

cīvitās, -ātis, F. (cīvis, *citizen*), *citizenship,* 41, 6: *the state,* 6, 1.

clādēs, -is, F. [CEL-, *strike*], *destruction, misfortune, disaster,* 30, 11: *defeat,* 21, 28. (W. G. 19.)

clam, adv. and prep. with acc., *secretly, privately, without the knowledge of others,* 43, 5.

clāmitō, 1, -āvī, -ātus (freq. of clāmō, *call*), *cry aloud, bawl, call loudly,* 4, 6. (W. G. 15.)

clāmō, 1, -āvī, -ātus [CAL-, *call*], *call, cry out, shout,* 55, 15. (W. G. 15.)

clāmor, -ōris, M. [CAL-, *call*], *loud call, shrieking, shouting,* 11, 24; 18, 8. (W. G. 15.)

clandestīnus, adj. (clam, *secretly*), *secret, hidden, concealed,* 10, 10.

clangor, -ōris, M. [CAL-, *call*], *sound, clang, noise: scream,* 10, 21: *cackling,* 21, 9.

clārus, adj. with comp. and sup. [CAL-, *call*], *clear, bright, shining,* 60, 18: *loud,* 24, 22: *famous, glorious, eminent,* 49, 17.

classis, -is, F. [CAL-, *call*], *class,* 12, 23: *fleet,* 30, 5.

Claudius, -ī, M., *Claudius,* name of a famous Roman gens, esp. *Appius Claudius,* the wicked decemvir, 17, 25: *Appius Claudius Caecus* who refused to make peace with Pyrrhus, 27, 19.

claudō, 3, -sī, -sus, *close, shut,* 15, 6: *shut in, imprison, confine,* 23, 24.

clausula, -ae, F. (claudō, *close*), *close, conclusion,* 71, 20.

clausus, adj. (P. of claudō), *closed, shut,* 6, 1.

clēmēns, -entis, adj. with comp. and sup., *mild, calm, gentle, merciful,* 66, 28.

clēmenter, adv. with comp. and sup. (clēmēns, *mild*), *mildly, with forbearance, mercifully,* 56, 9.

clēmentia, -ae, F. (clēmēns, *mild*), *moderation, mildness, forbearance, mercy,* 26, 10.

Cleopātra, -ae, F., *Cleopatra,* the famous queen of Egypt, 66, 2.

cliēns, -entis, M., *personal dependent, client,* 18, 1.

clīvus, -ī, M. [CLI-, *lean*], *declivity, slope, hill,* 40, 28.

VOCABULARY. 219

Clōdius, -ī, M., another form of *Claudius,* gentile name of *P. Clodius Pulcher,* Cicero's deadliest foe, 60, 24.

Clūsīnus, adj., *belonging to Clusium,* 16, 4. As subst. M., *an inhabitant of Clusium,* 20, 5.

Clūsium, -ī, N., *Clusium,* an ancient city of Etruria, Porsenna's capital, 20, 4.

Cn., abbreviation for *Gnaeus,* a Roman praenomen, 45, 21.

coāctus, P. of cōgō, 45, 10.

Coclēs, -itis, M., *one-eyed,* surname of Horatius, who defended the bridge against Porsenna's army, 16, 9.

(coepiō), 3, coepī, coeptus, *begin, commence,* 1, 19.

coërceō, 2, -cuī, -citus (com-, *completely;* arceō, *enclose*), *enclose on all sides, restrain, repress, hold in check, control,* 54, 21.

coetus, -ūs, M., for coitus [com-, *together;* I-, *go*], *coming together: assemblage, crowd, company,* 24, 5. (W. G. 46.)

cōgitātiō, -ōnis, F. (cōgitō, *think*), *thinking: thought, design, plan, project,* 10, 25; 60, 16.

cōgitō, 2, -āvī, -ātus (com-, *intensive;* agitō, *move violently*), *consider thoroughly, ponder: intend, plan,* 67, 20.

cōgnātiō, -ōnis, F. (cōgnātus, *kindred*), *blood-relationship, kindred,* 40, 24. (W. G. 41.)

cōgnōmen, -inis, N. (com-, *with,*

added; (gnōmen), *name*), *surname,* 16, 9. (W. G. 43.)

cōgnōminō, 1, -āvī, -ātus, (cōgnōmen, *surname*), *furnish with a surname, surname,* 67, 8.

cōgnōscō, 3, -gnōvī, -gnitus (com-. intensive; (g)nōscō, *know*), *become acquainted with, ascertain, learn,* 1, 6; 26, 8: perf. tenses, *know,* 26, 7. (W. G. 43.)

cōgō, 3, coēgī, coāctus [com-, *together;* AG-, *drive*], *drive together, collect: force, drive, compel,* 18, 26; 45, 10. (W. G. 2.)

Collātia, -ae, F., *Collatia,* a Sabine town near Rome, 14, 24.

Collātīnus, -ī, M., family name of *L. Tarquinius Collatinus,* husband of Lucretia, 14, 19.

collis, -is, M., *hill,* 5, 1.

collum, -ī, N., *neck,* 63, 24.

colō, 3, coluī, cultus [COL-, *till*], *till, cultivate: esteem, practise, cherish,* 4, 30: *honor, worship,* 5, 2. (W. G. 21.)

colōnia, -ae, F. (colōnus, *husbandman*), *colony, settlement,* 40, 15. (W. G. 21.)

columba, -ae, F., *dove, pigeon,* 63, 23.

com-, prep. = cum, used only in composition.

combūrō, 3, -ussī, -ūstus, *burn up, consume,* 56, 12,

comes, -itis, M. and F. [com-, *with;* I-, *go*], *companion, associate, comrade,* 26, 10. (W. G. 46.)

cŏmitās, -ātis, F. (cōmis, *kind*), *courtesy, kindness, good-fellowship,* 43, 5.

comitātus, -ūs, M. (comitor, *join as a companion*), *escort, train,* 68, 4.

Comitium, -ī, N. [com-, *together*; I-, *go*], *the Comitium, place of assembly,* the place next the Forum where the elections were held, 16, 17. (W. G. 46.)

comitor, 1, -ātus, dep. (comes, *companion*), *join as an attendant, accompany, attend,* 53, 23. (W. G. 46.)

commeātus, -ūs, M. (commeō, *go and come*), *going to and fro: leave of absence,* 18, 12 : *provisions, stores,* 32, 1.

commendō, 1, -āvī, -ātus (com-, *completely*; mandō, *intrust*), *commit for protection, intrust,* 40, 21: *commend, ask favor for,* 68, 4. (W. G. 51.)

commigrō, 1, -āvī, -ātus (com-, *with*; migrō, *go*), *remove, migrate,* 10, 19.

comminus, adv. (com-, *with*; manus, *hand*), *in close contest, hand to hand,* 30, 23: (W. G. 51.)

committō, 3, -mīsī, -missus (com-, *together*; mittō, *send, let go*), *bring together, unite: engage in, begin,* 25, 10 : *intrust, commit,* 62, 7 : *give occasion, cause,* 48, 13. (W. G. 53.)

commodē, adv. with comp. and sup. (commodus, *with due measure*), *duly, properly, well, completely,* 71, 19.

commodus, adj. with comp. and sup. (com-, *with*; modus, *measure*), *with due measure, full: suitable, fit, agreeable,* 55, 30.

commoveō, 2, -mōvī, -mōtus (com-, intensive; moveō, *move*), *move, shake: disturb, arouse, excite,* 20, 10. (W. G. 54.)

commūniō, 4, -īvī, -ītus (com-, *on all sides*; mūniō, *fortify*), *fortify on all sides, intrench,* 37, 6. (W. G. 55.)

commūnis, -e, adj. with comp. [com-, *together*; MV-, *bind*], *common, general, universal,* 50, 21. (W. G. 55.)

commūniter, adv. (commūnis, *common*), *together, in common, jointly,* 12, 26.

commūtō, 1, -āvī, -ātus (com-, *completely*; mūtō, *change*), *alter wholly, change entirely: exchange, change,* 49, 3. (W. G. 54.)

cōmō, 3, cōmpsī, cōmptus (com-, *together*; emō, *take*), *arrange, dress, adorn,* 71, 1.

compār, -paris, adj. (com-, *with*; pār, *equal*), *like, equal,* 3, 9.

comparātiō, -ōnis, F. (comparō, *prepare*), *preparing: gaining, acquisition,* 17, 19.

1 **comparō,** 1, -āvī, -ātus (com-, *completely*; parō, *prepare*), *prepare, make ready, furnish,* 11, 1: *gain, get, secure,* 41, 3.

2 **comparō,** 1, -āvī, -ātus (compār,

like), *bring together as equals, match, compare,* 2, 8.

1 compellō, 3, -pulī, -pulsus (com-, *together;* pellō, *drive*), *drive together: compel, force, impel,* 1, 21; 46, 21. (W. G. 59.)

2 compellō, 1, -āvī, -ātus (1 compellō, *urge*), *accost: reproach, rebuke,* 41, 12.

comperiō, 4, -perī, -pertus [com-, *thoroughly;* PER-, *try*], *obtain knowledge of, find out, learn,* 27, 30.

(compēs, -pedis), F., sing. only abl., *fetter, shackle, chain,* 59, 4.

compīlō, 1, -āvī, -ātus, *plunder, rob, pillage,* 29, 26.

complector, 3, -plexus, dep. [com-, *together;* PLEC-, *weave*], *clasp, embrace,* 10, 24. (W. G. 60.)

compleō, 2, -ēvī, -ētus [com-, intensive, *completely;* PLE-, *fill*], *fill up, fill full,* 32, 7.

complōrātiō, -ōnis, F. (complōrō, *bewail*), *loud complaint, lamentation,* 8, 1.

complūrēs, -a, or -ia, gen. -ium, adj. [com-, *intensive;* plūs, *more,* fr. PLE-, PLV-, *full*], *more than one, not a few, many,* 10, 8. (W. G. 62.)

compōnō, 3, -posuī, -positus (com-, *together;* pōnō, *put*), *bring together: adjust, settle, calm, appease,* 46, 28.

compos, -potis, adj. [com-, *completely;* POT-, *master*], *master of, powerful over,* 67, 13. (W. G. 63.)

compositum, -ī, N. (compōnō, *arrange*), *agreement, compact,* 11, 27.

comprehendō, 3, -dī, -hēnsus (com-, *together, completely;* prehendō, *seize*), *bind together: seize,* 30, 19: *arrest, capture,* 41, 24.

comprimō, 3, -pressī, -pressus (com-, *together;* premō, *press*), *press together, compress: restrain, put down, check, subdue,* 58, 26.

compulsus, P. of compellō, 1, 21.

concēdō, 3, -cessī, -cessus (com-, *completely;* cēdō, *go*), *go away, withdraw,* 20, 1: *concede, allow, grant,* 23, 29. (W. G. 14.)

concidō, 3, -cidī, — (com-, *together;* cadō, *fall*), *fall together: be slain, fall, perish,* 60, 9. (W. G. 14.)

conciliō, 1, -āvī, -ātus (concilium, *meeting*), *bring together, unite, reconcile: procure, win, obtain,* 4, 13; 40, 14: *cause, bring about,* 28, 21.

concipiō, 3, -cēpī, -ceptus (com-, *together;* capiō, *take*), *take hold of, take in: imagine, conceive,* 11, 12. (W. G. 17.)

concitātus, adj. with comp. and sup. (P. of concitō), *rapid, swift: roused,* 18, 23.

concitō, 1, -āvī, -ātus (com-, intensive; citō, *move*), *put in quick motion, rouse, urge, incite,* 8, 24: *cause, occasion,* 32, 20.

conclāmō, 1, -āvī, -ātus (com-, *together,* or intensive; clamō, *call out*), *cry out together, shout,* 7, 8. (W. G. 15.)

concoquō, 3, -cōxī, -coctus (com-, *together;* coquō, *boil*), *digest,* 17, 7.

concordia, -ae, F. (concors, *of the same mind*), *agreeing, together, union, harmony, concord,* 16, 19.

concupīscō, 3, -cupīvī, -ītus, inch. (com-, *forcibly:* cupiō, *desire*), *long for, aspire to, strive after,* 50, 6.

concurrō, 3, -currī, or -cucurrī, -cursus (com-, *together;* currō, *run*), *run together, assemble: meet, meet in battle, contend,* 7, 3; 45, 3. (W. G. 19.)

concursus, -ūs, M. (concurrō, *run together*), *running together, crowd, mob,* 18, 8: *attack,* 7, 4. (W. G. 19.)

condemnō, 1, -āvī, -ātus (com-, *together;* damnō, *convict*), *convict, condemn, find guilty,* 8, 7.

condiciō, -ōnis, F. [com-, *together;* DIC-, *show, point*], *agreement, condition, terms,* 26, 25. (W. G. 26.)

conditor, -ōris, M. (condō, *build*), *maker, builder, founder,* 21, 30. (W. G. 25.)

condō, 3, -didī, -ditus [com-, *together;* 2 DA-, *put*], *put together, found, establish, build,* 2, 15: *lay up, put away, conceal,* 15, 25. (W. G. 25.)

condūcō, 3, -dūxī, -ductus (com-, *together;* dūcō, *draw*), *draw together, assemble: contribute to, serve,* 42, 16. (W. G. 29.)

confectus, P. of cōnficiō, 46, 1.

cōnferō, cōnferre, contulī, conlātus, *bring together, collect,* 17, 15; 54, 17: *devote, apply, bestow,* 6a, 8: sē cōnferre, *to betake oneself, go,* 14, 5. (W. G. 34.)

cōnfessiō, -ōnis, F. (cōnfiteor, *confess*), *confession, acknowledgment,* 26, 16.

cōnfestim, adv., *immediately, forthwith,* 27, 20.

cōnficiō, 3, -fēcī, -fectus (com-, *completely;* faciō, *make*), *make ready, make,* 7, 29: *complete, accomplish, settle, close, finish,* 10, 15; 46, 1: *destroy, kill,* 7, 24: *grind, masticate,* 17, 3. (W. G. 33.)

cōnfidentia, -ae, F. (cōnfidēns, *bold*), *confidence, assurance, boldness,* 15, 20.

cōnfiteor, 2, -fessus, dep. (com-, *completely;* fateor, *confess*), *acknowledge, confess,* 34, 22.

cōnflagrō, 1, -āvī, -ātus (com-, *completely;* flagrō, *burn*), *burn, be consumed,* 9, 14. (W. G. 36.)

cōnflīgō, 3, -flīxī, -flīctus (com-, *together;* flīgō, *strike*), *come into collision: contend, fight,* 12, 10.

cōnflō, 1, -āvī, -ātus (com-, *together;* flō, *blow*), *blow together: accumulate, bring together,* 50, 23: *effect, cause, arouse,* 34, 5.

cōnfluō, 3, -flūxī, — (com-, *together;* fluō, *flow*), *flow together: gather, assemble,* 53, 22.

VOCABULARY. 223

cŏnfodiō, 3, -fōdī, -fossus (com-, completely; fodiō, dig), dig up: transfix, stab, **47**, 18.

cŏnfugiō, 3, -fūgī, — (com-, together; fugiō, flee), flee, flee for refuge, take refuge, **3, 4**. (W. G. 40.)

congredior, 3, -gressus, dep. (com-, together; gradior, come), come together, meet: fight, **33,** 18. (W. G. 44.)

congressus, -ūs, M. [com-, together; GRAD-, walk], meeting, interview, conference, **6**, 9. (W. G. 44.)

congruō, 3, -uī, —, coincide, agree, **2**, 10.

coniciō, 3, -iēcī, -iectus (com-, together; iaciō, throw), throw together, unite: throw, thrust, put, place, hurl, **1, 7; 18, 27; 43,** 9. (W. G. 47.)

coniungō, 3, -iūnxī, -iūnctus (com-, together; iungō, join), connect, join, unite, **10, 13**. (W. G. 48.)

coniūnx or coniux, -iugis, M. and F. [com-, together; IVG-, bind], married person, spouse, husband, wife, **1, 15**. (W. G. 48.)

coniūrātiō, -ōnis, F. (coniūrō, swear together), uniting in an oath, alliance, plot, conspiracy, **42,** 26. (W. G. 48.)

coniūrātus, adj. (P. of coniūrō) bound together by an oath, allied. Plur. M. as subst., conspirators, **55,** 12. (W. G. 48.)

coniūrō, 1, -āvī, -ātus (com-, together; iūrō, swear), swear together: form a conspiracy, **15,** 5. (W. G. 48.)

conlātus, P. of cōnferō, **17,** 15.

conlaudō, 1, -āvī, -ātus (com-, altogether; laudō, praise), praise highly, extol, **35,** 3.

conlēctus, P. of conligō, **21,** 25.

conlēga, -ae, M., colleague, associate, **37, 7,**

conligō, 3, -lēgī, -lēctus (com-, together; legō, gather), gather, collect, assemble, **21,** 25.

conlocō, 1, -āvī, -ātus (com-, together; locō, place), set right, arrange: station, settle, place, **45,** 30: give in marriage, **30,** 2.

conloquium, -ī, N. (conloquor, talk), conversation, conference, **6,** 5; **24,** 5.

conloquor, 3, -cūtus, dep. (com-, together; loquor, talk), talk, confer, **28,** 9.

cōnor, 1, -ātus, dep., undertake, endeavor, attempt, try, **55,** 18.

conqueror, 3, -questus, dep. (com-, altogether; queror, complain), complain, bewail, lament, **14,** 6.

conquīrō, 3, -quīsīvī, -quīsītus (com-, intensive, earnestly, eagerly; quaerō, seek), seek for, hunt up, search out: procure, collect, **30,** 12.

cōnsalūtō, 1, -āvī, -ātus (com-, intensive, cordially; salūtō, salute), greet, salute cordially, **44,** 21.

cōnscendō, 3, -endī, -ēnsus (com-, intensive, actively; **scandō,** *climb*), *mount, ascend : embark on ship,* 52, 26.

cōnscientia, -ae, F. (cōnsciō, *be conscious*), *knowledge, consciousness,* 59, 13.

cōnsciscō, 3, -scīvī, -scītus (com-, intensive ; sciscō, *approve*), *approve of, decree : adjudge, appropriate :* with mortem sibi, *to commit suicide,* 18, 28. (W. G. 66.)

cōnscrībō, 3, -īpsī, -īptus (com-, *together ;* scrībō, *write*), *write gether, enroll, enlist, levy,* 10, 7.

cōnscrīptus, -ī, M. (P. of cōnscrībō), *one enrolled,* esp. in the phrase patrēs (et) cōnscrīptī, referring to the senate, 67, 14.

cōnsecrō, 1, -āvī, -ātus (com-, *entirely;* sacrō, *consecrate*), *dedicate, devote, consecrate,* 5, 7.

cōnsēnsus, -ūs, M. (cōnsentiō, *agree*), *unanimity, concord, agreement, consent,* 21, 15 ; 45, 23.

cōnsentiō, 4, -sēnsī, -sēnsus (com-, *together ;* sentiō, *feel*), *agree, accord : conspire,* 42, 2.

cōnsequor, 3, -secūtus, dep. (com-, intensive, *sharply;* sequor, *follow*), *follow, follow up, pursue : overtake, reach,* 7, 19 : *obtain, win, get,* 11, 2.

cōnserō, 3, -seruī, -sertus (com-, *together ;* serō, *twine*), *connect, entwine, join,* 4, 2 : with manum, manūs, *fight hand to hand,* 7, 6.

cōnservō, 1, -āvī, -ātus (com-, intensive ; servō, *keep*), *keep safe, preserve, save,* 60, 15.

cōnsessus, -ūs, M. [com-, *together;* SID-, *sit*], *convention, meeting, assembly,* 27, 31. (W. G. 67.)

cōnsīderō, 1, -āvī, -ātus, *look at closely, regard attentively,* 2, 7.

cōnsīdō, 3, -sēdī, sessus [com-, *together ;* SID-, *sit*], *sit together, take seats,* 7, 1. (W. G. 67.)

cōnsilium, -ī, N. (cf. cōnsulō, *consult*), *council, deliberative assembly : counsel, deliberation,* 4, 18 : *plan, purpose, design,* 26, 30 : *prudence, wisdom, counsel,* 60, 12.

cōnsistō, 3, -stitī, -stitus (com-, *completely;* sistō, *stand*), *stand still : stand, halt, take a stand,* 21, 12 ; 34, 1. (W. G. 69.)

cōnsōbrīnus, -ī, M. (com-, *with, associated with ;* soror, *sister*), *mother's sister's son, first cousin,* 40, 23.

cōnsōlor, 1, -ātus, dep. (com-, *completely;* sōlor, *comfort*), *encourage, cheer : comfort, soothe, console,* 17, 16.

cōnspectus, -ūs, M. [com-, *together;* SPEC-, *see*], *seeing, sight, view,* 4, 24. (W. G. 68.)

cōnspiciō, 3, -spēxī, -spectus (com-, *together ;* speciō, *look at*), *look at attentively, perceive, see,* 8, 13. (W. G. 68).

cōnspicuus, adj. (cf. cōnspiciō), *visible, apparent : distinguished, remarkable,* 70, 21. (W. G. 68.)

cōnspīrō, 1, -āvī, -ātus (com-, *to-*

VOCABULARY. 225

gether; **spīrō**, *blow*), *blow together*: *plot, conspire*, 17, 1.
cōnstanter, adv. with comp. and sup. (cōnstāns, *firm*), *firmly, constantly, resolutely*, 70, 8.
cōnstantia, -ae, F. (cōnstāns, *firm*), *steadiness, firmness, constancy*, 15, 20; 64, 24. (W. G. 69.)
cōnstat, see cōnstō.
cōnsternō, 1, -āvī, -ātus, *confound, dismay, terrify*, 4, 5.
cōnstituō, 3, -uī, -ūtus (com-, intensive, *firmly*; **statuō**, *set*), *put, place*, 5, 1: *arrange, draw up*, 37, 8: *assign, select, appoint*, 4, 20: *manage, administer*, 64, 20: *determine, resolve, decide*, 33, 15. (W. G. 69.)
cōnstō, 1, -stitī, -stātūrus (com-, *together*; **stō**, *stand*), *agree, accord, be consistent with*, 41, 13: *be certain, be established, be known*, 15, 24; 55, 24: *be composed of, consist of*, 29, 11. (W. G. 69.)
cōnsuētūdō, -inis, F. (cōnsuētus, *accustomed*), *custom, habit*, 35, 8.
cōnsul, -ulis, M. (cf. cōnsulō, *consult*), *consul*, 17, 20.
cōnsulāris, -e, adj. (cōnsul), *of a consul, of consular rank*, 41, 8. As subst., *an ex-consul*, 37, 22.
cōnsulātus, -ūs, M. (cōnsul), *office of consul, consulship*, 47, 23.
cōnsulō, 3, -luī, -ltus, *deliberate, take counsel: inquire of, ask advice, consult*, 15, 27; 31, 12: *take measures, resolve, determine*, 56, 13.
contemnō, 3, -tempsī, -temptus (com-, intensive, *utterly*; **temnō**, *despise*), *esteem lightly, contemn, despise, disdain*, 36, 19.
contemptor, -ōris, M. (contemptus, *despised*), *he who disregards, contemner, despiser*, 29, 20.
contendō, 3, -dī, -tus (com-, intensive, *tight*; **tendō**, *stretch*), *draw tight, strain: march rapidly, hasten*, 13, 18: *ask, entreat*, 49, 9. (W. G. 71.)
contentiō, -ōnis, F. [com-, intens.; TEN-, *stretch*], *effort, exertion, struggle*, 41, 7: *contest, strife, dispute*, 2, 16. (W. G. 71.)
contineō, 2, -tinuī, -tentus (com-, *together*; **teneō**, *hold*), *hold together: shut in, keep, repress, restrain*, 6, 11; 46, 5: *include, contain*, 69, 20. (W. G. 71.)
contingō, 3, -tigī, -tāctus (com-, intensive, *on all sides*; **tangō**, *touch*), *touch, reach: happen, come to pass, fall to the lot of*, 25, 22. (W. G. 70.)
continuō, adv. (continuus, *joining*), *immediately, forthwith, directly*, 50, 16. (W. G. 71.)
continuus, adj. [com-, intensive, *on all sides*; TEN-, *stretch, reach*], *joining, uninterrupted, continuous*, 71, 10. (W. G. 71.)
cōntiō, -ōnis, F. [for conventiō, fr. com-, *together*; VEN-, *come*],

VOCABULARY.

gathering, meeting, assembly, 4, 21. (W. G. 73.)

contrā, adv. and prep. with acc.: adv., *opposite, face to face: on the contrary:* prep., *against, in the face of, contrary to,* 20, 8; 22, 15.

contrahō, 3, -trāxī, -tractus (com-, *together;* trahō, *draw*), *draw together, collect, assemble,* 49, 26.

contrārius, adj. (contrā, *over against*), *lying over against, contrary, opposite,* 51, 25.

contubernālis, -is, M. and F. (com-, *together;* taberna, *hut*), *tent-companion,* 43, 1: *comrade, companion,* 68, 19.

contumēlia, -ae, F., *insult, abuse, reproach,* 65, 21.

cōnūbium, -ī, N. (com-, *together;* nūbō, *marry*), *marriage, wedlock: right of marriage,* 3, 6.

convalēscō, 3, -luī, —, inch., *recover, regain health, grow strong,* 12, 18.

conveniō, 4, -vēnī, -ventus (com-, *together;* veniō, *come*), *come together, assemble,* 3, 11 : *meet, address, accost,* 68, 1. (W. G. 73.)

convertō, 3, -tī, -sus (com-, intensive, *completely;* vertō, *turn*), *turn around, turn: attract, fix, rivet, draw, direct,* 3, 13 ; 20, 26. (W. G. 74.)

convincō, 3, -vīcī, -vīctus (com-, *completely;* vincō, *conquer*), *overcome, convict,* 54, 11.

convīvium, -ī, N. [com-, *together;* vīv-, *live*], *meal in company, social feast, banquet,* 14, 23 (v. notes, fig. 20, p. 116). (W. G. 76.)

convocō, 1, -āvī, -ātus (com-, *together;* vocō, *call*), *call together, assemble, summon,* 40, 18. (W. G. 77.)

coorior, 4, -ortus, dep. (com-, intensive ; orior, *rise*), *come forth, arise,* 4, 23.

cophinus, -ī, M. (Gr., κόφινος), *basket,* 51, 3.

cōpia, -ae, F. (co- opia; com-, intensive ; ops, *wealth*), *abundance, plenty,* 54, 16. Plur., *forces, troops,* 31, 14 : cōpiam facere, *to give an opportunity,* 39, 7.

cōpiōsē, adv. with comp. and sup. (cōpiōsus, *rich*), *copiously, abundantly: at length, fluently,* 48, 15.

cōram, adv. and prep. with abl. (com-, *with ;* ōs, *face*), *in the presence of, before the eyes, before,* 36, 5.

Cornēlia, -ae, F., 1. *Cornelia,* daughter of Scipio Africanus and mother of the Gracchi, 40, 1. 2. *Cornelia,* daughter of Anna and wife of Caesar, 48, 23.

Cornēlius, -ī, M., *Cornelius,* name of a distinguished gens to which belonged many of the noblest families of Rome, *e.g.* Scipio, Sulla, etc.

corneus, adj. (cornū, *horn*), *of horn,* 29, 12.

VOCABULARY.   227

cornū, -ūs, N., *horn*, 33, 28.
corōna, -ae, F., *garland, wreath*, 49, 15 (v. notes, fig. 24, p. 125).
corpus, -oris, N., *body*, 7, 22: *dead body*, 13, 23.
corrigō, 3, -rēxī, -rēctus (com-, intensive; regō, *keep straight*), *make straight: improve, reform, correct*, 8, 23; 54, 6. (W. G. 65.)
corrumpō, 3, -rūpī, -ruptus (com-, intensive; rumpō, *break*), *destroy, ruin: corrupt, bribe*, 28, 19. (W. G. 64.)
corvus, -ī, M. [CAL-, *call*], *raven*, 68, 11: *grappling-iron*, 30, 19.
cōs, cōtis, F., *flint-stone, whetstone*, 11, 14.
cottīdiānus, adj. [cottīdiē (quot, *how many*; diēs, *day*)], *of every day, daily: usual, ordinary, common*, 66, 7; 69, 15. (W. G. 27.)
Crassus, -ī, M., family name of *M. Licinius Crassus*, surnamed *Dives* because of his wealth, one of the first triumvirate, 60 B.C.; killed by the Parthians 53 B.C., 50, 26.
crēber, -bra, -brum, adj., *frequent, repeated*, 69, 27.
crēdō, 3, -didī, -ditus [CRAT-, *faith*; DA-, *put*], *put faith in, trust: believe, suppose, think*, 4, 25.
cremō, 1, -āvī, -ātus, *burn, consume by fire*, 47, 22.
Cremōna, -ae, F., *Cremona*, a town in Cisalpine Gaul on the Po, 59, 7.

creō, 1, -āvī, -ātus, *bring forth, make: choose, appoint, elect*, 5, 9.
crepitus, -ūs, M. (crepō, *rattle*), *rattling, creaking, clashing, flapping*, 21, 10.
crēscō, 3, crēvī, crētus (inch. fr. creō, *make*), *come into being, spring up: rise, grow, flourish, increase*, 9, 3.
crīmen, -inis, N. [CER-, CRE-, *part*], *charge, accusation*, 19, 25. (W. G. 20.)
crīminor, 1, -ātus, dep. (crimen, *judgment*), *accuse of crime, complain of, denounce*, 34, 13.
crīnis, -is, M., *hair*, 4, 11; 7, 30.
cruciō, 1, -āvī, -ātus (crux, *cross*), *put to the rack, torture, torment*, 65, 7.
crūdēlis, -e, adj. (crūdus, *raw*), *unfeeling, cruel, severe*, 64, 23. (W. G. 22.)
crūdēlitās, -ātis, F. (crūdēlis, *cruel*), *severity, cruelty, barbarity*, 41, 27. (W. G. 22.)
crumēna, -ae, F., *money-bag, purse*, 69, 9.
cruor, -ōris, M. [CRV-, *raw*], *gore, blood*, 18, 22. (W. G. 22.)
crux, -ucis, F., *gallows, cross*, 31, 19.
crystallinum, -ī, N. (sc. vās, *vase*), *crystalline vase*, 69, 24.
crystallinus, adj., *of crystal, crystal*, 69, 18.
cubiculum, -ī, N. (cubō, *recline*), *room for reclining, bed-chamber*, 43, 5.

cŭbō, 1, cubuī, -itum, *lie down, recline, lie sick*, 48, 15.

culpa, -ae, F., *fault, error, blame, guilt*, 26, 17.

culter, -trī, M. [CEL-, *strike*], *knife, butcher's knife*, 15, 3 (v. notes, fig. 9, p. 96). (W. G. 19.)

cultus, -ūs, M. [COL-, *till*], *labor, care: style, luxury, refinement*, 70, 21. (W. G. 21.)

cum, prep. with abl., *with, together with, in the company of, at the same time with, accompanied by, and*, 3, 12; 3, 14; 4, 23; 23, 2.

cum, conj., of time, *when, at the time when, after, while, as long as, whenever*, 1, 19; 4, 21: of cause, *since, inasmuch as*, 1, 13; 3, 4: of concession, *though, although*, 40, 23: cum ... tum, *both ... and, while ... especially*, 42, 14.

Cūmae, -ārum, F., *Cumae*, an ancient Greek city on the coast of Campania, 22, 25.

cunctātiō, -ōnis, F. (cunctor, *delay*), *delay, hesitation*, 34, 10.

cunctātŏr, -ōris, M. (cunctor, *delay*), *delayer, loiterer, lingerer*, 34, 11: name given to *Fabius Maximus* because of his deliberate war policy, 33, 15.

cunctor, 1, -ātus, dep., *delay, linger, hesitate*, 13, 24.

cunīculus, -ī, M., *rabbit: mine, excavation*, 19, 23.

cupiditās, -ātis, F. (cupidus, *desirous*), *longing, desire, ambition*, 26, 29; 60, 15.

cupiō, 3, -īvī, -ītus, *long for, desire, wish*, 17, 19; 46, 3.

cūr, adv. interrog., *why? wherefore? for what reason?* 3, 8.

cūra, -ae, F. [for *cavira, fr. CAV-, *watch*], *trouble, care, diligence, attention*, 58, 26.

Curēs, -ium, F., *Cures*, the ancient chief town of the Sabines, 5, 4.

cūria, -ae, F., *curia*, one of the ten divisions into which each of the three tribes of patricians was divided, 4, 20: *senate-house, place of meeting of the senate*, 13, 18.

Curiātius, -ī, M., *Curiatius*, gentile name of the three Alban brothers who fought against the Horatii, 6, 23.

cūrō, 1, -āvī, -ātus (cūra, *care*), *care for, attend to: have done, command, see to*, 47, 22. (W. G. 18.)

cursus, -ūs, M. [CEL-, CVR-, *drive*], *running*, 7, 22: *course, march, voyage*, 5, 24; 32, 10. (W. G. 19.)

curūlis, -e, adj. (currus, *chariot*), *of a chariot: curule*, 20, 20: sella curūlis, *curule chair, official chair*, 5, 9. (See notes, fig. 1, p. 81).

custōdia, -ae, F. (custōs, *guard*), *watch, guard, protection*, 43, 6.

custōdiō, 4, -īvī, -ītus (custōs,

VOCABULARY.

guard), *watch, keep, defend, guard*, 5, 22.
custōs, -ōdis, M. and F., *guard, watch, defender*, 21, 5.

D

Dācī, -ōrum, M., the *Dacians*, a people living on the northern bank of the Danube, 54, 21.
damnō, 1, -āvī, -ātus (**damnum**, *hurt, loss*), *adjudge guilty, condemn, doom*, 19, 27; 56, 3: **capite damnāre**, *to condemn to death*, 70, 13.
dē, prep. with abl., *from:* of place and motion, *from, down from, out of*, 21, 19: of cause, *because of, according to*, 63, 5: of relation, *about, in respect to, concerning, over*, 11, 6; 14, 21; 63, 7.
dea, -ae, F. (**deus**, *god*), *goddess*, 6, 5. (W. G. 27.)
dēbeō, 2, -uī, -itus (**dē**, *from;* **habeō**, *have, hold*), *withhold: owe, be due*, 24, 11: *ought, must, should*, 13, 8. (W. G. 45.)
dēbilis, -e, adj. with comp. (**dē**, *not;* **habilis**, *manageable*), *lame, disabled*, 59, 2. (W. G. 45.)
dēcēdō, 3, -cessī, -cessus (**dē**, *from;* **cēdō**, *go*), *go away, depart, withdraw*, 13, 23: *die*, 17, 15. (W. G. 14.)
decem, num. adj. indecl., *ten*, 17, 21.
December, -bris, -bre, adj., *of the tenth: the tenth month* (from March), *December*, 63, 3.

Cȳrus, -ī, M., *Cyrus the Great*, the founder of the Persian empire, died 529 B.C., 55, 26.

decem virī or **decemvirī**, -ūm or -ōrum, M., *commission of ten men, decemviri: the compilers of the Twelve Tables*, 17, 21.
decennis, -e, adj. (**decem**, *ten;* **annus**, *year*), *of ten years*, 19, 18.
dēceptus, P. of **dēcipiō**, 46, 11.
dēcernō, 3, -crēvī, -crētus (**dē**, *from;* **cernō**, *separate*), *decide, determine, decree, vote*, 2, 17; 41, 19. (W. G. 20.)
Decimus, -ī, M., *Decimus*, a Roman praenomen, 63, 17.
decimus, adj. (**decem**), *tenth*, 20, 13.
dēcipiō, 3, -cēpī, -ceptus (**dē**, *away;* **capiō**, *take, catch*), *catch, deceive, cheat*, 46, 11.
dēclārō, 1, -āvī, -ātus (**dē**, *intensive;* **clārō**, *make clear*), *disclose, reveal: announce, declare*, 41, 17.
dēcrētus, P. of **dēcernō**, 56, 25.
dēcurrō, 3, -cucurrī or -currī, -cursus (**dē**, *down;* **currō**, *run*), *run down, run, hasten*, 40, 28. (W. G. 19.)
decus, -oris, N., *grace, honor: splendor: ornament, adornment*, 12, 24.
dēcutiō, 3, -cussī, -cussus (**dē**,

from; quatiō, *shake*), *shake off, strike down, strike off,* 14, 13.

dēditīcius, -ī, adj. (dēditus, *surrendered*), *surrendered.* As subst., *prisoner of war,* 65, 29.

dēditiō, -ōnis, F.(dēdō, *surrender*), *giving up, surrender,* 20, 10. (W. G. 24.)

dēditus, adj. (P. of dēdō, *surrender*), *given up, surrendered: engaged in;* lānae dēditus, *engaged in spinning,* 14, 25.

dēdō, 3, -didī, -ditus [dē, *away*; 2 DA-, *put*], *give away, give up, surrender,* 10, 1. (W. G. 24.)

dēdūcō, 3, -dūxī, -ductus (dē, *from, down;* dūcō, *lead*), *lead down, lead away: conduct, escort, accompany, lead,* 7, 26; 18, 15. (W. G. 29.)

dēfatīgātiō, -ōnis, F. (dēfatīgō, dē, *utterly;* fatīgō, *weary*), *weariness, fatigue, exhaustion,* 43, 17.

dēfendō, 3, -dī, -sus (dē, *from, off;* *fendō, *ward, strike*), *ward off, repel: defend, guard,* 1, 20; 17, 12.

dēferō, -ferre, -tulī, -lātus (dē, *down, from;* ferō, *bear*), *bring away, take, carry, carry down, remove,* 27, 21; 47, 20: *report, bring word, submit, announce,* 26, 14; 51, 1: *deliver, confer, give, offer,* 38, 24; 63, 22. (W. G. 34.)

dēficiō, 3, -fēcī, -fectus (dē, *from;* faciō, *make*), *withdraw, revolt, desert: leave, abandon: be wanting, fall short, fail, become weak,* 17, 4; 26, 20. (W. G. 33.)

dēflectō, 3, -flēxī, -flexus (dē, *from;* flectō, *bend*), trans. *bend aside, divert:* intrans. *turn aside, deviate,* 45, 13.

dēfōrmitās, -ātis, F. (dēfōrmis, *misshapen*), *ugliness, deformity,* 56, 24.

dēfūnctus, P. of dēfungor, 51, 30.

dēfungor, 3, -fūnctus, dep. (dē, *completely;* fungor, *perform*), *have done with, perform, finish: die,* 51, 30.

dēgō, 3, dēgī, — (dē, *along, by;* agō, *drive*), of time, *spend, pass,* 40, 29.

dehonestō, 1, -āvī, — (dē, *away from;* honestō, *honor*), *disgrace, dishonor,* 59, 11.

dēiciō, 3, -iēcī, -iectus (dē, *down;* iaciō, *throw*), *throw down, hurl down, bring down,* 11, 29; 13, 19; 21, 14. (W. G. 47.)

dein, see deinde, 34, 5.

deinceps, adv. [dein, *next;* CAP-, *take*], *one after another, in succession,* 6, 14.

deinde or dein, adv., *then, next, thereafter, hereafter,* 1, 16; 1, 17; 2, 23; 9, 6.

dēlābor, 3, -lapsus, dep. (dē, *down, from;* lābor, *glide, slip*), *fall, sink, glide down, descend,* 5, 17. (W. G. 49.)

dēlectō, 1, -āvī, -ātus (dē, *away;* laciō, *allure*), *allure, attract, delight, please,* 44, 10.

dēlēctus, adj. (P. of **dēligō**, *choose*), *picked, choice, select*, 35, 11.

dēleō, 2, -ēvī, -ētus, *erase, blot out: destroy*, 10, 8.

dēlīberābundus, adj. (**dēlīberō**, *consider*), *pondering, reflecting*, 14, 11.

dēlīberō, 1, -āvī, -ātus (**dē**, *thoroughly*; **lībrō**, *balance*), *weigh well, consider maturely, deliberate*, 24, 7.

dēliciae, -ārum, F. (cf. **dēlectō**), *delight, pleasure, charm, luxury*, 38, 12.

dēligō, 3, -lēgī, -lēctus (**dē**, *out from*; **legō**, *gather*), *choose, pick out*, 11, 22.

dēligō, 1, -āvī, -ātus (**dē**, *thoroughly*; **ligō**, *bind*), *tie, bind fast*, 33, 28.

dēlīrō, 1, —, —, *be crazy, be deranged*, 15, 17.

dēmigrō, 1, -āvī, -ātus (**dē**, *from*; **migrō**, *depart*), *migrate, move, depart*, 16, 6.

dēmissē, adv. with comp. and sup. (**dēmissus**, *low*), *low: abjectly humbly*, 44, 1. (W. G. 53.)

dēmittō, 3, -mīsī, -missus (**dē**, *down*: **mittō**, *send*), *send down, let down, let fall*, 5, 11; 28, 12· *thrust, put*, 69, 8. (W. G. 53.)

dēnārius, adj. (**dēnī**, *by tens*), *containing ten each: worth ten (asses)*. As subst. (sc. **nummus**), a silver coin worth originally ten, afterwards sixteen asses = about 16 cents, 69, 9.

dēnegō, 1, -āvī, -ātus (**dē**, *utterly*; **negō**, *refuse*), *reject, refuse, say no*, 49, 8.

dēnique, adv., *and thereafter, at last, at length, finally*, 19, 22 : *in fact, in a word*, 71, 10.

dēns, dentis, M., *tooth*, 17, 3.

dēnūdō, 1, -āvī, -ātus (**dē**, *utterly*; **nūdō**, *lay bare*), *lay bare, strip*, 19, 11.

dēnūntiō, 1, -āvī, -ātus (**dē**, *from*; **nūntiō**, *declare*), *declare, announce, order, command*, 21, 26; 53, 28.

dēnuō, adv. (**dē**, *from*; **novō**, *new, beginning*), *once more, anew, again*, 15, 18.

dēpereō, -īre, -iī, -itūrus (**dē**, *utterly*; **pereō**, *perish*), *perish, die*, 35, 23.

dēpōnō, 3, -posuī, -positus (**dē**, *away*; **pōnō**, *put*), *lay away, put aside, set down*, 61, 30: *put away, give up*, 19, 5.

dēposcō, 3, -poposcī, — (**dē**, intensive; **poscō**, *demand*), *demand*, 18, 1.

dēprecor, 1, -ātus, dep. (**dē**, *from, away*; **precor**, *pray*), *avert by prayer, deprecate*, 44, 2 : *pray, plead, offer a plea*, 42, 4 : *pray for, intercede in behalf of*, 49, 7.

dēprehendō, 3, -dī, -hēnsus (**dē**, *from*; **prehendō**, *take*), *take away, seize, intercept, capture*, 56, 9 : *discover, surprise*, 14, 24.

dēprimō, 3, -pressī, -pressus (**dē**,

down; premō, *press), press down, weigh down: sink,* **32,** 13.

dērīdeō, 2, -sī, -sus (dē, *down, to scorn;* rīdeō, *laugh), laugh to scorn, scoff at, deride,* **15,** 13.

dēscendō, 3, -dī, -ēnsus (dē, *down;* scandō, *climb), descend, come down,* **5,** 11: *go down, come down, go,* **13,** 8: *dismount,* **36,** 14.

dēscīscō, 3, -īvī, -ītus (dē, *from;* scīscō, *distinguish, separate), withdraw, revolt from, desert,* **40,** 13. (W. G. 66.)

dēscrībō, 3, -īpsī, -īptus (dē, *down;* scrībō, *write), write down: mark off, define, divide, fix,* **5,** 24.

dēserō, 3, -ruī, -rtus (dē, *un-;* serō, *bind), leave, forsake, abandon,* **7,** 9; **45,** 4.

dēsīderium, -ī, N. (cf. dēsīderō, *long for), longing, ardent desire, grief,* **61,** 4: *want, need,* **20,** 3.

dēsiliō, 4, -iluī, -ultus (dē, *down;* saliō, *leap), leap down, dismount,* **16,** 14; **36,** 18.

dēsipiō, 3, —, — (dē, *from, without;* sapiō, *be wise), be silly, act foolishly,* **15,** 12.

dēsistō, 3, -stitī, -stitus (dē, *from;* sistō, *stand), leave off, cease, desist from,* **20,** 7. (W. G. 69.)

dēspērātiō, -ōnis, F. (dēspērō, *be hopeless), hopelessness, despair.*

dēspērō, 1, -āvī, -ātus (dē, negative; spērō, *hope), be hopeless, despair of,* **38,** 19.

dēspondeō, 2, -spondī, -spōnsus (dē, *from;* spondeō, *promise), promise, pledge: promise in marriage,* **7,** 28.

dēstinō, 1, -āvī, -ātus [dē, intensive; STA-, *stand], make fast, bind: resolve, purpose, design, plan,* **27,** 3; **54,** 15. (W. G. 69.)

dēstringō, 3, -inxī, -ictus (dē, *from, off;* stringō, *strip), strip off: of a sword, draw,* **43,** 7.

dēsum, -esse, -fuī, -futūrus (dē, *away;* sum, *be), be absent, fail, be wanting,* **3,** 2. (W. G. 31.)

dēsūmō, 3, -ūmpsī, — (dē, *from;* sūmō, *take), take, choose: take upon oneself, assume,* **30,** 1.

dētegō, 3, -ēxī, -ēctus (dē, negative, *un-;* tegō, *cover), uncover, expose,* **57,** 3.

dēterreō, 2, -uī, -itus (dē, *from;* terreō, *frighten), frighten off: deter, restrain, hinder,* **11,** 8.

dētestor, 1, -ātus, dep. (dē, *down, against;* testor, *bear witness), curse, denounce,* **19,** 7.

dētineō, 2, -tinuī, -tentus (dē, *from, off;* teneō, *hold), keep back, delay, detain,* **52,** 6. (W. G. 71.)

dētrahō, 3, -trāxī, -tractus (dē, *off;* trahō, *draw), draw off, take off, pull down, take away, take down,* **23,** 30; **38,** 28.

dētrīmentum, -ī, N. (dēterō, *rub away), that which is worn away: loss, harm, damage,* **33,** 27.

dēturbō, 1, -āvī, -ātus (dē, *down;*

turbō, *move confusedly*), *beat down, overthrow, throw down*, 21, 13.

deūrō, 3, -ussī, -ūstus (dē, *down, completely;* ūrō, *burn*), *burn up, consume, destroy*, 15, 14.

deus, -ī, M. [DIV-, *bright, shine*], *god, deity*, 4, 24. (W. G. 27.)

dēvertō, 3, -tī, — (dē, *away;* vertō, *turn*), *turn away, turn aside, betake oneself*, 38, 11. (W. G. 74.)

dēvictus, P. of **dēvincō**, 47, 3.

dēvincō, 3, -vīcī, -victus (dē, *utterly;* vincō, *conquer*), *overcome, subdue, conquer completely*, 21, 28.

dēvolō, 1, —, -ātūrus (dē, *down;* volō, *fly*), *fly down*, 64, 4.

dexter, -tera, -terum, and -tra, -trum, adj. with comp. and sup., *the right*, 58, 29.

dextra, -ae, F. (dexter, sc. manus), *the right hand*, 40, 25.

diadēma, -atis, N. (Gr., διάδημα), *royal crown, diadem*, 40, 22.

Diāna, -ae, F. [for Dīvāna, DIV-, *bright*], *Diana*, Italian goddess of light and of the moon; identified with the Greek Artemis, goddess of the chase, 12, 25. (W. G. 27.)

(diciō), -ōnis, F. [DIC-, *show*], *dominion, sovereignty, authority*, 27, 1. (W. G. 26.)

dīcō, 3, dīxī, dictus [DIC-, *show*], *say, speak, tell*, 5, 10: *declare, assert*, 15, 10: *appoint*, 19, 27: *name, call*, 13, 26: **causam dīcere**, *to plead a case*, 58, 23: **iūs dīcere**, *to pronounce judgment*, 70, 13. (W. G. 26.)

dictātor, -ōris, M. (dictō, *dictate*), *dictator, chief magistrate with unlimited power*, 21, 16. (W. G. 26.)

dictātūra, -ae, F. (dictātor, *dictator*), *office of a dictator, dictatorship*, 67, 17.

dictitō, 1, -āvī, -ātus (intens. of dīcō, *say*), *say often, maintain, assert*, 40, 16. (W. G. 26.)

dictum, -ī, N. [DIC-, *show*], *remark, saying, word*, 44, 25: *command*, 12, 18.

diēs, gen. diēī or diē, M., sometimes F. in the singular [DI-, *shine*], *day, civil day*, 5, 25; 8, 29: *time*, 30, 6: **in diēs**, *day by day*, 54, 15. (W. G. 27.)

difficilis, -e, adj. with comp. and sup. (dis-, negative; facilis, *easy*), *hard, difficult, troublesome, perilous*, 27, 4. (W. G. 33.)

difficiliter, adv. with comp. and sup. (difficilis, *difficult*), *with difficulty*, 29, 1. (W. G. 33.)

difficultās, -ātis, F. (difficilis, *difficult*), *difficulty, distress, want, scarcity, need*, 58, 18. (W. G. 33.)

dīgerō, 3, -gessī, -gestus (dis-, *apart;* gerō, *carry*), *force apart, distribute, divide*, 17, 7. (W. G. 42.)

dīgnitās, -ātis, F. (dīgnus, *worthy*), *worth, merit: authority, distinc-*

tion, rank, reputation, honor, 11, 1; **52,** 4.

dignus, adj. with comp. and sup., *worthy, deserving,* **36,** 21.

dīgredior, 3, -gressus, dep. (dis-, *apart;* gradior, *walk), go apart, separate, depart,* **15,** 24. (W. G. 44.)

dīgressus, P. of dīgredior, **15,** 24.

dīligenter, adv. with comp. and sup. (dīligēns, *industrious), industriously, assiduously, diligently,* **58,** 2.

dīligentia, -ae, F. (dīligēns, *careful), attentiveness, earnestness, faithful care,* **39,** 26.

dīligō, 3, -lēxī, -lēctus (dis-, *apart;* legō, *choose), single out, esteem, love,* **43,** 13.

dīmicātiō, -ōnis, F. (dīmicō, *fight), fight, struggle, encounter,* **64,** 8.

dīmicō, 1, -āvī, -ātus (dis-, intensive; micō, *move to and fro), fight, struggle,* **4,** 4.

dīmissus, P. of dīmittō, **44,** 16.

dīmittō, 3, -mīsī, -missus (dis-, *apart;* mittō, *send), send different ways, send forth,* **49,** 22: *dismiss, let go, disband, release, send away,* **23,** 26; **25,** 9; **26,** 22; **44,** 16. (W. G. 53.)

dīrigō, 3, -rēxī, -rēctus (dis-, intensive; regō, *lay straight), arrange, send, aim, steer,* **52,** 28. (W. G. 65.)

dirimō, 3, -ēmī, -ēmptus (dis-, *apart;* emō, *take), take apart, separate: end, settle,* **61,** 11.

dīripiō, 3, -uī, -eptus (dis-, *apart;* rapiō, *seize), tear asunder, tear in pieces: lay waste, ravage, pillage, plunder,* **45,** 16; **59,** 17. (W. G. 64.)

dīruō, 3, -ruī, -rutus (dis-, *in different directions;* ruō, *clash, hurl), tear asunder, overthrow, destroy,* **9,** 2.

discēdō, 3, -cessī, -cessus (dis-, *apart;* cēdō, *go), go apart, scatter: go away, depart,* **45,** 25: *march away,* **19,** 22; **33,** 22.

discipulus, -ī, M. (discō, *learn), learner, disciple, follower,* **57,** 18. (W. G. 26.)

discō, 3, didicī, — [DIC-, *show], learn, become acquainted with,* **57,** 16: *learn how,* **66,** 5. (W. G. 26.)

discordia, -ae, F. (discors, *inharmonious), disunion, dissension, discord,* **17,** 9.

discordō, 1, -āvī, — (discors, *inharmonious;* dis-, *divided;* cor, *heart), be at variance, differ, quarrel,* **17,** 1.

discrīmen, -inis, N. [dis-, *apart;* CER-, CRE-, *separate], that which parts, interval: crisis, danger,* **41,** 21: *decisive battle,* **33,** 14. (W. G. 20.)

discurrō, 3, -currī and -cucurrī, -cursus (dis-, *in different directions;* currō, *run), run different ways,* **3,** 15: *run to and fro, wander, roam,* **34,** 1. (W. G. 19.)

discutiō, 3, -cussī, -cussus (dis-, *apart;* quatiō, *shake), dash to pieces, shatter: put an end to,* *thwart, dispel, remove,* 22, 5; 26, 17.

disertus, adj. with comp. and sup. (P. of **disserō,** *set in order*), *skillful, clever, fluent, eloquent,* 58, 12.

dispēnsātor, -ōris, M. (**dispēnsō,** *pay out*), *steward, treasurer, paymaster,* 69, 11.

dīspiciō, 3, -spēxī, -spectus (**dis-,** *apart;* **speciō,** *see*), *discern, perceive, distinguish,* 60, 21. (W. G. 68.)

displiceō, 2, -uī, -itus (**dis-,** negative; **placeō,** *please*), *displease, be unsatisfactory,* 50, 27.

dispōnō, 3, -posuī, -positus (**dis-,** *apart;* **pōnō,** *put*), *place here and there, arrange, dispose,* 45, 26.

dispositus, P. of **dispōnō,** 45, 26.

disputō, 1, -āvī, -ātus (**dis-,** intensive; **putō,** *think*), *argue, discuss, converse, explain,* 48, 15.

dissēnsiō, -ōnis, F. (**dissentiō,** *differ*), *difference of opinion, dissension, strife, discord,* 47, 10.

disserō, 3, -ruī, -rtus (**dis-,** *here and there, in order;* **serō,** *arrange*), *examine, argue, speak,* 27, 17.

dissimilis, -e, adj. with comp. and sup. (**dis-,** *not, un-;* **similis,** *like*), *unlike, dissimilar, different,* 6, 18.

dissimilitūdō, -inis, F. (**dissimilis,** *unlike*), *unlikeness, difference,* 29, 19.

dissimulō, 1, -āvī- -ātus (**dis-,** *not;* **simulō,** *make like*), *make unlike: hide, conceal,* 3, 10.

dissipō, 1, -āvī, -ātus (**dis-,** *apart;* * **supō,** *throw*), *spread abroad, scatter: waste, squander,* 41, 18.

dissuādeō, 2, -suāsī, -suāsus (**dis-,** *apart, from;* **suādeō,** *persuade*), *advise against, dissuade, oppose,* 27, 22.

distrahō, 3, -āxī, -actus (**dis-,** *apart;* **trahō,** *draw*), *pull asunder, divide,* 8, 30: *separate,* 7, 11.

distribuō, 3, -uī, -ūtus (**dis-,** *apart;* **tribuō,** *grant*), *divide, distribute, apportion,* 4, 20.

diū, adv. comp. **diūtius,** sup. **diūtissimē,** *all day: long, a long time,* 8, 20. (W. G. 27.)

diūturnus, adj. with comp. (**diū,** *a long time*), *of long duration, lasting, long,* 9, 10. (W. G. 27.)

dīversus, adj. with sup. (P. of **dīvertō,** *turn different ways*), *turned different ways: opposite, contrary, different,* 8, 30; 56, 11. (W. G. 74.)

dīvidō, 3, -vīsī, -vīsus [**dis-,** *apart;* VID-, *see*], *divide, part : distribute, share, apportion,* 19, 26; 68, 18.

dīvīnitus, adv. (**dīvīnus,** *divine*), *from heaven, by divine influence,* 4, 10. (W. G. 27.)

dīvīnus, adj. with comp. and sup. (**dīvus,** *god*), *of a god, of a deity, divine,* 15, 10. (W. G. 27.)

dīvitiae, -ārum, F. (**dīves,** *rich*),

wealth, riches, **17, 19.** (W. G. 27.)

dīvus, adj. [DIV-, *shine*], *of a deity: deified,* **65,** 29. (W. G. 27.)

dō, 1, dedī, datus [1 DA-, *give*], *hand over, give up, pay, surrender,* **27, 9:** *give, grant, intrust,* **1, 15; 5, 8:** *permit, allow,* **9, 8: poenās dare,** *to suffer punishment,* **31, 9: fīnem dare,** *to make an end,* **25, 17.** (W. G. 24.)

doceō, 2, -uī, -ctus [DIC-, *show*], *cause to know, teach, show, instruct,* **5, 12; 40, 1.** (W. G. 26.)

doctrīna, -ae, F. (for doctorīna, fr. doctor, *teacher*), *teaching, instruction, learning,* **40, 9:** *erudition, wisdom,* **57,** 20. (W. G. 26.)

doctus, adj. with comp. and sup. (P. of doceō, *teach*), *learned, skilled, trained,* **48, 3.** (W. G. 26)

dolor, -ōris, M., *pain, suffering,* **48, 14:** *grief, sorrow,* **18, 19.**

dolōsē, adv. (dolōsus, *crafty*), *craftily, deceitfully,* **3, 24.**

dolus, -ī, M. (cf. Gr., δόλος, *trick*), *device, artifice: deception, cunning,* **19, 23.**

domicilium, -ī, N. (domus, *house*), *habitation, dwelling,* **10, 26.**

dominātiō, -ōnis, F. (dominor, *be lord*), *rule, dominion, supremacy,* **50, 6.**

dominātus, -ūs, M. (dominor, *be lord*), *rule, command, sovereignty, tyranny,* **62, 10.**

dominor, 1, -ātus, dep. (dominus, *lord, master*), *be lord, have dominion, rule,* **59, 14.**

dominus, -ī, M. (cf. domō, *tame, master*), *master, possessor, ruler, lord,* **4,** 30; **41, 25.**

domō, 1, -uī, -itus, *domesticate, tame: vanquish, subdue,* **11, 5.**

domus, gen. -ūs or -ī, F., *house, dwelling-house, building,* **9, 14: home, 7, 26: domī,** *at home,* **9, 9.**

dōnātīvum, -ī, N. (dōnō, *give*), *largess, gift,* **68, 19.**

dōnec, conj., *as long as, while: until,* **16, 12.**

dōnō, 1, -āvī, -ātus (dōnum, *gift*), *give as a present, bestow, confer,* **11, 18.** (W. G. 24.)

dōnum, -ī, N. [1 DA-, *give*], *gift, present,* **27, 13.** (W. G. 24.)

dormiō, 4, -īvī, -ītus, *sleep,* **12, 5.**

dorsum, -ī, N., or dorsus, -ī, M., *back,* of a beast of burden: *ridge, cliff, range,* **54,** 20.

dōs, dōtis, F. [1 DA-, *give*], *marriage portion, dowry,* **29, 30.** (W. G. 24.)

Drepanum, -ī, N, *Drepanum,* a town on the western coast of Sicily, **31, 24.**

dubitō, 1, -āvī, -ātus (dubius, *doubtful*), *waver in opinion, be in doubt: hesitate,* **64, 16.** (W. G. 28.)

dubius, adj. [DVA-, *apart, two*], *moving two ways: doubtful, uncertain,* **15, 17.** (W. G. 28.)

dūcō, 3, -ūxī, -uctus [DVC-, *lead*],

lead, conduct, guide, **24,** 16 ;
65, 1 : *marry,* **48,** 23 : *construct,
make,* **12,** 22 : *draw, protract,
prolong,* **34,** 13: *consider, think,
regard,* **68,** 18 : *conduct, marshal,* **46,** 30. (W. G. 29.)

Duīlius, -ī, M., *Duilius,* name of
a Roman gens, e.g , *C. Duilius,*
the famous conqueror of the
Carthaginians, 260 B.C., **30,** 17.

dulcis, -e, adj. with comp. and
sup., *sweet: agreeable, pleasant,*
27, 9.

dum, conj., *while,* **2,** 11 : *until,*
12, 18 : *provided that, if only,*
43, 1. With **modo** often written
dummodo.

dummodo or **dum modo,** conj.,
provided, if only, **49,** 10.

duo, -ae, -o, num. adj. [DVA-,
two], *two,* **6,** 14. (W. G. 28.)

duodecim, num. adj. indecl. (duo,
two ; decem, *ten*), twelve, **2,** 19.
(W. G. 28.)

duodēnī, -ae, -a, num. adj. distr.
(cf. duodecim, *twelve*), *twelve
each, twelve apiece,* **59,** 8. (W.
G. 28.)

duplex, -icis, adj. [DVA-, *two ;*
PLEC-, *fold*], *twofold, double,*
65, 18. (W. G. 28 and 60.)

duplicō, 1, -āvī, -ātus (duplex,
twofold), *double,* **9,** 3. (W. G.
28 and 60.)

dux, ducis, M. and F. [DVC-, *lead*],
*leader, guide : commander,
general,* **3,** 21. (W. G. 29.)

Dyrrachium, -ī, N., *Dyrrachium,*
a coast town of Illyria, the
landing-place of those coming
from Italy, **52,** 21.

E

ē, prep. with abl., *from,* see **ex,
4,** 24.

eburneus, or **eburnus,** adj. (ebur,
ivory), *of ivory,* **20,** 21.

ecquid, adv. interrog.: direct,
at all, **55,** 9 : indirect, *whether,*
15, 14.

ēdictum, -ī, N. (ēdīcō, *declare, proclaim*), *proclamation, edict,* **61,**
30. (W. G. 26.)

edō, 3, ēdī, ēsus [ED-, *eat*], *eat,*
47, 27. (W. G. 30.)

ēdō, 3, -didī, -ditus [ex, *out, forth ;*
2 DA-, *put*], *give out, raise, put
forth,* **71,** 20 : *bear, produce,*

1, 6 : *publish, declare, tell,* **64,**
28 : *show, exhibit,* **50,** 20: *perform,* **52,** 25. (W. G. 25.)

ēdoceō, 2, -cuī, -ctus (ex, *thoroughly ;* doceō, *teach*), *teach thoroughly, instruct,* **30,** 11. (W. G. 26.)

ēducātiō, -ōnis, F. (ēducō, *rear*),
rearing, training, education, **39,**
26. (W. G. 29.)

ēdūcō, 3, -dūxī, -ductus (ex, *out,
forth ;* dūcō, *lead*), *lead forth,*
19, 3. (W. G. 29.)

ēducō 1, -āvī, -ātus (cf. ēdūcō),
bring up, rear, **1,** 16.

effēminātus, adj. with sup. (P.

VOCABULARY.

of **effēminō**, *make feminine*), *womanish*, *effeminate*, 45, 13.

efferō, efferre, extulī, ēlātus (**ex**, *out*, *forth*; **ferō**, *bear*), *carry out*, *take away*, 42, 20: *puff up*, *elate*, 9, 7. (W. G. 34.)

efficiō, 3, -fēcī, -fectus (**ex**, *thoroughly*, *successfully*; **faciō**, *do*), *work out*, *bring to pass*, *effect*, *make*, *cause*, 41, 31; 48, 14. (W. G. 33.)

efflāgitō, 1, -āvī, -ātus (**ex**, intensive; **flāgitō**, *demand*), *demand urgently*, *request*, *insist upon*, 30, 16.

effugiō, 3, -fūgī, — (**ex**, *from*, *away*; **fugiō**, *flee*), *flee away*, *avoid*, *escape*, 31, 8. (W. G. 40.)

effundō, 3, -fūdī, -fūsus (**ex**, *out*; **fundō**, *pour*), *pour out*, *pour forth*, *shed*, *spread abroad*, 1, 8; 51, 4; 54, 21: *empty*, *exhaust*, 41, 5. (W. G. 39.)

egeō, 2, -uī, —, *be needy*, *be in want*, 38, 30.

Ēgeria, -ae, F., *Egeria*, the nymph that met and instructed Numa, 6, 5.

ego, pron. pers., *I*, *me*, *we*, *us*, 9, 26; 36, 8.

ēgredior, ēgredī, -gressus, dep. (**ex**, *out*, *forth*; **gradior**, *walk*), *go out*, *march out*, *go away*, 20, 1; 24, 3. (W. G. 44.)

ēgregius, adj. (**ex**, *out*, *selected from*; **grex**, *herd*), *select*, *distinguished*, *excellent*, *eminent*, *noble*, 8, 13; 21, 10.

ēgressus, P. of **ēgredior**, 24, 3.

ēiciō, 3, -iēcī, -iectus (**ex**, *out*; **iaciō**, *cast*), *cast out*: with **sē**, *rush out*: of ships, *strand*, *wreck*, *cast ashore*, 30, 10. (W. G. 47.)

ēlābor, 3, ēlapsus, dep. (**ex**, *away*; **lābor**, *slip*), *slip away*, *get off*, *escape*, 49, 1. (W. G. 49.)

ēlabōrō, 1, -āvī, -ātus (**ex**, *out*, *thoroughly*; **labōrō**, *labor*), *labor*, *endeavor*, *take pains*, 62, 19.

ēlanguēscō, 3, -languī, —, inch. (**ex**, intensive; **languēscō**, *grow faint*), *grow faint*, *fail*, *slacken*, *relax*, 38, 12.

ēlātus, adj. (P. of **efferō**, *lift up*), *exalted*, *raised*, *uplifted*, 11, 29.

ēlegantia, -ae, F. (**ēlegāns**, *select*, *choice*), *taste*, *propriety*, *elegance*, 70, 23.

elephantus, -ī, M., nom. sing. usually **elephās**, or **elephāns**, *elephant*, 25, 11.

ēliciō, 3, -licuī, — (**ex**, *forth*, *out*; **laciō**, *allure*), *draw out*, *bring out*: *call down*, *evoke*, 5, 10.

ēligō, 3, -lēgī, -lēctus (**ex**, *out*; **legō**, *gather*), *pluck out*: *choose*, *select*, 4, 18.

ēloquentia, -ae, F. (**ēloquēns**, *eloquent*), *eloquence*, 26, 28.

ēmittō, 3, -mīsī, -mīssus (**ex**, *forth*, *out*; **mittō**, *send*, *let go*), *send out*, *send forth*, 28, 11: *hurl*, *cast*, 10, 2: *release*, *set free*, 63, 25. (W. G. 53.)

VOCABULARY. 239

emō, 3, ēmī, ēmptus, *buy, purchase*, 15, 15.

enim, conj., postpositive, *namely, that is to say, I mean*, 36, 27: *for, because*, 3, 9.

ēnītor, 3, -nīxus or -nīsus, dep. (**ex**, *forth*; **nītor**, *strain, struggle*), *force a way out, climb: endeavor, strive*, 61, 13.

ēnsis, -is, M., *two-edged sword*, 43, 7.

eō, īre, īvī or iī, itūrus [I-, *go*], *go, walk, move*, 3, 19; 7, 26: *fare, prosper*, 8, 4.

eō, adv., *for that reason, therefore*, 18, 16: *to that place, thither*, 3, 3: *so far, to that degree*, 35, 7.

Ephesius, adj., *Ephesian, of Ephesus*, 12, 25.

Ephesus, -ī, F., *Ephesus*, a celebrated city of Ionia in western Asia Minor, famed for its Diana temple.

epigramma, -atis, N. (Gr., ἐπίγραμμα, *inscription*), *inscription: epigram*, 56, 17.

Ēpīrus, -ī, F., *Epirus*, a province in the north of Greece, 25, 2.

epistula, -ae, F. (Gr., ἐπιστολή, *letter*), *a written communication, letter*, 56, 10.

epulor, 1, -ātus, dep. (**epulum**, *feast*), *feast, banquet, dine*, 38, 6. (See notes, fig. 20, p. 116.)

eques, -itis, M. (**equus**, *horse*), *horseman, rider: cavalryman, knight*, 4, 19; 37, 22; 39, 3.

equester, -tris, -tre, adj. (**eques**, *horseman*), *equestrian, of cavalry, of the knights*, 40, 27.

equitō, 1, -āvī, -ātus (**eques**, *horseman*), *ride*, 57, 1.

equus, -ī, -M., *horse, steed*, 14, 23.

ērēctus, adj. with comp. (P. of **ērigō**, *raise up*), *upright: attentive, on the alert, eager*, 18, 14.

ergā, prep. with acc., *towards, in respect of, in relation to, for*, 16, 15; 44, 3.

ergō, adv., *consequently, therefore, then, accordingly*, 11, 15; 14, 26.

ērigō, 3, -rēxī, -rēctus (**ex**, *out, up*; **regō**, *make straight*), *raise up*, 46, 22. (W. G. 65.)

error, -ōris, M. (cf. **errō**, *wander*), *wandering: error, doubt, uncertainty*, 60, 19.

ērubēscō, 3, -buī, —, inch. (**ex**, *without force*; **rubēscō**, *grow red*), *grow red: blush, feel ashamed*, 68, 8.

ērudiō, 4, -īvī, -ītus (**ex**, *out of*; **rudis**, *uncultivated*), *educate, teach*, 40, 2.

ērumpō, 3, -rūpī, -ruptus (**ex**, *forth*; **rumpō**, *break*), intrans., *burst forth, break out*, 23, 17. (W. G. 64.)

ēsca, -ae, F. [ED-, *eat*], *meat, food*, 69, 22. (W. G. 30.)

ēscendō, 3, -endī, -ēnsus (**ex**, *forth, up*; **scandō**, *climb*), *climb up, mount, ascend*, 18, 16.

Esquilīnus, -ī, M. (sc. **mōns**), the *Esquiline* hill, the largest of the seven hills of Rome, 12, 21.

VOCABULARY.

et, conj. and adv. 1. As conj., *and, and yet, but*, 1, 1: et ... et, *both ... and*, 3, 23. 2. As adv., *also, too, as well, even*, 3, 26; **68**, 28.

etiam, adv. (et, *and ;* iam, *now*), *even yet, still, even now, and also, also, even*, 3, 7; 3, 12: **etiam** nunc, *even yet, even at this time*, **52**, 14.

Etrūria, -ae, F., *Etruria*, a country of central Italy, **10**, 18.

Etrūscī, -ōrum, M., *the Etruscans*, the inhabitants of Etruria, **16**, 1.

etsī, conj. (et, *even ;* sī, *if*), *though, although*, **44**, 1.

Eurīpidēs, -is, M., *Euripides*, a celebrated Athenian tragic poet, 480–406, B.C., **50**, 7.

Eurōpa, -ae, F., *Europe*, **47**, 5.

ēvādō, 3, -sī, -sus (ex, *out ;* vādō, *go*), *come out, go forth : get away, escape*, **23**, 16: *rise, climb, mount*, **21**, 4: *turn out, become, prove to be*, **62**, 23.

ēveniō, 4, -vēnī, -ventus (ex, *out ;* veniō, *go, come*), *come out, come forth : happen*, **30**, 8.

ēventus, -ūs, M. [ex, *out ;* VEN-, *come*], *event, fortune : issue, outcome, result*, **12**, 4; **44**, 30.

ēvertō, 3, -tī, -sus (ex, *out, inside out ;* vertō, *turn*), *overturn, turn upside down, overthrow, ruin, destroy*, **32**, 23; **62**, 20.

ēvocō, 1, -āvī, -ātus (ex, *out ;* vocō, *call*), *call out, summon, call forth*, **13**, 21.

ex or before consonants **ē**, prep. with abl., *out, out of, from :* of place, *out of, from*, **4**, 24; **5**, 4: partitive uses, *of, among, from among*, **4**, 17; **28**, 1: of the cause, *by reason of, in consequence of*, **58**, 8: of measure and correspondence, *to, according to, with, by*, **11**, 27: of time, *following, after*, **31**, 10.

exārdēscō, 3, -ārsī, -ārsus, inch. (ex, *out ;* ārdēscō, *blaze*), *blaze out, take fire : be inflamed, be provoked, break out*, **47**, 11. (W. G. 8.)

exarō, 1, -āvī, -ātus (ex, *out ;* arō, *plough*), *plough out : raise, write*, **69**, 5.

exasperō, 1, -āvī, -ātus (ex, intensive ; asperō, *make rough*), *roughen : provoke, irritate*, **68**, 18.

excēdō, 3, -cessī, -cessus (ex, *out ;* cēdō, *go*), *go out, depart, withdraw*, **27**, 23.

excelsus, adj. (P. of excellō, *be eminent*), *elevated, tall, high*, **56**, 22: *noble, illustrious, eminent*, **10**, 24; **39**, 22.

excerpō, 3, -psī, -ptus (ex, *out ;* carpō, *pick*), *pick out, choose, select, gather*, **62**, 25.

excidium (exsci-), -ī, N. [ex, intensive ; SCID-, *split*], *overthrow, ruin, fall*, **19**, 24. (W. G. 66.)

excieō and **exciō**, 4, -īvī, -ītus and -itus (ex, *out ;* cieō, *call*), *call out : rouse, awaken*, **21**, 10.

excipiō, 3, -cēpī, -ceptus (**ex**, *out;* **capiō**, *take*), *take out, withdraw: welcome, entertain, receive,* 14, 6: *capture,* 64, 2; 69, 14: *meet, befall,* 53, 19.

excitō, 1, -āvī, -ātus (freq. of **exciō**), *call out, summon forth, wake, rouse,* 21, 6.

exclāmō, 1, -āvī, -ātus (**ex**, *out;* **clāmō**, *call, shout*), *call out, exclaim,* 29, 7.

excōgitō, 1, -āvī, -ātus (**ex**, *out;* **cōgitō**, *think*), *think out, contrive, devise, invent,* 30, 20.

excolō, 3, -coluī, -cultus (**ex**, intensive; **colō**, *till*), *cultivate, ennoble: refine, adorn, beautify,* 70, 27. (W. G. 21.)

excubiae, -ārum, F. (**ex**, *out;* cf. **cubō**, *lie, sleep*), *watching, keeping watch,* 71, 7.

excūsātiō, -ōnis, F. (**excūsō**, *excuse*), *excuse,* 42, 12.

excūsō, 1, -āvī, -ātus (**ex**, *free from;* **causa**, *judicial process*), *excuse,* 65, 27.

excutiō, 3, -cussī, -cussus (**ex**, *out;* **quatiō**, *shake*), *shake out, shake off, throw off,* 25, 16; 33, 3.

exemplum, -ī, N. (cf. **eximō**, *take out*), *sample, specimen: example, incident, case, precedent,* 39, 3; 64, 25: *kind, nature,* 65, 7.

exerceō, 2, -uī, -itus (**ex**, *out;* **arceō**, *shut*), *keep out of an enclosure; employ, train, exercise,* 43, 19: *carry into effect, administer,* 54, 13. (W. G. 9.)

exercitus, -ūs, M. (**exerceō**, *train*), *army,* 3, 22. (W. G. 9.)

exhauriō, 4, -hausī, -haustus (**ex**, *out;* **hauriō**, *draw*), *draw out, exhaust: impoverish,* 68, 23.

exhaustus, P. of **exhauriō**, 68, 23.

exhibeō, 2, -uī, -itus (**ex**, *out, forth;* **habeō**, *hold*), *hold forth, present: show, display,* 66, 28. (W. G. 45.)

exhorreō, 2, -uī, — (**ex**, intensive; **horreō**, *tremble*), *tremble before, shudder at, dread,* 67, 18.

exigō, 3, -ēgī, -āctus (**ex**, *out;* **agō**, *drive*), *drive out: spend, pass,* 29, 29. (W. G. 2.)

exiguus, adj. with sup., *little, small, inadequate, short,* 37, 17.

eximius, adj. (cf. **eximō**, *take out*), *taken out, excepted: uncommon, distinguished, select, choice,* 45, 6; 56, 14.

eximō, 3, -ēmī, -ēmptus (**ex**, *out, from;* **emō**, *take*), *take out, remove: deliver, release,* 59, 7.

existimō, 1, -āvī, -ātus (**ex**, *out, up;* **aestimō**, *reckon*), *value, estimate: judge, consider, think,* 29, 20.

exitium, -ī, N. [**ex**, *out;* I-, *go*], *destruction, ruin, death,* 15, 4; 17, 24. (W. G. 46.)

exitus, -ūs, M. [**ex**, *out;* I-, *go*], *going out, departure: close, end,* 47, 24: *death, lot, fate,* 53, 27. (W. G. 46.)

exōrdium, -ī, N. (**ex**, *starting from;* **ōrdō**, *row*), *beginning, origin,* 1, 1. (W. G. 56.)

exorior, 4, -ortus, dep. (**ex**, *forth, out*; **orior**, *rise*), *come forth, spring up, rise: begin*, 6, 20. (W. G. 56.)

expediō, 4, -īvī, -ītus (**ex**, *out*; **pēs**, *foot*), *set free, liberate*, 33, 27: *make ready, procure, prepare*, 21, 27; 29, 30. (W. G. 61.)

expellō, 3, -pulī, -pulsus (**ex**, *out*; **pellō**, *drive*), *drive out, drive away*, 45, 31. (W. G. 59.)

experīmentum, -ī, N. (**experior**, *try*), *trial, proof, test*, 11, 11.

experior, 4, -pertus, dep., *try, prove, make a trial*, 14, 22: *learn by experience, contend with, meet with*, 47, 8.

expiō, 1, -āvī, -ātus (**ex**, intensive; **piō**, *atone for*), *make amends for, atone for*, 8, 16.

expleō, 2, -ēvī, -ētus (**ex**, *completely*; **pleō**, *fill*), *fill up, fill*, 41, 31.

explōrātor, -ōris, M. (**explōrō**, *investigate*), *spy, scout*, 25, 7.

expōnō, 3, -posuī, -positus (**ex**, *out, forth*; **pōnō**, *put*), *put out, set forth: land, put on shore*, 49, 24: *expose, abandon*, 2, 15: *relate, tell, explain*, 13, 6; 35, 3.

exposcō, 3, -poposcī, — (**ex**, intensive; **poscō**, *demand*), *ask earnestly, beg: claim, demand*, 10, 2; 32, 25.

expositiō, -ōnis, F. (cf. **expōnō**, *set forth, a setting forth: abandonment, exposure*, 2, 10.

exprimō, 3, -pressī, -pressus (**ex**, *out*; **premō**, *press*), *press out, force out: express, utter*, 68, 16.

exprobrō, 1, -āvī, -ātus (**ex**, *out*; **probrum**, *reproach*), *blame for, find fault, reproach, upbraid*, 24, 2.

expūgnātiō, -ōnis, F. (**expūgnō**, *storm*), *taking by assault, storming*, 49, 14.

expūgnō, 1, -āvī, -ātus (**ex**, *out to the end*; **pūgnō**, *fight*), *take by assault, capture, subdue*, 14, 4; 26, 29; 30, 25: *overcome, conquer*, 49, 9.

exsilium, -ī, N. (**exsul**, *exile*), *banishment, exile*, 15, 6.

exsistō, 3, -stitī, — (**ex**, *forth*; **sistō**, *stand*), *step out, appear, arise*, 71, 8: *be, become*, 5, 1; 43, 15. (W. G. 69.)

exsolvō, 3, -solvī, -solūtus (**ex**, *from*; **solvō**, *release*), *loose, release, set free*, 22, 12.

exspectātiō, -ōnis, F. (**exspectō**, *await*), *awaiting, anticipation, expectation*, 18, 13. (W. G. 68.)

exspectō, 1, -āvī, -ātus (**ex**, *out*; **spectō**, *look*), *look out for, await, wait, wait to see*, 5, 16; 8, 25; 14, 14. (W. G. 68.)

exspīrō, 1, -āvī, -ātus (**ex**, *out*; **spīrō**, *breathe*), *breathe out, exhale: expire, perish, die*, 7, 7.

exstinguō, 3, -nxī, -nctus (**ex**, *completely*; **stinguō**, *quench*), *put out, extinguish: destroy, kill*, 6, 13.

exstō, 1, —, — (**ex**, *out*; **stō**,

stand), *stand out: be extant, exist, be*, 42, 15. (W. G. 69.)

exstruō, 3, -ūxī, ūctus (**ex**, *out, forth*; **struō**, *build*), *pile, heap up: build*, 65, 30.

exsultō, 1, -āvī, — (freq. of **exsiliō**, *leap*), *leap up, jump up: rejoice, exult*, 7, 23.

exterreō, 2, -uī, -itus (**ex**, intensive; **terreō**, *frighten*), *frighten*, 20, 5.

extimēscō, 3, -muī, —, inch. (**ex**, intensive'; **timēscō**, *become fearful*), *be greatly afraid, fear greatly, dread*, 44, 1.

extollō, 3, —, — (**ex**, *out, up*; **tollō**, *lift*), *lift up: laud, praise*, 27, 17.

extrā, prep. with acc. (**exter**, *on the outside*), *outside of, beyond*, 3, 19.

extraōrdinārius, adj. (**extrā**, *beyond*; **ōrdinārius**, *ordinary*), *out of the common order, unusual, extraordinary*, 45, 17.

extrēmus, adj. (sup. of **exter**, *outside*), *utmost, extreme, farthest, last*, 16, 10; 23, 3: *last part, end, extremity*, 57, 10.

exuō, 3, -uī, -ūtus, *take off, pull off: strip, despoil, deprive*, 65, 19.

exūrō, 3, -ussī, -ūstus (**ex**, *out*; **ūrō**, *burn*), *burn up, destroy*, 15, 18.

F

faber, -brī, M. [FAC-, *make*], *workman, smith*, 5, 19. (W. G. 33.)

Fabius, adj., name of a distinguished Roman gens, e.g., *Quintus Fabius Maximus*, 32, 26.

Fabricius, -ī, M., name of a famous Roman, *C. Fabricius Luscinus*, 28, 2. (W. G. 33.)

fabricō, 1, -āvī, -ātus (**fabrica**, *workshop*), *make, build, construct*, 5, 20. (W. G. 33.)

fābula, -ae, F. [FA-, *say*], *narrative, account, story*, 10, 19: *fable*, 17, 10. (W. G. 32.)

facētē, adv. with comp. and sup. (**facētus**, *fine*), *finely, gracefully: wittily*, 62, 26.

facile, adv. with comp. **facilius**, and sup. **facillimē** (**facilis**, *easy*), *easily, readily*, 18, 2; 21, 14.

facilis, -e, adj. with comp. and sup. [FAC-, *make*], *easy, without difficulty*, 30, 24. (W. G. 33.)

facinus, -oris, N. [FAC-, *do*], *deed, act, achievement*, 8, 6; 52, 24: *bad deed, crime*, 10, 9. (W. G. 33.)

faciō, 3, fēcī, factus [FAC-, *make, do*], pass. **fīō**, **fierī**, factus, *make, build*, 3, 1: *do, perform*, 6, 6: *cause, bring about*, 4, 25: *gain, take*, 35, 6: *give*, 39, 8: *choose, constitute, appoint*, 1, 5: pass. *be done*, 9, 23: *happen*, *come about, become,* 15, 20; **50**, 21. (W. G. 33.)

factum, -ī, N. (P. of faciō, *do*), *deed, achievement, event, act,* 14, 15. (W. G. 33.)

factus, adj. (P. of faciō, *make*), *elaborate, artistic,* 29, 28.

facultās, -ātis, F. (facilis, *easy to do*), *ability, means, chance, opportunity,* 46, 4. (W. G. 33.)

fācundia, -ae, F. (fācundus, *eloquent*), *eloquence, command of language,* 62, 22. (W. G. 32.)

fācundus, adj., *fluent, eloquent,* 16, 22. (W. G. 32.)

Falēriī, -ōrum, M., *Falerii,* the capital of the Falisci, a people of Etruria, 19, 1.

Falernus, adj., belonging to the *Falernian* territory, a district of Campania famous for its wines, 22, 23.

Faliscī, -ōrum, M., the *Faliscans,* a people of Etruria, 19, 5.

fallō, 3, fefellī, falsus, *trip: elude, escape the notice of,* 21, 5.

fāma, -ae, F. [FA-, *show*], *report, rumor, tradition,* 1, 10; 12, 26: *renown, fame, reputation, character,* 56, 18. (W. G. 32.)

famēs, -is, F., *hunger, want,* 21, 17.

familia, -ae, F. (famulus, *servant*), *the slaves in a household, family servants, domestics,* 41, 22: *household, family,* 48, 21.

familiāris, -e, adj. with comp. and sup. (familia, *family*), *belonging to a family: friendly,*

familiar, intimate, 26, 26: **rēs familiāris,** *estate, property,* 59, 12.

familiāritās, -ātis, F. (familiāris, *intimate*), *familiarity, intimacy, friendship,* 11, 2.

fāmōsus, adj. (fāma, *report*), *much talked of: slanderous, scandalous,* 56, 17.

famula, -ae, F. (famulus, *servant*), *maid-servant, female slave,* 12, 2.

fānum, -ī, N. (*for, speak*), *shrine, temple,* 12, 25. (W. G. 32.)

fascis, -is, M., *bundle, fagot:* plur., the *fasces,* 51, 4 (v. notes, fig. 25, p. 127).

fāstī, -ōrum, M. (fāstus, *not forbidden;* sc. **diēs**), *register of judicial days: almanac, calendar,* 54, 6.

fāstus, adj., *not forbidden:* **fāstus diēs,** *a day upon which court could be held,* 5, 25.

fātālis, -e, adj. (fātum, *fate*), *of fate, fated, fatal: dangerous,* 55, 7. (W. G. 32.)

fatīgō, 1, -āvī, -ātus [*fatis, *weary;* AG-, *drive*], *weary, harass,* 21, 21. (W. G. 2.)

faucēs, -ium, F., *throat,* 51, 24.

Faustulus, -ī, M., *Faustulus,* the shepherd that found and reared Romulus and Remus, 1, 14.

faveō, 2, fāvī, fautūrus, *be favorable, favor, befriend,* 44, 13.

favor, -ōris, M. (cf. **faveō,** *favor*), *favor, good-will,* 40, 13.

fax, facis, F., *torch,* 42, 7.

VOCABULARY.

fēlīx, -īcis, adj. with comp. and sup., *fruitful: prosperous, lucky, fortunate,* 38, 25.

fēmina, -ae, F., *female, woman,* 3, 8.

femur, -oris or -inis, N., *the thigh,* 24, 21.

ferē, adv., *about, nearly, almost,* 22, 2; 55, 24.

ferō, ferre, tulī, lātus [FER-, *bear*], *bear, lift, carry,* 1, 15; 25, 20: *conduct, lead,* 23, 10: *suffer, endure,* 8, 14: *report, say, tell,* 11, 8: *move, bring forward, carry, propose,* 6, 3; 41, 10: *bring, render,* 36, 1. (W. G. 34.)

ferōx, -ōcis, adj. with comp. and sup. (cf. **ferus**, *wild*), *bold, warlike, spirited,* 7, 30: *brave, fierce,* 6, 18: *confident,* 7, 21; 37, 4.

ferreus, adj. (**ferrum,** *iron*), *made of iron,* 30, 19.

ferrum, -ī, N., *iron, sword,* 6, 24.

ferus, adj., *wild, uncultivated: savage, barbarous,* 5, 6.

fessus, adj., *tired, worn out, feeble, infirm, weak,* 7, 22; 14, 14.

festīnātiō, -ōnis, F. (**festīnō,** *hasten*), *haste, hurry,* 23, 11.

festīnō, 1, -āvī, -ātus (**festīnus,** *hasty*), *hasten, be in haste, hurry,* 36, 2.

fētiālis, -e, adj., *speaking, diplomatic, negotiating: fetial,* 10, 4. Subst. M. (sc. **sacerdōs**), *fetial-* or *treaty-priest,* 10, 4; 24, 15. (W. G. 32.)

fictus, adj. (P. of **fingō,** *pretend*), *feigned, false,* 14, 7.

fidēlis, -e, adj. with comp. and sup. (**fidēs,** *trust*), *trustworthy, faithful, true,* 23, 9. (W. G. 35.)

fidēliter, adv. with comp. (**fidēlis,** *faithful*), *faithfully, loyally,* 61, 30.

Fīdēnātēs, -ium, M., *Fidenates,* inhabitants of Fidenae, a town on the Tiber, 8, 23.

fidēs, fideī or fidē [FID-, *trust*], *trust, faith, belief,* 4, 25; 10, 1: *good faith, faithfulness, conscientiousness,* 6, 10. (W. G. 35.)

fīdūcia, -ae, F. (**fīdus,** *trusty*), *trust, confidence, reliance,* 9, 6. (W. G. 35.)

fīlia, -ae, F., *daughter,* 1, 4.

fīlius, -ī, M., *son,* 1, 1.

fīniō, 4, -īvī, -ītus (**fīnis,** *limit*), *limit, enclose: end, finish,* 40, 30: *determine, settle, decide,* 6, 21.

fīnis, -is, M., *boundary, limit,* 52, 11: *territory, country,* 9, 23: *close, end,* 25, 17.

fīnitimus, adj. (**fīnis,** *limit*), *adjoining, neighboring.* Subst., **fīnitimī,** -ōrum, M., *neighbors,* 3, 11.

fīō, fierī, factus, used as pass. of **faciō**; see **faciō**, 9, 23.

firmō, 1, -āvī, -ātus (**firmus,** *strong*), *make firm: strengthen, secure, fortify,* 37, 20; 46, 17.

firmus, adj. with comp. and sup., *strong, true, faithful,* 43, 6.

flāgitō, 1, -āvī, -ātus [freq. FLAG-,

VOCABULARY.

blaze], *demand urgently, entreat*, 61, 4.

flāmen, -inis, M. [for *flagmen, fr. FLAG-, *blaze*], *priest, flamen*, 5, 8.

Flāminius, -ī, M., *Flaminius*, gentile name of C. Flaminius Nepos, consul 217 B.C., and slain at Lake Trasumenus, 33, 9.

flamma, -ae, F. [for *flagma, FLAG-, *blaze*], *blazing fire, flame*, 12, 4. (W. G. 36.)

flēbiliter, adv. (flēbilis, *to be wept over*), *mournfully, dolefully*, 44, 2.

flectō, 3, flexī, flexus, *bend, turn: move, prevail upon, persuade*, 17, 10.

fleō, 2, flēvī, flētus [FLV-, *flow*], *weep, cry, wail*, 7, 29.

flōreō, 2, -uī, — (flōs, *flower*), *bloom: flourish: be prosperous, be successful*, 58, 24.

flōs, -ōris, M., *blossom, flower*, 22, 19.

fluctus, -ūs, M. [FLV-, *flow*], *flood, wave, billow*, 53, 2. (W. G. 37.)

flūmen, -inis, N. [FLV-, *flow*], *flood, stream, river*, 1, 9. (W. G. 37.)

fluvius, -ī, M. [FLV-, *flow*], *river*, 20, 12. (W. G. 37.)

foculus, -ī, M. (dim. of focus, *fire-place*), *sacrificial hearth, brazier, fire-pan*, 15, 13.

focus, -ī, M., *fire-place, hearth*, 29, 13.

foedē, adv. with comp. and sup. (foedus, *foul*), *foully, cruelly, basely*, 59, 11.

foederātus, adj. (foedus, *treaty*), *confederated, allied*, 32, 23.

foedus, adj. with comp. and sup. *foul, ugly, horrible: terrible, destructive*, 30, 9.

foedus, -eris, N. [FID-, *bind, trust*], *league, treaty, agreement*, 4, 14; 6, 24. (W. G. 35.)

fōns, fontis, M. [FV-, *pour*], *spring, fountain*, 6, 7. (W. G. 39.)

forās, adv., *out of doors, forth, out*, 11, 30.

fore, see sum, 26, 23.

forem, see sum, 3, 9.

foris, -is, F., *door, gate:* plur., **forēs**, *the two leaves of a door, double door, entrance*, 48, 9.

fōrma, -ae, F., *form, shape, figure, looks, appearance*, 4, 28: *condition*, 51, 15.

Formiae, -ārum, F., *Formiae*, a city of Latium near the borders of Campania. Cicero had a beautiful villa there. 22, 24.

forte, adv. (abl. of fors, *chance*), *by chance, as it happens, by accident*, 1, 8; 7, 10. (W. G. 34.)

fortis, -e, adj. with comp. and sup., *strong: fearless, brave, manly*, 53, 20.

fortiter, adv. with comp. and sup. (fortis, *strong*), *strongly: boldly, bravely*, 4, 4.

fortitūdō, -inis, F. (fortis, *strong*), *strength: manliness, bravery, courage*, 12, 8.

fortūna, -ae, F. (fors, *chance*), *chance, fate, fortune*, 8, 25:

the goddess *Fortuna*, 53, 27. (W. G. 34.)

forum, -ī, N. (cf. forīs, *out of doors*), *an open space, market-place*. Forum Rōmānum, an open space between the Capitoline and Palatine hills surrounded by porticoes and shops, where the life of Rome centered, 4, 2.

fossa, -ae, F. (fossus, *digged*), *ditch, trench*, 12, 22.

foveō, 2, fōvī, fōtus, *warm: favor, assist, support*, 61, 18.

frāgmentum, -ī, N. [FRAG-, *break*], *piece broken off, piece, fragment*, 40, 28. (W. G. 38.)

fragor, -ōris, M. [FRAG-, *break*], *crash, noise: thunder*, 4, 23. (W. G. 38.)

frangō, 3, frēgī, frāctus [FRAG-, *break*], *break in pieces, break, shatter*, 51, 4: *subdue, crush, weaken, overcome, check*, 9, 11; 23, 25; 39, 20. (W. G. 38.)

frāter, -tris, M., *brother*, 1, 3.

frāternus, adj. (frāter, *brother*), *of a brother, a brother's*, 41, 3.

fraudō, 1, -āvī, -ātus (fraus, *fraud*), *defraud, cheat, rob*, 11, 21.

fraus, fraudis, F., *cheating, imposition, stratagem*, 14, 3: *foul play, crime*, 13, 15.

frēnum, -ī, N., plur. frēnī, -ōrum, M., or frēna, -ōrum, N., *bridle, bit*, 13, 24.

frequenter, adv. with comp. and sup. (frequēns, *often*), *often, frequently*, 9, 5.

frūgālitās, -tātis, F. (frūgālis, *thrifty*), *economy, thriftiness, frugality*, 47, 25.

frūmentārius, adj. (frūmentum, *corn*), *of corn: for distributing grain*, 41, 9.

frūmentum, -ī, N., *corn, grain, harvested grain*, 41, 5.

fruor, 3, frūctus, dep., *enjoy, delight in*, 27, 10.

frūstrā, adv. (cf. fraus, *deception*), *in error: without effect, in vain*, 48, 14.

Fūfetius, -ī, M., gentile name of *Mettius Fufetius*, the leader of the Albans, 6, 20.

fuga, -ae, F. [FVG-, *flee*], *flight*, 7, 12. (W. G. 40.)

fugiēns, -entis, adj. (P. of fugiō, *flee*), *fleeing*. As subst., M., *a fugitive*, 51, 22.

fugiō, 3, fūgī, fugitūrus [FVG-, *flee*], *flee, fly, take flight*, 4, 5: *avoid, shun*, 24, 4. (W. G. 40.)

fugō, 1, -āvī, -ātus (fuga, *flight*), *cause to flee, put to flight*, 49, 28. (W. G. 40.)

fulgeō, 2, fulsī, — [FVLG-, *blaze*], *lighten: flash, gleam*, 7, 5. (W. G. 36.)

fulmen, -inis, N. [FVLG-, *blaze*], *lightning flash, thunderbolt*, 5, 11. (W. G. 36.)

Fulvius, -ī, M., gentile name of *A. Fulvius*, one of Catiline's followers, 59, 26.

VOCABULARY.

fūnāle, -is, N. [fūnis, *rope;* fr. FID-, *bind*], *a wax torch,* 31, 5.

fūnctus (P. of fungor), 51, 13.

fundō, 3, fūdī, fūsus [FVD-, *pour*], *pour, pour out: scatter, vanquish, put to flight, rout,* 10, 7. (W. G. 39.)

fungor, 3, fūnctus, dep., *busy oneself, be engaged, perform, discharge,* 51, 13.

fūnus, -eris, N., *funeral procession, burial, funeral,* 55, 27.

fūrāx, -ācis, adj. with sup. (fūror, *steal*), *given to stealing, thievish,* 29, 20. (W. G. 34.)

Furculae, -ārum, F. (dim. of furca, *fork*), the *Furculae Caudīnae,* the fork-like defiles where the Romans were defeated by the Samnites, 321 B.C., 23, 13.

Fūrius, -ī, M., *Furius,* name of a Roman gens, 19, 1.

furor, -ōris, M. (furō, *rage*), *rage, madness, fury, passion,* 41, 1.

fūrtō, adv. (fūrtum, *theft*), *by stealth, secretly,* 5, 19. (W. G. 34.)

futūrus, adj. (P. of sum, *be*), *going to be, coming, future,* 55, 4.

G

Gabiī, -ōrum, M., *Gabii,* an ancient city of Latium, 14, 3.

Gabīnī, -ōrum, M., *the Gabini,* the inhabitants of Gabii, 14, 5.

Gādēs, -ium, F., *Gades,* a town in southern Spain, now Cadiz, 50, 11.

Gāius, -ī, M., *Gaius,* a Roman praenomen, abbreviated *C.,* 23, 5.

Gallia, -ae, F., *Gaul,* the country comprising substantially all that is now Holland, Belgium, Switzerland, and France, 51, 13.

Gallus, adj., *of Gaul, Gallic,* 20, 4. As subst., M., *a Gaul,* 20, 7; 21, 12.

gaudium, -ī, N. (gaudeō, *rejoice*), *inward joy, joy, delight,* 7, 8.

Gaurus, -ī, M., *Gaurus,* a mountain in Campania, famous for its wine, 22, 23.

gemīnātus, adj. (P. of geminō, *double*), *double,* 7, 21.

geminus, adj., *twin-born: double,* 5, 26; plur. M. as subst., *twins,* 1, 5.

gener, -erī, M. [GEN-, *beget*], *daughter's husband, son-in-law,* 12, 13. (W. G. 41.)

genitus, P. of gīgnō, 12, 1.

gēns, gentis, F. [GEN-, *beget*], *race, family, house,* 57, 11: *people, nation, tribe,* 3, 5; 4, 30. (W. G. 41.)

genū, -ūs, N. *knee,* 24, 21.

genus, -eris, N. [GEN-, *beget*], *race, family,* 25, 3: *rank, class, order, kind,* 31, 20; 57, 8. (W. G. 41.)

Germānī, -ōrum, M., *the Germans,* 51, 16.

Germānia, -ae, F., *Germania, Germany,* 71, 5.

gerō, 3, gessī, gestus [GES-, *carry*], *bear about, carry, wear, have, display,* 3, 23; 7, 3: *accomplish, manage, wage, carry on,* 6, 12; 51, 14; 62, 6: with *sē, act, conduct oneself, behave,* 1, 12; 43, 13: **magistrātum gerere,** *to fill* or *occupy an office,* 20, 20. (W. G. 42.)

gestō, 1, -āvī, -ātus (freq. of gerō, *bear*), *have, wear,* 56, 27.

gestus, -ūs, M. [GES-, *carry*], *bearing, gesture, movement, sign,* 69, 7. (W. G. 42.)

gīgnō, 3, genuī, genitus [GEN-, *beget*], *produce, give birth to, beget, bear,* 12, 1; 60, 2. (W. G. 41.)

gladius, -ī, M., *sword,* 7, 5 (v. n. fig. 29).

glōria, -ae, F., *glory, fame, renown, honor,* 9, 14.

glōrior, 1, -ātus, dep. (glōria, *glory*), *pride oneself, boast,* 36, 5.

glōriōsē, adv. with comp. and sup. (glōria, *glory*), *gloriously,* 40, 29.

glōriōsus, adj. with comp. and sup. (glōria, *glory*), *full of glory, glorious, famous: to be gloried in,* 26, 23.

Gnaeus, -ī, M., *Gnaeus,* a Roman praenomen; abbreviation *Cn.,* 42, 23.

Gracchus, -ī, M., *Gracchus,* family name of the Sempronian gens, e.g., *Tiberius Sempronius Gracchus,* 39, 23.

gradus, -ūs, M. [GRAD-, *walk*], *step, pace,* 23, 16: *stage, grade, degree,* 70, 30: *stairs, steps,* 13, 19. (W. G. 44.)

Graecia, -ae, F., *Greece,* 17, 21.

Graeculus, adj. (dim. of Graecus), *Grecian, Greek.* As subst. M. and F., *a worthless, insignificant Greek,* 69, 1.

Graecus, adj., *of the Greeks, Greek, Grecian,* 40, 1.

grandis, -e, adj. with comp., *fullgrown, large, great,* 69, 12.

grānum, -ī, N., *grain, seed,* 57, 10.

graphium, -ī, N. (Gr., γραφίον), *writing-style, pen,* 55, 18.

grātia, -ae, F. (grātus, *pleasing*), *favor, esteem, regard, friendship,* 17, 8: *thanks, gratitude,* 29, 24: *return, recompense,* 50, 22: abl. **grātiā,** after a gen., *on account, for the sake,* 12, 12.

grātulor, 1, -ātus, dep. (grātus, *pleasing*), *manifest joy, congratulate,* 7, 25.

grātus, adj. with comp. and sup., *dear, agreeable, acceptable, pleasing,* 31, 2: *grateful, thankful,* 16, 15.

gravis, -e, adj. with comp. **gravior,** and sup. **gravissimus,** *heavy, laden, burdened,* 32, 9: *serious, dangerous, severe,* 12, 16; 52, 22: *earnest, weighty,* 22, 4: *harsh, annoying, disagreeable,* 26, 20; 52, 4: *eminent, great,* 41, 17.

graviter, adv. with comp. **gravius,** and sup. **gravissimē,**

250 VOCABULARY.

(**gravis**, *heavy*), *heavily: greatly, seriously, severely,* 48, 6: *deeply, impressively,* 48, 15.

gubernātor, -ōris, M. (**gubernō**, *steer*), *steersman, helmsman,* 52, 29.

H

habeō, 2, -uī, -itus [HAB-, *have*], *have, hold, occupy,* 1, 2; 4, 22; 28, 23: *treat,* 25, 18: *hold, converse,* 59, 21: *have in mind, regard, look upon, consider,* 27, 25; 70, 9. (W. G. 45.)

habitō, 1, -āvī, -ātus (freq. of **habeō**, *have*), *dwell, abide, inhabit,* 9, 5; 9, 6. (W. G. 45.)

habitus, -ūs, M. [HAB-, *have*], *condition, appearance: attire, dress, apparel,* 66, 20.

Hamilcar, -aris, M., *Hamilcar Barca,* the famous Carthaginian general, the hero of the first Punic war, the father of the great Hannibal, 32, 6.

Hannibal, -alis, M., *Hannibal,* a common Carthaginian name (31, 6), esp. the great Carthaginian commander, who brought Rome to the verge of destruction in the second Punic war (218–202 B.C), 32, 18.

Hannō, -ōnis, M., a very common Carthaginian name, *e.g.*, the commander of the fleet at the Ægatian islands, 241 B.C., 32, 4.

haruspex, -icis, M. [*haru, entrails;* SPEC-, *see*], *inspector of the entrails of victims, soothsayer, diviner,* 55, 6. (W. G. 68.)

hasta, -ae, F., *staff: spear,* 10, 2.

haud, adv., *not, not at all,* 2, 8; 7, 15.

herba, -ae, F. [*ferba, FER-, bear*], *grass, greens, herb,* 29, 13. (W. G. 34.)

Herculāneum, -ī, N., *Herculaneum,* a town of Campania, near Naples, buried by Vesuvius 79 A.D., 22, 25.

Herculēs, -is, M., *Hercules,* the Greek Heracles, son of Jupiter and Alcmena, and god of strength, 26, 3.

hērēditās, -ātis, F. (**hērēs**, *heir*), *heirship, inheritance,* 63, 16.

Hērennius, -ī, M., *Herennius,* name of a Samnite, afterwards of a Roman gens. *Herennius Pontius,* father of C. Pontius, the Samnite general, 23, 22.

hērēs, -ēdis, M. and F., *heir,* 61, 17.

herī, adv., *yesterday,* 28, 13.

hībernācula, -ōrum, N. (dim. of **hīberna**, *winter-quarters*), *tents for winter-quarters, an encampment for winter,* 19, 19.

hīc, haec, hōc, pron. dem., *this, the present,* 3, 16: *the following,* 2, 23: *the aforesaid,* 10, 6: *he, she, it,* 1, 16: **hīc** . . . **ille,** *the former . . . the latter,* 52, 4.

VOCABULARY. 251

hīc, adv., *in this place, at this point, here,* 22, 8.

hiemō, 1, -āvī, -ātūrus (hiems, winter), *pass the winter,* 19, 19.

hiems, -emis, F., *winter, winter time,* 70, 22 : *storm,* 52, 22.

Hierosolyma, -ōrum, N., *Jerusalem,* chief city of the Jews, 46, 26.

hilarē, adv. with comp. (hilarus, *gay*), *gayly, merrily,* 43, 4.

hilaritās, -ātis, F. (hilaris, *cheerful*), *cheerfulness, gayety, merriment, hilarity,* 71, 16.

hinc, adv., *from this place, hence,* 8, 3 : hinc . . . hinc, *on this side . . . on that,* 4, 12.

Hispānia, -ae, F., *Spain,* 32, 22.

Hispāniēnsis, -e, adj. (Hispānia, *Spain*), *of Spain, Spanish,* 53, 19.

hodiē, adv. (contracted from hōc diē, *on this day*), *to-day,* 28, 14. (W. G. 27.)

homō, -inis, M. and F., *human being, man, person,* 10, 9.

honestās, -ātis, F. (honōs, *honor*), *honor, reputation : integrity, virtue,* 29, 2.

honestē, adv. with comp. and sup. (honestus, *honorable*), *properly, creditably, honorably,* 62, 15.

honestus, -adj. with comp. and sup. (honōs, *honor*), *regarded with honor, respected: becoming, honorable, worthy,* 48, 16.

honōrificē, adv., comp. honōrificentius, sup. honōrificentissimē (honōrificus, *honorable*), *honorably, with honor,* 26, 6.

honōrificus, adj., comp. -ficentior, sup. -ficentissimus [honōs, *honor;* FAC-, *do*], *that does honor, honorable,* 45, 24.

honōs or honor, -ōris, M., *honor, distinction, esteem,* 25, 18: *public honor, office,* 20, 20 ; 38, 24: honōris causā, *out of respect,* 48, 10.

hōra, -ae, F., *hour,* 53, 10.

Horātius, -ī, M., *Horatius,* name of a Roman gens, 6, 22.

horrendus, adj. (P. of horreō, *shudder*), *dreadful, terrible, fearful, horrible,* 28, 11.

horror, -ōris, M. (cf. horreō, *shudder*), *shaking, shudder: horror, fear,* 7, 5.

hortor, 1, -ātus, dep., *urge, incite, encourage, exhort,* 38, 4.

hortus, -ī, M., *garden,* 14, 12.

hospes, -itis, M. (cf. hostis, *stranger, enemy*), *entertainer, host,* 4, 6.

hospita, -ae, F. (cf. hospes, *host*), *she who entertains, a hostess: visitor, guest, stranger,* 15, 8.

hospitālis, -e, adj. with sup. (hospes, *guest, host*), *hospitable, kind,* 22, 20.

hostia, -ae, F., *animal sacrificed, victim,* 65, 30.

hostīlis, -e, adj. (hostis, *enemy*), *of an enemy, hostile,* 23, 13.

hostīliter, adv. (hostīlis, *hostile*), *like an enemy,* 64, 12.

VOCABULARY.

Hostīlius, -ī, M., name of a Roman gens, 4, 4. *Tullus Hostilius,* third king of Rome, **6,** 17.

hostis, -is, M. and F., *stranger, foreigner: enemy,* 4, 7.

hūc, adv. (cf. **hīc,** *this*), *to this place, hither,* 33, 30.

hūmānitās, -ātis, F. (hūmānus, *human*), *human nature: kindness, sympathy, good nature,* 26, 10: *culture, refinement,* 57, 17.

hūmānus, adj. with comp. and sup. (homō, *man*), *of man, human,* 16, 24.

hydra, -ae, F. (Gr., ὕδρα), *water-serpent: the Hydra,* a mythical monster having fifty heads, slain by Hercules, 26, 3.

I

iaceō, 2, -cuī, — [IAC-, *go, send;* cf. iaciō, *throw*], *lie, be prostrate,* 25, 20: *lie dead,* 7, 24. (W. G. 47.)

iactātiō, -ōnis, F. (iactō, *throw*), *tossing, shaking, motion,* 61, 26. (W. G. 47.)

iactō, 1, -āvī, -ātus (freq. of iaciō, *throw*), *throw, cast, hurl,* 52, 16: *toss,* 21, 20: *boast of, vaunt, take pride in,* 42, 9. (W. G. 47.)

iam, adv., *at the present moment, then, now,* 7, 20: *by this time, already,* 4, 5: *immediately, straightway, directly, presently,* 65, 22: **iam nunc,** *at this very moment, even at this time,* 27, 11.

iam prīdem, adv., *long ago, long since,* 52, 3.

Iāniculum, -ī, N. (Iānus), *the Ianiculum,* one of the hills of Rome, site of the mythical citadel of Janus, 6, 13. (W. G. 27.)

Iānus, -ī, M. [for *Diānus = Divānus, fr. DIV-, *shine*], *Janus,* an old Italian sun deity, later god of doors, passages, and entrances, of all beginnings, and of the month of January, 5, 25. (W. G. 27.)

Iarbās, -ae, M., *Iarbas,* a king of Mauritania in Northern Africa, 44, 12.

ibi, adv., *in that place, there,* 6, 25: *then, thereupon,* 27, 21.

ibīdem, adv. (ibi, *in that place;* -dem, demonst. suffix), *in the same place, on the spot,* 15, 17.

(īcō), 3, īcī, ictus (only in perf. system), *strike, hit,* 9, 13; 40, 29: with **foedus,** *to make a treaty, enter into a league,* 4, 14.

ictus, -ūs, M. (cf. īcō, *strike*), *blow, stroke, thrust,* 43, 8.

īdem, eadem, idem, pron. dem., *the same,* 1, 14: *likewise, also,* etc., 4, 28; 10, 11; 34, 27.

ideō, adv., *for that reason, on that account,* 22, 19.

Īdūs, Īduum, F., *the Ides, middle of the month*, the 15th of March, May, July, and October, and the 13th of the other months, 55, 3.

igitur, conj., *then, therefore, thereupon*, 18, 4; 23, 16: *so then, as I was saying*, 38, 26.

ignāvia, -ae, F. (ignāvus, *idle*), *laziness, sloth, worthlessness*, 50, 13.

ignāvus, adj. with comp. and sup. (in-, *not;* (g)nāvus, *busy*), *inactive, lazy, without spirit, cowardly.*

ignis, -is, M., *fire*, 5, 7.

ignōbilis, -e, adj. (in-, *not;* (g)nōbilis, *known*), *unknown, inglorious, obscure*, 30, 15. (W. G. 43.)

ignōrō, 1, -āvī, -ātus [*ignōrus, *ignorant;* GNO-, *know*], *not to know, be ignorant*, 56, 19. (W. G. 43.)

ignōscō, 3, -nōvī, -nōtus (in-, *not;* (g)nōscō, *come to know*), *pardon, forgive, overlook, indulge*, 18, 18; 54, 3. (W. G. 43.)

ignōtus, adj. with comp. and sup. (in-, *not;* (g)nōtus, *known*), *unknown, unfamiliar, strange*, 46, 6. (W. G. 43.)

īlicō, adv. (in, *on;* locō, *the spot*), *on the spot, instantly, immediately*, 55, 13.

ille, illa, illud, pron. dem., *that*, 7, 23: *he, she, it, they*, 3, 22; 34, 13; 38, 6; 49, 8: *the famous, well known*, 40, 3: ille . . . hīc, *the former . . . the latter*, 6, 14.

illīc, adv. (cf. ille, *that*), *yonder, in that place, there*, 50, 4.

illūc, adv. (cf. ille, *that*), *to that place, thither*, 34, 1.

imāgō, -inis, F. (cf. imitor, *imitate*), *imitation, copy, likeness, statue, bust, picture*, 3, 1; 50, 13.

imbellis, -e, adj. (in-, *not;* bellum, *war*), *unwarlike*, 4, 6. (W. G. 28.)

imber, -bris, M., *rain, violent rain, shower*, 34, 25.

imbuō, 3, -uī, -ūtus, *wet, soak: infect, imbue, fill*, 6, 9.

imitātor, -ōris, M. (imitor, *imitate*), *imitator, mimic*, 22, 24.

imitor, 1, -ātus, dep., *imitate, act like*, 39, 3.

immātūrus, adj. (in-, *not;* mātūrus, *ripe*), *untimely, unripe, premature*, 8, 3; 10, 15.

immemor, -oris, adj. (in-, *not;* memor, *mindful*), *unmindful, forgetful, regardless, heedless*, 23, 20.

immēnsus, adj. [in-, *not;* mēnsus, P. of mētior, *measure*], *immeasurable, vast, immense*, 15, 12. (W. G. 51.)

immineō, 2, —, —, *project over, overhang: menace, threaten*, 29, 22.

immō, adv., *no indeed, on the contrary: and even, nay more*, 67, 19.

immōbilis, -e, adj. with comp.

(in, *not;* mōbilis, *movable*), *immovable,* 23, 17. (W. G. 54.)

immŏlō, 1, -āvī, -ātus (in, *upon;* mola, *meal*), *sprinkle with sacrificial meal, offer, sacrifice,* 13, 5.

immortālis, -e, adj. (in-, *not;* mortālis, *mortal*), *immortal,* 15, 27.

immōtus, adj. (in-, *not;* mōtus, *moved*), *unmoved, undisturbed, firm,* 62, 2. (W. G. 54.)

impăr, -aris, adj. (in-, *not;* păr, *equal*), *uneven, dissimilar: unequal to, no match for,* 7, 11.

impatiēns, -entis, adj. (in-, *not;* patiēns, *bearing*), *that cannot bear, impatient,* 52, 25.

impediō, 4, -īvī, -ītus (in, *in;* pēs, *foot*), *entangle, ensnare: hinder, prevent,* 27, 10. (W. G. 61.)

impedītus, adj. with comp. and sup. (P. of impediō, *hinder*), *hindered, embarrassed, burdened, encumbered,* 32, 9. (W. G. 61.)

impendium, -ī, N. (impendō, *weigh out*), *money laid out, expense, cost,* 68, 22.

impēnsa, -ae, F. (impēnsus, P. of impendō), *expenditure, outlay,* 50, 21.

imperātor, -ōris, M. (imperō, *command, order*), *commander-in-chief, general,* 29, 21: *imperator, emperor,* 68, 12.

imperfectus, adj., *unfinished,* 52, 6.

imperium, -ī, N. (imperō, *command, order*), *command, order: authority, power,* 13, 4: *dominion, empire, supreme command,* 2, 17: *realm, empire, state,* 38, 10.

imperō, 1, -āvī, -ātus (in, *upon;* parō, *put*), *command, order,* 28, 8: *rule, govern,* 29, 16: *impose, levy,* 51, 19.

impetrō, 1, -āvī, -ātus (in, without force; patrō, *bring about*), *gain one's end, get, obtain, procure by request,* 20, 11; 39, 10.

impetus, -ūs, M. (in, *against;* petō, *strive*), *attack, assault, onset,* 4, 3: *fury, impulse, violence,* 7, 15.

impietās, -ātis, F. (impius, *irreverent*), *irreverence, impiety, disloyalty to parents,* 64, 24.

impius, adj. (in-, *not;* pius, *dutiful, pious*), *undutiful, unpatriotic, wicked,* 3, 26.

implicō, 1, -āvī, -ātus [in, *in;* PLEC-, *fold*], *infold, grasp, seize: disable,* 9, 10. (W. G. 60.)

implōrō, 1, -āvī, -ātus, *invoke with tears, beseech, entreat,* 18, 15.

impōnō, 3, -posuī, -positus (in, *upon;* pōnō, *place*), *place upon, set on,* 54, 29: *put on board, embark,* 1, 7: *impose, assign, put,* 31, 23.

imprīmīs, adv. (in, *in;* prīmus, *first*), *especially,* 45, 19.

impūgnō, 1, -āvī, -ātus (in, *against;* pūgnō, *fight*), *fight against, attack: oppose,* 61, 18.

VOCABULARY. 255

impūnītus, adj. with comp. (in-, un-; pūnītus, *punished*), *unpunished*, 70, 7.

in, prep. with acc. or abl.: with acc., (1) of place after verbs of motion, *into, to, upon*, 1, 7; 1, 15; 11, 29: *against, towards, among*, 7, 16; 12, 11: *in*, 1, 6: (2) of purpose, *in order to, for*, 8, 24: (3) of other relations, *to, respecting, towards*, 14, 5: with abl., (1) of place, *in, within*, 1, 10: *on, over, at*, 1, 9; 10, 13: *of, among*, 41, 8: (2) of time, *during, in, at*, 41, 21.

inambulō, 1, —, — (in, *in, on*; ambulō, *walk*), *walk up and down, pace to and fro*, 14, 12. (W. G. 73.)

inānis, -e, adj. with comp. and sup., *empty*, 42, 20.

incalēscō, 3, -caluī, —, inch. (in, without force; calēscō, *grow warm*), *grow warm, be heated*, 26, 13.

incautus, adj. with comp. (in-, *not*; cautus, *careful*), *incautious, heedless, off one's guard*, 35, 14.

incēdō, 3, -cessī, -cessus (in, *on*; cēdō, *move*), *advance, march, go*, 67, 30.

incendium, -ī, N. [in, *to*; CAND-, *glow*], *flame, conflagration*, 59, 22. (W. G. 16.)

incendō, 3, -dī, -cēnsus [in, *to*; CAND-, *glow*], *set fire to, burn*, 33, 28; 43, 2: *rouse, incite*, 59, 14. (W. G. 16.)

inceptum, -ī, N. (P. N. of incipiō, *begin*), *beginning, attempt, undertaking*, 60, 3. (W. G. 17.)

incidō, 3, -cidī, — (in, *in, on*; cadō, *fall*), *fall in, fall: arise, come upon*, 14, 21: *happen, occur*, 59, 19. (W. G. 14.)

incitō, 1, -āvī, -ātus (in, *on*; citō, *urge*), *set in rapid motion, hasten: spur on, incite*, 13, 16.

inclāmō, 1, -āvī, -ātus (in, *to, against*; clāmō, *call*), *give a cry, appeal, call out to, call upon*, 7, 17; 36, 17.

inclīnō, 1, -āvī, -ātus (in, *to*; *clīnō, lean*), *bend, incline: be favorable to*, 27, 18.

inclūdō, 3, -sī, -sus (in, *in*; claudō, *shut*), *shut up, shut in, confine*, 63, 24.

inclutus, adj., *celebrated, famous*, 11, 10: *renowned*, 5, 3.

incōgnitus, adj. (in-, *not*; cōgnitus, *known*), *unknown*, 15, 8. (W. G. 43.)

incola, -ae, M. and F. [in, *in*; COL-, *till, dwell*], *inhabitant*, 3, 2. (W. G. 21.)

incolō, 3, -luī, — (in, *in*; colō, *till, dwell*), *be at home, dwell*, 51, 16. (W. G. 21.)

incolumis, -e, adj., *sound, uninjured, safe*, 16, 14; 23, 26.

incrēdibilis, -e, adj. (in-, *not*; crēdibilis, *to be believed*), *not to be believed, incredible*, 44, 19.

increpō, 1, -uī, -itus (in, intensive; crepō, *rattle*), *sound, make resound: rattle, crash*,

7, 4; 21, 24: *chide, rebuke, scold,* 2, 23; 8, 2.

incrēscō, 3, -ēvī, — (in, *upon;* crēscō, *grow*), *grow upon, increase,* 10, 11.

incumbō, 3, -cubuī, -cubitus (in, *upon;* *cumbō, *lie, lean*), *lean: exert oneself, apply oneself, attend to,* 57, 24.

incūriōsus, adj. (in-, *not;* cūriōsus, *careful*), *careless, negligent,* 71, 1. (W. G. 18.)

incursiō, -ōnis, F. [in, *in, against;* CEL-, CVR-, *drive*], *running against, attack: incursion, invasion,* 9, 20. (W. G. 19.)

incutiō, 3, -cussī, -cussus (in, *into, against;* quatiō, *shake*), *wield against, strike,* 20, 28.

inde, adv., *from that place, thence,* 14, 24; 19, 2: *then, thereupon,* 10, 22: *therefore, from this fact,* 17, 5.

index, -dicis, M. and F. [in, *to;* DIC-, *point*], *one who points out: sign, mark, indication,* 5, 26. (W. G. 26.)

indicium, -ī, N. [in, *to;* DIC-, *point*], *notice, information: indication, proof, sign,* 55, 4. (W. G. 26.)

indicō, 1, -āvī, -ātus (index, *one who points out*), *point out, inform, show, reveal,* 1, 21; 19, 18.

indīcō, 3, -dīxī, -dictus (in, *to;* dīcō, *say*), *declare publicly, announce, proclaim, appoint,* 71, 7: **bellum indīcere,** *declare war against,* 9, 7. (W. G. 26.)

indictus, adj. (in-, *not;* dictus, *said*), *not said:* **indictā causā,** *without a hearing,* 60, 25.

indigeō, 2, -uī, — (indu (= in), *without force;* egeō, *need*), *need, want,* 29, 17.

indīgnātus, adj. (P. of indīgnor, *deem unworthy*), *angered, indignant,* 59, 14.

indīgnē, adv. with comp. and sup. (indīgnus, *unworthy*), *unworthily: angrily, impatiently,* 14, 4.

indīgnus, adj. with comp. and sup., *unworthy, unbecoming, undeserving,* 62, 11.

indō, 3, -didī, -ditus [in, *into, on;* 2 DA-, *put*], *put into: give, confer,* 57, 11.

indolēs, -is, F. [indu (= in) *in;* OL-, *grow*], *inborn quality, nature, character, bearing, disposition,* 2, 7; 39, 25. (W. G. 56.)

indūcō, 3, -dūxī, -ductus (in, *in;* dūcō, *lead*), *lead in,* 23, 6: *persuade, mislead, induce,* 44, 9. (W. G. 29.)

industria, -ae, F. (industrius, *active*), *diligence, industry, zeal,* 11, 1.

industrius, adj., *active, diligent, careful, industrious,* 29, 21.

ineō, -īre, -īvī and -iī, -itus (in, *into;* eō, *go*), *go into: begin, enter upon,* 51, 24: *devise, meditate, form, engage in,* 41, 4. (W. G. 46.)

īnfāmis, -e, adj. (in-, negative; fāma, *reputation, fame*), *of ill*

VOCABULARY. 257

repute, *in disgrace, infamous*, 27, 25. (W. G. 32.)

infans, -fantis, adj. with comp. and sup. (-in, *not*; *fans, *speaking*), *that cannot speak, mute.* As subst. M. and F., *infant*, 1, 11. (W. G. 32.)

infelix, -icis, adj. with comp. and sup. (in-, *not*; felix, *fruitful*), *unfruitful: unsuccessful, ill-fated, unfortunate*, 31, 10.

infero, -ferre, intuli, inlatus (in, *in, against*; fero, *bear*), *bring in, carry in*, 35, 13: *bring against, wage, direct*, 46, 13: with se, *betake oneself, go*, 4, 12. (W. G. 34.)

infesto, 1, —, — (infestus, *disturbed*), *annoy, make unsafe, disturb, ravage*, 2, 4; 45, 15.

infestus, adj. with comp. and sup., *made unsafe, disturbed: hostile*, 7, 2.

inflatus, adj. with comp. (P. of inflo, *blow into*), *swelled up, inflated*, 57, 7.

informo, 1, -avi, -atus (in, *to*; formo, *give shape*), *shape, fashion: inform, instruct, educate*, 57, 17.

infra, adv. and prep. with acc., *below, beneath*, 55, 17.

infundo, 3, -fudi, -fusus (in, *in, upon*; fundo, *pour*), *pour upon, pour in*, 41, 30. (W. G. 39.)

ingemo, 3, -ui, — (in, *at, over*; gemo, *groan*), *groan over, mourn, bewail*, 50, 13.

ingenium, -i, N. [in, *in*; GEN-, *be born*], *nature, innate quality: disposition, character*, 13, 14; 36, 22: *talent, ability, capacity, genius*, 59, 27. (W. G. 41.)

ingens, -entis, adj. with comp.[in-, *not*; GEN-, *beget*], *not natural: vast, huge, enormous, very great*, 5, 11; 7, 5. (W. G. 41.)

ingenuus, adj. [in, *in*; GEN-, *beget, be born*], *native: free-born, of free parents*, 11, 18. (W. G. 41.)

ingratus, adj. with comp. and sup.(in-, *not*; gratus, *pleasant*), *unthankful, ungrateful*, 20, 3.

ingredior, -i, -essus, dep. (in, *on, forward*; gradior, *walk*), *advance, go forward: enter*, 10, 26. (W. G. 44.)

ingressus, P. of ingredior, 20, 23.

inhibeo, 2, -ui, -itus (in, *in*; habeo, *hold*), *hold in, hold back*, 13, 24. (W. G. 45.)

inicio, 3, -ieci, -iectus (in, *in, upon*; iacio, *throw*), *throw upon: throw over, apply, put on*, 8, 8: *lay hands on, seize*, 18, 6: *inspire, infuse, suggest*, 60, 13. (W. G. 47.)

inimicitia, -ae, F. (inimicus, *unfriendly*), *enmity, hostility*, 61, 11.

inimicus, adj. (in-, *not*; amicus, *friendly*), *unfriendly, hostile*, 29, 25. As subst., *enemy, personal foe*, 43, 29. (W. G. 5.)

inique, adv. with comp. and sup. (iniquus, *unequal*), *unequally: unjustly, unfairly*, 19, 26.

iniquus, adj. with comp. and sup. (in-, *not;* aequus, *even*), *uneven: unfair, unjust,* 21, 23: *hostile, adverse, unkind,* 62, 1.

initium, -ī, N. [in, *into;* 1-, *go*], *going in, entrance: beginning,* 20, 29: abl. sing. initiō as adv., *in the beginning, at first,* 58, 18. (W. G. 46.)

iniūria, -ae, F. (in, *against;* iūs, *law*), *injustice, wrong, injury, insult,* 20, 2; 56, 15; 70, 5. (W. G. 48.)

(iniūssus, -ūs), M., only in the abl. (in-, *without;* iūssus, *order*), *without command, without orders,* 24, 10.

inlīdō, 3, -sī, -sus (in, *upon, against;* laedō, *strike*), *dash against,* 71, 11.

inligō, 1, -āvī, -ātus (in, *on;* ligō, *bind*), *bind on, fasten, tie,* 19, 13.

inlūdō, 3, -sī, -sus (in, *at, with;* lūdō, *play*), *play at, sport with: jeer at, mock, ridicule,* 24, 3.

inlūstris, -e, adj. with comp. [in, intensive; LVC-, *shine*], *lighted, bright: famous, distinguished, renowned,* 47, 2. (W. G. 50.)

innītor, 3, -nīxus, dep. (in, *on, upon;* nītor, *strive*), *lean upon, support oneself by,* 57, 7.

innōtēscō, 3, -tuī, —, inch. (in, without force; nōtēscō, *become known*), *become known,* 39, 18.

innoxius, adj. (in-, *not;* noxius, *harmful*), *harmless: not guilty, innocent,* 20, 2.

innuō, 3, -uī, — (in, *to;* *nuō, *nod*), *nod, hint, intimate,* 44, 25.

inopia, -ae, F. (inops, *needy*), *want, famine, need, poverty,* 21, 7.

inopīnātus, adj. (in-, *not;* opīnātus, *supposed*), *unexpected,* 56, 1.

inops, -opis, adj. (in-, *without;* (ops), *resources*), *without resources, helpless: needy, poor, destitute,* 29, 30.

inquam, defective, always postpositive, *say*, 9, 25; 38, 7.

inquiētus, adj. (in-, *not;* quiētus, *quiet*), *restless, disturbed, sleepless,* 69, 26.

inrīdeō, 2, -rīsī, -rīsus (in, *at;* rīdeō, *laugh*), *laugh at, joke, mock, jeer, ridicule,* 2, 21; 66, 8.

inruō, 3, -ruī, — (in, *in;* ruō, *rush*), *rush in, make an attack,* 40, 27.

inruptiō, -ōnis, F. (in, *in;* cf. rumpō, *break*), *breaking in, invasion, assault,* 19, 23. (W. G. 64.)

īnscientia, -ae, F. (in-, negative; scientia, *knowledge*), *want of knowledge, ignorance,* 60, 19.

īnscrībō, 3, -īpsī, -īptus (in, *upon;* scrībō, *write*), *write upon, inscribe,* 63, 21.

īnscrīptus, P. of īnscrībō, 63, 21.

īnsequor, 3, -cūtus, dep. (in, *on;* sequor, *follow*), *follow, come next, follow after,* 9, 7: *pursue,* 47, 14.

īnsideō, 2, -sēdī, — (in, *on, upon;*

sedeō, *sit*), *sit upon*, 10, 21 : *occupy, take possession of, camp upon*, 18, 24. (W. G. 67.)

īnsidiae, -ārum, F. [**in**, *against;* SED-, *sit*], *snare, trap : ambuscade*, 23, 6 : *plot*, 11, 21. (W. G. 67.)

īnsidior, 1, -ātus, dep. (**īnsidiae**, *ambush*), *lie in ambush, lie in wait for*, 1, 19. (W. G. 67.)

īnsīgne, -is, N. (**īnsīgnis**, *remarkable*), *mark, proof, sign*, 11, 19 : *costume, regalia, badge, decoration*, 20, 21: *honor, distinction*, 51, 20.

īnsīgnis, -e, adj. with comp. (**in**, *on, upon;* **sīgnum**, *mark*), *distinguished by a mark, eminent, distinguished, remarkable, conspicuous, splendid*, 4, 3 ; 5, 9 ; 46, 30.

īnsitus, adj. (P. of **īnserō**, *implant*), *ingrafted: innate, inborn, fixed*, 36, 22.

īnsolēns, -entis, adj. (**in**-, *un-;* **solēns**, *usual*), *unaccustomed, unusual : arrogant, haughty, insolent*, 33, 14.

īnsolenter, adv. with comp. (**īnsolēns**, *unusual*), *unusually : insolently, arrogantly*, 54, 24.

īnsolentia, -ae, F. (**īnsolēns**, *unusual*), *unusualness : arrogance, insolence*, 17, 23.

īnstituō, 3, -uī, -ūtus (**in**, *into;* **statuō**, *place, set*), *put in place, fix : institute, found, establish, organize*, 5, 6 : *train, teach, educate*, 40, 3. (W. G. 69.)

īnstitūtum, -ī, N. (N. of P. of **īnstituō**, *establish*), *purpose, intention, decree, ordinance, institution :* 6, 4. (W. G. 69.)

īnstruō, 3, -ūxī, -ūctus (**in**, *in, on ;* **struō**, *build*), *build in : draw up, array*, 21, 27: *equip, fit out, furnish*, 45, 6.

īnsula, -ae, F., *island, isle*, 32, 10.

īnsum, inesse, īnfuī (**in**, *in ;* **sum**, *be*), *be in*, 62, 25. (W. G. 31.)

īnsusurrō, 1, -āvī, -ātus (**in**, *to;* **susurrō**, *whisper*), *whisper to, suggest*, 69, 16.

intāctus, adj. with comp. (**in**-, *not ;* **tāctus**, *touched*), *untouched, uninjured*, 7, 21 ; 30, 6. (W. G. 70.)

integer, -gra, -grum, adj. with comp. and sup. [**in**-, *not ;* TAG-, *touch*], *untouched, unhurt*, 7, 11. (W. G. 70.)

intellegō, 3, -ēxī, -ēctus (**inter**, *between ;* **legō**, *choose*), *come to know, perceive, understand*, 8, 26 ; 14, 15.

intendō, 3, -dī, -tus (**in**, *on, to ;* **tendō**, *stretch*), *stretch out, extend : bend, turn, aim, direct*, 32, 10. (W. G. 71.)

intentus, adj. with comp. and sup. (P. of **intendō**, *give attention to*), *intent, attentive*, 11, 28.

inter, prep. with acc. (comp. form of **in**, *in*), *between, betwixt*, 2, 16: *among, in the midst of*, 1, 16 ; 4, 3 : *during,* *at, while, in, in the course of*, 26, 15; **69,** 6.

intercalārius, adj. (**intercalāris,** *to be inserted*), *for insertion, intercalary,* **54,** 8.

intercalō, 1, -āvī, -ātus (**inter,** *between ;* **calō,** *call*), *insert in the calendar, intercalate,* **54,** 9.

intercipiō, 3, -cēpī, -ceptus (**inter,** *between ;* **capiō,** *take*), *seize in passing, intercept : usurp,* 11, 3.

interdīcō, 3, -dīxī, -dictus (**inter,** *between ;* **dīcō,** *speak*), *interpose by speaking, forbid, interdict,* 61, 1. (W. G. 26.)

interdiū, adv. (**inter,** *during ;* **diū,** *by day*), *during the day, by day,* **46,** 5. (W. G. 27.)

interdum, adv. (**inter,** *during ;* **dum,** *while*), *sometimes, occasionally, now and then,* 71, 11.

intereā, adv. (**inter,** *among ;* **ea,** *these things*), *meanwhile,* 2, 3.

interēmptus, P. of **interimō,** 2, 12.

interfector, -ōris, M. [**inter,** *between ;* FAC-, *make*], *slayer, murderer, assassin,* **53, 5.** (W. G. 33.)

interficiō, 3, -fēcī, -fectus (**inter,** *between ;* **faciō,** *make*), *put out of the way, destroy, kill,* **2,** 22. (W. G. 33.)

intericiō, 3, -iēcī, -iectus (**inter,** *between ;* **iaciō,** *throw*), *throw between, set between, interpose,* **15,** 1. (W. G. 47.)

interim, adv. (**inter,** *between, during ;* **im,** old acc. of **is,** *this*), *meanwhile, in the meantime,* 9, 3.

interimō, 3, -ēmī, -ēmptus (**inter,** *within, from within ;* **emō,** *take*), *take from the midst, do away with, abolish,* **40,** 16 : *kill,* **2,** 12.

interitus, -ūs, M. [**inter,** *among ;* I-, *go*], *overthrow, destruction, death,* **4,** 5. (W. G. 46.)

internūntius, -ī, M. (**inter,** *between ;* **nūntius,** *announcing*), *messenger,* 63, 23.

interpretor, 1, -ātus, dep. (**interpres,** *a middle-man*), *explain, interpret, conclude, understand,* **39,** 18.

interrogō, 1, -āvī, -ātus (**inter,** *between, among ;* **rogō,** *ask*), *ask, inquire, question,* 11, 11; **44,** 7.

interrumpō, 3, -rūpī, -ruptus (**inter,** *between ;* **rumpō,** *break*), *break apart, break to pieces, break through : destroy,* **16,** 12. (W. G. 64.)

intersum, -esse, -fuī, -futūrus (**inter,** *between ;* **sum,** *be*), *be between : be present, attend,* **57,** 15. (W. G. 31.)

intervāllum, -ī, N. (**inter,** *between ;* **vāllum,** *palisades*), *space between palisades, intermediate space, distance,* **33,** 17 : *per intervālla, at intervals,* 7, 12.

interveniō, -īre, -vēnī, -ventus (**inter,** *between ;* **veniō,** *come*), *come between, intervene, interrupt,* **21,** 25. (W. G. 73.)

intrā, adv. and prep. with acc.

(for **interā**, *within*), *within, in, into, during,* 10, 14; **44**, 14.

intrō, 1, -āvī, -ātus (cf. **intrā,** *within*), *go into, enter,* 31, 12.

intrōdūcō, 3, -dūxī, -ductus (**intrō,** *within;* **dūcō,** *lead*), *lead in, admit, introduce,* 27, 15. (W. G. 29.)

intrōductus, P. of **intrōdūcō,** 27, 15.

intrōmittō, 3, -mīsī, -mīssus (**intrō,** *in;* **mittō,** *send*), *send in, admit, let in,* 16, 23. (W. G. 53.)

intueor, 2, -itus, dep. (**in,** *upon;* **tueor,** *look*), *look upon, look at, gaze at,* 23, 16.

intumēscō, 3, -muī, —, inch. (**in,** *without force;* **tumēscō,** *begin to swell*), *be swollen, rise, swell up: rage, become angry,* 52, 27.

inūsitātus, adj. with comp. (**in-,** *not;* **ūsitātus,** *usual*), *unusual, uncommon, very rare, extraordinary,* 47, 1.

invādō, 3, -vāsī, -vāsus (**in,** *into, against;* **vādō,** *go*), *go into: attack, assail, invade,* 23, 2: *seize, take possession of,* 16, 4.

invalidus, adj. (**in-,** *not;* **validus,** *strong*), *not strong, infirm, weak, feeble,* 65, 17.

invehō, 3, -vēxī, -vectus (**in,** *in;* **vehō,** *carry*), *carry in:* pass. *be carried in, ride into, sail into, enter,* 49, 26. (W. G. 72.)

inveniō, 4, -vēnī, -ventus (**in,** *upon;* **veniō,** *come*), *come upon, find,* 14, 26: *find out, learn, discover,* 23, 15. (W. G. 73.)

invicem, adv. (**in,** *in;* **vicis,** *turn*), *by turns, in turn, one after another,* 11, 27; 21, 3.

invīctus, adj. with sup. (**in-,** *not;* **victus,** *conquered*), *unconquered, unsubdued, invincible,* 31, 3.

invideō, 2, -vīdī, -vīsus (**in,** *at, askance at;* **videō,** *look*), *look askance at: envy, hate, grudge,* 42, 25. (W. G. 75.)

invidia, -ae, F. (**invidus,** *envious*), *envy, jealousy, ill-will, unpopularity,* 34, 5; 34, 12. (W. G. 75.)

invidiōsus, adj. with comp. and sup. (**invidia,** *envy*), *full of envy, invidious: hateful, odious, unpopular,* 8, 21. (W. G. 75.)

inviolātus, adj. (**in-,** *un-;* **violātus,** *hurt*), *uninjured, unhurt,* 24, 26.

invīsus, adj. with comp. (P. of **invideō,** *envy*), *hated, detested,* 42, 25.

invītō, 1, -āvī, -ātus (for ***invocitō,** freq. of **invocō,** *call upon, appeal to*), *invite, feast, entertain,* 69, 14 : *ask, urge,* 28, 16.

invītus, adj. with sup., *against the will, reluctant,* 37, 7.

iocus, -ī, M., plur., **iocī** or **ioca,** *jest, joke:* inter or per iocum, *jokingly,* 49, 30; 50, 3.

ipse, -a, -um, pron. intens., *that* or *this very: self, in person, he, she, himself, herself, itself,* etc., 1, 6 ; 3, 4 ; 5, 10 : to emphasize possession, *own,* 17, 23 ; 30, 23 : often freely translated by *mere, very, just, exactly, even,* etc., 13, 24 ; 16, 12 ; 44, 11.

īrāscor, 3, īrātus, dep. (ira, *anger*), *be angry, be in a rage,* 70, 4.

īrātus, adj. with comp. and sup. (P. of īrāscor, *be angry*), *angered, enraged,* 2, 22.

is, ea, id, pron. demonstr., *he, she, it, the one mentioned,* 1, 3 : *this, that, such,* 1, 6; 6, 9; 8, 6 : in gen. case, *his, her, its, their,* 6, 6.

iste, -a, -ud, pron. demonstr., *this, that: he, she, it,* 42, 9.

ita, adv., *in this manner, in such a way, so, thus, accordingly,* 2, 24 ; 4, 16 ; 4, 21 ; 6, 9.

Italia, -ae, F., *Italy,* 22, 17.

Italicus, adj., *of Italy, Italian,* 41, 6.

itaque, conj. (ita, *thus;* -que, *and*), *and so, and thus, accordingly,* 2, 5 ; 4, 10 ; 8, 1.

item, adv., *likewise, further, moreover, too,* 54, 13.

iter, itineris, N. [I-, *go*], *a going: journey, march,* 25, 26 ; 61, 6 : *way, path, road, means of access,* 16, 8 ; 61, 22. (W. G. 46.)

iterum, adv., *again, a second time,* 25, 24.

Iuba, -ae, M., *Juba,* a king of Numidia, in northern Africa, 53, 15.

iubeō, 2, iussī, iussus, *order, command,* 3, 11 : *wish, entreat, urge, invite,* 10, 25 ; 24, 8.

iūcundus, adj. with comp. and sup. [DIV-, *bright*], *pleasant,* *agreeable, delightful,* 61, 7. (W. G. 27.)

Iūdaea, -ae, F., *Judea,* the country of the Jews, Palestine, 46, 25.

Iūdaeus, adj. *of Judea, of the Jews.* As a subst., M. plur., *the Jews,* 46, 25.

iūdex, -icis, M. and F. [iūs, *right;* DIC-, *point out*], *judge, juror,* 8, 7 ; 18, 3. (W. G. 26 and 48.)

iūdicium, -ī, N. (iūdex, *judge*), *judgment, trial : court,* 58, 1. (W. G. 26 and 48.)

iūdicō, 1, -āvī, -ātus (iūdex, *judge*), *judge : deem, consider,* 28, 18 : *declare, proclaim,* 14, 26. (W. G. 26 and 48.)

iugulum, -ī, N. (dim. of iugum, *yoke*), *throat, neck,* 41, 24. (W. G. 48.)

iugum, -ī, N. [IVG-, *bind together*], *yoke,* 8, 18 : *height, range, ridge,* 33, 6. (W. G. 48.)

Iūlia, -ae, F., *Julia :* (1) daughter of Julius Caesar, 52, 1 ; (2) sister of Julius Caesar, 63, 10.

Iūlius, -ī, M., name of the famous gens to which *C. Julius Caesar* belonged, 4, 25.

iungō, 3, iūnxī, iūnctus [IVG-, *yoke*], *join together, unite,* 13, 14 : *make by joining, enter into,* 50, 26. (W. G. 48.)

iūnior, comp. of iuvenis, 62, 30.

Iūnius, -ī, M., gentile name of the Brutus family, e.g. *M. Junius Brutus,* 55, 2.

Iūnō, -ōnis, F., *Juno,* daughter of

VOCABULARY. 263

Saturn, sister and wife of
Jupiter, goddess of marriage,
21, 8. (W. G. 27.)
Iuppiter, Iovis, M. [DIV-, *shine;*
pater, *father*], *Jupiter*, son of
Saturn, the supreme god, 4, 9.
iūrō, 1, -āvī, -ātus (iūs, *right*),
swear, take an oath, 32, 19. (W.
G. 48.)
iūs, iūris, N. [IV-, *bind*], *that
which is binding, law, right,
justice*, 8, 15; 10, 4; 11, 4:
court of justice, 8, 7; 18, 10:
permission, prerogative, 46, 27:
iūs dīcere, *to pronounce judgment*, 54, 9: iūre, *justly*, 8, 10.
(W. G. 48.)
iūsiūrandum, iūrisiūrandī, N. (iūs,
right; iūrō, *swear*), *oath*, 4, 27.
(W. G. 48.)

iūssus, P. of iubeō, 24, 8.
(iūssus, -ūs), M. (iubeō, *order*),
only abl. sing., *order, command*,
8, 27.
iūstitia, -ae, F. (iūstus, *just*),
justice, equity, 5, 3. (W. G. 48.)
iūstus, adj. (iūs, *right*), *righteous,
just*, 24, 24: *perfect, complete*,
24, 19. (W. G. 48.)
iuvenis, -is, adj. with comp.
iūnior [DIV-, *bright, shine*],
young, youthful, 43, 2. As
subt., M. and F., *young person,
youth* (between twenty and
forty years), 3, 14. (W. G. 27.)
iuventūs, -ūtis, F. (iuvenis,
young), *age of youth, youth*.
Often used collectively, *youth,
young people*, 20, 17. (W. G.
27.)

K

Kalendae, -ārum, F. [CAL-, *call*],
*day of proclamation, Calends,
first day of the month*, 5,
22.

L

L., abbreviation for *Lucius*, a
Roman praenomen, 19, 27.
labor, -ōris, M., *labor, toil: hardship*, 43, 17.
labōriōsē, adv. with comp. and
sup. (labōriōsus, *toilsome*),
laboriously, industriously, 54,
10.
labōrō, 1, -āvī, -ātus (labor, *labor*),
labor: suffer, be afflicted, 48, 7:
be in difficulty, be in danger,
45, 9.

lacerō, 1, -āvī, -ātus (lacer,
mangled), *tear to pieces,
mangle: wreck, shatter*, 30, 9:
censure, slander, abuse, 56, 18.
lacessō, 3, -īvī, -ītus, *excite, provoke*, 19, 10.
lacrima, -ae, F., *tear*, 8, 14.
lacrimābundus, adj. (lacrimō,
weep), *bursting into tears, weeping*, 18, 14.
lacrimō, 1, -āvī, -ātus (lacrima,
tear), *shed tears, weep*, 67, 12.

VOCABULARY.

lacus, -ūs, M., *hollow, lake,* 22, 22.
laedō, 3, -sī, -sus, *hurt, injure: annoy, offend,* 19, 10.
laesus, P. of laedō, 19, 10.
laetitia, -ae, F. (laetus, *joyful*), *joy, pleasure, delight,* 67, 6.
laetus, adj. with comp. and sup., *joyful, cheerful, glad, happy,* 5, 15; 44, 20.
laeva, -ae, F. (laevus, *left;* sc. manus), *left hand,* 3, 26.
Laevīnus, -ī, M., family name of P. *Valerius Laevinus,* consul 280 B.C., 25, 7.
lambō, 3, —, —, *lick,* 1, 11.
lāmina, -ae, F., *thin slice, plate,* 63, 20.
lāna, -ae, F., *wool: spinning,* 14, 25 (v. notes, fig. 8).
lanius, ī, M. [for *lacnius, LAC-, tear*], *butcher,* 18, 20.
lapideus, adj. (lapis, *stone*), *of stone, consisting of stones,* 11, 7.
lapis, -idis, M., *stone: mile-stone,* 25, 27 (v. notes, fig. 13).
laqueus, -ī, M., *noose,* 8, 8.
Lārentia, -ae, F., *Acca Larentia,* wife of Faustulus, the shepherd who found Romulus and Remus, 1, 15.
largītiō, -ōnis, F. (largior, *bestow*), *generosity, giving freely, granting,* 40, 13.
latebra, -ae, F. (lateō, *be hidden*), *hiding place, retreat,* 49, 3.
lateō, 2, -uī, —, *lie hid, be concealed,* 65, 4.
laterīcius, adj. (later, *brick*), *made of bricks,* 70, 28.

Latīnus, adj., *of Latium, Latin,* 54, 18. Subst. Latīnus, -ī, M., *a Latin,* 9, 18.
latrō, -ōnis, M., *freebooter, robber, bandit,* 1, 18.
latus, -eris, N., *side, flank,* 47, 17.
laudō, 1, -āvī, -ātus (laus, *praise*), *praise, laud, commend,* 14, 22.
laurea, -ae, F., *the laurel tree: laurel crown, bay wreath,* 56, 27.
laus, laudis, F., *praise, commendation, fame, glory,* 17, 18; 58, 14.
laxē, adv. with comp. (laxus, *wide*), *widely: loosely,* 24, 18.
laxitās, -ātis, F. (laxus, *wide*), *width, spaciousness, size,* 70, 20.
lectīca, -ae, F. (lectus, *couch*), *litter, sedan, palanquin,* 27, 21 (v. notes, fig. 14).
lectulus, -ī, M. (dim. of lectus), *small couch, bed,* 65, 12.
lectus, -ī, M., *couch, bed,* 43, 7.
lēgātiō, -ōnis, F. (lēgō, *send with a commission*), *embassy, legation,* 3, 7.
lēgātus, -ī, M. (lēgō, *send with a commission*), *ambassador,* 3, 5: *lieutenant,* 36, 10.
legiō, -ōnis, F. (cf. legō, *gather*), *body of soldiers, legion,* 24, 2.
legō, 3, lēgī, lēctus [LEG-, *gather*], *gather, collect: choose, appoint,* 5, 21: *read,* 56, 12.
lēnōcinium, -ī, N. (lēnō, *seducer*), *allurement, enticement: ornament, finery,* 70, 30.

Lentulus, -ī, M., family name of P. *Cornelius Lentulus*, 62, 26.
lentus, adj. with comp. and sup. (cf. **lēnis**, *soft*), *pliant, flexible: lingering, slow*, 55, 28.
Lepidus, -ī, M., family name of *M. Aemilius Lepidus*, one of the second triumvirate, 64, 19.
lētālis, -e, adj. (**lētum**, *death*), *deadly, fatal, mortal*, 12, 17.
levis, -e, adj. with comp. and sup., *light: small, trivial*, 33, 22.
levō, 1, -āvī, -ātus (**levis**, *light*), *lift up, raise: lighten, relieve*, 32, 6.
lēx, lēgis, F., *motion, bill, measure, law*, 6, 3; 41, 5; 54, 12 : *condition*, 6, 24; 23, 29.
libēns, -entis, adj. with sup. (P. of **libet**, *it pleases*), *willing, with pleasure, glad*, 38, 30.
libenter, adv. with comp. and sup. (**libēns**, *willing*), *willingly, cheerfully, gladly*, 56, 27.
līber, -era, -erum, adj. with comp. and sup., *free, unrestrained: frank*, 44, 10.
Līber, -erī, M., *Liber*, an Italian deity of planting and fructification, identified with the Greek Bacchus, 22, 19.
liber, -brī, M. *book*, 15, 9.
līberālitās, -ātis, F. (**līberālis**, *of freedom*), *characteristic of a freeman: liberality, generosity*, 26, 8.
līberāliter, adv. with comp. and sup. (**līberālis**, *of freedom*), *like a freeman, courteously, graciously*, 28, 5.
līberē, adv. with comp. (**līber**, *free*), *freely, openly*, 26, 13.
līberī, -ōrum or -ūm (**līber**, *free*), *free persons: children*, 3, 12.
līberō, 1, -āvī, -ātus (**līber**, *free*), *set free, free*, 2, 12 : *release*, 39, 17.
lībertās, -ātis, F. (**līber**, *free*), *freedom: political freedom, liberty*, 17, 12 : *freedom of speech*, 58, 3.
lībertus, -ī, M. (**līber**, *free*), *freedman*, 49, 4.
licet, 2, -cuit and -citum est, impers., *it is lawful, is allowed, is permitted*, 41, 16.
līctor, -ōris, M., *lictor*, official attendant upon a magistrate, 8, 8 (v. notes, fig. 3).
līneāmentum, -ī, N. (**linea**, *string*), *line, mark: feature, lineament*, 2, 9.
lingua, -ae, F. (for old **dingua**, cf. Eng. *tongue*), *tongue*, 1, 11.
liquefaciō, 3, —, -factus (**liqueō**, *be fluid;* **faciō**, *make*), *make liquid, melt, dissolve*, 66, 14.
lītigātor, -ōris, M. (**lītigō**, *dispute*), *a party to a lawsuit, litigant*, 68, 4.
littera, -ae, F., *a letter of the alphabet:* plur., *a letter, epistle*, 44, 16 : *learning, education, letters*, 18, 5.
lītus, -oris, N., *sea-shore, beach*, 30, 10.

Līvius, -ī, M., gentile name of *M. Livius Salinator*, consul 219 and 207 B.C., **35**, 18.

Locrī, -ōrum, M., *Locri Epizephyrii*, a Greek city in Bruttium in southern Italy, **30**, 5.

locuplēs, -ētis, adj. with comp. and sup. (**locus**, *place*; cf. **pleō**, *fill*), *rich, wealthy*, **17**, 18.

locus, -ī, M., plur., **locī** and **loca**, *place, spot*, **1**, 10: *station, position*, **60**, 7: *cause, occasion, opportunity*, **50**, 4; **56**, 13: *place, position, rank*, **55**, 22.

longē, adv. with comp. and sup. (**longus**, *long*), *a long way off, far*, **4**, 7: *greatly, by far*, **44**, 3.

longus, adj. with comp. and sup., *long*, **23**, 10: *of long duration, tedious*, **32**, 11.

loquor, 3, -cūtus, dep., *speak, talk*, **26**, 16.

lōrum, -ī, N., *thong, strap*, **24**, 19. (W. G. 78.)

Lūceria, -ae, F., *Luceria*, a town in Apulia, on the borders of Samnium, **23**, 7.

Lūcerīnī, -ōrum, M., *the inhabitants of Luceria*, **23**, 9.

Lūcius, -ī, M., *Lucius*, often written *L.*, a Roman praenomen, **10**, 17.

Lucrētia, -ae, F., *Lucretia*, wife of Tarquinius Collatinus, **14**, 24.

Lucrīnus, adj. (sc. **lacus**, *lake*), the *Lucrine Lake*, on the coast of Campania, **22**, 21.

lūctor, 1, -ātus, dep. (**lūcta**, *a wrestling*), *wrestle, struggle, strife*, **43**, 20.

lūctus, -ūs, M. (cf. **lūgeō**, *mourn*), *sorrow, mourning, grief, distress*, **37**, 16.

Lūcullus, -ī, M., family name of *L. Licinius Lucullus*, consul 74 B.C., and a distinguished soldier, **47**, 28.

lūcus, -ī, M. [LVC-, *shine*], *sacred grove: wood, grove*, **3**, 2. (W. G. 50.)

lūdibrium, -ī, N. (**lūdus**, *play*), *mockery, derision*, **3**, 7.

(**lūdicer**), -cra, -crum, adj. (**lūdus**, *play*), *belonging to play, done in sport, sportive*, **1**, 17.

lūdus, -ī, M., *play, game: school*, **18**, 5: plur., *public games, shows*, **3**, 10.

lūgeō, 2, lūxī, lūctus, *mourn, lament, bewail*, **8**, 5.

lūgubris, -e, adj. (cf. **lūgeō**, *mourn*), *of mourning, mournful*, **71**, 13.

lūmen, -inis, N. [LVC-, *shine*], *light*, **60**, 18. (W. G. 50.)

lūna, -ae, F. [LVC-, *shine*], *moon*, **5**, 24. (W. G. 50.)

lupa, -ae, F. (**lupus**, *wolf*), *she-wolf*, **1**, 10.

lūstrō, 1, -āvī, -ātus (**lūstrum**, *purification*), *light up: review*, **4**, 21. (W. G. 50.)

Lutātius, -ī, M., gentile name of *Lutatius Catulus*, consul 242 B.C., who brought the first Punic war to a close in 241 B.C., **31**, 22.

VOCABULARY. 267

lūx, lūcis, F. [LVC-, *shine*], *light*, 64, 1: *daylight, day*, 18, 12: *life*, 24, 3. (W. G. 50.)

lūxus, -ūs, M., *excess, indulgence: magnificence, splendor*, 14, 24; 66, 4.

M

M., abbreviation for *Marcus*, a Roman praenomen, 22, 11.

Macedonia, -ae, F., *Macedonia*, a country north of Greece, 61, 24.

māchina, -ae, F. (Gr., μηχανή), *machine, device*, 30, 19.

mactō, 1, -āvī, -ātus (mactus, *honored*), *magnify, honor: sacrifice, offer*, 65, 30.

mactus, adj., *worshipped, honored*: **macte virtūte estō,** *be increased in your merit, go on and prosper in your valor, well done*, 37, 17.

Maecēnās, -ātis, M., *C. Cilnius Maecenas*, the intimate friend and prime minister of Augustus, 70, 9.

maestus, adj. with sup., *sad, sorrowful, dejected, gloomy*, 60, 26.

magis, adv. comp. (**māgnus,** *great*), *more, in a higher degree: rather, in preference*, 3, 1.

magister, -trī, M., *master, commander*, 34, 12: *teacher*, 19, 2.

magistrātus, -ūs, M. (**magister,** *master*), *office of master, civil office, magistracy*, 18, 25: *magistrate*, 38, 25.

māgnificus, adj., comp. **māgnificentior,** sup. **māgnificentissimus** [**māgnus,** *great;* FAC-, *make*], *great, noble: splendid, magnificent*, 66, 7.

māgnitūdō, -inis, F. (**māgnus,** *great*), *greatness, size, magnitude*, 13, 2.

māgnopere, adv.(abl. of **māgnum opus**), *very much, greatly, exceedingly*, 66, 23.

māgnus, adj., comp. **māior, -ōris,** sup. **māximus,** *large, great*, 6, 4: *strong, loud*, 4, 23: *aged*, 1, 2: *noble, eminent*, 26, 10.

Māgnus, -ī, M., *Magnus*, surname of *Cn. Pompeius Magnus*, 44, 21.

Maharbal, -alis, M., *Maharbal*, the commander of Hannibal's cavalry, 38, 3.

māiestās, -ātis, F. (**māior,** *greater*), *greatness, dignity, majesty*, 20, 24.

māior, comp. of **māgnus,** *greater*, 6, 4: *older*, 1, 2.

male, adv., comp. **pēius** sup. **pessimē** (**malus,** *bad*), *badly, wrongly: unsuccessfully*, 31, 20: *scarcely*, 7, 23.

mālō, mālle, māluī, — (**magis,** *rather;* **volō,** *wish*), *choose rather, prefer*, 26, 21. (W. G. 79.)

malum, -ī, N. (**malus,** *evil*), *an*

evil, mischief, misfortune, calamity, 32, 24.

malus, adj., comp. **pĕior,** -us, gen. -ōris; sup. **pessimus,** *bad, evil, not good,* 28, 19: *pernicious, dangerous,* 41, 4.

Māmurius, -ī, M., *Mamurius Veturius,* the maker of the sacred shields, 5, 19.

mandō, 1, -āvī, ātus [**manus,** *hand;* 2 DA-, *put*], *put in hand, intrust: order, command,* 42, 2. (W. G. 25 and 51.)

maneō, 2, mānsī, mānsus [MAN-, *stay*], *stay, remain, abide,* 22, 8: *last, continue, endure,* 8, 20. (W. G. 52.)

manifestus, adj., *palpable, clear, open, evident,* 8, 16.

manipulāris, -e, adj. [**manipulus,** *handful, maniple;* fr. **manus,** *hand;* PLE-, *fill*], *belonging to a maniple of a company.* As subst., M., *common soldier,* 22, 7.

Mānlius, -ī, M., *Manlius,* name of a Roman gens, 20, 17.

mānō, 1, -āvī, —, *flow, run: extend, spread,* 57, 20.

mānsuētūdō, -inis, F. (cf. **mānsuēscō,** *tame*), *tameness, mildness, gentleness,* 66, 29. (W. G. 51.)

manūmittō, 3, -mīsī, -missus (**manus,** *hand;* **mittō,** *send*), *release, set at liberty, emancipate,* 38, 29. (W. G. 51.)

manus, -ūs, F. [MA-, *measure*], *hand,* 3, 23: *hook,* 30, 19: *band, force, troops,* 59, 20. (W. G. 51.)

Mārcius, -ī, M., name of a Roman gens, as *Ancus Marcius,* fourth king of Rome, 9, 16.

Mārcus, -ī, M., *Marcus,* a Roman praenomen, 19, 1.

mare, -is, N. (cf. Eng. *mere*), *sea,* 22, 20 : **Mare Superum,** *the upper sea, the Adriatic,* 54, 20.

margarīta, -ae, F., *pearl,* 66, 11.

maritimus, adj. (**mare,** *sea*), *of the sea, sea, maritime,* 31, 14.

Marius, -ī, M., name of a Roman gens, as *C. Marius,* 44, 13.

marmoreus, adj. (**marmor,** *marble*), *made of marble, marble,* 70, 27.

Mārs, Mārtis, M., *Mars,* father of Romulus and god of war, with whose month, Martius, the Roman year began, 5, 21 : *war, battle,* 53, 25.

Mārtius, adj., *of Mars: of March,* 5, 22.

Massicus, adj., *of Mount Massicus* in Campania, 22, 23.

māter, -tris, F., *mother,* 1, 12.

mātrimōnium, -ī, N. (**māter,** *mother*), *wedlock, marriage, matrimony,* 13, 14: **in mātrimōnium dare,** *give in marriage,* 13, 13.

mātrōna, -ae, F. (**māter,** *mother*), *married woman, wife, matron,* 40, 2.

māximē, adv. (**māximus,** *greatest*), *in the highest degree, especially,* 3, 12.

māximus, sup. of **māgnus,** *greatest, extreme,* 11, 5 ; 40, 2. As subst. M., family name of *Q. Fabius Maximus*, 36, 21.

medicāmentum, -ī, N. (medicō, *medicate*), *drug, remedy, medicine*, 46, 17.

medicus, -ī, M., *medical man, physician, surgeon*, 28, 23.

meditor, 1, -ātus, dep., *consider, meditate: plan, devise*, 54, 23.

medium, -ī, N. (medius, *middle*), *middle, center, intervening space*, 6, 26: *midst, public*, 39, 1.

medius, adj. [MED-, *mean, middle*], *in the middle*, 6, 7: *middle part, midst*, 10, 10.

melior, adj. comp. of bonus, *better*, 71, 9.

membrum, -ī, N., *limb, member*, 17, 7.

Memmius, -ī, M., name of a Roman gens, as *C. Memmius Gemellus*, 56, 19.

memorābilis, -e, adj. with comp. (memorō, *call to mind*), *that may be heard of: worth telling, remarkable*, 50, 14.

memoria, -ae, F. (memor, *mindful*), *memory, remembrance*, 15, 7.

memorō, 1, -āvī, -ātus (memor, *mindful*), *bring to remembrance, relate, tell*, 9, 13.

Menēnius, -ī, M., *Menenius*, name of a Roman gens, whose most famous member was *Menenius Agrippa Lanatus*, consul 503 B.C., 16, 19.

mēns, mentis, F. [MAN-, MEN-, *mind;* cf. meminī], *mind*, 11, 12: *feeling, attention*, 3, 14: *plan, purpose*, 27, 6. (W. G. 52.)

mēnsa, -ae, F., mēnsus [P. of mētior (MA-), *measure*], *table: meal, course*, 66, 9.

mēnsis, -is, M. [MA-, *measure*], *month*, 54, 8. (W. G. 51.)

mentiō, -ōnis, F. [MAN-, MEN-, *mind*], *calling to mind, mention*, 14, 21. (W. G. 52.)

mercor, 1, -ātus, dep. (merx, *goods*), *trade, purchase, buy*, 15, 22.

mereō, 2, -uī, -itus, *deserve, merit: win, earn*, 33, 16.

mergō, 3, mersī, mersus, *dip, plunge, sink*, 30, 26.

meritō, adv. (abl. of meritum, *merit*), *deservedly, justly*, 40, 3.

merx, -cis, F., *goods, wares, commodities*, 54, 12.

Metellus, -ī, M., *Metellus*, name of an illustrious Roman family of the Caecilian gens, 44, 28.

Mettius, -ī, M., praenomen of *Mettius Fufetius*, the Alban general, 8, 20.

metus, -ūs, M., *fear, dread*, 6, 11.

meus, pron. poss. (mē, *me*), *of me, my*, 2, 24.

mī, voc. of meus, 27, 8.

micāns, -antis, adj. (P. of micō, *dart to and fro*), *gleaming, flashing*, 7, 4.

mīles, -itis, M. and F., *soldier*, 12, 10: collect., *soldiery, army*, 19, 21.

Milētus, -ī, F., *Miletus*, a large Ionian city, on the western coast of Asia Minor, 49, 25.

mīlia, plur. of mīlle, 37, 24.

mīliēns or **mīliēs**, adv. (mīlle, *thousand*), *a thousand times*, 50, 24.

mīlitāris, -e, adj. (mīles, *soldier*), *of a soldier, of war*: rēs mīlitāris, *the art of war*, 4, 30.

mīlitia, -ae, F. (mīles, *soldier*), *military service*, 16, 21: locative, mīlitiae, *in war, on the field*, 9, 9.

mīlle, plur. mīlia or mīllia, num. adj., *thousand, ten hundred*, 21, 21.

mīmus, -ī, M. (Gr., μῖμος), *mimic actor: farce*, 71, 19.

minimē, adv. sup. of parum (minimus, *least*), *least of all, least, very little: not at all, by no means*, 2, 7.

minimus, adj. sup. of parvus, *least, smallest, trifling, insignificant*, 62, 24.

minister, -tra, -trum, adj., *subordinate, ministering*. As subst. M., *attendant, servant*, 66, 10.

ministerium, -ī, N. (minister, *subordinate*), *service, occupation, work, employment*, 17, 6.

minitor, 1, -ātus, dep. (freq. of minor, *threaten*), *threaten, menace*, 59, 23.

minor, 1, -ātus, dep. (minae, *projections: threats*), *jut forth, project: threaten*, 18, 7.

minor, minus, -ōris, adj. (comp. of parvus, *small*), *smaller, less*, 15, 22.

Minucius, -ī, M., gentile name of *M. Minucius Rufus*, 34, 12.

minuō, 3, -uī, -ūtus, *make small, lessen, diminish*, 44, 25.

minus, adv. comp. of parum (N. of minor, *less*), *less*, 6, 10.

mīrābilis, -e, adj. with comp. (mīror, *wonder at*), *wonderful, marvellous, strange*, 12, 4.

mīrāculum, -ī, N. (mīror, *wonder*), *marvellous thing, wonderful sight*, 34, 2.

mīrandus, adj. (P. of mīror, *wonder*), *wonderful, strange*, 29, 26.

mīrificus, adj. with sup. [mīrus, *wonderful*; FAC-, *make*], *wonderful, marvellous*, 63, 8.

mīror, 1, -ātus, dep. (mīrus, *wonderful*), *wonder, marvel, admire*, 68, 12; 69, 6.

mīrus, adj., *wonderful, astonishing, amazing*, 3, 3; 41, 27.

Mīsēnum, -ī, N., *Misenum*, a promontory of Campania, 22, 21.

miseror, 1, -ātus, dep. (miser, *wretched*), *lament, deplore*, 26, 12.

missiō, -ōnis, F. (mittō, *send*), *sending: release, discharge from service*, 50, 16. (W. G. 53.)

Mithridātēs, -is, M., *Mithridates the Great*, king of Pontus, 46, 2.

Mithridāticus, adj., *of Mithridates, Mithridatic*, 48, 4.

mītigō, 1, -āvī, -ātus [mītis, *mild*;

VOCABULARY. 271

AG-, *make*], *soften, ripen : civilize, tame,* 5, 6.

mītis, -e, adj. with comp. and sup., *mild : gentle, kind,* 13, 11.

mittō, 3, mīsī, missus [MIT-, *send*], *cause to go, send,* 3, 5 : *let go, release, dismiss,* 69, 24 : *throw, hurl,* 12, 11. (W. G. 53.)

Mitylēnae, -ārum, F., *Mitylene,* a famous Greek city on the island of Lesbos in the Aegean sea, 49, 15.

moderātiō, -ōnis, F. (moderor, *set bounds to*), *moderation, self-control,* 56, 7.

moderātus, adj. with comp. and sup. (P. of moderor, *set a measure to*), *within bounds, moderate,* 44, 3.

modicus, adj. (modus, *measure*), *in proper measure, moderate,* 33, 17 : *middling, ordinary,* 70, 20.

modius, -ī, M. (modus, *measure*), *a grain measure, peck,* 37, 26.

modo, adv. (abl. of modus, *measure*), *only, merely,* 22, 16 : modo ... modo, *sometimes ... sometimes,* 61, 25.

modus, -ī, M. [MA-, *measure*], *measure, extent: manner, way,* 9, 23 : *code,* 54, 15 : quō modo, *in the manner that, as,* 42, 15.

moenia, -ium, N. [MV-, *shut, fasten*], *defensive walls, city walls, walls,* 2, 24. (W. G. 55.)

mōlēs, -is, F., *shapeless mass, huge bulk, weight,* 25, 13.

molestē, adv. with comp. and sup. (molestus, *troublesome*), *with trouble, with difficulty, with annoyance, with vexation,* 48, 11.

molestia, -ae, F. (molestus, *troublesome*), *trouble, annoyance, vexation,* 43, 18.

molestus, adj. with comp. and sup. (mōlēs, *mass*), *troublesome, annoying,* 48, 19.

mōlior, 4, -ītus, dep. (mōlēs, *mass*), *make exertion, endeavor: do, undertake,* 52, 13.

mollis, -e, adj. with comp. and sup., *soft, mild, gentle,* 22, 18 : *weak, effeminate,* 45, 13.

Molō, -ōnis, M., *Molo,* surname of Apollonius of Rhodes, the famous Greek rhetorician, 49, 16.

mōmentum, -ī, N. [MOV-, *move*], *movement: brief space of time, instant, moment,* 53, 11 : *cause, circumstance,* 35, 21. (W. G. 54.)

moneō, 2, -uī, -itus [MAN-, *mind*], *remind, admonish, advise, warn,* 20, 7 ; 35, 3. (W. G. 52.)

monitus, -ūs, M. (moneō, *warn*), *reminding, warning, admonition, advice,* 6, 6. (W. G. 52.)

mōns, montis, M. [MAN-, *project*], *mountain,* 6, 13.

mora, -ae, F., *delay,* 32, 12.

morbus, -ī, M. (cf. morior, *die*), *sickness, disease,* 6, 13.

moriēns, -entis, adj. (P. of morior, *die*), *dying,* 65, 27.

VOCABULARY.

morior, morīrī and morī, mortuus, dep. [MAR-, *die*], *die, expire*, **17, 13**.

moror, 1, -ātus, dep. (mora, *delay*), *delay, remain: retard, detain, hinder*, **57, 6**.

mors, -tis, F. [MAR-, *die*], *death*, **10, 15**.

morsus, -ūs, M. (cf. mordeō, *bite*), *biting, sting, bite*, **66, 25**.

mortuus, adj. (P. of morior, *die*), *dead*, **6, 17**.

mōs, mōris, M. [MA-, *measure*], *habit, usage, custom*, **9**, 22: *nature, manner, mode*, **53, 10**: *conduct, character*, **13, 15**. (W. G. 51.)

moveō, 2, mōvī, mōtus [MOV-, *move*], *move: expel, remove*, **29, 27**: *affect, inspire, influence*, **7, 30**; **22, 5**; **43, 3**. (W. G. 54.)

mox, adv., *soon*, **25, 10**: *thereupon, then*, **41, 25**.

mucrō, -ōnis, M., *sharp point, edge: sword*, **47, 18**.

muliebriter, adv. (muliebris, *feminine*), *in the manner of a woman, like a woman*, **40, 5**.

mulier, -eris, F., *woman*, **4, 11**.

muliercula, -ae, F. (dim. of mulier, *woman*), *little woman: young woman, girl*, **35, 23**.

mūliō, -ōnis, M. (mūlus, *mule*), *mule-driver*, **13, 23**.

multiplex, -icis, adj. [multus, *many*; PLEC-, *fold*], *with many folds, manifold, many*, **53, 8**. (W. G. 60.)

multitūdō, -inis, F. (multus, *much*), *great number, multitude, crowd*, **10, 9**.

multō, adv. (abl. N. of multus, *much*), *by much, much, a great deal*, **4, 16**; **17, 17**.

multō, 1, -āvī, -ātus (multa, *fine*), *punish*, **18, 26**.

multum, adv. (multus, *much*), *much, very much*, **26, 26**.

multus, adj., comp. plūs, sup. plūrimus, *much*: plur., *many*, **16, 14**. As a subst. M., *many men*, **3, 11**.

mūniō, 4, -īvī, -ītus (moenia, *ramparts*), *defend with a wall, fortify: protect*, **37, 19**: *make, build, construct*, **54, 19**. (W. G. 55.)

mūnus, -eris, N. [MV-, *fasten*], *service, office: reward, gift*, **3, 21**; **27, 15**.

mūraena, -ae, F., *a murena* (a sea-fish), **69, 20**.

mūrus, -ī, M. [MV-, *shut, fasten*], *wall, city wall*, **11, 6**. (W. G. 55.)

Mutina, -ae, F., *Mutina*, city in Cisalpine Gaul, **63, 18**.

Mutinēnsis, -e, adj., *belonging to Mutina, at Mutina*, **64, 6**.

mūtō, 1, -āvī, -ātus (freq. of moveō, *move*), *move: change, alter*, **11, 8**. (W. G. 54.)

N

nam, conj., *for, seeing that, inasmuch as,* **2, 9; 49,** 12.

namque, conj., *for, seeing that, inasmuch as,* **18,** 5; **21,** 9.

nancīscor, -ī, nactus or nanctus, dep., *get, meet with, find,* **3,** 18.

nārrō, 1, -āvī, -ātus [GNA-, *know*], *make known, tell, say,* **16, 23; 51,** 20. (W. G. 43.)

Nāsīca, -ae, M., surname of *Publius Cornelius Scipio Nasica Serapio*, who led the senate against Ti. Gracchus, **40,** 23.

nāscor, -ī, nātus, dep. [GNA-, *beget*], *be born, be born to,* **13,** 3 : *rise, derive origin, spring from,* **14,** 20 : *begin, arise, spring up,* **55,** 29. (W. G. 41.)

nāsus, -ī, M., *nose,* **57,** 10.

nātūra, -ae, F. [GNĀ-, *beget*], *birth: nature, natural disposition,* **40,** 9.

nātus, adj. (P. of nāscor, *be born*), *born: of the age of,* **32,** 18. (W. G. 41.)

(**nātus**, -ūs), M., only abl. sing. [GNA-, *be born*], *birth, age,* **1,** 2.

naufragium, -ī, N. [nāvis, *ship;* FRAG-, *break*], *shipwreck,* **56,** 4. (W. G. 38.)

nāvālis, -e, adj. (**nāvis**, *ship*), *nautical, naval,* **30,** 17.

nāvicula, -ae, F. (dim. of **nāvis**, *ship*), *small vessel, boat, skiff,* **52,** 28.

nāvigium, -ī, N. [nāvis, *ship;* AG-, *drive*], *vessel, ship, boat,* **52,** 28.

nāvis, -is, F., *ship,* **30,** 7.

Nāvius, -ī, M., *Attus Navius*, the augur under Tarquinius Priscus, **11,** 9.

nē, adv. and conj. (1) As adv., *no, not :* nē . . . quidem, *not even,* **21,** 5. (2) As conj., in clauses of purpose, *that not, lest,* **5,** 18.

-ne, adv. enclit. interrog. : added as an interrogation mark to the first or principal word of the clause. Not translatable, **42,** 8.

Neāpolis, -is, F., *Naples*, on the coast of Campania, **22,** 25.

nec or **neque**, adv. and conj. (nē, *not;* -que, *and*) (nec emphasizes negation, neque connection), *and not, but not, also not, nor,* **7,** 23; **46,** 3 : nec . . . nec, *neither . . . nor,* **7,** 20 : nec . . . et, *on the one hand not . . . and on the other,* **70,** 8.

necessārius, adj. (necesse, *necessary*), *needful, indispensable, necessary,* **17,** 18.

necessitās, -ātis, F. (necesse, *necessary*), *necessity,* **1,** 21.

necō, 1, -āvī, -ātus (cf. **nex**, *death*), *kill, slay,* **28,** 25.

nefārius, adj. (nefās, *impious act*), *impious, execrable, abominable,* **42,** 11.

nefāstus, adj. (nefās, *impious act*), *contrary to religion, unhallowed, unpropitious*, referring to days

VOCABULARY.

upon which no legal business could be done, 5, 25; 20, 13.

neglegēns, -entis, adj. with comp. (P. of **neglegō**, *disregard*), *heedless, careless*, 71, 1.

neglegō, 3, -ēxī, -ēctus (nec, *not;* legō, *gather*), *not gather, disregard, neglect, be indifferent to*, 15, 21.

negō, 1, -āvī, -ātus, *say no, deny, refuse, say not*, 11, 10.

nēmō, —, dat. **nēminī**, acc. **nēminem**, M. and F. (nē, *not;* homō, *man*), *no man, no one, nobody*, 36, 24.

nemus, -oris, N., *woodland, forest, pasture, grove*, 5, 12.

nepōs, -ōtis, M., *grandson*, 2, 8.

neptis, -is, F. (cf. nepōs, *grandson*), *granddaughter*, 70, 25.

neque, see nec, 18, 16.

nēsciō, 4, -īvī, — (nē, *not;* sciō, *know*), *not to know, be ignorant, not know how*, 38, 9. (W. G. 66.)

neuter, -tra, -trum, adj. pron. (nē, *not;* uter, *either*), *neither the one nor the other, neither*, 23, 27.

nēve or **neu**, adv., *and not, nor, and that not, and lest*, 17, 2.

nex, necis, F. (cf. necō, *kill*), *death, murder, slaughter*, 41, 3; 49, 1.

nexus, adj. (P. of nectō, *bind*), *imprisoned*, 22, 12.

nī, conj., *if not, unless*, 18, 7.

niger, -gra, -grum, adj. comp. nigrior, sup. nigerrimus, *black, dark*, 56, 23.

nihil or **nīl**, N., indecl. (nē, *not;* hīlum, *a whit*), *nothing*, 14, 11.

nihildum, N., indecl., *nothing as yet*, 50, 14.

nihilum, -ī, N. (nē, *not;* hīlum, *a whit*), *not a shred, nothing*, 15, 22; 44, 21.

Nīlus, -ī, M., *the Nile*, 47, 19.

nīmīrum, adv. (nē, *not;* mīrum, *strange*), *without doubt, doubtless, surely, truly*, 38, 7.

nimis, adv.[nē, *not;* MA-, *measure*], *beyond measure, too much, too*, 17, 19.

nimius, adj. (nimis, *too much*), *beyond measure, excessive, too great*, 15, 11.

nisi, conj. (nē, *not;* sī, *if*), *if not, unless, except*, 9, 12; 11, 10.

nitēns, -entis, adj. with comp. (P. of niteō, *shine*), *shining, brilliant: illustrious, distinguished*, 59, 28.

nō, 1, -āvī, —, *swim*, 57, 6.

nōbilis, -e, adj. with comp. and sup. [GNO-, *know*], *well-known, famous, celebrated, renowned*, 4, 26; 48, 7: *of noble birth, high-born*, 12, 2; 32, 5. (W. G. 43.)

nōbilitās, -ātis, F. (nōbilis, *known*), *celebrity, fame: the nobility, aristocracy*, 17, 12. (W. G. 43.)

noceō, 2, -cuī, -citūrus (cf. necō, *kill*), *harm, hurt, injure*, 70, 12.

noctū, adv. (cf. nox, *night*), *at night, by night*, 30, 15.

noctua, -ae, F. (nox, *night*), *night-owl, owl*, 69, 27.

nocturnus, adj. (nox, *night*), *by night, nocturnal*, 6, 5.
Nōla, -ae, F., *Nola*, a town in central Campania, 71, 21.
nōlō, nōlle, nōluī, — (nē, *not;* volō, *wish*), *wish ... not, not to wish, be unwilling*, 41, 14. (W. G. 79.)
nōmen, -inis, N. [GNO-, *know*], *means of knowing, name*, 2, 16; *fame, renown*, 16, 5. (W. G. 43.)
nōminō, 1, -āvī, -ātum (nōmen, *name*), *call by name, name*, 4, 19. (W. G. 43.)
nōn, adv. (nē, *not;* ūnum, *one*), *not, by no means, not at all*, 3, 4 : nōn sōlum ... sed etiam, *not only ... but also*, 27, 14.
nōndum, adv., *not yet*, 27, 6.
nōnnūllus or nōn nūllus, adj. (nōn, *not;* nūllus, *no*), *some, several:* plur. M. as subst., *some, several*, 26, 15.
nōnnumquam, adv. (nōn, *not;* numquam, *never*), *sometimes*, 57, 2.
nōs, plur. of ego, *we, us*, 27, 9.
nota, ae, F. [GNO-, *know*], *means of recognition, mark*, 64, 27. (W. G. 43.)
nōtus, adj. with comp. and sup. (P. of nōscō, *come to know, learn*), *known, familiar*, 35, 12. (W. G. 43.)
novācula, -ae, F. (novō, *make new*), *sharp knife, razor*, 11, 15.
novem, num. adj. indecl., *nine*, 15, 9.
novus, adj., *new, young*, 2, 16; 67, 23 : *novel, unusual, strange*, 47, 1.
nox, noctis, F. (cf. noceō, *harm*), *night*, 21, 3.
nūbēs, -is, F. [NVB-, *cloud*], *cloud, mist*, 34, 24.
nūbō, 3, nūpsī, nūptus (cf. nūbēs, *cloud, veil*), *veil oneself: be married, marry*, 52, 1.
nūdus, adj. *naked*, 24, 12.
nūllus, gen. nūllīus, dat. nūllī, adj. (nē, *not;* ūllus, *any*), *not any, none, no*, 6, 12. As subst. M. and F., *no one, nobody*, 58, 8.
num, adv. interrog., usually expecting a negative answer. In an indirect question, *whether*, 11, 14.
Numa, -ae, M., *Numa Pompilius*, the second king of Rome, 5, 3.
numerō, 1, -āvī, -ātus (numerus, *number*), *count, reckon: pay*, 49, 24 : *esteem, consider, regard*, 22, 27.
numerus, -ī, M., *number*, 9, 4 : *quantity, sum, amount*, 32, 4.
Numidia, -ae, F., *Numidia*, a country in northern Africa, now Algiers, 44, 12.
Numitor, -ōris, M., king of Alba Longa, 1, 1.
nummus, -ī, M., *piece of money, coin*, 68, 13.
numquam, adv. (nē, *not;* umquam, *at any time*), *at no time, never*, 36, 8.
nunc, adv. (num, *now;* -ce, de-

monst. suffix), *now, at present, at this time,* 4, 2.

nūntiō, 1, -āvī, -ātus (nūntius, *messenger*), *announce, make known, report,* 5, 15.

nūntius, adj., *that announces, making known.* As subst., M., *bearer of tidings, messenger,* 9, 26.

nurus, -ūs, F., *daughter-in-law,* *young woman, married woman,* 14, 23.

nusquam, adv. (nē, *not;* usquam, *anywhere*), *nowhere, in no place,* 3, 6: *on no occasion,* 37, 11.

nūtō, 1, -āvī, -ātus (freq. of nuō, *nod*), *nod: waver,* 51, 21.

nūtrīx, -īcis, F. (nūtriō, *nourish*), *nurse,* 18, 8.

O

ō, interj. of feeling or surprise, often best untranslated, *O!* 27, 3.

ob, prep. with acc., *on account of, for,* 3, 16.

obeō, -īre, -īvī, -itus (ob, *before, towards;* eō, *go*), *go to meet, go in opposition: perish, die,* 10, 16. (W. G. 46.)

obiciō, 3, -iēcī, -iectus (ob, *before, against;* iaciō, *throw*), *throw before, cast, offer, expose,* 65, 2; 69, 19: *set against, place before, oppose,* 16, 7. (W. G. 47.)

oblātus, P. of offerō, 28, 17.

obligō, 1, -āvī, -ātus (ob, *to;* ligō, *bind*), *bind up, bind, put under obligations,* 23, 26.

oblītus, adj. (P. of oblīvīscor, *forget*), *forgetful, unmindful,* 8, 4.

oblīviō, -ōnis, F. (cf. oblīvīscor, *forget*), *forgetfulness, oblivion,* 67, 5.

oblīvīscor, -ī, -lītus, *forget,* 39, 14.

obnoxius, adj. (ob, *to;* noxius, *hurtful*), *liable, exposed,* 56, 24.

obruō, 3, -uī, -utus (ob, without force; ruō, *throw down*), *overwhelm, cover, bury,* 3, 25: *destroy, slay,* 37, 12.

obsequor, -ī, -cūtus, dep. (ob, intensive; sequor, *follow*), *comply, yield, submit to,* 42, 8.

obses, -idis, M. and F. [ob, *before, by;* SED-, *sit*], *hostage,* 51, 19. (W. G. 67.)

obsideō, 2, -ēdī, -essus (ob, *before, against;* sedeō, *sit*), *sit, remain: besiege, blockade,* 14, 18. (W. G. 67.)

obsidiō, -ōnis, F. (cf. obsideō, *sit before*), *siege, blockade,* 19, 18. (W. G. 67.)

obsistō, 3, -stitī, -stitus (ob, *before, in the way;* sistō, *place oneself*), *stand in the way: oppose, resist,* 41, 7. (W. G. 69.)

obstinātus, adj. with comp. (P. of obstinō, *resolve*), *resolved upon, determined, resolute,* 20, 19. (W. G. 69.)

obstrepō, 3, -uī, — (ob, *against;* strepō, *make a noise*), *make a noise against, roar at, clamor at,* 11, 26.

obstringō, 3, -strinxī, -strictus (ob, *upon;* stringō, *draw tight*), *shut in, confine: bind, tie, hamper, involve,* 22, 12; 24, 9.

obstupefaciō, 3, -fēcī, -factus (ob, *before;* stupefaciō, *astonish*), pass. obstupefīō, -fierī, -factus, *astonish, amaze, stupefy,* 16, 13.

obtingō, 3, -tigī, — (ob, *to;* tangō, *touch*), *fall to the lot of, befall,* 55, 25. (W. G. 70.)

obtrectātor, -ōris, M. (obtrectō, *belittle*), *detractor, traducer, disparager,* 56, 24.

obtruncō, 1, —, -ātus (ob, *down, completely;* truncō, *cut*), *cut down, cut to pieces, kill,* 35, 16.

obveniō, 4, -vēnī, -ventus (ob, *toward, against;* veniō, *come, go*), *come up to, go to meet: befall, happen, fall to one's lot,* 50, 1. (W. G. 73.)

obviam, adv. (ob viam, *in the way*), *in the way, towards, against, to meet,* 26, 1. (W. G. 72.)

obvius, adj. (ob, *before;* via, *way*), *in the way, meeting, to meet,* 7, 27. (W. G. 72.)

obvolvō, 3, -vī, -lūtus (ob, *completely;* volvō, *roll*), *wrap around, envelop, cover over,* 52, 26. (W. G. 78.)

occāsiō, -ōnis, F. [ob, *to;* CAD-, *fall*], *occasion, favorable moment, favorable opportunity,* 33, 20. (W. G. 14.)

occāsus, -ūs, M. [ob, *down;* CAD-, *fall*], *falling, going down, setting,* 20, 15.

occidēns, -entis, adj. (P. of occidō, *go down*), *setting, sinking,* 44, 24.

occidō, 3, -cidī, -cāsus (ob, *down;* cadō, *fall*), *fall down: perish, be slain,* 37, 23: *sink, set,* 44, 24. (W. G. 14.)

occīdō, 3, -cīdī, -cīsus (ob, *down;* caedō, *strike*), *strike down: cut down, kill,* 4, 16; 42, 1. (W. G. 66.)

occumbō, 3, -cubuī, -cubitus (ob, *down;* *cumbō, *sink*), *fall in death, die,* 30, 15.

occupō, 1, -āvī, -ātus [ob, *completely;* CAP-, *take*], *take into possession, seize, occupy,* 14, 1; 43, 29.

occurrō, 3, -currī, -cursus (ob, *against;* currō, *run*), *run to meet, go to meet, meet,* 68, 10: *answer, reply,* 65, 28. (W. G. 19.)

Octāvia, see Octāvius.

Octāviānus, -ī, M., *C. Julius Caesar Octavianus,* the Roman emperor. He received the surname *Augustus* 27 B.C., 63, 10.

Octāvius, adj., name of the *Octavian* gens, originally plebeian, but made patrician by Julius Caesar. To it belonged the emperor Augustus, and his sister Octavia, wife of Mark Antony. 61, 17; 66, 2.

oculus, -ī, M. [AC-, *sharp*], *eye*, 3, 14.

odium, -ī, N., *hatred, aversion, enmity*, 31, 9.

odor or **odōs**, -ōris, M., *smell, scent, perfume*, 25, 15; 47, 22.

offendō, 3, -fendī, -fēnsus (ob, *against*; *fendō, strike*), *strike against: offend, displease*, 66, 30.

offēnsus, adj. with comp. (P. of offendō, *offend*), *offended, displeased*, 54, 30.

offerō, offerre, obtulī, oblātus (ob, *before*; ferō, *bear*), *bring before, present, show, offer*, 28, 6; 55, 4. (W. G. 34.)

officiōsus, adj. with comp. and sup. (officium, *service*), *full of courtesy, obliging, obedient*, 68, 12.

officium, -ī, N. [for opificium, opus, *work*; FAC-, *do*], *service, kindness, duty, office*, 64, 8: *official duty, business*, 55, 13. (W. G. 33.)

ōlim, adv., *at that time, some time, once upon a time, once*, 16, 24: *this long time*, 27, 20.

ōmen, -inis, N. (old osmen, for ausmen), *foreboding, sign, omen*, 22, 6.

omittō, 3, -īsī, -issus (ob, *over, past*; mittō, *send*), *let go: let alone, disregard, lose sight of*, 33, 18. (W. G. 53.)

omnis, -e, adj., *all, every, every kind, the whole*, 4, 17; 24, 3; 38, 20. As subst., M. and F. pl., *all men, all persons*, 5, 15. As subst., N., pl., *all things*, 4, 18.

onus, -eris, N., *load, burden*, 32, 6.

onustus, adj. (onus, *load*), *loaded, burdened*, 32, 2.

opera, -ae, F. (opus, *work*), *service, effort, work*, 62, 8: *assistance, agency*, 36, 7: operam dare, *see to, give attention to, listen to*, 9, 13; 49, 17.

opifex, -icis, M. and F. [opus, *work*; FAC-, *make*], *workman, mechanic*, 68, 10. (W. G. 33.)

Opīmius, -ī, M., *L. Opimius*, consul 121 B.C., 41, 19.

opīniō, -ōnis, F. (opīnor, *suppose*), *opinion, supposition, expectation*, 47, 6.

oportet, 2, -uit, impers., *it is necessary, is proper, behooves*, 31, 16.

oppidum, -ī, N. (ob, *on, over*; *pedum (cf. Gr. πέδον), *ground*), *town*, 5, 4. (W. G. 61.)

oppleō, 2, -ēvī, -ētus (ob, *completely*; pleō, *fill*), *fill completely, fill up: cover*, 37, 13.

opportūnus, adj. with comp. and sup. (ob, *before*; *portūnus, fr. portus, *harbor*), *fit, suitable, opportune, favorable*, 46, 4.

oppositus, adj. (P. of oppōnō, *set against*), *opposed, opposite*, 52, 21.

opprimō, 3, -essī, -essus (ob, *down, against*; premō, *press*), *press*

VOCABULARY. 279

together, press down: put down, overthrow, crush, 36, 27.

oppūgnātiō, -ōnis, F. (oppūgnō, *storm*), *storming, attack, assault, siege,* 20, 7.

oppūgnō, 1, -āvī, -ātus (ob, *against;* pūgnō, *fight*), *fight against, attack, storm, besiege,* 19, 11.

(ops), opis, F., no nom. or dat. sing., *aid, succor,* 7, 17 : *power, influence, strength,* 52, 3: *means, property, riches,* 38, 30.

optimās, -ātis, adj. (optimus, *best*), *of the best, aristocratic.* As subst., M., *aristocrat, patrician,* 40, 26.

optimē, adv., sup. of bene, *very well, best of all,* 22, 8.

optimus, adj., sup. of bonus, *best, most excellent,* 39, 26.

optiō, -ōnis, F. (cf. optō, *choose*), *choice,* 3, 21.

optō, 1, -āvī, -ātus, *choose, prefer: wish, pray for,* 55, 28.

opus, -eris, N., *work, labor: need, want, necessity,* 38, 26.

ōrāculum or **ōrāclum**, -ī, N. (ōrō, *speak*), *divine announcement, oracle,* 15, 10. (W. G. 57.)

ōrātiō, -ōnis, F. (ōrō, *speak*), *speaking, speech, oration,* 22, 5. (W. G. 57.)

orbis, -is, M., *ring, circle: the earth,* 25, 21 : orbis terrae or terrārum, *the whole earth,* 22, 17; 45, 27.

orbus, adj., *deprived, destitute: bereaved, childless,* 8, 13.

ōrdinō, 1, -āvī, -ātus (ōrdō, *row,* *line*), *set in order, arrange, institute,* 4, 21 ; 12, 22. (W. G. 56.)

ōrdior, 4, ōrsus, dep. [OL-, OR-, *grow*], *begin, commence,* 11, 28. (W. G. 56.)

ōrdō, -inis, M. [OL-, OR-, *grow*], *row, line, order, rank,* 40, 27; 46, 10. (W. G. 56.)

oriēns, -entis, M. (P. of orior, *rise*), *rising sun: the East,* 37, 9. As adj., *rising,* 44, 24.

orīgō, -inis, F. (orior, *rise*), *beginning, source, birth, origin,* 25, 4. (W. G. 56.)

orior, 4, ortus, dep. [OL-, OR-, *rise*], *arise, rise,* 44, 24 : *proceed, start, begin,* 2, 16 ; 20, 29. (W. G. 56.)

ōrnāmentum, -ī, N. (ōrnō, *fit out*), *decoration, ornament, jewel,* 40, 2 ; 47, 1.

ōrnātus, adj. with comp. and sup. (P. of ōrnō, *fit out*), *fitted out, furnished: adorned, decorated,* 70, 26 : *eminent, illustrious,* 49, 7.

ōrnātus, -ūs, M. (ōrnō, *adorn*), *splendid dress, fine attire, apparel,* 20, 24.

ōrnō, 1, -āvī, -ātus, *fit out, furnish, equip: ornament, adorn,* 20, 20.

ōrō, 1, -āvī, -ātus (ōs, *mouth*), *speak: plead, pray, beg,* 4, 13. (W. G. 57.)

ōs, ōris, N., *mouth,* 1, 12 ; 10, 13: *face, features, countenance,* 15, 19. (W. G. 57.)

ostendō, 3, -dī, -tus [ob(s), *before;*

tendō, *stretch*], *stretch out before, expose to view, hold out, show, exhibit, display,* 25, 8; 58, 4. (W. G. 71.)
ostentō, 1, -āvī, -ātus (freq. of ostendō, *stretch out*), *present to view: display, show off, parade, exhibit,* 8, 11. (W. G. 71.)
Ōstia, -ae, F. (ōs, *mouth*), *Ostia, the seaport of Rome at the mouth of the Tiber,* 10, 14. (W. G. 57.)

ōtiōsē, adv. (ōtiōsus, *at leisure*), *at leisure,* 38, 27.
ōtiōsus, adj. with sup. (ōtium, *leisure*), *at leisure, disengaged, idle,* 16, 24 : *free from public affairs,* 62, 18.
ōtium, -ī, N. [AV-, *delight*], *leisure, freedom from business : ease, rest, repose,* 27, 10 : **per ōtium,** *at one's ease,* 49, 16.
ovō, 1, —, —, *exult, rejoice,* 7, 25.

P

pācātus, adj. with comp. and sup. (P. of pācō, *pacify*), *pacified, peaceful,* 6, 1.
paene, adv., *nearly, almost,* 16, 8.
paeniteō, 2, -uī, — (cf. poena, *penalty*), *make sorry.* Impers., *it repents : discontents, dissatisfies,* 33, 24.
palam, adj., *openly, plainly, publicly,* 34, 22.
Palātium, -ī, N. (Palēs, an Italian shepherd-god), *Palatine hill :* in plural, *a palace,* 69, 1.
palūdāmentum, -ī, N., *military cloak, soldier's cloak,* 7, 29.
palūs, -ūdis, F., *swamp, marsh, pool,* 4, 22.
pānis, -is, M. [PA-, *feed*], *bread,* 21, 19.
papāver, -eris, N., *a poppy,* 14, 13.
pār, paris, adj., *equal,* 47, 11 : *similar, like, well-matched,* 7, 20 ; 13, 12.

parābilis, -e, adj. (parō, *prepare*), *easily procured, at hand,* 48, 2.
parātus, adj. with comp. and sup. (P. of parō, *prepare*), *prepared, ready,* 22, 3.
parcō, 3, pepercī or parsī, parsus, *spare, treat with forbearance,* 44, 11.
parcus, adj. with comp. and sup. (cf. parcō, *spare*), *sparing, frugal,* 43, 18.
parēns, -entis, M. and F. (P. of pariō, *beget*), *father, mother, parent,* 21, 30.
pāreō, 2, -uī, —, *appear : obey, comply, be subject to,* 42, 11.
pariter, adv. (pār, *equal*), *equally, alike,* 17, 13.
parō, 1, -āvī, -ātus, *make ready, prepare, provide,* 3, 10 : *plan, intend, purpose,* 35, 2.
parricīdium, -ī, N. (parricīda, *a parricide*), *murder of a father,*

parricide, 58, 4. (W. G. 58 and 66.)

pars, partis, F., *part, piece, portion, share*, 12, 16; 41, 16: *some, many*, 56, 4: *direction*, 51, 25: *party, faction*, 43, 12: *office, duty*, 30, 1: **trēs partēs**, *three fourths*, 47, 3.

Parthī, -ōrum, M., the *Parthians*, a brave people living south of the Caspian sea, 51, 30.

partior, 4, -ītus, dep. (pars, *part*), *share, distribute, divide*, 45, 7.

parum, adv., comp. minus, sup. minimē (cf. parcō, *spare*), *too little, not enough, insufficiently*, 26, 15.

parvulus, adj. dim. (parvus, *small*), *very small*. As subst., *infant*, 1, 7.

pāscō, 3, pāvī, pāstus [PA-, *feed*], *feed, support: graze, pasture*, 35, 4.

passim, adv. (cf. **passus**, *outstretched*), *scattered about far and wide, generally, in every direction*, 35, 17.

passus, adj. (P. of pandō, *spread out*), *outspread, extended: dishevelled*, 4, 12.

pāstor, -ōris, M. [PA-, *feed*], *herdsman, shepherd*, 1, 14. (W. G. 58.)

patefaciō, 3, -fēcī, -factus (pateō, *lie open*; faciō, *make*), *lay open, open: disclose, expose, bring to light*, 59, 20. (W. G. 33.)

patella, -ae, F. (dim. of patina, *pan*), *small pan, little dish*, 29, 11.

patēns, -entis, adj. with comp. (P. of pateō, *lie open*), *open*, 20, 23.

pater, -tris, M. [PA-, *feed*], *father*, 3, 20: plur., *senators*, 4, 26. (W. G. 58.)

paternus, adj. (pater, *father*), *of a father, fatherly, paternal*, 11, 20. (W. G. 58.)

patiēns, -entis, adj. with comp. and sup. (P. of **patior**, *endure*), *able to bear, enduring, patient*, 57, 2.

patior, 3, passus, dep., *bear, support, endure*, 61, 26: *meet with, suffer, endure*, 59, 15: *allow, permit*, 37, 21.

patria, -ae, F. (fem. of **patrius**, *ancestral*; sc. terra, *land*), *fatherland, native land*, 6, 24. (W. G. 58.)

patrimōnium, -ī, N. (pater, *father*), *inheritance from a father, inheritance, patrimony*, 41, 18. (W. G. 58.)

patrius, adj. (pater, *father*), *of a father, paternal*, 18, 19. (W. G. 58.)

patrō, 1, -āvī, -ātus, *bring to pass, accomplish, perform*, 11, 22.

patrōnus, -ī, M. (pater, *father*), *protector, patron, advocate, pleader*, 58, 24. (W. G. 58.)

paucus, adj. with comp. and sup., *few*, 10, 15: plur. M. as subst., *few, a few*, 6, 21.

paulātim, adv. (paulum, *a little*), *by degrees, gradually*, 14, 6.

paulō, adv. (abl. N. of **paulus**,

little), as ablative of difference in expressions of comparison, *by a little, somewhat, a little*, 8, 12.

paulum, adv. (paulus, *little*), *a little, somewhat, a little while,* 52, 12; 55, 17.

Paulus, -ī, M., name of a famous Roman family; see *Aemilius,* 37, 2.

pauper, -eris, adj. with comp. and sup., *of small means, poor,* 28, 4: *insignificant, small,* 50, 2. As subst., M., *a poor man,* 17, 17.

paupertās, -ātis, F. (pauper, *poor*), *poverty,* 17, 14.

pavidus, adj. (paveō, *tremble with fear*), *trembling, fearful, timid,* 18, 8.

pavor, -ōris, M., *trembling, shaking, terror, dread,* 38, 14.

pāx, pācis, F., *compact, agreement, treaty, peace, reconciliation,* 4, 13; 64, 19.

peccātum, -ī, N. (peccō, *miss*), *fault, mistake, sin,* 42, 12.

peccō, 1, -āvī, -ātus, *miss, transgress, offend, sin,* 42, 12.

pectus, -oris, N., *breast,* 18, 21.

pecūnia, -ae, F. (pecū, *cattle;* the earliest form of wealth), *property, wealth, riches: money,* 11, 1.

pecus, -oris, N., *cattle* of all kinds: *flock: herd,* 1, 18.

pedīculus, -ī, M. (dim. of pēs, *foot*), *a little foot,* 29, 12.

pelliciō, 3, -lexī, -lectus, *allure, tempt, entice,* 17, 26.

pellis, -is, F., *skin, hide, leather: winter tent,* 19, 20 (v. notes, fig. 10, p. 97).

pellō, 3, pepulī, pulsus [PEL-, *drive*], *push, drive, hurl: drive out, banish, put to flight, drive away, expel,* 1, 3; 41, 23. (W. G. 59.)

pendō, 3, pependī, pēnsus, *suspend, weigh: pay,* 32, 17.

penitus, adv. [PA-, *feed*], *inwardly, into the inmost part, far within,* 11, 24.

per, prep. with acc.: of space, *through, across, through the midst of, throughout, among,* 5, 22; 8, 17; 17, 7; 45, 26: of time, *during, for,* distr. *by,* 23, 2; 49, 3: of agency and means, *by the agency of, by means of, through the instrumentality of,* 34, 28; 35, 25; 40, 17: of an apparent or pretended cause, *under pretence of,* 34, 30: of manner, *in,* 50, 3.

peragō, 3, -ēgī, -āctus (per, *through;* agō, *drive*), *thrust through: go through with, accomplish, finish, complete,* 8, 17; 19, 23: *set forth, enumerate,* 10, 1.

peragrō, 1, -āvī, -ātus (per, *through;* ager, *field*), *wander through, traverse, pass through,* 1, 18.

percellō, 3, -culī, -culsus [per, *thoroughly;* CEL-, *strike*], *beat down, overturn: strike, smite, hit,* 24, 22: *astound, strike with* *consternation*, **44**, 27. (W. G. 19.)

percontor or **percūnctor**, 1, -ātus, dep. (per, *by*; **contus**, *pole*, i.e., hunt with a pole), *question strictly, ask, inquire*, **15**, 11.

perculsus, P. of **percellō**, **44**, 27.

percussor, -ōris, M. (cf. **percutiō**, *strike through*), *striker, murderer, assassin*, **56**, 1.

percutiō, 3, -cussī, -cussus (per, *thoroughly*; **quatiō**, *strike*), *strike through and through, pierce*, **43**, 8; *strike, knock at*, **48**, 9; *slay, kill*, **11**, 17.

perdō, 3, -didī, -ditus [per, *through;* 2 DA-, *put*], *make away with, destroy, squander, waste, lose*, **37**, 18; **58**, 29. (W. G. 25.)

perdūcō, 3, -dūxī, -ductus (per, *through;* **dūcō**, *lead*), *lead through, lead, conduct*, **2**, 3. (W. G. 29.)

peregrīnus, adj. (**peregre**, fr. per, *through;* **ager**, *field*), *from foreign parts, foreign*, **54**, 11.

perennis, -e, adj. with comp. (per, *through*; **annus**, *year*), *lasting through the year, everlasting, unceasing, perpetual, never failing*, **6**, 7; **32**, 19.

pereō, -īre, -iī or -īvī, -itūrus (per, *through;* **eō**, *go*), *pass away, disappear: die, perish*, **56**, 4: *be lost, be wasted, be spent in vain*, **68**, 24: *be ruined*, **17**, 9. (W. G. 46.)

perferō, -ferre, -tulī, -lātus (per, *through*; **ferō**, *bear*), *bear through: keep, retain*, **67**, 16. (W. G. 34.)

perficiō, 3, -fēcī, -fectus (per, *thoroughly;* **faciō**, *do*), *accomplish, carry out, complete*, **35**, 22.

perfidia, -ae, F. (**perfidus**, *faithless*), *faithlessness, treachery, perfidy*, **9**, 1. (W. G. 35.)

perfidus, adj. [per, *breaking through, disregarding;* FID-, *trust*], *promise-breaking, dishonest, treacherous, faithless*, **4**, 6. (W. G. 35.)

perfruor, 3, -ūctus, dep. (per, *thoroughly;* **fruor**, *enjoy*), *enjoy fully, be delighted with*, **67**, 7.

perfuga, -ae, M. [per, *thoroughly, entirely;* FVG-, *flee*], *deserter*, **35**, 25. (W. G. 40.)

perfugiō, 3, -fūgī, — (per, *through, entirely;* **fugiō**, *flee*), *flee for refuge*, **37**, 22. (W. G. 40.)

pergō, 3, perrēxī, perrēctus (per, *through;* **regō**, *conduct*), *go on, press on, hasten, march*, **11**, 25; **38**, 5. (W. G. 65.)

perīclitor, 1, -ātus, dep. (**perīculum**, *trial*), *try, prove, test: incur danger, be in peril*, **34**, 20.

perīculōsus, adj. with comp. and sup. (**perīculum**, *trial*), *dangerous, perilous*, **23**, 11.

perīculum, -ī, N., *trial, experiment: peril, danger, risk*, **23**, 3.

perītus, adj. with comp. and sup. (P. of **perior**, *try*), *experienced, trained, skillful, expert*, **10**, 23.

permāgnus, adj. (per, *very;* māgnus, *great*), *very great, very large, immense*, 32, 3.

permoveō, 2, -mōvī, -mōtus (per, *thoroughly;* moveō, *move*), *move deeply, induce, persuade*, 61, 15. (W. G. 54.)

permulceō, 2, -mulsī, -mulsus (per, without force; mulceō, *stroke*), *rub gently, stroke*, 20, 27.

permūtō, 1, -āvī, -ātus (per, *thoroughly;* mūtō, *change*), *change throughout: exchange*, 65, 11. (W. G. 54.)

perōrō, 1, -āvī, -ātus (per, *to the end;* ōrō, *speak*), *speak from beginning to end, plead at length*, 58, 1. (W. G. 57.)

perpellō, 3, -pulī, — (per, *through;* pellō, *strike*), *urge, compel, prevail upon, induce*, 35, 26. (W. G. 59.)

perpetuō, adv. (perpetuus, *continuous*), *constantly, ever, uninterruptedly*, 5, 7.

perpetuus, adj., *continuous, perpetual:* in perpetuum, *forever, for all time*, 54, 24.

perrumpō, 3, -rūpī, -ruptus (per, *through;* rumpō, *break*), *break through, force a way through*, 70, 15. (W. G. 64.)

persaepe, adv. (per, *very;* saepe, *often*), *very often*, 57, 5.

perscrībō, 3, -scrīpsī, -scrīptus (per, *to the end, in full;* scrībō, *write*), *write in full: enter, record*, 17, 23.

persecūtus, P. of persequor.

persequor, 3, -cūtus, dep. (per, *throughout;* sequor, *follow*), *follow perseveringly, follow after, pursue*, 44, 13.

perspiciō, 3, -spēxī, -spectus (per, *through;* speciō, *look*), *look through, look into: perceive clearly, note, see through, understand*, 27, 6. (W. G. 68.)

perstringō, 3, -inxī, -ictus (per, *thoroughly;* stringō, *bind*), *bind closely, press hard: affect deeply, touch, move*, 7, 5.

persuādeō, 2, -suāsī, -suāsus (per, *completely;* suādeō, *persuade*), *convince, persuade*, 29, 8.

pertaedet, 2, -taesum est, impers. (per, *completely;* taedet, *it wearies*), *it wearies, disgusts, makes sick*, 50, 13.

perterrēfaciō, 3, -fēcī, -factus (per, *thoroughly;* terreō, *frighten;* faciō, *make*), *frighten thoroughly*, 28, 14.

pertināciter, adv. (pertināx, *persevering*), *perseveringly, obstinately, stubbornly*, 49, 8. (W. G. 71.)

pertineō, 2, -uī, — (per, *through, to the end;* teneō, *hold*), *stretch out, reach, extend*, 46, 10. (W. G. 71.)

perturbō, 1, -āvī, ātus (per, *thoroughly;* turbō, *disturb*), *confuse, disturb, confound*, 40, 11.

perveniō, 4, -vēnī, -ventus (per, *through, to;* veniō, *come*), *arrive, come to, reach*, 11, 25. (W. G. 73.)

pēs, pedis, M., *foot*, 57, 3 : **pedem referre**, *to retreat*, 25, 11.

pessimē (pessimus), sup. of malє, *worst*, 41, 4.

pessimus, see malus.

pestilentia, -ae, F. (pestilēns, *infected*), *infectious disease, plague, pestilence*, 9, 7.

pestis, -is, F., *infectious disease, plague: pest, curse, bane*, 45, 27.

petītiō, -ōnis, F. (petō, *seek*), *attack, aim: application, candidacy, petition*, 56, 20.

petō, 3, -īvī or -iī, petītus, *strive for, seek*, 3, 19: *go to*, 40, 20: *attack, aim at*, 20, 11: *demand*, 15, 23: *beg, ask*, 3, 6; 3, 22.

phalerae, -ārum, F. (Gr., τὰ φάλερα), *a metal plate for the breast:* for horses, *a metal breast decoration, breast-plate*, 45, 6.

Pharnacēs, -is, M., *Pharnaces*, son of Mithridates, king of Pontus, 46, 13.

Pharsālicus or Pharsālius, adj., *Pharsalian, of Pharsalus* (in Thessaly), 53, 3.

Pharsālos or -us, -ī, F., *Pharsalus* or *Pharsalia*, the Thessalian town near which Pompey was defeated by Julius Caesar, 48 B.C., 47, 15.

philosophia, -ae, F. (Gr., φιλοσοφία), *philosophy*, 62, 16.

philosophus, adj., *philosophical.* As subst., M. and F., *a philosopher*, 48, 7.

pietās, -ātis, F. (pius, *dutiful*), *dutiful conduct, devotion, piety*, 6, 9 : *duty, love, loyalty* to kin and country, 50, 10.

pignus, -oris and -eris, N., *pledge, security, token, proof*, 5, 14; 39, 9.

pilleus, -ī, M., and pilleum, -ī, N., *close-fitting felt cap, skull-cap*, 10, 20.

pīrāta, -ae, M., *sea-robber, corsair, pirate*, 45, 15.

pīrāticus, adj., *of pirates, piratical*, 46, 1.

piscīna, -ae, F. (piscis, *fish*), *fish-pond*, 69, 20.

piscis, -is, M., *fish*, 69, 22.

Pīsō, -ōnis, M., family name of *L. Calpurnius Piso*, an enemy of C. Gracchus, 41, 8.

plācābilis, -e, adj. with comp. (plācō, *quiet, soothe*), *easily pacified, placable*, 26, 9.

Placentia, -ae, F., *Placentia*, a city in Cisalpine Gaul, on the Po, 59, 7.

placeō, 2, -uī or placitus sum, -citus, *please, be pleasing, be agreeable, suit*, 33, 1 : *seem right, seem best*, 23, 23. Impers., *it is believed, is settled, is agreed*, 6, 21.

placidē, adv. with comp. (placidus, *gentle*), *gently, quietly, calmly*, 15, 18.

plācō, 1, -āvī, -ātus, *quiet, soothe: reconcile, conciliate*, 43, 10.

plāga, -ae, F., *blow, stroke, wound*, 55, 21.

plaga, -ae, F. [PLEC-, *weave*], *hunting-net, snare: region, district*, **22**, 18.

Plancus, -ī, M., *Plancus*, family name of *C. Plotius Plancus*, proscribed 43 B.C., **65**, 3.

plēbēius, adj. (**plēbs**, *the common people*), *of the common people, plebeian*, **17**, 25. (W. G. 62.)

plēbs, plēbis, or **plēbēs**, -ēī or -ī, F. [PLE-, *fill*], *the common people, commons, plebeians*, **4**, 26. (W. G. 62.)

plēnus, adj. with comp. and sup. [PLE-, *fill*], *full, filled*, **42**, 19. (W. G. 62.)

plērusque, -raque, -rumque, adj. (a strengthened form of **plērus**, *a very great part*), *a very great part, the majority*. As subst., plur. M., **plērīque**, *most people, very many*, **46**, 29. (W. G. 62.)

Plīnius, -ī, M., *Plinius*, Roman gens to which belonged *C. Plinius Secundus*, or *Pliny*, the famous writer on natural history. Perished 79 A.D., in the eruption of Vesuvius, **58**, 28.

Plōtius, -ī, M., gentile name of *C. Plotius Plancus*, **65**, 3.

plumbeus, adj. (plumbum, *lead*), *of lead, leaden*, **63**, 20.

plumbum, -ī, N., *lead*, **41**, 30.

plūrēs, see 1 **plūs**.

plūrimum, adv. (acc. N. of **plūrimus**, *most*), *very much:* plūrimum posse, *to be very influential, all powerful*, **14**, 8; **31**, 3.

plūrimus, adj., sup. of **multus** (**plūs**, *more*), *most, very much, very many*, **5**, 6. (W. G. 62.)

1 **plūs**, plūris, adj. [PLE-, *fill*], sing. N. as subst., *more*, **42**, 17: plur., *more, in greater number*, **10**, 14; **44**, 24: plūrēs, M. subst., *the majority*, **67**, 21.

2 **plūs**, adv. (acc. N. of **plūs**, the adj.), *more*, **53**, 25. (W. G. 62.)

poena, -ae, F., *satisfaction, punishment, penalty*, **3**, 27; **6**, 11.

Poenus, -ī, M., *a Carthaginian*, **32**, 5: plur., *the Carthaginians*, **30**, 17.

poēta, -ae, M., *poet*, **50**, 8.

polliceor, 2, -itus, dep. (prō, *forth;* liceor, *bid*), *hold forth, offer, promise*, **28**, 24.

Pōlliō, -ōnis, M., family name of *Vedius Pollio*, punished by Augustus for cruelty to a slave, **69**, 17.

Pompēiānus, adj., *of Pompey, Pompeian*, **52**, 4.

Pompēiī, -ōrum, M., *Pompeii*, the well-known Campanian city destroyed by an eruption from Vesuvius in 79 A.D., **22**, 25.

Pompēius, -ī, M., the Pompeian gens, to which *Cn. Pompeius Magnus* or *Pompey* belonged, **42**, 23.

Pompilius, -ī, M., *Pompilius*, gentile name of *Numa Pompilius*, **5**, 3.

Pomptīnus, adj., *Pomptine*, referring to the Pomptine marshes

VOCABULARY. 287

along the coast of Latium, 54, 19.

pondō, adv. (old abl. of **pondus**, *weight*), *by weight, in weight*, 21, 21.

pondus, -eris, N. (cf. pendō, *weigh*), *weight*, 21, 23.

pōnō, 3, posuī, positus (for posinō, fr. por (prō), *forth, down;* sinō, *set*), *put down, put, place, fix, deposit*, 62, 5; 66, 11: *set up, erect*, 16, 18: *give, spend, employ*, 62, 9: **castra pōnere**, *to pitch camp*, 26, 1.

pōns, -ontis, M., *bridge*, 10, 12.

ponticulus, -ī, M. (dim. of pōns, *bridge*), *little bridge*, 52, 15.

Ponticus, adj., *of Pontus, Pontic*, 53, 13.

Pontius, -ī, M., name of a Samnite and Roman gens, e.g., *C. Pontius*, the famous Samnite who captured the Roman army at the Caudine Forks, 23, 5.

Pontus, -ī, M., *Pontus*, the kingdom of Mithridates in northeastern Asia Minor, 46, 13.

populus, -ī, M. [PLE-, *fill*], *people, nation*, 3, 4; 6, 2. (W. G. 62.)

porrigō, 3, -rēxī, -rēctus (por (prō), *forth, out;* regō, *stretch*), *stretch out, extend: offer, hand, present*, 69, 2. (W. G. 65.)

Porsena, -ae, M., *Porsenna*, king of Etruria, whose capital was Clusium, 16, 1.

porta, -ae, F., *city-gate, gate, door*, 5, 25; 15, 6.

portendō, 3, -dī, -tus [por (prō), *forth;* tendō (TEN-), *stretch*], *point out, reveal, foretell, predict*, 10, 24. (W. G. 71.)

porticus, -ūs, F. (porta, *gate*), *covered walk between columns, colonnade, portico*, 50, 19.

portō, 1, -āvī, -ātus, *bear, carry, bring*, 10, 26; 64, 10.

portōrium, -ī, N. (cf. porta, *gate*), *tax, duty, custom, tariff*, 54, 12.

portus, -ūs, M. (cf. porta, *gate*), *harbor, haven*, 22, 20.

poscō, 3, poposcī, —, inch., *ask urgently, beg, demand*, 15, 12.

Posīdōnius, -ī, M., *Posidonius*, a famous Stoic philosopher, 48, 5.

possum, posse, potuī, irr. v. (potis, *able;* sum, *be*), *be able, have power, can*, 5, 19. (W. G. 31 and 63.)

post, adv., and prep. with acc.: as adv., *after, behind, later*, 4, 16: as prep., *behind*, 19, 12: *after, since*, 26, 24: *next to*, 12, 1.

posteā, adv. (post, *after;* ea, *these things*), *after this, thereafter, later*, 2, 18; 38, 23.

(posterus), adj., comp. **posterior**, sup. **postrēmus** (post, *after*), *coming after, following, next, subsequent*, 8, 29; 15, 2: **ad postrēmum**, *at last*, 14, 9. Plur. M. as subst., *coming generations, descendants, posterity*, 9, 22.

postīcus, adj. (**post**, *after*), *in the rear, behind.* As subst., N., *a back door,* 65, 12.

postmodum, adv. (**post**, *after;* **modus**, *extent, measure*), *after a while, a little later,* 19, 25.

postquam, conj., *after, as soon as, when,* 12, 8.

postrēmō, adv. (abl. of **postrēmus**, *last*), *at last, finally, last of all,* 49, 5.

postrēmus, sup. of **posterus**, *last,* 14, 9.

postrīdiē, adv. (for **posterī diē**; * **posterus**, *next;* **diēs**, *day*), *on the day after, the next day,* 5, 15. (W. G. 27.)

postulātum, -ī, N. (P. N. of **postulō**, *demand*), *demand, request, claim,* 10, 1.

postulō, 1, -āvī, -ātus, *ask, demand, claim, desire,* 32, 14; 39, 9.

Postumius, -ī, M., Roman gentile name, as *Spurius Postumius Albinus,* consul 321 B.C., 23, 4.

potentātus, -ūs, M. (**potēns**, *able*), *might, power, rule, dominion,* 4, 16.

potentia, -ae, F. (**potēns**, *able*), *might, force, power,* 41, 3. (W. G. 63.)

potestās, -ātis, F. (**potis**, *able*), *ability, sovereignty, sway, dominion, power,* 14, 3; 45, 5 : *office, authority,* 40, 15. (W. G. 63.)

potior, 4, -ītus, dep. (**potis**, *able*), *become master of, take posession of, get, obtain,* 2, 24. (W. G. 63.)

potius, adv. comp. [**potis**, *able;* fr. POT-, *master*], *rather, preferably,* 32, 9. (W. G. 63.)

prae, prep. with abl., *before, in front of,* 7, 27 : *compared with,* 28, 4.

praebeō, 2, -uī, -itus (**prae**, *forth;* **habeō**, *hold*), *hold forth, offer, tender,* 41, 25 : *afford, give, present,* 47, 3. (W. G. 45.)

praeceptor, -ōris, M. [**prae**, *before;* CAP-, *take*], *teacher, instructor,* 57, 18.

praeceptum, -ī, N. (P. N. of **praecipiō**, *advise*), *maxim, rule, order, command,* 62, 23.

praecīdō, 3, -cīdī, -cīsus (**prae**, *before, in front;* **caedō**, *cut*), *cut off in front, cut off,* 26, 4. (W. G. 66.)

praecinō, 3, -uī, — (**prae**, *before;* **canō**, *make music*), *play before,* 31, 5.

praecipiō, 3, -cēpī, -ceptus (**prae**, *beforehand;* **capiō**, *take*), *take beforehand, get in advance : advise, warn, direct, order,* 4, 29. (W. G. 17.)

praecipuē, adv. (**praecipuus**, *special, chief*), *chiefly, principally, eminently,* 47, 25. (W. G. 17.)

praeclārus, adj. with comp. and sup. (**prae**, *intensive;* **clārus**, *bright*), *very bright, brilliant: eminent, excellent, famous,* 45, 20. (W. G. 15.)

praeda, -ae, F., *property taken in*

war, booty, spoil, plunder, 19, 26.

praedicātiō, -ōnis, F. (praedicō, *make known*), *public proclamation: praise, boast*, 53, 12. (W. G. 26.)

1 **praedicō**, 1, -āvī, -ātus (prae, *before;* dicō, *make known*), *make known by proclamation, proclaim: declare openly, make known, relate*, 60, 12. (W. G. 26.)

2 **praedīcō**, 3, -dīxī, -dictus (prae, *before;* dicō, *say*), *say before, foretell, predict: advise, admonish, warn*, 55, 7. (W. G. 26.)

praedō, -ōnis, M. (praeda, *spoil*), *one that makes booty, plunderer, robber, pirate*, 45, 28.

praefectus, -ī, M. (P. of praeficiō, *put over*), *overseer. commander, governor*, 35, 6. (W. G. 33.)

praeferō, -ferre, -tulī, -lātus (prae, *before;* ferō, *bear*), *bear before, carry in front*, 53, 14: *offer, present*, 60, 18: *place before, prefer*, 40, 24. (W. G. 34.)

praeferōx, -ōcis, adj. (prae, *intensive;* ferōx, *violent*), *very violent, insolent*, 53, 8.

(**praefor**), 1, -fātus, dep. (prae, *before;* *for, *say*), *say beforehand*, 59, 30. (W. G. 32.)

praelūceō, 2, -lūxī, — (prae, *before;* lūceō, *shine*), *shine before, shed light before*, 31, 5. (W. G. 50.)

praemittō, 3, -mīsī, -missus (prae, *before;* mittō, *send*), *send forward, despatch in advance*, 21, 2. (W. G. 53.)

praemium, -ī, N., *advantage, favor: reward*, 28, 24.

praeripiō, 3, -ripuī, -reptus (prae, *before;* rapiō, *take away*), *snatch away, carry off*, 10, 15. (W. G. 64.)

praesēns, -entis, adj. with comp. (P. of praesum, *be before*), *at hand, in person, present*, 59, 21. (W. G. 31.)

praesidium, -ī, N. [praeses, fr. prae, *before;* SID-, *sit*], *defence, protection, aid: troops, guard, garrison*, 16, 6; 23, 15. (W. G. 67.)

praestō, 1, -itī, -itus (prae, *before;* stō, *stand*), *stand out, stand before, excel, surpass*, 14, 26. (W. G. 69.)

praesum, -esse, -fuī (prae, *before;* sum, *be*), *be before, be set over, have charge of*, 3, 20. (W. G. 31.)

praeter, prep. with acc., *past, by: contrary to, against*, 45, 5: *beyond, besides, in addition to*, 39, 1: *except, apart from*, 24, 10.

praetereā, adv. (praeter, *besides;* ea, *these things*), *in addition, further, moveover*, 5, 13; 27, 24.

praetereō, -īre, -iī, -itus (praeter, *by, past;* eō, *go*), *go by, go past, pass by*, 36, 15. (W. G. 46.)

praeteritus, adj. (P. of praetereō, *go by*), *gone by, past, departed*, 67, 5.

praetervehor, 3, -vectus, dep. (praeter, *by;* vehor, *be carried*), *be borne past, sail by, pass by,* 30, 5.

praetextātus, adj. (praetexta, *toga praetexta*), *wearing the toga praetexta,* 20, 24.

praetextus, adj. (P. of praetexō, *border, fringe*), *bordered, edged.* As subst., F., *the toga praetexta,* 11, 17.

praetor, -ōris, M. [for praeitor; prae, *before;* I-, *go*], *leader, chief, magistrate: praetor:* as governor of a province, *propraetor, ex-praetor,* 58, 22. (W. G. 46.)

praetōrius, adj. (praetor, *praetor*), *of the praetor, praetorian,* 30, 26. As subst., M., *one who has been praetor, ex-praetor,* 37, 23. (W. G. 46.)

praeveniō, 4, -vēnī, -ventus (prae, *before;* veniō, *come*), *come before, precede, outstrip, anticipate, prevent,* 32, 8; 57, 5. (W. G. 73.)

prāvus, adj. with comp. and sup., *crooked, deformed: wrong, bad, wicked,* 59, 28.

precor, 1, -ātus, dep. (* prex, *prayer*), *ask, beg, entreat, pray,* 20, 1.

prehendō, and **prēndō**, 3, -hendī, -hēnsus, *lay hold of, catch,* 69, 30.

pretiōsus, adj. with comp. and sup. (pretium, *price*), *of great value, costly, precious,* 47, 22.

pretium, -ī, N., *price, money, ransom,* 15, 11; 26, 7: *pay, reward,* 17, 26.

(**prex**, precis), nom. and gen. sing. not in use, F., *prayer, request, entreaty,* 43, 10.

prīdem, adv., *long ago, long since,* 52, 3.

prīdiē, adv., *on the day before, the previous day,* 55, 29. (W. G. 27.)

prīmō, adv. (primus, *first*), *at first, at the beginning, first,* 1, 16; 11, 25.

(**prīmōris**, -e), adj. (primus, *first*), *first,* 7, 4. Plur. M. as subst., *the chiefs, nobles, leaders,* 14, 16.

prīmum, adv. (N. of prīmus, *first*), *at first, first: for the first time,* 19, 18: **quam prīmum**, *as soon as possible,* 50, 17: **ut primum**, *as soon as,* 63, 14.

prīmus, adj. sup., *the first, first,* 4, 3; 46, 25. As subst., M. plur., *the foremost,* 31, 25.

prīnceps, -cipis, adj. [prīmus, *first;* CAP-, *take*], *first in order, foremost,* 7, 26: *chief, eminent, most noble,* 56, 7. As subst., M., *leader, foremost man, chief,* 27, 12; 44, 4: *ruler, emperor,* 69, 10. (W. G. 17.)

prīncipium, -ī, N. (prīnceps, *first in order*), *beginning,* 33, 28. (W. G. 17.)

prior, neut. prius, -ōris, adj. comp., *former, prior, first,* 2, 18; 33, 12.

VOCABULARY. 291

Priscus, -ī, M. (priscus, *of former times*), *Priscus*, cognomen of Tarquinius Priscus, 11, 5.

prius, adv. comp. (sing. N. of **prior**, *former*), *before, sooner, first*, 13, 7 : with quam, *earlier than, sooner than, before,* 7, 18.

priusquam, see prius, 7, 18 ; 31, 10.

prīvātim, adv. (prīvātus, *private*), *apart from state affairs, in private, privately,* 58, 2.

prīvātus, adj. (P. of prīvō, *take from, withdraw*), *apart from the state, personal, private,* 39, 5. As subst., M., *man in private life, private citizen,* 67, 20.

prīvō, 1, -āvī, -ātus (prīvus, *one's own*), *deprive, rob,* 1, 4.

prō, prep. with abl., *before, in front of: for the sake of, in behalf of,* 6, 23; 22, 27; 54, 29: *in place of, instead of,* 17, 20: *for, the same as, as,* 5, 2: *in proportion to, in comparison with, according to,* 36, 12: *for, in exchange for,* 15, 23.

proavus, -ī, M. (prō, *before;* avus, *grandfather*), *great-grandfather,* 58, 27.

probō, 1, -āvī, -ātus (probus, *good*), *esteem good, approve, commend,* 38, 7.

proboscis, -idis, F., *proboscis,* 28, 11.

Proca, -ae, M., *Proca,* an Alban king, father of Numitor and Amulius, 1, 1.

prōcēdō, 3, -cessī, — (prō, *before;* cēdō, *go*), *go forward, proceed, advance, go forth,* 4, 1; 4, 27.

procella, -ae, F. [prō, *forth;* CEL-, *drive*], *violent wind, storm, tempest,* 34, 25. (W. G. 19.)

prōclāmō, 1, -āvī, -ātus (prō, *out, forth;* clāmō, *call*), *call, cry out,* 8, 10; 40, 25.

procul, adv. [prō, *forth, away;* CEL-, *drive*], *at a distance, away, far, afar off,* 2, 8; 35, 2. (W. G. 19.)

Proculus, -ī, M., *Proculus,* a Roman surname, 4, 25.

prōcumbō, 3, -cubuī, -cubitus (prō, *forward;* *cumbō, *fall*), *fall forward, sink down, fall prostrate,* 46, 21.

prōcūrō, 1, -āvī, -ātus (prō, *for;* cūrō, *care*), *take care of, attend to: avert, expiate by sacrifice,* 5, 13. (W. G. 18.)

prōdigium, -ī, N., *prophetic sign, token, omen, prodigy,* 10, 23.

prōditiō, -ōnis, F. [prō, *forth, away;* 1 DA-, *give*], *betrayal, treason, treachery,* 3, 26.

prōditor, -ōris, M. [prō, *forth, away;* 1 DA-, *give*], *betrayer,* 19, 6. (W. G. 25.)

prōdō, 3, -didī, -ditus [prō, *forth;* 2 DA-, *put*], *exhibit, reveal: relate, hand down, transmit,* 15, 7. (W. G. 25.)

proelior, 1, -ātus, dep. (proelium, *battle*), *join battle, fight,* 59, 7.

proelium, -ī, N., *battle, combat,* 4, 10.

VOCABULARY.

profectō, adv. (prō, *according to;* factum, *fact*), *actually, indeed, certainly, surely*, 59, 9. (W. G. 33.)

profectus, P. of proficīscor, 10, 7.

prōferō, -ferre, -tulī, -lātus (prō, *out, forth;* ferō, *carry*), *carry out, bring forth*, 39, 1. (W. G. 34.)

prōficiō, 3, -fēcī, -fectus (prō, *forth;* faciō, *make*), *make headway, succeed*, 30, 3.

proficīscor, 3, -fectus, dep. (prō, *forth, off;* *faciscor (faciō), *begin to make*), *set forward, set out, go, march forth, depart*, 10, 7; 10, 18; 46, 2. (W. G. 33.)

profiteor, 2, -fessus, dep. (prō, *forth, publicly;* fateor, *confess*), *declare publicly, avow, profess*, 29, 5.

prōflīgō, 1, -āvī, -ātus (prō, *forward, down;* flīgō, *strike*), *strike to the ground, overthrow, defeat, conquer*, 33, 9.

profugiō, 3, -fūgī, — (prō, *forth;* fugiō, *flee*), *flee, run away, escape*, 18, 22; 41, 24. (W. G. 40.)

profugus, adj. [prō, *forth;* FVG-, *flee*], *fugitive, banished.* As subst. M., *a fugitive*, 59, 3. (W. G. 40.)

profundō, 3, -fūdī, -fūsus (prō, *forth;* fundō, *pour*), *pour out, pour forth: waste, squander*, 59, 12. (W. G. 39.)

profūsus, adj. (P. of profundō, *pour out*), *lavish, extravagant*, 40, 13. (W. G. 39.)

prōgredior, 3, -gressus, dep. (prō, *forth;* gradior, *go*), *go forth, come forth, advance*, 36, 12. (W. G. 44.)

prohibeō, 2, -uī, -itus (prō, *forth, away from;* habeō, *hold*), *keep away from, check, hinder, debar, prevent*, 63, 19.

prōiciō, 3, -iēcī, -iectus (prō, *forth;* iaciō, *throw*), *throw forth, throw*, 40, 31: *extend*, 46, 9. (W. G. 47.)

proinde, adv. (prō, *forth;* inde, *from that time*), *hence, accordingly, therefore*, 53, 29.

prōmineō, 2, -uī, —, *stand out, jut, overhang, lean out, bend forward, stretch out*, 62, 2.

prōmissum, -ī, N. (prōmittō, *promise*), *promise*, 66, 8.

prōmittō, 3, -mīsī, -missus (prō, *forth;* mittō, *send*), *let go, put forth: promise, assure*, 5, 14. (W. G. 53.)

prōmptus, adj. with comp. and sup. (P. of prōmō, *bring forth*), *disclosed, manifest: ready, prompt, quick*, 36, 22.

pronepōs, -ōtis, M. (prō, *before;* nepōs, *grandson*), *great-grandson*, 59, 12.

prōnūntiō, 1, -āvī, -ātus (prō, *forth, abroad;* nūntiō, *announce*), *publish, proclaim, decide, declare*, 66, 15.

prope, adv. with comp. propius, *about, nearly, almost*, 49, 3.

prōpellō, 3, -pulī, -pulsus (prō, *forth;* pellō, *drive*), *drive forth, drive out*, 35, 5. (W. G. 59.)

VOCABULARY.

prōpēnsus, adj. with comp. (P. of prōpendeō, *hang down*), *hanging down: inclined, disposed,* 27, 16.

properō, 1, -āvī, -ātus (properus, *quick*), *make haste, go quickly, hasten,* 2, 2.

propinquus, adj. with comp. (prope, *near*), *near, neighboring,* 46, 11. As subst., M. and F., *relation, kinsman,* 49, 6.

propius, adv., comp. of prope, *nearer,* 55, 14.

prōpōnō, 3, -posuī, -positus (prō, *forth;* pōnō, *put*), *put forth, display: report, propose,* 17, 22: *offer,* 28, 24.

prōpositum, -ī, N. (P. N. of prōpōnō, *propose*), *plan, design,* 44, 23.

propriē, adv. (proprius, *own, personal*), *personally: especially, peculiarly,* 36, 23.

propter, prep. with acc. (prope, *near*), *near, hard by: on account of, from, because of,* 4, 19; 9, 1.

prōripiō, 3, -puī, -reptus (prō, *forth;* rapiō, *drag*), *drag forth:* with sē, *hurry forth, rush,* 11, 30. (W. G. 64.)

prōrogō, 1, -āvī, -ātus (prō, *forward;* rogō, *ask*), *prolong, continue, extend,* 40, 16.

prōscrībō, 3, -scrīpsī, -scrīptus (prō, *forth, publicly;* scrībō, *write*), *proclaim, publish, outlaw, proscribe,* 61, 21.

prōscrīptiō, -ōnis, F. (prōscrībō, *make public*), *notice of sale, advertisement: proscription,* 64, 22.

prōscrīptus, -ī, M. (prōscrībō, *proscribe*), *outlaw, proscribed person,* 64, 26.

prōsequor, 3, -cūtus, dep. (prō, *forth, out;* sequor, *follow*), *follow, accompany, attend,* 60, 30.

Prōserpina, -ae, F., *Proserpina,* the wife of Pluto, and queen of the lower world, 30, 6.

prōsiliō, 4, -uī, — (prō, *forth;* saliō, *jump*), *leap forward, spring up,* 55, 18.

prōsperus, adj. with comp. (prō, *according to;* spēs, *hope*), *according to hope, favorable, prosperous.* As subst., N., *good fortune, prosperity,* 30, 14.

prōsum, prōdesse, prōfuī, — (prō, *for;* sum, *be*), *be useful, benefit, profit,* 6, 12. (W. G. 31.)

prōtinus, adv. [prō, *forward;* TEN-, *stretch*], *forward, right onward: forthwith, at once,* 52, 28. (W. G. 71.)

prōvehō, 3, -vēxī, -vectus (prō, *forward;* vehō, *carry*), *carry forward:* pass., *move forward, sail,* 61, 25. (W. G. 72.)

prōvincia, -ae, F., *office, duty: territory, province,* 40, 14.

prōvocō, 1, -āvī, -ātus (prō, *forth;* vocō, *call*), *call forth, summon: make an appeal, appeal,* 8, 9. (W. G. 77.)

proximē, adv. sup. (proximus, *nearest*), *nearest, next,* 49, 25.

proximus, adj. sup. (prope, *near*), *nearest*, 35, 29; 36, 16: *last*, 6, 18. As subst., M., *those nearest, the bystanders*, 52, 13: in proximō, *near by*, 3, 2.

prūdentia, -ae, F. (prūdēns), *foreseeing: sagacity, caution, good sense*, 36, 23. (W. G. 75.)

psittacus, -ī, M. (Gr., ψίττακος), *parrot*, 68, 20.

Ptolemaeus, -ī, M., *Ptolemaeus, Ptolemy*, name of several kings of Egypt, 47, 16.

pūblicē, adv. (pūblicus, *of the people*), *publicly, officially, in behalf of the state*, 15, 27: *by order of the state*, 16, 16.

pūblicō, 1, -āvī, -ātus (pūblicus, *public*), *make public: open to the public*, 54, 19. (W. G. 62.)

pūblicus, adj. (populus, *people*), *of the people, of the state, public, common*, 8, 1; 9, 26. As subst., N., *state treasury*, 39, 5. (W. G. 62.)

Pūblius, -ī, M., *Publius*, a Roman praenomen, 25, 6.

pudor, -ōris, M., *shame, disgrace*, 24, 4.

puella, -ae, F. (dim. of puer, *boy*), *girl, maiden*, 8, 2.

puer, -erī, M., *boy, young man*, 12, 5; 45, 11: *slave*, 69, 21:

plur. puerī, *children*, 11, 18: ā puerīs, *from childhood*, 40, 1.

puerīlis, -e, adj. with comp. (puer, *boy*), *boyish, childish, youthful*, 57, 16.

pugiō, -ōnis, M., *short dagger, dirk*, 55, 20.

pūgna, -ae, F., *hand-to-hand fight, battle, combat*, 4, 2.

pūgnō, 1, -āvī, -ātus (pūgna, *fight*), *fight, give battle, engage*, 4, 8; 46, 4.

pulcher, -chra, -chrum, adj., comp. pulchrior, sup. pulcherrimus, *beautiful*, 22, 17: *noble, glorious, honorable*, 46, 24.

pulsus, P. of pellō, 1, 3.

pulvis, -eris, M. or F., *dust*, 37, 9.

pungō, 3, pupugī, punctus, *prick: afflict, sting*, 48, 18.

Pūnicus, adj., *Punic, Carthaginian*, 30, 18.

pūniō, 4, -īvī, -ītus (poena, *penalty*), *punish, correct, chastise*, 44, 7.

Puteolī, -ōrum, M., *Puteoli*, famous sea-port town of Campania, 22, 25.

putō, 1, -āvī, -ātus, *clean: judge, suspect, believe, think*, 21, 18.

Pyrēnaeus, adj., *Pyrenaean*. Subst., M., *the Pyrenees*, 33, 6.

Pyrrhus, -ī, M., *Pyrrhus*, king of Epirus, 25, 2.

Q

quā, see quā rē.

quadrāgēsimus, adj. (quadrāgintā, *forty*), *the fortieth*, 45, 31.

quadrāgintā, num. adj. indecl. (quattuor, *four*), *forty*, 6, 16.

quadrīgae, -ārum, F. (for quadri-

VOCABULARY. 295

iugae, cf. quattuor, *four;* iugum, *yoke*), *a team of four, four-horse team,* **8,** 30. (W. G. 48.)

quadringentī, -ae, -a, num. adj. (quattuor, *four ;* centum, *hundred*), *four hundred,* **32,** 1.

quaerō, 3, -sīvī, -sītus, *seek, look for,* **32,** 22: *ask, inquire,* **27, 29.**

quaesō, 3, —, ⲧ, archaic form of quaerō, found only in 1st per. sing. and plu. indic. pres., *beg, pray, beseech,* **18,** 18.

quaestor, -ōris, M. (for quaesītor, fr. quaerō, *question*), *quaestor,* a Roman magistrate whose duties consisted mainly in caring for the public money and the military stores. There were at first but two quaestors, but their number increased until there were forty in Caesar's time. **50,** 1.

quaestūra, -ae, F. (quaestor, *quaestor*), *the office of quaestor, quaestorship,* **58,** 17.

quālis, -e, pronom. adj. interrog., *of what sort, what kind of,* **27, 29.**

quam, adv. (case form of quī, *who*), *in what manner, how,* **17,** 18 : after a comp. or word of comparison, *than,* **3,** 1: tam ... quam, *so ... as :* quam diū, *as long as,* **29,** 15 : quam prīmum, *as soon as possible,* **50,** 17. (W. G. 27.)

quamquam, conj., *though, although,* **44,** 18.

quamvīs, conj. (quam, *as;* vīs, *you will*), *however much, although,* **48,** 19 ; **52, 7.**

quantum, adv. (quantus, *how much*), *as much as, as far as,* **33,** 19.

quantus, pronom. adj.: relat., *as much as, as great as,* **24,** 21 ; **41,** 7 : interrog., *how great?* **19, 18.** As subst., N., *how much? as much,* **16,** 16 ; **52,** 13.

quāpropter, adv., *on account of which, wherefore,* **32,** 23.

quā rē, rel. adv. (quā, *by what;* rē, *means*), *in order that, so that, therefore, by reason of which,* **1,** 19.

quartānus, adj. (quartus, *fourth*), *occurring on the fourth day, quartan,* **49,** 2.

quartus, adj. (quattuor, *four*), *fourth,* **28,** 17.

quasi, adv. (quam, *as ;* sī, *if*), *as if, just as if, on the ground that,* **2,** 4 ; **11, 4.**

quater, adv. num. (cf. quattuor, *four*), *four times,* **59,** 5.

quattuor, num. adj. indecl., *four,* **13, 26.**

-que, conj. enclit., *and, but, accordingly,* **1,** 12.

querella, -ae, F., *lament: accusation, complaint,* **23,** 18.

queror, 3, questus, dep., *complain, lament, bewail,* **68,** 28.

quī, quae, quod, adj. pron. interrog., *which? what? what kind of?* **5,** 12 ; **53, 29.**

quī, quae, quod, pron. rel., *who, which,* **1,** 2 ; **1, 8.**

VOCABULARY.

quī, quae or qua, quod, pron. indef., used after sī, nisi, nē, num, *any*, 33, 20.
quī, adv. interrog., *how?* 41, 13.
quia, conj., *because*, 7, 11.
quīcumque, quaecumque, quodcumque, indef. rel. pron. (quī, *who;* -cumque, indef. suff.), *whoever, whatever, every one who, everything that,* 2, 23; 25, 9; 35, 8.
quid, adv. interrog. (acc. N. of quis, *who*), *how? why? what?* 42, 6.
quīdam, quaedam, quoddam, and as subst. quiddam, pron. indef., *a certain, a, somebody, one,* 12, 9; 29, 4 : plur., *some, some things,* 8, 16 ; 55, 27.
quidem, adv., *to be sure, certainly, indeed,* 6, 11 : nē ... quidem, *not even,* 21, 5.
quidquam, see quisquam, 24, 10.
quiēs, -ētis, F., *rest, repose,* 9, 8 : *sleep,* 23, 19.
quiētus, adj. with comp. and sup. (P. of quiēscō, *rest*), *at rest, calm, inactive, quiet,* 62, 1.
quīn, conj. (abl. quī, *why;* nē, *not*), interrog., *why not? wherefore not?* 24, 18 : corroborative, *but, indeed, nay, in fact,* 38, 16 : in a dependent clause, *so that not, but, but that, from,* 2, 8 ; 19, 5.
Quīnctilius, -ī, M., *P. Quinctilius Varus*, a general of Augustus, defeated by the Germans 9 B.C., 71, 12.

quīndecim, num. adj. (quīnque, *five ;* decem, *ten*), *fifteen,* 15, 26.
quīngentī, -ae, -a, num. adj. (quīnque, *five ;* centum, *hundred*), *five hundred,* 37, 25.
quīnquāgintā, num. adj. indecl., *fifty,* 23, 2.
quīnque, num. adj. indecl., *five,* 54, 8.
quīnquennium, -ī, N. (quīnque, *five ;* annus, *year*), *a period of five years,* 64, 20.
quīnquiēns, adv. (quīnque, *five*), *five times,* 54, 3.
quīntus, num. adj. (quīnque, *five*), *fifth,* 20, 12.
Quīntus, -ī, M., a Roman praenomen, 32, 25.
Quirīnālis, -e, adj. (Quirīnus), *of Quirinus, of Romulus, Quirinal,* referring to the *Quirinal hill,* one of the seven hills, 5, 1.
Quirīnus, -ī, M. (Quirīs, i.e. Curēs), *Quirinus, the deified Romulus,* 5, 2.
quis, quid, pron. interrog., *who? which one? what man? what thing? what?* 2, 1; 5, 17.
quis, qua, quid, pron. indef., with sī, nisi, nē, num, *any one, anything, some one, something,* 41, 20 ; 67, 23.
quisnam, or (as adj.) quīnam, quaenam, quidnam or (as adj.) quodnam, pron. interrog. (quis, *who ;* -nam, intens.), *who then? who in the world? what in the*

VOCABULARY.

world? what, pray? 40, 19; 44, 8.

quisquam, M., quicquam, N., pron. indef. (quis, *any one;* -quam, indef. suff.), *any, any one, anything,* 24, 10; 56, 2.

quisque, quaeque, quidque, and (as adj.) quodque, pron. indef. (quis, *who;* -que, indef. suff.), *whoever it be, each, each one, everybody, everything, all,* 6, 23; 54, 16.

quisquis, quicquid, and (as adj.) quodquod, pron. rel. indef. (quis, *who,* doubled), *whoever, whatever, every one who, everything which,* 42, 5.

quō, adv. and conj. (old dat. and abl. form of quī), *whither,* 50, 1: *in order that,* 9, 4; 41, 30.

quod, adv. and conj. (acc. N. sing. of rel. quī, *as to which*), as adv., *as to what, in what:* quod sī, *but if,* 52, 14: as conj., *that, in that, because,* 11, 17; 42, 5; 47, 2; 51, 21.

quōminus, conj. (quō, *by which;* minus, *less*), *that not, lest, from,* 27, 10.

quō modo, rel. adv. (quō, *in what;* modō, *manner*), *in the manner that, as,* 42, 15.

quondam, adv. (cum, *when, since;* -dam, demonstr. suff.), *once, formerly, on a time,* 5, 10; 55, 25.

quoniam, adv. (quom, *when, since;* iam, *now*), *since now, since, because,* 24, 9.

quoque, conj. (placed after an emphatic word), *also, too,* 6, 3.

quōrsum and **quōrsus**, adv. (quō, *whither;* versus, *turned*), *to what place, whither,* 51, 26.

quot, rel. adj. plur. indecl., *as, as many as,* 26, 4: quot . . . tot, *as many . . . as.*

quotannīs (quot, *how many;* annus, *year*), *every year, annually,* 71, 13.

quousque, adv. (quō, *whither;* usque, *up to*), *until what time, till when,* 40, 6.

R

radius, -ī, M., *staff, rod: beam, ray,* 37, 9.

rādīx, -īcis, F., *root,* 29, 13.

rapīna, -ae, F. [RAP-, *snatch*], *robbery, plunder,* 1, 18. (W. G. 54.)

rapiō, 3, -puī, raptus [RAP-, *snatch*], *seize and carry off, snatch, drag,* 3, 15; 12, 11; 69, 19 : rapere in iūs, *drag before the court,* 8, 7. (W. G. 64.)

rārō, adv. with comp. (rārus, *rare*), *seldom, rarely,* 70, 24.

rārus, adj. with comp. and sup., *thin, rare: infrequent, uncommon,* 56, 7.

ratiō, -ōnis, F. (cf. reor, *reckon*),

reckoning, account: course, conduct, plan, **33**, 12.
ratis, -is, F., *raft, float: vessel,* **30**, 23.
rebellō, 1, -āvī, -ātus (**re-**, *again;* **bellō,** *wage war*), *wage war again, revolt, rebel,* **19**, 17. (W. G. 28.)
recēdō, 3, -cessī, -cessus (**re-**, *back;* **cēdō,** *go*), *go back, retire, retreat, withdraw,* **45**, 10: *desist,* **33**, 14. (W. G. 14.)
receptus, -ūs, M. [**re-**, *back;* CAP-, *take*], *taking back: retiring, retreat,* **34**, 21.
recessus, -ūs, M. [**re-**, *back;* CAD-, *fall*], *going back, retreat: nook, recess,* **45**, 26. (W. G. 14.)
recidō or **reccidō,** 3, reccidī or recidī, recāsūrus (**re-**, *back;* **cadō,** *fall*), *fall back: pass, return, fall to,* **4**, 17. (W. G. 14.)
recipiō, 3, -cēpī, -ceptus (**re-**, *back;* **capiō,** *take*), *take back, recover,* **12**, 11; **36**, 7: with pron. reflex., *withdraw, retire,* **26**, 5: *accept, admit, receive, welcome,* **4**, 15. (W. G. 17.)
reconciliō, 1, -āvī, -ātus (**re-**, *again;* **conciliō,** *procure*), *procure again, reëstablish, restore,* **64**, 10: *reunite, reconcile,* **43**, 11.
recreō, 1, -āvī, -ātus (**re-**, *again, anew;* **creō,** *make*), *make anew, revive, encourage,* **46**, 22.
rēctē, adv. with comp. and sup. (**rēctus,** *straight*), *in a straight line: properly, well,* **12**, 20. (W. G. 65.)

recubō, 1, —, —, (**re-**, *back;* **cubō,** *lie*), *lie upon the back, lie back, recline,* **38**, 23.
recuperō, 1, -āvī, -ātus (**re-**, *again;* cf. **capiō,** *take*), *regain, rescue, recover, save,* **21**, 29.
reddō, 3, -didī, -ditus (**red-**, *back;* **dō,** *give*), *give back, restore, return,* **22**, 2: *deliver, give,* **44**, 16. (W. G. 24.)
redeō, -īre, -iī, -itus (**red-**, *back;* **eō,** *go*), *go back, return,* **7**, 16; **24**, 26. (W. G. 46.)
redigō, 3, -ēgī, -āctus (**red-**, *back;* **agō,** *drive*), *drive back, lead back: reduce, force, subdue,* **14**, 3; **51**, 15.
redimō, 3, -ēmī, -ēmptus (**red-**, *back;* **emō,** *buy*), *buy back, redeem, ransom,* **26**, 6.
redintegrō, 1, -āvī, -ātus (**red-**, *again;* **integrō,** *make whole*), *make whole again, renew,* **4**, 10. (W. G. 70.)
reditus, -ūs, M. [**red-**, *back;* 1-, *go*], *going back, return,* **39**, 17. (W. G. 46.)
redūcō, 3, -dūxī, -ductus (**re-**, *back;* **dūcō,** *lead*), *lead back; bring back,* **19**, 13. (W. G. 29.)
referō, -ferre, rettulī, relātus (**re-**, *back;* **ferō,** *bear*), *bear back, bring back, bring,* **41**, 29; **42**, 20: with **sē,** *return,* **62**, 16: **pedem referre,** *withdraw, retreat,* **25**, 11: *give back, restore,* **30**, 13: *gain, win,* **12**, 13: *report, relate,* **58**, 28: *refer, attribute, ascribe,* **29**, 6: *number,*

count, reckon, 20, 14: *lift, raise,* 40, 20. (W. G. 34.)

refoveō, 2, -fōvī, — (re-, *again;* foveō, *warm*), *warm again, restore, revive,* 53, 16.

refrāctus, P. of refringō, 35, 30.

refringō, 3, -frēgī, -frāctus (re-, intensive; frangō, *break*), *break up, batter down, break open,* 35, 30. (W. G. 38.)

refugiō, 3, -fūgī, — (re-, *back;* fugiō, *flee*), *flee back, flee for safety, flee,* 13, 20. (W. G. 40.)

rēgālis, -e, adj. (rēx, *king*), *kingly, royal, regal,* 66, 21. (W. G. 65.)

rēgia, -ae, F. (rēgius, *royal*), *royal palace,* 9, 5. (W. G. 65.)

rēgīna, -ae, F. (rēx, *king*), *queen,* 66, 2. (W. G. 65.)

regiō, -ōnis, F. [REG-, *guide*], *direction: region, district,* 23, 1. (W. G. 65.)

rēgius, adj. (rēx, *king*), *kingly, royal, belonging to the king,* 1, 14; 41, 3. (W. G. 65.)

rēgnō, 1, -āvī, -ātus (rēgnum, *royal power*), *to have royal power, be king, reign,* 1, 3.

rēgnum, -ī, N. [REG-, *guide*], *kingly government, royalty: sovereignty, supreme power,* 1, 2: *realm, kingdom,* 11, 21. (W. G. 65.

regō, 3, rēxī, rēctus [REG-, *guide*], *keep straight, guide: govern, rule,* 2, 17. (W. G. 65.)

regredior, 3, -gressus, dep. (re-, *back;* gradior, *go*), *go back, return,* 17, 11: *withdraw, retreat,* 20, 18. (W. G. 44.)

rēiciō, 3, rēiēcī, -iectus (re-, *back;* iaciō, *throw*), *throw back,* 64, 15. (W. G. 47.)

relābor, 3, -lāpsus, dep. (re-, *back;* lābor, *slide*), *slide back, flow back, sink back,* 1, 9. (W. G. 49.)

relātus, P. of referō, 20, 14.

relictus, P. of relinquō, 22, 3.

religiō, -ōnis, F. (re-, *back;* cf. ligō, *bind*), *conscientiousness, duty: piety, reverence,* 5, 4; 9, 18: *pledge of faith, oath,* 24, 13: *worship, religion,* 5, 6.

religō, 1, -āvī, -ātus (re-, *back;* ligō, *bind*), *bind back, fasten on, bind fast,* 8, 30; 59, 7.

relinquō, 3, -līquī, -lictus (re-, *behind;* linquō, *leave*), *leave behind, leave, abandon,* 1, 9; 21, 22: *bequeath, leave by will,* 1, 2; 11, 3: *leave alive,* 21, 28: *permit to remain,* 34, 7.

reliquiae, -ārum, F. (reliquus, *remaining*), *what is left, remnants, remains,* 21, 25.

reliquus, adj. (cf. relinquō, *leave*), *left, left over, remaining,* 15, 14.

remaneō, 2, -mānsī, — (re-, *behind;* maneō, *stay*), *stay behind, remain,* 59, 25. (W.G. 52.)

remittō, 3, -mīsī, -missus (re-, *back;* mittō, *let go*), *let go back, send back: give up,* 71, 16. (W. G. 53.)

removeō, 2, -mōvī, -mōtus (re-, *back;* moveō, *move*), *move back,* *withdraw, remove,* **28,** 10. (W. G. 54.)

Remus, -ī, M., *Remus,* the brother of Romulus, **1,** 5.

renāscor, 3, -nātus, dep. (re-, *again* ; (g)nāscor, *be born*), *be born again, grow again,* **26,** 4. (W. G. 41.)

renūntiō, 1, -āvī, -ātus (re-, *back* ; nūntiō, *bring word*), *bring back word, report,* **25,** 9 : *declare elected, announce,* **63,** 4 : (re- with negative force) *refuse, decline,* **38,** 25.

renuō, 3, -uī, — (re-, *back ;* nuō, *nod*), *nod backwards : decline, refuse,* **55,** 14.

reor, 2, ratus, dep., *reckon, believe, think,* **7,** 13.

repellō, 3, reppulī, repulsus (re-, *back ;* pellō, *drive*), *drive back, drive away : repulse, repel, reject, remove,* **54,** 30. (W. G. 59.)

rependō, 3, -pendī, -pēnsus (re-, *back ;* pendō, *weigh*), *weigh back : pay by same weight,* **41,** 29.

repente, adv. (repēns, *sudden*), *suddenly, unexpectedly,* **2,** 11.

repentīnus, adj. (repēns, *sudden*), *sudden, unexpected,* **56,** 1.

reperiō, 4, repperī, repertus, *find, meet with,* **57,** 21 : *get, procure, obtain,* **47,** 28.

repetō, 3, -īvī, -ītus (re-, *again ;* petō, *seek*), *seek again, return to,* **23,** 14 : *demand back, claim,* **13,** 17: rēs repetere, *demand restitution,* **9,** 22.

repetundae, -ārum, F. (repetō, *demand back*), sc. pecūniae, *extortion,* **54,** 10.

repleō, 2, -ēvī, -ētus (re-, *again ;* pleō, *fill*), *fill again : fill, fill up,* **40,** 15.

repōnō, 3, -posuī, -positus (re-, *back ;* pōnō, *put*), *put back, replace,* **10,** 22.

reportō, 1, -āvī, -ātus (re-, *back ;* portō, *bear*), *carry back, take back, bear back,* **29,** 17.

reprimō, 3, -pressī, -pressus (re-, *back ;* premō, *press*), *press back, restrain, check,* **34,** 21.

repudiō, 1, -āvī, -ātus (repudium, *a putting away*), *put away, cast off,* **48,** 25 : *refuse, scorn,* **28,** 6.

repūgnō, 1, -āvī, -ātus (re-, *back, in opposition ;* pūgnō, *fight*), *fight back, oppose, resist,* **50,** 29.

repulsa, -ae, F. (P. of repellō, *drive back*), *rejection, repulse,* **59,** 15.

repulsus, P. of repellō, **54,** 30.

reputō, 1, -āvī, -ātus (re-, *again, over ;* putō, *think*), *count over, calculate : think over, meditate, reflect upon,* **52,** 13.

rēs, reī, F., *thing, object, matter, affair, business, event, fact, circumstance, deed,* **1,** 6; **1,** 14; **1,** 19; **2,** 10; **6,** 21; **10,** 3; **10,** 14: *condition,* **39,** 21: *property, estate,* **59,** 12: *interest, advantage,* **50,** 17: *cause, reason,* **10,** 6: *state, commonwealth,* **16,**

4; 36, 24: **rēs pūblica**, *the state, the republic*, 37, 11.

rescindō, 3, -scidī, -scissus (**re-**, *back*; **scindō**, *cut*), *cut off, cut down, break down*, 16, 13. (W. G. 66.)

resistō, 3, -stitī, — (**re-**, *back*; **sistō**, *stand*), *stand back, stand still, halt, stop*, 4, 10: *oppose, resist*, 44, 22. (W. G. 69.)

resolvō, 3, -solvī, -solūtus (**re-**, *back* to the original condition; **solvō**, *loose*), *untie, unfasten: dissolve, melt*, 66, 11.

respergō, 3, -sī, -sus (**re-**, *again, over*; **spargō**, *scatter*), *sprinkle over, besprinkle*, 18, 22.

respiciō, 3, -spēxī, -spectus (**re-**, *back*; **speciō**, *look*), *look back, look back upon, look at, gaze at*, 7, 14; 54, 26. (W. G. 68.)

respīrō, 1, -āvī, -ātus (**re-**, *back*; **spīrō**, *blow*), *blow back, breathe: revive, be refreshed, be relieved*, 38, 27.

respondeō, 2, -spondī, -spōnsus (**re-**, *in return*; **spondeō**, *promise*), *answer, respond*, 10, 5.

respōnsum, -ī, N. (P. N. of **respondeō**, *answer*), *answer, reply*, 41, 16: *opinion, oracle*, 13, 3.

restinguō, 3, -nxī, -nctus (**re-**, *back* to its original state; **stinguō**, *quench*), *put out, quench, extinguish*, 59, 23.

restituō, 3, -uī, -ūtus (**re-**, *again*; **statuō**, *set up*), *set up again, replace, rebuild*, 61, 9: *give back, restore*, 2, 13: *revive, repair*, 36, 25. (W. G. 69.)

retineō, 2, -tinuī, -tentus (**re-**, *back*; **teneō**, *hold*), *hold back: keep possession of, retain, keep*, 36, 6. (W. G. 71.)

retrahō, 3, -trāxī, -tractus (**re-**, *back*; **trahō**, *draw*), *draw back, call back: drag back, bring back*, 59, 30.

retrō, adv., *backward, to the rear*, 23, 14.

reus, adj. (**rēs**, *thing*), *concerned in a thing, party to an action*: often as subst., M., *the accused*, 59, 22.'

reversus, P. of **revertor**, 31, 1.

revertō, 3, -vertī, —, or **revertor**, 3, -versus (**re-**, *back*; **vertō**, *turn*), *turn back, return*, 1, 14; 44, 19.

revocō, 1, -āvī, -ātus (**re-**, *again*; **vocō**, *call*), *call again, recall, call back*, 61, 6. (W. G. 77.)

rēx, **rēgis**, M. [REG-, *guide*], *absolute monarch, king*, 1, 1. (W. G. 65.)

Rhēa, -ae, F., *Rhea*, praenomen of Rhea Silvia, the mother of Romulus and Remus, 1, 4.

Rhēnus, -ī, M., *the Rhine*, river of Germany, 51, 16.

rhētor, -oris, M. (Gr., ῥήτωρ), *teacher of oratory, rhetorician, orator*, 58, 12.

Rhodos (rarely **Rhodus**), -ī, F., *Rhodes*, an island in the Mediterranean, south of Asia Minor, 48, 5.

rīdeō, 2, -sī, -sus, *laugh, smile,* 36, 8 : *laugh at, ridicule,* 15, 16.

rigō, 1, -āvī, -ātus, *wet, moisten,* 6, 7.

rīpa, -ae, F., *bank,* 1, 8.

rīsus, -ūs, M. (cf. rīdeō, *laugh*), *laughing, laughter,* 69, 11.

rīte, adv. (old abl. for rītū; see rītus), *according to religious usage, with due observance, duly,* 5, 23.

rītus, -ūs, M., *form of religious observance, ceremony, formula, rite,* 10, 4.

rixa, -ae, F., *quarrel, dispute,* 11, 23.

rōbur, -oris, N., *hard-wood: hardness, vigor, strength,* 30, 24 : *the best part, the flower,* 25, 24.

rogō, 1, -āvī, -ātus, *ask, question,* 23, 23: *beg, request,* 15, 18.

Rōma, -ae, F., *Rome,* 2, 20.

Rōmānī, -ōrum, M. (Rōma, *Rome*), *the Romans,* 3, 17.

Rōmānus, adj. (Rōma, *Rome*), *of Rome, Roman,* 3, 15. As subst., M. and F., *a Roman,* 30, 22.

Rōmulus, -ī, M., *Romulus,* the mythical founder of Rome, 1, 5.

Rōscius, -ī, M., *Roscius,* gentile name of Sextius Roscius, whom Cicero defended against a charge of parricide, 58, 4.

rōstrum, -ī, N. (rōdō, *gnaw*), *beak: ship's beak:* plur., *the rostra,* the speaker's stand in the Forum, 54, 29 (v. notes, fig. 27, p. 129).

Rubicō, -ōnis, M., *the Rubicon,* a small stream marking the boundary between Cisalpine Gaul and Italy, 52, 11.

Rūfīnus, -ī, M., family name of P. Cornelius Rufinus, 29, 18.

ruīna, -ae, F. (cf. ruō, *fall with violence*), *rushing down, falling down, ruin: calamity, fall, destruction,* 9, 3; 59, 22 : plur., *ruins,* 22, 3.

rumpō, 3, rūpī, ruptus [RVP-, *break*], *break, burst, tear: break in upon, cut short, interrupt,* 69, 27. (W. G. 64.)

ruō, 3, ruī, rutus, *fall with violence, go to ruin: hurry, hasten,* 59, 29.

rūrsus or rūrsum, adv. (revorsus or revorsum, P. of revertō, *turn back*), *turned back, back: again, anew,* 10, 22. (W. G. 74.)

rūs, rūris, N., *country* (as opposed to the city), *fields,* 62, 12.

S

Sabīnī, -ōrum, M., *Sabines,* an ancient Italian people, dwelling in central Italy, north of Latium, 3, 12.

sacer, -cra, -crum, adj. with sup. [SAC-, *fasten*; cf. sanciō, *make sacred*], *sacred,* 16, 21.

sacerdōs, -ōtis, M. and F. [sacer, *sacred;* DA-, *give*], *priest, priestess,* 1, 5. (W. G. 24.)

VOCABULARY. 303

sacrārium, -ī, N. (**sacrum**, *a holy thing*), *a depository of holy things, shrine*, 15, 25.

sacrificium, -ī, N. (**sacrificus**, *of sacrifices*), *sacrifice*, 8, 17. (W. G. 33.)

sacrum, -ī, N. (**sacer**, *consecrated*), *something consecrated, a holy thing:* plur. *religious rites, sacrifices*, 5, 6.

saeculum, -ī, M., *race, generation: century, age, time*, 40, 5.

saepe, adv. with comp. and sup., *often, many times, frequently*, 1, 13; 35, 7.

saepiō, 4, -psī, -ptus (**saepēs**, *hedge*), *to surround with a hedge, hedge in, fortify, surround*, 16, 6.

saeviō, 4, -iī, -ītus (**saevus**, *fierce*), *be fierce, be furious, rage*, 24, 12.

saevitia, -ae, F. (**saevus**, *furious*), *harshness, cruelty, severity*, 14, 5.

saevus, adj. with comp. and sup., *raging, furious, violent*, 52, 27.

saginō, 1, -āvī, -ātus (**sagīna**, *food*), *fatten*, 47, 29.

sagulum, -ī, N. (dim. of **sagum**, *military cloak*), *a small military cloak*, 64, 15.

Saguntum, -ī, N., or **Saguntus**, -ī, F., *Saguntum*, a town in the eastern part of Spain, near the coast. Its capture by Hannibal led to the second Punic war. 32, 22.

Salernitānus, adj., *belonging to* *Salernum*, a town in Campania, 65, 4.

Salii, -ōrum, M., *Salii*, a college of priests founded by Numa for the service of Mars. They danced in procession through the city every March. 5, 20 (v. notes, fig. 2, p. 82).

Salinātor, -ōris, M., *Salinator*, a Roman surname, 35, 18.

salīnum, -ī, N. (**sāl**, *salt*), *a vessel for salt, salt-cellar*, 29, 11.

saltō, 1, -āvī, -ātus (freq. of **saliō**, *leap*), *dance*, 5, 23.

(**saltus**, -ūs), M. (cf. **saliō**, *leap*), only acc. and abl. sing., and plur., *leap, spring, jump, bound*, 2, 22; 31, 7.

saltus, -ūs, M., *glen, ravine*, 1, 18; 23, 24.

salūbris, -e, adj. with comp. and sup. (**salūs**, *soundness*), *health-giving, healthful: healthy, vigorous*, 9, 9.

salūs, -ūtis, F. (**salvus**, *sound*), *soundness, health: safety*, 21, 9.

salūtātiō, -ōnis, F. (**salūtō**, *greet*), *greeting, saluting, salutation*, 68, 22.

salūtātor, -ōris, M. (**salūtō**, *greet*), *a saluter*, 68, 27.

salūtō, 1, -āvī, -ātus (**salūs**, *health*), *greet, pay respects, call upon, salute*, 13, 22; 63, 5.

salvus, adj., *in good health, safe, uninjured*, 40, 25.

Samnīs -ītis, adj., *of, or belonging to, the Samnites*, 24, 22.

Samnītēs, -ium, M. plur., *Sam-*

nites, *the people of Samnium*, a rugged district of central Italy, east of Latium, **22**, 15.

sapiēns, -entis, adj. with comp. and sup. (P. of **sapiō**, *have taste*), *wise, sensible, discreet, judicious*, **40**, 3. As subst., *man of sense, philosopher*, **29**, 5.

Sardinia, -ae, F., *Sardinia*, a large island in the Mediterranean, west of Italy, **42**, 13.

sarmentum, -ī, N., *twig, fagot*, **33**, 27.

satis, adj.; N. indecl., only nom. and acc.; adv.: as adj., *enough, sufficient*, **38**, 9: as noun, *enough*, **37**, 16: as adv., *sufficiently, enough*, **49**, 6.

saucius, adj., *wounded, hurt*, **64**, 9.

saxum, -ī, N. [SAC-, *split*], *split rock, rock*, **21**, 4. (W. G. 66.)

scālae, -ārum, F. (cf. **scandō**, *climb*), *ladder, scaling-ladder*, **19**, 22.

scapha, -ae, F. (Gr., σκάφη), *light boat, skiff*, **31**, 7.

scelerātus, adj. with comp. and sup. (P. of **scelerō**, *pollute*), *polluted, profaned, defiled*, **13**, 25.

scelestē, adv. (**scelestus**, *wicked*), *wickedly, impiously*, **14**, 1.

scelus, -eris, N., *wicked deed, crime, sin*, **59**, 12.

schola, -ae, F. (Gr., σχολή), *leisure for learning, lecture, school*, **40**, 6.

sciō, **4**, -īvī, -ītus [SAC-, SCI-, *divide, distinguish*], *know, understand, perceive, be skilled in, know how*, **4**, 7; **23**, 22; **38**, 8. (W. G. 66.)

Scīpiō, -ōnis, M. (**scīpiō**, *staff*), *Scipio*, a very distinguished Roman family of the Cornelian gens, **33**, 7.

scīpiō, -ōnis, M., *staff, walking-stick*, **20**, 27.

scīscitor, **1**, -ātus, dep. (freq. fr. **scīscō**, *seek to know*), *seek to know, ask, inquire*, **14**, 10. (W. G. 66.)

scissus, adj. (P. of **scindō**, *tear*), *rent, riven*, **5**, 18.

scrība, -ae, M. (cf. **scrībō**, *write*), *official scribe, clerk*, **39**, 4.

scrībō, **3**, scrīpsī, scrīptus, *scratch, engrave: write*, **51**, 10.

scrīnium, -ī, N., *case, book-box*, **56**, 9 (v. notes, fig. 28, p. 130).

Scultenna, -ae, M., *the Scultenna*, a river in Cisalpine Gaul, **63**, 22.

scūtum, -ī, N., *shield, buckler*, **3**, 25 (v. notes, fig. 26, p. 127).

sē, acc. and abl. of **suī**.

sēcēdō, **3**, -cessī, -cessus (**sē-**, *apart from*; **cēdō**, *go*), *go apart, go away, withdraw*, **16**, 21.

secō, **1**, -cuī, -ctus [SAC-, SEC-, *divide*], *cut, cut in two*, **11**, 14. (W. G. 66.)

sēcrētō, adv. (**sēcrētus**, *separate*), *in secret, secretly*, **28**, 15.

sēcrētus, adj. with comp. (P. of **sēcernō**, *sever*), *severed, apart: hidden, private, secret*, **5**, 22. (W. G. 20.)

VOCABULARY. 305

sector, 1, -ātus, dep. (freq. of sequor, *follow*), *follow eagerly, attend*, 58, 1.

secundus, adj. with comp. and sup. (sequor, *follow*), *in time, order or rank, following, next, second*, 50, 5.

secūris, -is, acc. im or em, abl. -ī, F. [SAC-, SEC-, *split*], *axe, hatchet, cleaver*, 11, 29. (W. G. 66.)

secus, adv., *otherwise, differently*, 12, 7.

sed, conj., *but, on the contrary, but also, but in fact*, 1, 3; 36, 19.

sedeō, 2, sēdī, sessum [SED-, *sit*], *sit, seat oneself*, 37, 13: *settle, lie, lower over*, 34, 24. (W. G. 67.)

sēdēs, -is, F. [SED-, *sit*], *seat, bench, chair*, 20, 29: *site, location*, 9, 5. (W. G. 67.)

sēditiō, -ōnis, F. [sēd, *apart, aside*; I-, *go*], *a going aside, dissension, civil discord, sedition, mutiny*, 4, 27; 43, 9. (W. G. 46.)

sēdūcō, 3, -dūxī, -ductus (sē-, *apart, aside*; dūcō, *lead*), *lead aside, take apart, draw aside*, 18, 20.

sēdulō, adv. (sēdulus, *busy*), *busily, industriously: deliberately, purposely*, 34, 14.

sēgnis, -e, adj. with comp., *slow, sluggish, lazy*, 17, 6.

sēgniter, adv. (sēgnis, *slow*), *slowly, tardily, sluggishly, without spirit*, 12, 10; 40, 22.

sella, -ae, F. [SED-, *sit*], *seat, chair, magistrate's seat*, 5, 9; 43, 25 (v. notes, fig. 1, p. 81). (W. G. 67.)

semel, adv. num., *once, a single time*, 67, 20.

sēmet, see suī, 41, 25.

semper, adv., *ever, always, at all times, forever*, 50, 7.

Semprōnius, -ī, M., *Sempronius*, name of a Roman gens, 33, 8.

senātor, -ōris, M. (cf. **senātus**, *senate*), *a member of the senate, senator*, 4, 18.

senātōrius, adj. (senātor, *senator*), *of a senator, senatorial*, 42, 23.

senātus, -ūs, M. (cf. **senex**, *old*), *the council of elders, senate*, 13, 17.

Seneca, -ae, M., surname of *L. Annaeus Seneca*, a famous Stoic philosopher, instructor of Nero, died 65 A.D., 65, 14.

senectūs, -ūtis, F. (**senex**, *old*), *old age, extreme age*, 4, 19.

senex, senis, adj. with comp., *senior, old, aged*, 8, 10. As subst., M., *old man*, 4, 17.

senior, -ōris, comp. of **senex**, 4, 17.

Senonēs, -um, M., *the Senones*, a people in Cisalpine Gaul, 20, 4.

sententia, -ae, F. (cf. **sentiō**, *think*), *a way of thinking, sentiment, opinion, decision, wish, desire*, 23, 27; 55, 25.

sentiō, 4, sēnsī, sēnsus, *discern by sense, feel: think, believe*, 67, 24.

sēparātim, adv. (**sēparātus,** *separated*), *apart, separately,* 50, 20.
sepeliō, 4, -pelīvī, -pultus, *bury, inter,* 6, 13.
septem, num. adj. indecl., *seven,* 6, 15.
Septimulēius, -ī, M., *L. Septimuleius,* a friend of C. Gracchus, 41, 28.
septimus, num. adj. (**septem,** *seven*), *the seventh,* 14.
septirēmis, -e, adj. (**septem,** *seven;* rēmus, *oar*), *with seven banks of oars,* 30, 26 (v. notes, fig. 16, p. 109).
septuāgēsimus, adj. num. ord. (**septuāgintā,** *seventy*), *seventieth,* 71, 22.
sepulcrum, -ī, N. (cf. **sepeliō,** *bury*), *place where a corpse is buried, grave, tomb,* 17, 16.
sepultūra, -ae, F. (cf. **sepeliō,** *bury*), *burial, interment,* 65, 21.
sepultus, P. of **sepeliō,** 6, 13.
sequor, 3, secūtus, *follow, come after, attend, accompany,* 14, 12: *chase, pursue,* 7, 13: *favor, conform to, adopt, follow,* 8, 26; 24, 15.
Sergius, -ī, M., *Sergius,* the name of a Roman gens, 58, 25.
sēriō, adv. (**sērius,** *earnest*), *in earnest, seriously,* 50, 4.
sērius, adj. (for *sevĕrius, from **sevērus,** *grave*), *grave, earnest, serious,* 15, 20.
sermō, -ōnis, M., *continued speech, talk, conversation,* 26, 30: *report, rumor,* 34, 16.

sērō, adv. with comp. and sup. (**sērus,** *late*), *late, at a late hour,* 24, 5.
Sertōrius, -ī, M., *Q. Sertorius,* the famous general of the Marian party, who maintained himself in Spain, and defied the power of Rome, until he was assassinated. 44, 29.
serva, -ae, *female slave, maid,* 18, 6.
servīlis, -e, adj. (**servus,** *slave*), *of a slave, slavish, servile,* 2, 7.
servitūs, -ūtis, F. (**servus,** *slave*), *the condition of a servant, slavery,* 18, 1.
Servius, -ī, M., a Roman praenomen, e.g., *Servius Tullius,* 12, 1.
servō, 1, -āvī, -ātus, *make safe, save, rescue, preserve, keep, deliver,* 42, 24; 53, 27.
servus, -ī, M., *slave, servant,* 38, 29; 47, 27.
sēsē, acc. and abl. of **suī,** 7, 15.
sessor, -ōris, M. [SED-, *sit*], *one who sits: rider,* 25, 16. (W. G. 67.)
sēstertius, adj. num. (**sēmis,** *half;* **tertius,** *third*), *two and a half.* As subst., M. (sc. **nummus**), *a sesterce,* a small silver coin, originally two and a half asses, worth 4.1 cents. 50, 24.
sētius, adv. comp., *the less, in a less degree,* 18, 16.
seu, see **sīve,** 4, 10.
sevērē, adv. with comp. and sup.

VOCABULARY. 307

(sevērus, *grave*), *gravely, seriously, severely*, 54, 10.
sex, adj. num. indecl., *six*, 2, 18.
sexāgintā, adj. num. indecl., *sixty*, 54, 7.
sextāns, -antis, M. (sex, *six*), *the sixth, a sixth part;* a small coin, one sixth of an as, worth less than a cent, 17, 15.
Sextīlis, -e, adj. (sextus, *sixth;* sc. mēnsis, *month*), *the sixth month* counting from March, *August*, 20, 13.
Sextus, -ī, M., *Sextus*, a Roman praenomen, 14, 3.
sextus, adj. num. ord. (sex, *six*), *the sixth*, 48, 22.
sī, conj., *if, on condition that, when*, 3, 21 ; 50, 9.
sībilus, -ī, M., plur. sībilī, -ōrum, M., also sībila, -ōrum, N., *whistling*, 35, 9.
Sibyllīnus, adj. (Sibylla, *the Sibyl*), *of a Sibyl, Sibylline*, 15, 25.
sīc, adv., *thus, in this way*, 2, 19; 2, 23.
siccō, 1, -āvī, -ātus (siccus, *dry*), *to make dry, dry, drain*, 54, 19.
siccus, adj., *dry*. As subst., siccum, -ī, N., *dry land*, 1, 9.
Sicilia, -ae, F., *Sicily*, 27, 3.
Siculī, -ōrum, M., *the Sicilians*, 58, 19.
sīcut or sīcutī, adv. (sīc, *so;* ut, *as*), *so as, just as*, 19, 8.
sīgnifer, -fera, -ferum, adj. [sīgnum, *sign;* FER-, *bear*], *sign-bearing*. As subst., M.,

standard-bearer, ensign, 22, 7 (v. notes, fig. 12, p. 99).
sīgnificō, 1, -āvī, -ātus [sīgnifex, *image-maker*, fr. sīgnum, *sign;* FAC-, *make*], *make signs, show by signs: mean, indicate, signify*, 6, 2.
sīgnō, 1, -āvī, -ātus (sīgnum, *mark*), *set a mark upon, mark, seal, sign*, 51, 9.
sīgnum, -ī, N., *mark, sign: ensign, standard*, 12, 11 (v. notes, fig. 6, p. 89): *signal*, 3, 14 : sīgna īnferre, *attack*, 59, 24.
silēns, -entis, adj., *in silence, silent*, 5, 16.
silentium, -ī, N. (silēns, *still*), *stillness, silence*, 14, 15.
sileō, 2, -uī, —, *be noiseless, be still, keep silence*, 23, 17.
silva, -ae, F., *wood, forest*, 33, 30.
Silvia, -ae, F., v. Rhēa, 1, 4.
similis, -e, adj., comp. similior, sup. simillimus, *like, resembling, similar*, 2, 9.
similiter, adv., comp. similius, sup. simillimē (similis, *like*), *likewise, similarly*, 68, 19.
similitūdō, -inis, F. (similis, *like*), *likeness, resemblance, similitude*, 13, 16.
simplex, -icis, adj. with comp. [cf. semel, *once;* PLEC-, *fold*], *simple, plain: open, frank*, 26, 16. (W. G. 60.)
simul, adv., *at the same time*, 8, 2.
simulācrum, -ī, N. (simulō, *make like*), *likeness, image, portrait, statue*, 20, 26.

simulō, 1, -āvī, -ātus (**similis,** *like*), *make like, imitate: feign, counterfeit, pretend,* 6, 5; 62, 30.

simultās, ātis, F. (**simul,** *at the same time*), *hostile encounter, dissension: rivalry, jealousy, grudge,* 29, 18; 56, 15.

sīn, conj. (**sī,** *if;* **nē,** *not*), *if however, if on the contrary, but if,* 28, 19.

sine, prep. with abl., *without,* 6, 8.

singulāris, -e, adj. (**singulī,** *one at a time*), *one by one: singular, remarkable,* 58, 26.

singulī, -ae, -a, adj., *one at a time, single, separate, several, one on a side,* 7, 12; 7, 20; 24, 1; 39, 1.

sinister, -tra, -trum, adj. with comp., *left,* 3, 23.

sinō, 3, sīvī, situs, *let down, fix: let, suffer, allow,* 18, 19.

sinus, -ūs, M., *bent surface, curve, fold: the fold of the toga about the breast,* 32, 27.

sistō, 3, stitī, status, *cause to stand:* **sistere gradum,** *stop, halt,* 23, 15. (W. G. 69.)

situs, adj. (P. of **sinō,** *set, fix*), *placed, situated,* 57, 10.

sīve, or **seu,** conj. (**sī,** *if;* -ve, *or*), *or if: or, or rather,* 30, 19; **sīve . . . sīve,** or **seu . . . seu,** *whether . . . or,* 4, 10.

sōbrius, adj. (**sē-,** *apart from, not;* **ēbrius,** *drunk*), *not drunk, sober,* 56, 30.

socer, -erī, M., *father-in-law,* 52, 1.

societās, -ātis, F. (**socius,** *fellow*), *fellowship, association: league, alliance,* 3, 5; 50, 25.

sociō, 1, -āvī, -ātus (**socius,** *sharer*), *hold in common, share,* 4, 15.

socius, -ī, M., *fellow, comrade, associate,* 59, 25: *ally,* 23, 9.

sōl, sōlis, M., *the sun,* 5, 17.

soleō, 2, solitus, semi-dep., *use, be wont, be accustomed,* 2, 5.

solidus, adj. with sup., *undivided, whole: genuine, true, real,* 17, 18.

sōlitūdō, -inis, F. (**sōlus,** *alone*), *desert, wilderness,* 1, 10.

solitum, -ī, N. (P. of **soleō,** *be wont*), *the customary, what is usual,* 43, 4.

solitus, adj. (P. of **soleō,** *be wont*), *wonted, accustomed, usual,* 27, 20.

solium, -ī, N. [SED-, *sit*], *seat, official seat, chair of state, throne,* 66, 21. (W. G. 67.)

sollicitō, 1, -āvī, -ātus (**sollicitus,** *disturbed*), *disturb, agitate: arouse, incite, move,* 68, 21.

sollicitus, adj. with comp., *thoroughly moved, agitated, disturbed: sensitive, watchful, on the alert,* 21, 6.

sōlum, adv. (**sōlus,** *alone*), *alone, only, merely,* 21, 5: **nōn sōlum . . . sed etiam,** *not only . . . but also,* 6, 18.

sōlus, gen. **sōlīus,** dat. **sōlī,** *alone, only, single-handed,* 2, 24; 16, 11.

solvō, 3, solvī, solūtus (**sē-,** *apart;*

VOCABULARY. 309

luō, *loose*), *loosen, unbind*, 7, 30.
somnium, -ī, N. (somnus, *sleep*), *dream*, 13, 3.
somnus, -ī, M. (for sopnus; cf. sōpiō, *put to sleep*), *sleep*, 43, 18.
sōpiō, 4, -īvī, -ītus, *deprive of sense, put to sleep:* in pass., *sleep*, 35, 16.
soror, -ōris, F., *sister*, 7, 27.
sorōrius, adj. (soror, *sister*), *of a sister, sisterly, sister's*, 8, 19.
sors, -tis, F., *lot: fate, fortune, destiny*, 26, 12; 62, 1.
sortior, 4, -ītus, dep. (sors, *lot*), *cast lots, draw lots*, 65, 24.
spatium, -ī, N., *space; distance*, 7, 13: *period of time, interval*, 49, 20.
speciēs, —, acc. -em, abl. -ē, F. [SPEC-, *see*], *sight, look, appearance*, 25, 14: *semblance, pretence, pretext*, 12, 4; 55, 12. (W. G. 68.)
spectāculum, -ī, N. (spectō, *look at*), *place in the theatre: show, spectacle*, 3, 11. (W. G. 68.)
spectō, 1, -āvī, -ātus (freq. of speciō, *look*), *look on, look at, behold, watch*, 7, 5. (W. G. 68.)
speculum, -ī, N. [SPEC-, *see*], *reflector, looking-glass, mirror*, 71, 17. (W. G. 68.)
spernō, 3, sprēvī, sprētus, *despise, reject, spurn*, 27, 14.
spērō, 1, -āvī, -ātus (spēs, *hope*), *hope, look for, expect*, 10, 25.
spēs, speī, *hope*, 7, 9: *expectation*, 17, 26.

spīritus, -ūs, M. (cf. spīrō, *breathe*), *breathing, breath: spirit, energy, courage*, 9, 12.
splendor, -ōris, M., *brightness, splendor: honor, lustre, dignity*, 57, 14.
spoliō, 1, -āvī, -ātus (spolium, *skin*), *strip: plunder, strip, spoil*, 7, 24; 48, 26.
spolium, -ī, N., *the skin;* plur., *the arms stripped from an enemy, booty, spoil*, 7, 27; 38, 29.
spondeō, 2, spopondī, spōnsus, *promise sacredly, vow: agree, promise, engage*, 28, 27; 49, 24.
(spōns, spontis), F. (cf. spondeō, *promise*), only abl. sing., usu. with pron. poss., *of one's own accord, freely, willingly, voluntarily*, 60, 21.
spōnsiō, -ōnis, F. (spondeō, *promise*), *solemn promise, engagement, covenant*, 24, 8.
spōnsus, -ī, M. (P. of spondeō, *promise*), *betrothed man*, 7, 29.
sprētus, P. of spernō, 27, 14.
Spūrinna, -ae, M., *Vestritius Spurinna*, the seer who warned Julius Caesar to beware the Ides of March, 55, 6.
Spurius, -ī, M., *Spurius*, a Roman praenomen, 23, 4.
statim, adv. [STA-, *stand*], *steadily: on the spot, at once, instantly*, 2, 1. (W. G. 69.)
statiō, -ōnis, F. [STA-, *stand*], *a standing: station, post*, 21, 20. (W. G. 69.)

statua, -ae, F. (**status,** P. of **sistō,** *place, set*), *an image, statue,* 16, 17. (W. G. 69.)

statuō, 3, -uī, -ūtus (**status,** *station*), *cause to stand, set up, plant,* 22, 7 : *determine, decide,* 21, 1. (W. G. 69.)

statūra, -ae, F. [STA-, *stand*], *height, size, stature,* 56, 22. (W. G. 69.)

status, -ūs, M. [STA-, *stand*], *station, position : rank, state, condition,* 27, 27. (W. G. 69.)

stercus, -oris, N., *filth,* 51, 3.

sternō, 3, strāvī, strātus, *spread out, scatter : throw to the ground,* 21, 13.

Sthenius, -ī, M., *Sthenius,* a Sicilian, a friend of C. Marius, 44, 4.

stīpendium, -ī, N. (for **stipipendium** ; **stips,** *small coin;* *pendium, cf. pendere, pay), a paying of tax : pay, wages,* 19, 20 : *military service, campaign,* 49, 14.

stirps, -pis, F. or M., *stalk, root: offspring, family, stock, lineage,* 8, 13 ; 42, 23.

stō, -āre, stetī, status [STA-, *stand*], *stand,* 18, 14 : *stand by, persist in,* 66, 8. (W. G. 69.)

strāgēs, -is, F., *overthrow, destruction, defeat, slaughter,* 37, 20.

strāgulum, -ī, N. (**strāgulus,** *for spreading out*), *spread, covering, bed-spread,* 43, 8.

strēnuē, adv. (**strēnuus,** *prompt*), *promptly, actively, strenuously,* 31, 25.

strēnuus, adj. with sup., *active, vigorous,* 14, 2.

strepitus, -ūs, M. (**strepō,** *make a noise*), *noise, clash, crash, alarm,* 21, 6 ; 71, 20.

strīdor, -ōris, M. (cf. **strīdō,** *make a harsh noise*), *harsh noise, roar,* 28, 11.

stringō, 3, -inxī, -ictus, *draw tight, bind tight : unsheathe, draw, of a sword,* 8, 2.

studeō, 2, -uī, —, *give attention, be eager, take pains, desire,* 67, 23.

studiōsē, adv. with comp. and sup. (**studiōsus,** *eager*), *eagerly, studiously,* 58, 1.

studium, -ī, N. (cf. **studeō,** *give attention*), *application, eagerness, desire, exertion, effort,* 3, 11 ; 32, 5 : *study, pursuit,* 57, 24 : *good-will, friendliness, devotion,* 61, 5.

stupeō, 2, -uī, —, *be struck senseless, be confused, be astounded, be stupefied, be paralyzed,* 18, 8.

suādeō, 2, -sī, -sus, *advise, recommend, exhort, urge, persuade,* 12, 7 ; 57, 12.

sub, prep. with acc. and abl : with abl., *under, below, beneath,* 15, 3 ; 67, 4 : with acc., with verbs of motion, *under,* 8, 18.

subdō, 3, -didī, -ditus [**sub,** *under;* 2 DA-, *put*], *put under, apply,* 42, 8. (W. G. 25.)

subdūcō, 3, -dūxī, -ductus (**sub,**

under, away; dūcō, *lead), lead away, withdraw, steal away, remove,* 8, 25; 43, 6. (W. G. 29.)

subeō, -īre, -iī, -itus (sub, *under;* eō, *come, go), come under, go under: take up, carry,* 64, 10: *submit to, suffer, undergo,* 45, 1 : *penetrate, take effect,* 46, 16. (W. G. 46.)

subiciō, 3, -iēcī, -iectus (sub, *under;* iaciō, *throw), throw under, place under: make subject,* 27, 2. (W. G. 47.)

subigō, 3, -ēgī, -āctus (sub, *from below, up;* agō, *drive), drive up, bring up: subdue, subjugate, conquer,* 12, 20. (W. G. 2.)

subitō, adv. (subitus, *sudden), suddenly,* 4, 22. (W. G. 46.)

subitus, adj., *sudden, unexpected,* 28, 8. (W. G. 46.)

sublātus, P. of tollō, 40, 25.

sublevō, 1, -āvī, -ātus (sub, *from below;* levō, *lift), lift from beneath, raise up, hold up, support,* 21, 3.

sublicius, adj. (sublica, *stake, pile), resting upon piles,* 10, 13.

sublīmis, -e, adj. with comp., *uplifted, high, on high, aloft,* 10, 22.

sublūstris, -e, adj. [sub, *a little;* *lūstrus, fr. LVC-, *shine*], *giving some light, faintly luminous, glimmering,* 21, 3.

submittō, 3, -mīsī, -missus (sub, *down, secretly;* mittō, *send), let down, send down, let grow,* 38, 23. (W. G. 53.)

subolēs, -is, F. [sub, *from below;* OL-, *grow], sprout, shoot: offspring, progeny, posterity,* 1, 4.

subōrnō, 1, -āvī, -ātus (sub, *without force,* or *secretly;* ōrnō, *fit out), fit out, furnish: incite secretly, suborn,* 18, 1.

subrīdeō, 2, -sī, — (sub, *a little;* rīdeō, *laugh), smile,* 26, 22.

subsellium, -ī, N. (sub, *less in size;* sella, *seat), low bench, seat,* 40, 29 (v. notes, fig. 22, p. 119). (W. G. 67.)

subsequor, 3, -cūtus, dep. (sub, *below, after;* sequor, *follow), follow after, follow up,* 52, 22.

subsistō, 3, -stitī, — (sub, *under;* sistō, *stand still), take a stand, stop, halt: remain, stay,* 55, 6. (W. G. 69.)

substituō, 3, -uī, -ūtus (sub, *under;* statuō, *set), place under: substitute, put in place of,* 45, 23. (W. G. 69.)

subterrāneus, adj. (sub, *under;* terra, *ground), underground, subterranean,* 19, 23.

subtexō, 3, -xuī, — (sub, *under;* texō, *weave), weave under, sew on: add,* 68, 29.

succēdō, 3, -cessī, -cessus (sub, *below;* cēdō, *go), go below, come under: follow, succeed, take place of,* 5, 3. (W. G. 14.)

successor, -ōris, M. (cf. succēdō, *take the place of), follower, successor,* 44, 17. (W. G. 14.)

successus -ūs, M. (succēdō, *come*

up), *a coming up, approach: success,* 33, 13. (W. G. 14.)

succlāmō, 1, -āvī, -ātus (sub, *after;* clāmō, *call*), *cry out in response,* 33, 2.

succurrō, 3, -currī, -cursus (sub, *under;* currō, *run*), *run under, run to help, aid, assist,* 36, 26. (W. G. 19.)

sufficiō, 3, -fēcī, -fectus (sub, *under;* faciō, *make, put*), *put under, lay a foundation for: suffice, satisfy, be large enough,* 2, 20; 39, 4. (W. G. 33.)

suffīgō, 3, -fīxī, -fīxus (sub, *beneath:* fīgō, *fasten*), *fasten beneath, attach, nail to,* 49, 30.

suffodiō, 3, -fōdī, -fossus (sub, *under;* fodiō, *dig*), *dig under: stab underneath,* 59, 6.

suffrāgātor, -ōris, M. (suffrāgor, *favor by voting*), *favorer, supporter, partisan,* 56, 20.

suī, dat. sibi, acc. and abl. sē, emphatic form, sēsē, or sēmet, sing. and plur. pron. of 3d pers., always reflexive, *himself, herself, itself, themselves,* 1, 12; 1, 20; 4, 12; 41, 25.

Sulla, -ae, M., a family name in the Cornelian gens, especially *L. Cornelius Sulla,* dictator B.C. 82. 43, 12.

Sullānus, adj. (Sulla), *of Sulla.* As subst., M., *follower of Sulla,* 58, 3.

sum, esse, fuī, futūrus [ES-, *be*], *be, exist, live,* 1, 2; 41, 29: *be present, be found,* 6, 21: *be of, consist of,* 54, 8.

summa, -ae, F. (summus, *highest;* sc. rēs, *thing*), *top, summit: chief place, leadership, highest rank,* 13, 4: *amount, sum,* 69, 12.

summus or suprēmus, adj. sup. (for * supimus, sup. of superus, *upper*), *uppermost, supreme, highest,* 12, 6: *last, final,* 71, 17: *greatest, utmost, best, extreme,* 21, 7; 25, 18; 33, 16; 36, 20. As subst., N., *the top, the summit,* 21, 12.

sūmō, 3, sūmpsī, sūmptus (sub, *up from below;* emō, *take*), *take, lay hold of: take, drink, eat, consume,* 46, 15: *adopt, assume,* 63, 16: *begin, undertake,* 3, 17: *obtain, get, receive,* 18, 12: *select, choose,* 33, 2.

sūmptuārius, adj. (sūmptus, *outlay*), *of expense, sumptuary,* 54, 12.

sūmptus, P. of sūmō, 18, 12.

sūmptus, -ūs, M. (sūmō, *lay out*), *outlay, expense,* 42, 19.

supellex, -lectilis, F., *domestic utensils, household stuff, furniture,* 29, 10; 70, 23.

super, prep. with acc. and abl: with abl., *over, above, on:* with acc., *over, above, on, upon,* 7, 7; 7, 28; 28, 12: *beyond,* 1, 8: *during, at,* 55, 30.

superadstō, -āre, -stitī, — (super, *upon;* ad, *near;* stō, *stand*), *stand upon,* 25, 14. (W. G. 69.)

superbē, adv. with comp. and sup. (**superbus**, *proud*), *haughtily, proudly, arrogantly*, 10, 5.

superbia, -ae, F. (**superbus**, *proud*), *loftiness, haughtiness, pride, arrogance*, 17, 12.

superbus, adj. with comp. and sup. (**super**, *above*), *haughty, proud, arrogant, insolent*, 14, 1; 30, 12.

superiaciō, 3, -iēcī, -iectus (**super**, *upon, over*; **iaciō**, *throw*), *throw over*, 30, 22. (W. G. 47.)

superincidō, 3, —, — (**super**, *from above*; **in**, *upon*; **cadō**, *fall*), *fall from above, fall down upon*, 16, 14.

superior, -ius, gen. -ōris, comp. of **superus**, *superior, victorious*, 33, 22; 47, 10.

superō, 1, -āvī, -ātus (**superus**, *over, above*), *go over, rise above: ascend, mount, cross*, 33, 6: *subdue, conquer*, 27, 2 : *surpass, outstrip, excel*, 30, 19.

supersum, -esse, -fuī (**super**, *over*; **sum**, *be*), *be over and above, be left, remain*, 7, 20 : *outlive, survive*, 11, 20 ; 35, 19. (W. G. 31.)

superus, adj. with comp. and sup., *that is above, upper, higher*, 12, 16.

superveniō, 4, -vēnī, -ventus (**super**, *upon, in addition;* **veniō**, *come*), *come in addition, come up, arrive*, 45, 11 : *come upon, surprise*, 2, 12. (W. G. 73.)

supervīvō, 3, -vīxī, — (**super**, *over, beyond;* **vīvō**, *live*), *outlive, survive*, 56, 2.

suppliciter, adv. (**supplex**, *petitioner*), *like a petitioner, humbly, suppliantly*, 65, 21. (W. G. 60.)

supplicium, -ī, N. (**supplex**, *kneeling in entreaty*), *kneeling, bowing down : death penalty, punishment*, 2, 5; 44, 2. (W. G. 60.)

suprēmus, see **summus**, 71, 17.

surgō, 3, surrēxī, and subrēxī, — (**sub**, *from below;* **regō**, *make straight*), *rise, get up, stand up*, 70, 17. (W. G. 65.)

suscipiō, 3, -cēpī, -ceptus [**sub(s)**, *from under;* **capiō**, *take*], *take up, take : receive, assume, take upon oneself, undertake, begin*, 12, 1; 22, 15; 43, 1.

suspectus, adj. with comp. (P. of **suspiciō**, *mistrust*), *subject to suspicion, mistrusted, suspected*, 52, 3. (W. G. 68.)

sustineō, 2, -tinuī, -tentus [**sub(s)**, *from under, up;* **teneō**, *hold*], *hold up, bear up*, 7, 24 : *keep up, support*, 7, 24; 29, 12 : *withstand, sustain, bear, endure*, 16, 11; 65, 6. (W. G. 71.)

sūtor, -ōris, M. (**suō**, *sew*), *shoemaker, cobbler*, 68, 21.

suus, pron. poss. 3d pers. (cf. **suī**, *of himself, herself, itself, themselves*), reflexive adj., *of oneself, belonging to oneself, his own, her own, his, her, its,* *their*, 3, 22; 6, 23; 17, 12. As subst., **suī**, *his friends, their friends*, 14, 9: **sua mors**, *a natural death*, 56, 3.

Syria, -ae, F., *Syria*, on the eastern shore of the Mediterranean, 48, 4.

T

T., *Titus*, a Roman praenomen, 64, 25.

tabella, -ae, F. (dim. of **tabula**, *board*), *small board: writing-tablet*, 70, 17 (v. notes, fig. 21, p. 117).

taberna, -ae, F. [TA-, *stretch*], *hut: shop, stall*, 18, 5.

tabernāculum, -ī, N. (**taberna**, *hut*), *tent*, 43, 1 (v. notes, fig. 10, p. 97).

tābēs, -is, F., *wasting, decline, decay*, 17, 5.

tabula, -ae, F. [TA-, *stretch*], *board: writing-tablet*, 39, 4 (v. notes, fig. 21, p. 117): *table of the law*, 17, 22.

tacitus, adj. (P. of **taceō**, *be silent*), *passed in silence, kept secret: in silence, without speaking*, 36, 15.

taedium, -ī, N. (**taedet**, *it wearies*), *weariness, tediousness, disgust*, 43, 17.

talentum, -ī, N. (Gr. τάλαντον), *talent, half a hundred-weight*, a Grecian standard of value equal to about $1080 in gold. 49, 23.

tālis, -e, adj., *such, of such a kind*, 25, 22.

tam, adv., *in such a degree, such, so*, 12, 12; 44, 9: **tam** . . .

quam, *as much . . . as, as well . . . as*, 69, 7.

tamen, adv., *notwithstanding, nevertheless, for all that, however, yet, still*, 1, 5; 8, 16; 9, 8.

tamquam, adv. (**tam**, *as much;* **quam**, *as*), *as much as, just as, like as, as if*, 46, 11.

Tanaquil, -īlis, F., *Tanaquil*, the wife of Tarquinius Priscus, 10, 22.

tandem, adv. (**tam**, *to such a degree;* -**dem**, demonstr. ending), *at length, at last, finally*, 30, 11.

tantopere, adv. (abl. of **tantum opus**), *so earnestly, so greatly, so much*, 49, 11.

tantum, adv. (**tantus**, *so great*), *only, merely*, 63, 1 : **tantum modo**, *only, merely*, 33, 15.

tantus, adj., *so great, such*, 8, 1. As subst., **tantum**, -ī, N., *so much*, 16, 16; 38, 14: as gen. of price, *of such value, worth so much*, 42, 5.

tardē, adv. with comp. and sup. (**tardus**, *slow*), *slowly*, 46, 16.

tardō, 1, -āvī, -ātus (**tardus**, *slow*), *make slow, hinder, delay, retard*, 55, 19.

Tarentīnus, adj., *of Tarentum*,

VOCABULARY. 315

Tarentine, 34, 30. As subst.,
M. plur., **Tarentīnī**, -ōrum, *the inhabitants of Tarentum*, 25, 1.

Tarentum, -ī, N., *Tarentum*, a famous and powerful Greek city in southern Italy on the gulf of Tarentum, 34, 28.

Tarpēia, -ae, F., *Tarpeia*, name of the Roman maiden who opened the gates to the Sabines, 3, 18.

Tarpēius, adj., *of Tarpeia, Tarpeian*, 22, 13.

Tarquinius, -ī, M., *Tarquinius, Tarquin*, name of a family prominent in the history of the kings of Rome, 10, 17.

Tarquiniī, -ōrum, M., *Tarquinii*, a town in southern Etruria. 10, 17.

Tatius, -ī, M., gentile name of *Titus Tatius*, leader of the Sabines, 3, 20.

tegō, 3, tēxī, tēctus, *cover, cover over*, 60, 7.

tēlum, -ī, N., *missile, spear, shaft, javelin, weapon*, 4, 12; 11, 30; 16, 14.

temerārius, adj. (temerē, *rashly*), *rash, indiscreet, imprudent*, 37, 4.

temerē, adv., *rashly, heedlessly, indiscreetly*, 30, 15.

temeritās, -ātis, F. (temerē, *rashly*), *hap, chance: rashness, indiscretion*, 23, 18.

temperāns, -antis, adj. with comp. and sup. (P. of **temperō**, *abstain*), *observing moderation, sober, moderate, temperate*, 43, 18.

tempestās, -ātis, F. (tempus, *time*), *portion of time, time*, 11, 9: *storm, tempest*, 4, 23.

templum, -ī, N., *open place for observation: consecrated place: fane, temple*, 27, 30.

temptō, 1, -āvī, -ātus (intens. of **tendō**, *stretch*), *handle: make trial of, attempt*, 21, 2.

tempus, -oris, N., *portion of time, time, season*, 2, 10; 47, 28.

tendō, 3, tetendī, tentus, or tēnsus [TEN-, *stretch*], *stretch: reach out, extend*, 51, 26: *direct, aim*, 53, 6. (W. G. 71.)

tenebrae, -ārum, F., *darkness, gloom*, 60, 19.

teneō, 2, tenuī, — [TEN-, *stretch*], *hold, grasp*, 30, 20: *bind, hold fast, restrain*, 24, 9: *keep*, 2, 11. (W. G. 71.)

tentōrium, -ī, N. [TA-, TEN-, *stretch*], *tent*, 43, 6 (v. notes, fig. 10, p. 97). (W. G. 71.)

tepeō, 2, —, —, *be moderately warm, be lukewarm: steam*, 22, 21.

ter, adv. num. (cf. **trēs**, *three*), *three times, thrice*, 58, 30.

Terentius, -ī, M., gentile name of *C. Terentius Varro*, consul 216 B.C., 37, 3: Pompey's tent-companion, 42, 26.

tergiversor, 1, —, dep. (tergum, *back*; **vertō**, *turn*), *turn the back, decline, refuse*, 32, 25.

VOCABULARY

tergum, -ī, N., *back,* **19,** 13: **ā tergō,** *in the rear,* **8,** 27; **46,** 9.

ternī, -ae, -a, adj. num. distrib. (**ter,** *thrice*), *three each, by threes,* **7,** 2.

terō, 3, trīvī, trītus, *rub, wear away: use up, spend, waste,* **34,** 14.

terra, -ae, F. (cf. **torreō,** *dry up*), *earth, ground: land,* **30,** 7: **orbis terrae** or **terrārum,** *the earth,* **22,** 17; **45,** 27.

terreō, 2, -uī, -itus, *frighten, alarm, terrify,* **8,** 28,

terribilis, -e, adj. (**terreō,** *frighten*), *frightful, dreadful, terrible,* **25,** 13.

territus, P. of **terreō,** **55,** 5.

terror, -ōris, M. (cf. **terreō,** *frighten*), *great fear, dread, alarm, terror,* **10,** 11.

tertiō, adv. (**tertius,** *third*), *for the third time,* **47,** 5.

tertius, adj. num. ord. (**ter,** *thrice*), *third,* **7,** 18.

testimōnium, -ī, N. (**testis,** *witness*), *witness, evidence, testimony,* **45,** 25: *proof,* **37,** 25.

testor, 1, -ātus (**testis,** *witness*), *cause to testify: make known, attest, bear witness,* **51,** 9.

thēsaurus, -ī, M. (Gr. θησαυρός), *something laid up, treasure,* **30,** 5.

Thessalia, -ae, F., *Thessaly,* a district in northern Greece, **47,** 13.

Tiberis, -is, M., *the Tiber,* the chief river of Latium, on which Rome was built, **1,** 7.

Tiberius, -ī, M., contracted **Ti.,** *Tiberius,* a Roman praenomen, **39,** 23.

tībīcen, -inis, M. (**tībia,** *pipe;* **canō,** *sing* or *play*), *piper, flute-player,* **31,** 5 (v. notes, fig. 17, p. 109).

Tīcīnus, -ī, M., *Ticinus,* a river in Cisalpine Gaul, **33,** 7.

tigillum, -ī, N. (dim. of **tignum,** *beam*), *small bar of wood, little beam,* **8,** 17.

Tigrānēs, -is, M., *Tigranes,* a king of Armenia, **46,** 19.

timeō, 2, -uī, —, *fear, be afraid, dread, apprehend,* **46,** 15; **46,** 29.

timidus, adj. with comp. and sup. (cf. **timeō,** *fear*), *fearful, afraid, cowardly, timid,* **34,** 11.

titulus, -ī, M., *superscription, inscription,* **53,** 14.

Titus, -ī, M., *Titus,* Roman praenomen, **3,** 20.

toga, -ae, F. (cf. **tegō,** *cover*), *toga, gown,* **32,** 26 (v. notes, fig. 18, p. 111).

tolerō, 1, -āvī, -ātus (cf. **tollō,** *lift*), *bear, endure, support,* **16,** 22.

tollō, 3, sustulī, sublātus, *lift, raise,* **4,** 9: *lift, cheer, encourage,* **9,** 19: *take away, carry off, remove,* **10,** 20.

tonitrus, -ūs, M. (**tonō,** *make a loud noise*), *thunder,* **4,** 23.

tōnsor, -ōris, M. (**tondeō,** *shear*),

shearer, hair-cutter, barber, 71, 2.

Tŏrānius, -ī, M., *T. Toranius,* who betrayed his father to death 43 B.C. **64,** 25.

torqueō, 2, torsī, tortus, *turn, twist: torture,* **65,** 5.

tot, adj. num. indecl., *so many, such a number of,* **26,** 4.

totidem, adj. num. indecl. (tot, *so many;* -dem, demonstr. ending), *just so many, the same number of,* **47,** 23.

totiēns, adv. num. (tot, *so many*), *so often, so many times,* **33,** 10.

tōtus, gen. tōtīus, dat. tōtī, adj., *all, the whole, entire,* **7, 9; 17,** 4.

trādō, 3, -didī, -ditus (trāns, *across;* dō, *deliver*), *give up, hand over, deliver, surrender,* **2, 6; 19,** 4: *betray,* **14, 17:** *hand down, transmit, report, say,* **1, 10; 41,** 30. (W. G. 24.)

trādūcō, 3, -dūxī, -ductus (trāns, *across;* dūcō, *lead*), *lead across, conduct across, carry over, transfer,* **10, 8:** *spend, pass,* **23,** 20: *lead in disgrace,* **23,** 30. (W. G. 29.)

trahō, 3, -trāxī, -tractus, *draw, pull, drag,* **7, 22:** *obtain, derive,* **25,** 4: *delay, detain,* **40,** 6.

trāiciō, 3, -iēcī, -iectus (trāns, *across;* iaciō, *throw*), *throw across, transfer: lead across, take across, transport,* **52, 17:** *pierce, stab through, transfix,*

55, 18: *pass over, cross over,* **2, 22.**

trānō, 1, -āvī, — (trāns, *across;* nō, *swim*), *swim over, swim across,* **16,** 15.

trāns, prep. with acc., *across, over, to the farther side of,* **51,** 16.

trānscendō, 3, -dī, — (trāns, *over;* scandō, *climb*), *climb over, pass over, cross,* **35,** 29.

trānseō, -īre, -iī, -itus (trāns, *over;* eō, *go*), *go over, cross over, pass over, pass by, pass,* **9, 2; 68, 26:** *pass over, be changed, be transformed,* **4, 24.** (W. G. 46.)

trānsfīgō, 3, -fīxī, -fīxus (trāns, *through;* fīgō, *fasten*), *pierce through, transfix,* **8, 2.**

trānsfuga, -ae [trāns, *across;* FVG-, *flee*], *one who joins the enemy, deserter,* **23,** 6. (W. G. 40.)

trānsgredior, 3, -gressus, dep. (trāns, *across;* gradior, *step*), *step across, pass over, cross,* **30, 22.** (W. G. 44.)

trānsigō, 3, -ēgī, -āctus (trāns, *through;* agō, *drive*), *drive through: finish, carry through, complete,* **65, 18.**

trānsiliō, 4, -uī, — (trāns, *across;* saliō, *leap*), *leap across, jump over,* **2, 24.**

trānsmarīnus, adj. (trāns, *beyond;* marīnus, *of the sea*), *from over the sea,* **25,** 5.

trānsmigrō, 1, —, — (trāns, *across;* migrō, *depart*), *move, migrate,* **22,** 4.

trānsmittō, 3, -mīsī, -missus (trāns, *across;* mittō, *send*), *send across, put across, throw across,* 8, 17 : *pass over, cross over,* 52, 22. (W. G. 53.)

trānsvehō, 3, -vēxī, -vectus (trāns, *across;* vehō, *carry*), *carry across, convey over, transport,* 31, 24. (W. G. 72.)

trānsversus, adj. (trāns, *across;* versus, *turned*), *turned across, crosswise, transverse,* 61, 22. (W. G. 74.)

Trasumēnus, -ī, M., *Trasumenus,* lake in Etruria, celebrated for Hannibal's defeat of the Romans, 217 B.C. 33, 9.

Trebia, -ae, M., *Trebia,* river of Cisalpine Gaul, tributary to the Po, 33, 8.

trecentēsimus, adj. num. ord. (trecentī, *three hundred*), *three-hundredth,* 17, 20.

trecentī, -ae, -a, num. adj. (trēs, *three;* centum, *hundred*), *three hundred,* 17, 20.

tredecim, num. adj. indecl. (trēs, *three;* decem, *ten*), *thirteen,* 11, 16.

trepidātiō, -ōnis, F. (trepidō, *hurry with alarm*), *confused hurry, alarm, agitation, confusion,* 51, 28.

trepidō, 1, -āvī, -ātus (trepidus, *restless*), *hurry with alarm, be in confusion,* 21, 11 : *hesitate, tremble, fear,* 52, 29.

trēs, tria, adj. num., *three,* 4, 19.

tribūnal, -ālis, N. (tribūnus, *head of a tribe*), *raised platform for the seats of magistrates, judgment-seat, tribunal,* 18, 16.

tribūnātus, -ūs, M. (tribūnus, *tribune*), *office of a tribune, tribuneship,* 41, 2.

tribūnīcius, adj. (tribūnus, *tribune*), *of a tribune,* 40, 15.

tribūnus, -ī, M. (tribus, *tribe*), *head of tribe: tribune,* 17, 11 ; 18, 24.

tribuō, 3, -uī, -ūtus (tribus, *tribe*), *confer, bestow, give, yield,* 43, 27.

tribus, -ūs, F. (cf. trēs, *three*), *third part of the people: tribe,* 39, 4.

tribūtum, -ī, N. (P. N. of tribuō, *give*), *stated payment, contribution, tribute,* 16, 21.

triennium, -ī, N. (trēs, *three;* annus, *year*), *three years' time, three years,* 56, 2.

trigeminus, adj. (trēs, *three;* geminus, *born together*), *born three at a birth,* 6, 22. Plur. M. as subst., *triplets,* 6, 26.

trīgintā, num. adj. indecl., *thirty,* 4, 20.

trīstis, -e, adj. with comp. and sup., *sad, sorrowful: bitter, severe, terrible,* 24, 4.

triumphō, 1, -āvī, -ātus (triumphus, *triumphal procession*), *march in triumphal procession, celebrate a triumph, triumph,* 11, 6 ; 19, 26.

triumphus, -ī, M., *triumphal procession, triumph, celebration of*

VOCABULARY. 319

victory by a public entrance into Rome, 31, 2.

triumvir, -virī, M. (trēs, *three;* vir, *man*), *one of three associates in office, a member of a board of three*, 64, 20.

trucīdō, 1, -āvī, -ātus [trux, *wild;* SCID-, *cut*], *cut to pieces, slaughter, butcher*, 20, 30. (W. G. 66.)

truncus, -ī, M., *stem, stock : trunk, body*, 47, 19.

trux, -ucis, adj., *wild, savage, fierce*, 25, 19.

tū, pers. pro., *thou, you*, 19, 7.

tueor, 2, tūtus, dep., *look at, gaze upon: watch, guard, protect*, 33, 15.

Tullia, -ae, F., name of the daughter of Servius Tullius, also of Cicero's daughter, 13, 16.

Tullius, -ī, M., name of a Roman gens, e.g., *Servius Tullius, Marcus Tullius Cicero*, 12, 1.

Tullus, -ī, M., praenomen of *Tullus Hostilius*, the third king of Rome, 6, 17.

tum, adv., *then, at that time, in those times*, 1, 10; 1, 20; 8, 9; 12, 25.

tumultuor, 1, -ātus, dep. (tumultus, *uproar*), *make a disturbance, be in confusion*, 11, 24; 43, 10.

tumultus, -ūs, M., *uproar, disturbance, disorder*, 13, 22.

tunc, adv. (tum, *then;* -ce, dem. suff.), *then, at that time*, 1, 8 ; 4, 8.

turba, -ae, F., *turmoil, disorder: throng, crowd*, 13, 22.

turbō, 1, -āvī, -ātus (turba, *turmoil*), *disturb, throw into disorder*, 25, 14.

turbulentus, adj. with comp. and sup. (turba, *commotion*), *full of commotion, disturbed, stormy*, 60, 22.

turdus, -ī, M., *thrush*, 47, 26.

turpis, -e, adj. with comp. and sup., *ugly, unsightly : shameful, dishonorable, disgraceful*, 24, 8.

tūtēla, -ae, F. (tueor, *look at*), *defence, protection*, 2, 20.

tūtor, -ōris, M. (tueor, *look at*), *watcher, defender : tutor, guardian*, 11, 3.

tūtor, 1, -ātus, dep. (tueor, *look at*), *watch, protect, defend*, 59, 8.

tūtus, adj. with comp. and sup. (P. of tueor, *look at*), *guarded, safe, secure*, 16, 7 ; 46, 5.

tuus, pron. poss. (tū, *thou*), *thy, thine, your, yours*, 28, 13.

U

ūber, -eris, N. (cf. Eng. *udder*), *teat, udder, breast*, 1, 12.

ūber, -eris, adj., comp. ūberior, sup. ūberrimus (ūber, *richness*), *abounding, rich, fruitful, fertile*, 22, 18.

ubi, adv. rel. and interrog.: rel., *in which place, in what place, where*, 2, 15 : *when*, 3, 13; 41, 11 : interrog., *where?* 65, 5.

ulcīscor, 3, ultus, dep., *avenge oneself on: take revenge for, avenge,* 64, 12.

ūllus, gen. ūllīus, dat. ūllī, adj. (for ūnulus, dim. of ūnus), *any*, 14, 17. As subst., M., *any one,* 50, 27.

ulterior, -ius, adj. comp., *farther, more remote,* 50, 1 : neut. ulterius, as adv., *longer, farther,* 65, 7.

ūltimum, adv. (ūltimus, *last*), *for the last time,* 18, 19.

ūltimus, adj., sup. of ulterior, *farthest, most distant, uttermost, last,* 55, 8 ; 67, 16 : *greatest, extreme, utmost,* 66, 20.

ūltrā, prep. with acc., *beyond: above, past, exceeding,* 57, 2.

ūltrō, adv. (dat. and abl. of *ulter, far ;* sc. locō, *place*), *to the farther side, beyond: voluntarily,* 56, 16.

umbō, -ōnis, M., *knob, boss,* 21, 12 (v. notes, fig. 11, p. 98).

umbra, -ae, F., *shade, shadow,* 46, 9.

umerus, -ī, M., *the upper arm, shoulder,* 7, 28.

umquam, adv., *at any time, ever,* 16, 3.

unde, relat. adv., *from whom, from which, where, on which side,* 6, 25; 11, 18 : *whence, from what source,* 29, 30.

ūndecim, adj. num. indecl. (ūnus, *one ;* decem, *ten*), *eleven,* 5, 19.

undique, adv. (unde, *whence;* -que, indef. suff., *-soever*), *from every quarter, on all sides, all around,* 53, 21.

ūniversus, adj. (ūnus, *one, together;* versus, *turned*), *all together, whole, entire,* 31, 15. Plur. M. as subst., *all men, everybody,* 61, 8. (W. G. 74.)

ūnus, gen. ūnīus, dat. ūnī, adj. num., *one, a single,* 7, 10; 7, 15: *only, alone,* 24, 12: *the same, one and the same,* 65, 28.

ūnusquisque, ūnaquaeque, ūnumquodque (ūnus, *one ;* quisque, *each*), adj., *each one, every one,* 14, 22.

urbānus, adj. with comp. and sup. (urbs, *city*), *of the city.* As subst., M., *inhabitant of a city : a wit, a wag,* 51, 8.

urbs, urbis, F., *walled town, city,* 2, 14 : *Rome,* 59, 17.

urgueō or urgeō, 2, ursī, —, *press, force: press hard, beset, assail,* 21, 18.

ūrīnātor, -ōris, M. (ūrīnor, *dive*), *diver,* 63, 21.

usquam, adv., *at any place, anywhere,* 18, 18.

usque, adv., *all the way, right on, continuously, even,* 46, 10.

ūsūrpō, 1, -āvī, -ātus [ūsus, *use ;* RAP-, *seize*], *seize for use, seize, upon, make use of,* 56, 27.

ūsus, -ūs, M. (cf. ūtor, *use*), *use: profit, benefit, advantage,* 42, 15 : *occasion, need, want,* 29, 12.

ut or utī, adv., *when, as soon as*, 7, 4: *as*, 1, 10: ut ... ita, *as ... so*, 22, 1; 36, 25.

ut, conj. with subj. of purpose or result: of purpose, *in order that, that, to, so as to*, 1, 3; 4, 29; 5, 26; 7, 17: of result, *that, so that*, 4, 30.

ūter, -tris, M. (cf. uterus, *womb*), *bag of hide, leathern bottle, skin*, 57, 7.

uter, utra, utrum, gen. utrīus, dat. utrī, adj., *which of two, which*, 2, 16: *whichever one, the one which*, 33, 1.

uterque, utraque, utrumque, adj., *each, either, each one, both*, 11, 25; 55, 14.

ūtilis, -e, adj. with comp. and sup. (ūtor, *use*), *useful, serviceable, profitable*, 6, 3.

utinam, adv., *I wish that! if only! would that!* 29, 7.

utique, adv., *in any case, at any rate.: in particular, especially*, 64, 3.

ūtor, 3, ūsus, dep., *use, employ, profit by*, 38, 9; 43, 5.

utrimque, adv. (uterque, *each of two*), *on each side, on either hand*, 7, 1.

uxor, uxōris, F., *wife, spouse*, 3, 4.

V

vacō, 1, -āvī, -ātus, *be empty, be vacant: be unoccupied, be at leisure*, 63, 14.

vae, interj., *alas! woe!* 21, 24.

vāgītus, -ūs, M. (vāgiō, *cry*), *crying, squalling*, 1, 11. (W. G. 77.)

valeō, 2, -uī, -itūrus (cf. Eng. *well*), *be strong, be vigorous*, 17, 9: *have power, have influence*, 26, 27.

Valerius, -ī, M., *Valerius*, name of a Roman gens, 25, 7.

valētūdō, -inis, F.(valeō,*be strong*), *state of health, health*, 71, 15: *ill health, sickness*, 55, 26.

validus, adj. with comp. and sup. (cf. valeō, *be strong*), *strong, able, powerful*, 16, 4; 43, 20.

vāllum, -ī, N. (vāllus, *palisade, stake*), *line of palisades, rampart, intrenchment*, 2, 21; 34, 2.

vānus, adj. with comp. and sup. (for *vacnus, cf. vacō, *be empty*), *containing nothing: empty, groundless, vain*, 53, 12.

varius, adj., *variegated, mottled: diverse, various*, 44, 29.

Varrō, -ōnis, M., surname in the Terentian gens, as *C. Terentius Varro*, the consul defeated at Cannae, 37, 3.

Varus, -ī, M., see Quīnctilius, 71, 6.

vās, vāsis, N., plur. vāsa, -ōrum, *vessel, dish*, 66, 10.

vāstō, 1, -āvī, -ātus (vāstus, *empty*), *make empty, devastate, lay waste, ravage*, 25, 27; 34, 6.

vāstus, adj. with comp. and sup.

(cf. Eng. *waste*), *empty, uninhabited, waste*, 1, 9: *vast, huge, immense*, 25, 13.

vectīgal, -ālis, N. [VEH-, *carry*], *payment to the state, tax, tribute*, 32, 17.

vectus, P. of **vehō**, 13, 20.

vegetus, adj., *enlivened, animated, bright*, 56, 23.

vehementer, adv. with comp. and sup. (**vehemēns**, *eager*), *eagerly, violently, earnestly, vehemently*, 48, 6. (W. G. 72.)

vehō, 3, vēxī, vectus [VEH-, *carry*], *bear, carry, convey*, 52, 30; 69, 8: *ride*, 13, 20. (W. G. 72.)

Vēiēns, -entis, adj. (**Vēiī**), *of* or *belonging to Veii*, 8, 23. As subst., *an inhabitant of Veii*, 19, 17.

Vēiī, -ōrum, M., *Veii*, an Etruscan town, 19, 11.

vel, conj. and adv. (old imper. of **volō**, *wish*), *or if you will, or*: **vel** ... **vel**, *either ... or*, 25, 16: *even*, 66, 30.

vēlō, 1, -āvī, -ātus (**vēlum**, *sail, covering*), *cover, wrap, veil*, 9, 24.

vēlōcitās, -ātis, F. (**vēlōx**, *swift*), *swiftness, fleetness, speed*, 30, 18.

vēlōx, -ōcis, adj. with comp. and sup., *swift, quick, rapid, fleet*, 43, 20.

velut or **velutī**, adv. (**vel**, intensive, *even*; **ut**, *as*), *even as, just as, like*, 1, 13: *as if, just as if, as though*, 6, 8; 8, 18.

vēnābulum, -ī, N. (**vēnor**, *hunt*), *hunting-spear*, 35, 15.

vēnātiō, -ōnis, F. (**vēnor**, *hunt*), *hunting: hunting spectacle*, 50, 19.

vēndō, 3, -didī, — [**vēnum**, *sale*; 2 DA-, *put, expose*], *sell*, 34, 8. (W. G. 25.)

venēnum, -ī, N., *strong potion, drug: poison*, 28, 25.

vēneō, -īre, -iī, — (**vēnum**, *sale*; **eō**, *go*), *go to sale, be sold*, 29, 26.

venerātiō, -ōnis, F. (**veneror**, *reverence*), *reverence, respect, veneration*, 49, 21.

venia, -ae, F., *indulgence, kindness, permission*, 18, 20: *forgiveness, pardon*, 49, 6.

veniō, 4, vēnī, ventus [VEN-, *come, go*], *come, go*, 3, 13; 43, 14: *come to, reach*, 17, 5. (W. G. 73.)

vēnor, 1, -ātus, dep., *hunt*, 1, 17.

venter, -tris, M., *belly, stomach*, 16, 24.

ventus, -ī, M. *wind*, 37, 9.

vēnum, N., *that which is sold*; usually acc. in a phrase with **dō**, as **vēnum dō**, 15, 10.

vēnum dō, -are, -dedī, -atus, *sell as a slave, sell*, 15, 10.

Venusia, -ae, F., *Venusia*, a town on the borders of Apulia and Lucania, 37, 22.

venustus, adj. with comp. (**venus**, *charm*), *charming, pleasing, handsome*, 70, 30.

(**verber**), -eris, N., *lash, whip, scourge, rod*, 45, 11.

verberō, 1, -āvī, -ātus (verber, *lash*), *beat, scourge, strike*, 19, 15.

verbum, -ī, N. (cf. Eng. *word*), *word*, 2, 23 : *saying, expression*, 56, 29.

vērē, adv. with comp. and sup. (vērus, *true*), *truly*, 38, 13.

verēcundia, -ae, F. (cf. vereor), *fear, modesty: sense of shame*, 53, 30 : *reverence, respect*, 24, 18.

vereor, 2, -itus, dep., *reverence, respect: fear*, 31, 8.

veritus, P. of vereor, 31, 8.

vernō, 1, —, — (vernus, *of spring*), *spring, be verdant, bloom*, 22, 19.

vērō, adv. (vērus, *true*), *in truth, certainly, surely*, 9, 11 : *indeed*, 18, 21 : *but, however*, 3, 4; 6, 4.

verrūca, -ae, F., *wart*, 57, 10.

versiculus, -ī, M. (dim. of versus, *line*), *little line, short verse*, 56, 18. (W. G. 74.)

versō, 1, -āvī, -ātus (freq. of vertō, *turn*), *turn often, keep turning*: pass., *be engaged in, be busy, conduct oneself*, 42, 14; 57, 25. (W. G. 74.)

versus, P. of vertō, 46, 28.

versus, -ūs, M. [VERT-, *turn*], *line*, 50, 8. (W. G. 74.)

vertō, 3, -tī, -sus [VERT-, *turn*], *turn, change*: pass., *be turned: turn about, return*, 46, 28. (W. G. 74.)

vērum, adv. (vērus, *true*), *truly, certainly: but, yet*, 4, 15.

vērus, adj. with comp. and sup., *true, actual, genuine*, 63, 1.

Vesta, -ae, F., *Vesta*, daughter of Saturn and Ops, goddess of flocks and herds, and of the household, guardian of the city. 1, 4.

vester, -tra, -trum, pron. poss. (vōs, *you*), *your, yours, of you*, 60, 20.

vestibulum, -ī, N., *enclosed space before a house, entrance*, 11, 23.

vestīgium, -ī, N. (cf. vestīgō, *track*), *bottom of foot, sole: footstep, track*, 53, 28.

vestis, -is, F., sing. collect., *clothes, clothing, attire*, 5, 9.

Vesuvius, -ī, M., *Vesuvius*, the famous volcano, 22, 24.

veterānus, adj. (vetus, *old*), *old, veteran*, 68, 2. As subst., M. plur., *veteran soldiers, veterans*, 63, 17.

vetō, 1, -uī, -itus (cf. vetus, *old*), *not to suffer, not to permit, forbid, prohibit*, 34, 3.

vetus, -eris, adj. with sup., veterrimus, *old, aged: of a former time, ancient, former*, 27, 27; 38, 28.

via, -ae, F. [VEH-, *carry*], *way, highway, road, street*, 8, 17; 18, 21; 23, 14: *march, journey*, 57, 4. (W. G. 72.)

vicārius, adj. (vicis, *change*), *substituted*. As subst., M., *substitute, proxy*, 68, 6.

vīcēsimus, adj. num. ord. (**vīgintī,** *twenty*), *twentieth,* **25, 27.**

vīciēns, adv. num. (**vīgintī,** *twenty*), *twenty times,* **58,** 30.

vīcīnus, adj. with comp. (**vīcus,** *row of houses*), *of the neighborhood, near, neighboring,* **3,** 5.

victor, -ōris, M. (**vincō,** *conquer*), *conqueror, vanquisher, victor,* **2,** 19. In apposition, with adj. force, *victorious,* **20,** 15.

victōria, -ae, F. (**victor,** *victor*), *victory,* **6,** 25.

victus, P. of **vincō, 19,** 16.

vīcus, -ī, M., *row of houses, street, quarter,* **13, 25** : *village,* **37,** 5.

vidēlicet, adv. (**vidēre,** *to see ;* **licet,** *it is allowed*), *one may see, clearly, obviously,* **3,** 23.

videō, 2, vīdī, vīsus [VID-, *see*], *see, discern, perceive,* **2,** 19 : *see to, provide for,* **41,** 19 : *go to see, visit,* **3, 12** : *consider, reflect upon,* **53,** 20: pass., *be seen,* **15, 24** : *seem, appear, seem good,* **2,** 21 ; **8,** 6. (W. G. 75.)

vigil, -ilis, adj., *awake, on the watch.* Assubst., M., *watchman, sentinel,* **35,** 13.

vigilantia, -ae, F. (**vigilāns,** *watchful*), *watchfulness, vigilance,* **63,** 8.

vigilia, -ae, F. (**vigil,** *awake, alert*), *watching: a watch, time of keeping watch,* **35,** 26.

vīgintī, num. adj. indecl., *twenty,* **32,** 17.

vīlla, -ae, F. (dim. of **vīcus,** *village*), *country-house, country-seat, farm, villa,* **61,** 2.

Vīminālis, -e, adj., sc. **collis,** *the Viminal hill,* one of the seven hills of Rome, **12,** 21.

vinciō, 4, vinxī, vinctus, *bind, fetter, tie, fasten,* **24,** 12 ; **24,** 17.

vincō, 3, vīcī, victus, *conquer, defeat, subdue, be victorious,* **4,** 6 ; **8, 28** : *gain one's end, succeed,* **18, 2.**

vinctus, P. of **vinciō, 24,** 12.

vinculum, -ī, N. (**vinciō,** *bind*), *fetter, chain:* plur., *prison,* **1, 6.**

vindicō, 1, -āvī, -ātus (**vindex,** *a maintainer*), *assert a claim to: avenge, punish,* **3,** 27 ; **18,** 23.

vīnum, -ī, N., *wine,* **26,** 13 ; **42,** 21.

violentus, adj. with comp. and sup. (cf. **vīs,** *strength*), *violent, impetuous,* **13, 14.**

violō, 1, -āvī, -ātus (cf. **vīs,** *strength*), *treat with violence, injure, break,* **24, 24** ; **50, 9.**

vir, virī, M., *male person, man,* **4, 26** : *husband,* **4, 13** : *man of courage,* **4, 3.**

virga, -ae, F., *slender green branch, twig, rod,* **19, 14.**

Virginia, -ae, F., *Virginia,* daughter of Virginius, **18, 17.**

Virginius, -ī, M., gentile name of L. *Virginius,* the Roman centurion, father of Virginia, **18, 3.**

virgō, -inis, F., *virgin, maid, maiden,* **3, 18.**

VOCABULARY. 325

virītim, adv. (**vir**, *man*), *man by man, singly, individually*, **41**, 15.

virtūs, -ūtis, F. (**vir**, *man*), *manliness, manhood: courage, valor*, **8**, 15: *goodness, virtue*, **28**, 15; **47**, 25.

vīs, vīs, —, vim, vī ; plur., **vīrēs**, -ium, etc., F., *vigor, strength, vehemence, force*, **1**, 17 ; **18**, 7 ; **67**, 17 : *violence*, **15**, 2 : *quantity, number*, **3**, 3 : plur., *troops*, **9**, 6.

vīsō, 3, -sī, -sus (freq. of **videō**, *see*), *view, behold: go to see, visit*, **48**, 8. (W. G. 75.)

vīsus, P. of **video**, **7**, 28.

vīsus, -ūs, M. (**videō**, *see*), *looking, power of sight: sight, appearance*, **12**, 4 : *apparition, vision*, **55**, 5. (W. G. 75.)

vīta, -ae, F. [VIV-, *live*], *life*, **29**, 29 : *way of living*, **29**, 9: *career*, **17**, 13. (W. G. 76.)

vītis, -is, F., *vine, grape-vine*, **22**, 22.

vīvō, 3, vīxī, — [VIV-, *live*], *live, be alive*, **36**, 20 : *reside, dwell*, **28**, 16. (W. G. 76.)

vīvus, adj. [VIV-, *live*], *alive, living*, **66**, 23: of water, *running, fresh*, **13**, 7. (W. G. 76.)

vix, adv., *with difficulty, hardly, scarcely*, **39**, 4.

vōbīs, see **tū**.

vōciferō, or **vōciferor**, 1, -ātus, dep. [* **vōciferus**, fr. **vōx**, *voice*; FER-, *bear*], *cry out, shout, bawl*, **11**, 26. (W. G. 77.)

vōcitō, 1, -āvī, -ātus (freq. of **vocō**, *call*), *be wont to call, name*, **34**, 12. (W. G. 77.)

vocō, 1, -āvī, -ātus [VOC-, *call*], *call, summon*, **11**, 25; **18**, 10: *call by name, name*, **2**, 20. (W. G. 77.)

volāns, -antis, P. of **volō**, **4**, 12.

volgō, adv. (**volgus**, *the mass*), *in the throng, commonly, generally*, **4**, 25.

volitō, 1, -āvī, -ātus (freq. of **volō**, *fly*), *fly to and fro, flutter*, **10**, 21 : *move, fly*, **51**, 22.

volnerō, 1, -āvī, -ātus (**volnus**, *wound*), *wound, hurt, injure*, **7**, 8.

volnus, -eris, N., *wound*, **7**, 22.

volō, velle, voluī [VOL-, *wish*], *will, be willing, wish, desire, want, purpose*, **12**, 24; **27**, 1. (W. G. 79.)

volō, 1, -āvī, -ātūrus, *fly*, **4**, 12.

Volscī, -ōrum, M., *the Volscians*, the most important people of ancient Latium, **57**, 9.

voltur, -uris, M., *vulture*, **2**, 18.

voltus, -ūs, M. [VOL-, wish], *an expression of countenance, features, looks, air, face*, **2**, 6; **25**, 20.

volucer, -ucris, -ucre, adj., *flying, winged*. As subst., F. (sc. **avis**) *bird*, **65**, 22.

volūmen, -inis, N. [VOLV-, *roll*], *that which is rolled: roll of writing, book, volume*, **67**, 26. (W. G. 78.)

voluntārius, adj. (**voluntās**, *will*),

willing, voluntary, **65**, 26. (W. G. 79.)

volŭntās, -ātis, F. [1 VOL-, *wish*], *will, choice, desire, inclination*, **42**, 8. (W. G. 79.)

volŭptās, -ātis, F. [cf. **volup**, *agreeably;* VOL-, *will*], *satisfaction, pleasure, delight*, **29**, 6. (W. G. 79.)

vōs, plur. of **tū**, **31**, 13.

vŏtum, -ī, N. (P. N. of **voveō**, *vow*), *promise to a god, vow: desire, prayer*, **67**, 13.

vŏveō, 2, vōvī, vōtus, *vow, promise solemnly*, **4**, 9.

vōx, vōcis, F. [VOC-, *call*], *voice, cry, call*, **8**, 26 ; **35**, 12 : *utterance, word, speech, saying*, **22**, 5; **25**, 21. (W. G. 77.)

X

Xenophōn, -ōntis, M., *Xenophon*, the Athenian, **55**, 26.

Z

zōna, -ae, F. (Gr., ζώνη), *woman's girdle, belt: money-belt*, **42**, 19.

www.ingramcontent.com/pod-product-compliance
Lightning Source LLC
Chambersburg PA
CBHW020335240426
43673CB00039B/940